Models of Proposal Planning & Writing

Models of Proposal Planning & Writing

Second Edition

Jeremy T. Miner and Kelly C. Ball-Stahl

An Imprint of ABC-CLIO, LLC

Santa Barbara, California • Denver, Colorado

Library of Congress Cataloging-in-Publication Data

Names: Miner, Jeremy T., author. | Ball-Stahl, Kelly C., author.
Title: Models of proposal planning & writing / Jeremy T. Miner, Kelly Ball-Stahl.
Other titles: Models of proposal planning and writing
Description: Second edition. | Santa Barbara : Greenwood, 2016. | Revised edition of Models of proposal planning & writing, 2005.
Identifiers: LCCN 2015043599 | ISBN 9781440833892 (hardback) | ISBN 9781440833939 (paperback) | ISBN 9781440833908 (ebook)
Subjects: LCSH: Proposal writing for grants—United States. | Proposal writing for grants—United States—Case studies. | BISAC: BUSINESS & ECONOMICS / Business Communication / General. | BUSINESS & ECONOMICS / Strategic Planning.
Classification: LCC HG177.5.U6 M558 2016 | DDC 658.15/224—dc23
LC record available at http://lccn.loc.gov/2015043599

ISBN: 978-1-4408-3389-2 (hardcover)
978-1-4408-3393-9 (paperback)
EISBN: 978-1-4408-3390-8

20 19 18 17 16 1 2 3 4 5

This book is also available on the World Wide Web as an eBook.
Visit www.abc-clio.com for details.

Greenwood
An Imprint of ABC-CLIO, LLC

ABC-CLIO, LLC
130 Cremona Drive, P.O. Box 1911
Santa Barbara, California 93116-1911

This book is printed on acid-free paper ♾
Manufactured in the United States of America

Contents

Preface

"Do you have any sample proposals that you'd be willing to share?" is a common request that we have received over the past two decades from individuals all across the country who have participated in our grant writing workshops. Successful grantseekers know that examining copies of funded proposals is an effective way to begin preparing to write their own proposals.

Inevitably, though, these individuals with whom we have shared sample proposals contact us again later and ask two questions: "How did you know what to write?" and "Why did you write it like that?" In reality, these grantseekers are asking us to put the proposals in context; they want to understand better the processes that led to the final products.

Many grants manuals, including our own *Proposal Planning & Writing* (Greenwood Press), employ a "how-to" or "systems approach" to developing grant proposals. These books tell you *what* to write and *how* to write it. They frequently provide examples from successfully funded proposals. In a few cases, brief summary analyses of the proposals are also included. More often, however, the sample proposals stand on their own as "self-explanatory."

While these sample proposals are useful, they leave gaps. Namely, they neglect to explain *why* specific proposal elements are persuasive to a sponsor. As a result, you must figure out independently what made the proposals successful and then determine how to incorporate similar elements into your own grant proposals. Said differently, these proposals are samples, not models.

Models of Proposal Planning & Writing, second edition, attempts to bridge this gap. The purpose of this book is to walk you step-by-step, from beginning to end, through an integrated process of planning and writing persuasive proposals. You will see the questions that we asked of ourselves and those asked of sponsors *before* we developed a complete grant application. You will read the actual proposals we submitted to private and public sponsors, including in-depth analyses of the key features that made them persuasive. You will examine the verbatim reviewer comments and award letters we received back from the sponsors. As a whole, these annotated models serve as a springboard from which you can begin to develop your own fundable proposals.

It is fairly easy to secure copies of federally funded proposals—they are public information. A few public sponsors post a sampling of awarded proposals on their Web sites. Some federal program officers are willing to share them with you directly when you make a specific request. You can also obtain copies under the Freedom of Information Act. On the other hand, it's more difficult to secure samples of funded proposals from private foundations. There are two main reasons why: (1) foundations consider proposals they receive to be the proprietary intellectual property of individual applicants, and (2) foundations are not required by law to share them. When you are able to obtain samples of private and public proposals, they seldom include an explanation of the thought processes behind proposal development or an explanation of why they were funded.

The models included in this book provide a solid framework for planning and practical strategies for writing that grantseekers can use to improve the quality—and persuasiveness—of their proposals. This means going beyond explaining the *what* and *how* of a grant project to describing the *why* of the project, using the available means of logical and psychological persuasion.

NEW TO THIS EDITION

While the second edition retains the essential features of the previous edition for planning and writing successful proposals, the following additions are designed to better meet the emerging needs of today's grantseekers in an era of increased competition for limited resources.

New Chapter on Stewardship and Persistence

In one sense, a grant award notification signifies that your relationship with the sponsor is just beginning. Nevertheless, it's not too early to be thinking about the long term. This new chapter identifies specific actions you can take internally at your organization and externally with the program officer to establish a relationship grounded in trust and open communication. In essence, responsible stewardship in the present will better position you, your project, and your organization for additional funding from the same and other sponsors in the future.

More Annotated Models

Our book readers and workshop participants repeatedly call for more annotated models. That's why nearly 70 percent of the book content is new and covers a broader range of health, education, and social service topics. Furthermore, annotations are easier to read; call-out thought bubbles highlight the questions asked internally of organizations and externally of sponsors before the complete application was developed and pinpoint specific passages where persuasive themes were woven into the fabric of the narrative. Comprehensive annotations provide practical information that can guide efforts to develop your own persuasive proposals.

Introduction to Logic Models

Assessment and evaluation are instrumental to project success; they pinpoint what is really happening in your project and allow you to be accountable to sponsors. Logic models are graphical displays that illustrate the relationship between a current situation, processes, and resulting outputs and outcomes. Logic models demonstrate, often in one page, the depth of your project planning, implementation, evaluation, and reporting. New to this edition is a sample logic model that follows a template common to many sponsors.

Real Reviewer Comments

It is essential to get feedback on your grant application, regardless of whether or not it was funded. Securing verbatim copies of reviewer comments, when they are available, will highlight specific aspects that the sponsor liked about the project as well as potential areas of weakness to be addressed. Written reviewer comments were available for two of the complete grant applications presented in this second edition, and they are included in their entirety immediately following their respective proposals. Further, comprehensive annotations of the real reviewer comments are also provided, calling attention to dimensions where reviewers were on target and might have missed the mark.

New Appendix of Preproposal Contact Questions

One takeaway message of this book is that you need to ask a lot of questions before you start writing a proposal. Preproposal contact with past grant winners, past grant reviewers, and program officers can help you to fine-tune your proposal, so that it matches the sponsor's priorities. Candidly, some grantseekers are reluctant to make the call. They rationalize, "Program officers are so busy, I don't want to intrude on them," when the real stumbling block is that they don't know what to ask. The new appendix draws out of the chapters 124 examples of questions and organizes them into four types that consider past action as well as future intentions. The examples also serve to stimulate composition of your own preproposal contact questions.

TARGET AUDIENCES

The people who have attended our grant writing workshops and who are currently using the ideas presented in this book represent a wide variety of professions and disciplines. Nine major categories stand out:

- **Economic Development:** City planning, land use, urban revitalization, workforce development, and job creation.
- **Education:** Day care programs, adult education, public and private schools, special education departments, colleges and universities, English as foreign language programs, libraries.
- **First Responders:** Police, fire, emergency medical services.
- **Government:** Local, state, and federal agencies; courts, human services, parks and recreation.
- **Health Care:** Hospitals, nursing homes, public health organizations, Veterans Administration, International Health, families, maternal and child health.
- **Philanthropy:** Foundations, charitable organizations, service clubs.
- **Religions:** Churches, synagogues, mosques, and other houses of worship; faith-based organizations, religious education.
- **Social Services:** Community development, rehabilitation, mental health, welfare, senior citizens.
- **Other:** Fine and performing arts, senior citizens' advocates and agencies, special interest groups.

Grantseekers are a diverse group with different missions and service recipients; however, each must present ideas clearly to the public and private sponsors that fund worthy recipients. Health care systems, institutions of higher education, and agencies that are involved with the development and submission of numerous grant proposals will find the information in this book useful for strengthening the capacity of their faculty, staff, administrators, and collaborators to secure extramural funding for programs that fulfill their organizational missions.

STRUCTURE AND CONTENT

In this book you will find five model proposals: four sponsored by private, independent grantmakers and one sponsored by a federal agency. By topic, the proposals represent a community health project, a gerontology research project, a community awareness project, a library special collections project, and health sciences research project. By applicant, the proposals represent a community-based coalition affiliated with a pediatric hospital, a public institution of higher education, a food bank in collaboration with university partners, an academic library, and an individual affiliated with comprehensive public higher education. By type, the proposals represent a planning grant, a research grant, a partnership development grant, a preservation assistance grant, and an international teaching and research fellowship.

Models of Proposal Planning & Writing, second edition, illustrates in specific detail grants processes *and* products. The first three chapters in the book present a framework for developing persuasive proposals. This includes introducing the "Persuasion Intersection" and identifying the "Roads to the Persuasion Intersection," describing the "RFP Analysis Process," and outlining the "Complete Grant Application." The next five chapters contain actual grant applications that were funded, along with in-depth analyses of

- Request for Proposal (RFP) guidelines
- Cover letters
- Application forms
- Project summaries
- Letters of intent
- Full proposals
- Budgets and budget narratives
- Reviewer comments
- Grant award notifications

The last chapter offers final thoughts about grant stewardship, steps to take after the grant award notification arrives. In the appendix you will find a collated listing of the preproposal contact questions from each chapter, which you can use as a reference tool to consult as you begin to formulate questions for past grant winners, past grant reviewers, and program officers. Whether you are a novice, intermediate, or experienced grantseeker, the models presented in this book are ones that you can follow for planning and writing persuasive proposals of your own.

ACKNOWLEDGMENTS

American science fiction writer Frank Herbert once remarked, "There is no real ending. It's just the place where you stop the story." In this second edition of *Models of Proposal Planning & Writing*, we picked up where we left off and stayed true to the form of the first edition. The RFP guidelines, proposals, and reviewer comments presented in this book are real—so much so, in fact, that we did not correct ex post facto errors in grammar, spelling, or punctuation. In some cases, the sponsors made minor mistakes; in other instances, we did. We preserved these mistakes in their original forms to demonstrate to you that proposals do not need to be perfect in order to attract funding. Persuasion is the key to successful grant seeking.

Models of Proposal Planning & Writing, second edition, would not have been possible without the talented and dedicated individuals who were responsible for conceptualizing and implementing the projects described in this book. For their roles in controlling pediatric asthma, we wish to thank Dr. John R. Meurer, professor of pediatrics (community care) and director of the Institute for Health and Society, Medical College of Wisconsin; Dr. Kevin J. Kelly, professor of pediatrics (allergy, immunology, and rheumatology) and pediatrician-in-chief, University of North Carolina Children's Hospital; and Dr. Ramesh C. Sachdeva, associate executive director, American Academy of Pediatrics.

We gratefully acknowledge Dr. Peter A. Lichtenberg, director of both the Institute of Gerontology and the Merrill Palmer Skillman Institute, Wayne State University, for his contributions to improving the quality of life for older adults.

We recognize Emily Moore, executive director, Feed My People Food Bank; Nancy Coffey, nutrition coordinator, University of Wisconsin Extension; and Dr. Mary Canales, professor of nursing, University of Wisconsin–Eau Claire for their efforts to change community views on hunger.

For her dedication to preserving significant archival collections for the benefit of future generations, we extend sincere thanks to Felice Maciejewski, university librarian, Dominican University.

And finally, for his commitment to accelerating global learning and understanding, we say *paljon kiitoksia*—many thanks—to Dr. Crispin Pierce, professor of environmental public health, University of Wisconsin–Eau Claire.

THE INFAMOUS BOTTOM LINE

Successful grantseekers are often individuals who are so dedicated to their ideas that they will invest both passion and time in order to find the means to carry them out. Sponsors have clear objectives and expectations that they hope to realize by providing financial support to such dedicated persons. A persuasively written grant proposal is the link between them. This book provides detailed models to help you forge that link.

CHAPTER 1

Introduction to Persuasive Proposal Writing

In today's competitive grants environment, "good" proposals seldom get funded; "excellent" proposals get funded. Excellent proposals *persuade* sponsors to open up their checkbooks to invest in you, your project, and your organization. To increase the competitiveness of your grant applications and chances for funding success, this book models a systematic process for identifying and incorporating persuasion throughout your proposals.

Inevitably, sponsors (grantmakers) receive more proposals than they can possibly fund. In a stack of applications, grant reviewers quickly discern between proposals that are responsive to Request for Proposal (RFP) guidelines and those that are not; nonresponsive proposals are rejected immediately. Good proposals provide information to demonstrate that they comply with *every* requirement in the RFP. Excellent proposals, however, stand out from the competition because they go beyond merely complying with the requirements of the RFP to satisfying the needs of the sponsor. Proposals are persuasive when they connect your project ideas to the values of the sponsor. Connecting with the values of the sponsor means that your proposal must present the right balance of logic, emotion, and relationships.

THE PERSUASION INTERSECTION

As a grantseeker, your job is to secure extramural funding for projects that are important to your organization. However, sponsors rarely award grant funding just because you support a specific cause or work for a specific organization. You must persuade them to invest in your projects and organization. Providing information about your project is a necessary but not sufficient condition to win grant funding; do not expect sponsors to immediately understand the value of your project. Information is not persuasion. Persuasion is the key to funding success. Persuasion occurs at the intersection of the sponsor's values, applicant credibility, proposal logics, and proposal psychologics. As illustrated in Fig. 1 and subsequently defined, these four elements make up the Persuasion Intersection.

Sponsor Values

Sponsors have a particular view of the world. They are vitally concerned about specific problems, injustices, or inequities. They are so concerned, in fact, that they are willing to commit their own money to address these problems. In essence, they see a gap between a current situation and an improved situation, between "what is" and "what ought to be." Their mission is to close this gap. The gap represents sponsor values, how they view problems of interest to them.

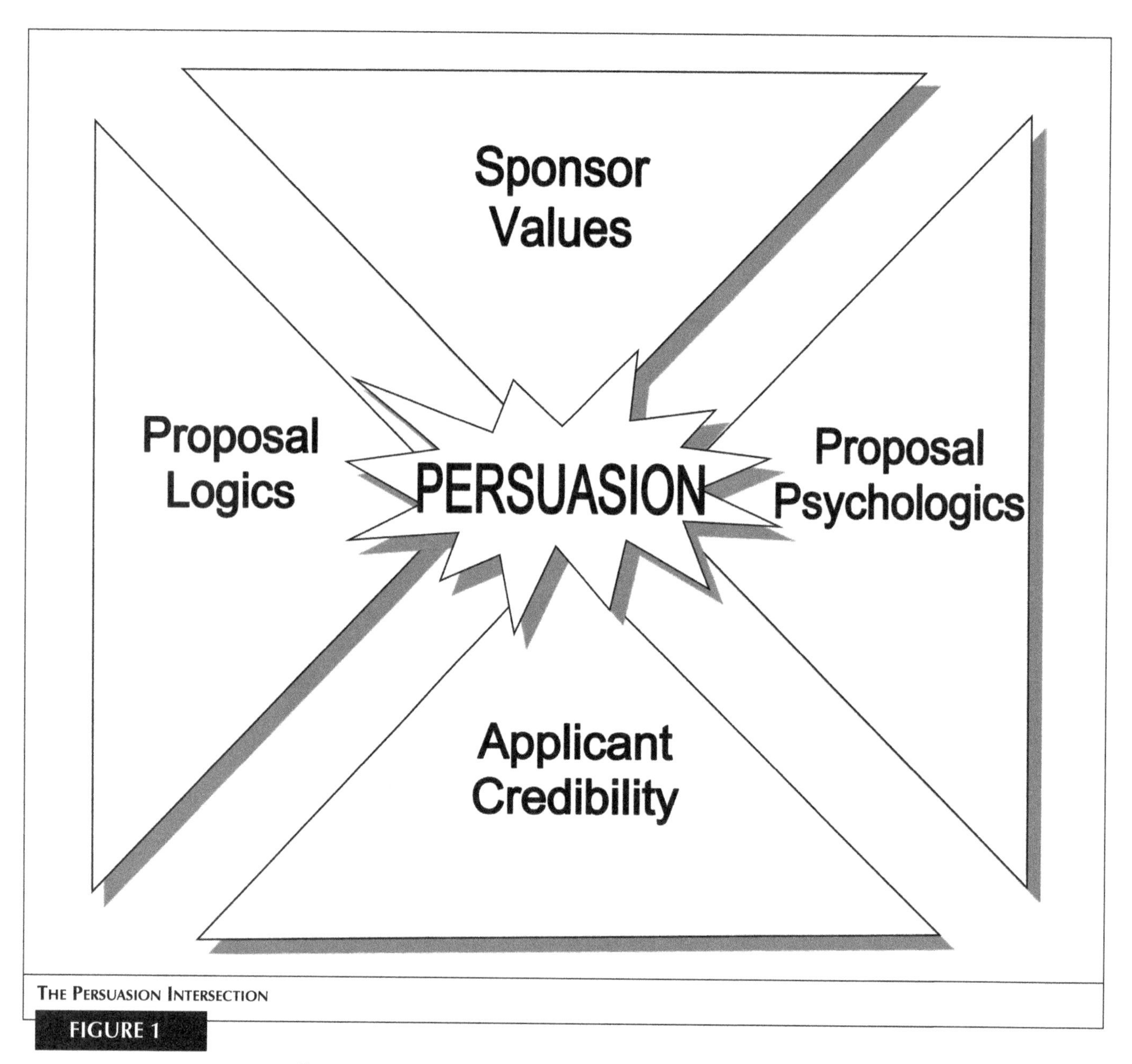

THE PERSUASION INTERSECTION

FIGURE 1

For instance, one private foundation concerned about preventing child abuse describes its values:

> The Prevent Abuse Foundation is committed to ensuring a safe environment for children through support of primary prevention activities throughout the state, advocating support for children and families, as well as educating professionals and communities about the role of prevention in eliminating child abuse. Over the last 20 years, the Prevent Abuse Foundation has become a vital resource to communities across the state by supporting a variety of family support strategies, including parent education, home visitation, family resource centers and public awareness campaigns. The Prevent Abuse Foundation also provides grass roots, community-based groups with technical and professional assistance, sharing the best program practices and evaluation techniques.

Applicant Credibility

As the applicant, your job is to establish three types of credibility: organizational, individual, and project. You have a creditable organization proposing a creditable idea to be directed by a creditable project director. Enhance your credibility by establishing your uniqueness. Differentiate yourself from your potential competition. What makes your organization stand out from others? What can your project director do better than anyone else? What makes your project innovative? Uniqueness is a strength when it relates to your exceptional ability to conduct the proposed project.

The following example illustrates how a university biology department seeking funding for genetics research describes itself:

> The biology department at Major State University is uniquely suited to conduct this crucial genetics research. Stemming from the department's solid past of 30 years of doctoral studies in biological science, its faculty includes Drs. Kwasny, Lee, and Dilworth. This distinguished academic core cumulatively represents 117 years of productive research experience at our university. With a special focus on the molecular basis of oncogenesis, our current research uses unique systems to analyze the genetic and hormonal factors responsible for gene regulation. While these systems are not widely studied in established programs of cell biology, they are most suitable for answering the cutting-edge questions of gene expression and regulation—and our department is endowed with the intellectual talent to succeed.

Proposal Logics

Proposal logics include the *systematic* development of proposal components to show the relationship between an identified gap, an improved situation, and resulting benefits to the target population. Problems represent gaps between what exists today and what could exist tomorrow. Objectives are the specific, measurable activities that will help solve the problem. Benefits represent the good things that will occur by achieving the objectives. These elements must reflect a direct relationship between the proposed project and the values of the sponsor.

As an illustration, the RFP guidelines from one private foundation that supports medical, cultural, civic, and educational programs benefiting youth under the age of 18 indicate:

> Please provide a concise description of the need or problem to be addressed. Include the overall goals and purpose of your organization or specific department concerned, the specific purpose of the funds, and how your objectives will be accomplished. Include a project timeline. Please summarize your target population in measurable terms. Indicate how your organization will evaluate the program.

Proposal Psychologics

Sponsors fund projects for psychological as well as for logical reasons. Proposal psychologics respond to the emotional needs of the sponsor. Successful proposals go beyond addressing the minimum performance standards outlined in the application materials; they also display intangible elements: trust, energy, passion, ownership, and commitment. Sponsors' emotions store the lessons of experience. They don't want to take a lot of risks with their money. Sponsors view grants as investments in an improved future. Thus, before they award funding, they need to feel comfortable with you, to trust that you understand their concerns and share their values.

In a proposal to a federal agency, a private college describes its lengthy history of success collaborating with community partners, directing national programs that serve the targeted minority population, and institutionalizing project activities:

> For more than a decade project partners have collaborated on a variety of grant-related initiatives, including a six-year joint teacher education program between the College of Native Americans and Midwestern Regional College. The project director has led several successful national intervention projects for Native American middle school students, including Kids Math Camp, Achievement in Math, and Math and Science Immersion. Each one of these projects has been sustained beyond the conclusion of its granting period through the generosity of individual philanthropy and in-kind contributions from partner institutions.

Successful proposal writers understand the relationship between sponsor values and their own organizational capabilities and between proposal logics and proposal psychologics. Proposals are more persuasive when they reflect the priorities of the sponsor. Novice proposal writers often focus on their own need for funds instead of matching their project's goals with the sponsor's priorities. Proposals are funded when they express the values shared by the sponsor. Projects are rejected when they do not precisely reflect the priorities of the sponsor.

Exhibit 1 illustrates how proposals with seemingly self-oriented needs can be recast to reflect sponsor-oriented values. Rather than focusing on your organization's need for funding,

Self-Oriented Needs	Sponsor-Oriented Values
The Family Welfare Agency requests a grant of $25,000 to meet its operating expenses.	The Family Welfare Agency invites your investment of $25,000 to sustain the delivery of crucial services to victims of violence and abuse.
Top Flite High School invites you to share in a $100,000 project to buy new tablet computers.	Top Flite High School invites your participation in a $100,000 project to reduce student achievement gaps in science and mathematics.
La Casa de Esperanza requests your support of $50,000 to hire a case manager.	La Casa de Esperanza invites you to share in a $50,000 project to improve the quality of life for Hispanics with chronic health conditions.
Fairview Middle School, recently recognized by the governor as a "Center for Educational Excellence," requests a $5,000 grant to pay for a guest speaker who will talk about teen bullying.	Fairview Middle School, recently recognized by the governor as a "Center for Educational Excellence," requests a $5,000 grant to help decrease bullying behavior among teens.
Nature Academy is seeking a grant of $17,500 to replace 300 trees that were lost during the August 2016 EF2 tornado.	Nature Academy seeks $17,500 to build the capacity of individuals for creating an environmentally sustainable community.
An International Society grant of $10,000 will allow me to travel to the national research archives in Munich, Germany and ultimately publish a manuscript on "EU Exchange: Spaniards with German Passports."	An International Society grant of $10,000 will advance research on and understanding of the European Union's export and import process.
A "Partnerships for Health" grant of $300,000 over four years will enable Midwestern Health System, ranked by *U.S. News & World Report* as one of the nation's elite providers, to build a multidisciplinary network and research base for policy on healthy food retail.	Midwestern Health System, ranked by *U.S. News & World Report* as one of the nation's elite providers, seeks $300,000 over four years from the "Partnerships for Health" grant program to prevent obesity among at-risk groups in low-income communities.

EXHIBIT 1

equipment, and staff, think about who will ultimately benefit from these human, physical, and financial resources and the difference that will be produced in their lives. In all seven examples, the message is clear and simple: sponsors usually give money to organizations that help other people; sponsors seldom give money to organizations that help only themselves. You should select a sponsor that shares your view of the world and tailor proposals to them.

ROADS TO THE PERSUASION INTERSECTION

Persuasion is an interaction of elements. Proposal logics or proposal psychologics alone are not sufficient to persuade a sponsor to fund a project. The sponsor must also be involved and have a vested interest in your project and its outcomes. The Roads to the Persuasion Intersection bring together objective and subjective writing approaches to fine-tune your proposal so that it more closely matches sponsor values. As illustrated in Figure 2, this means navigating among RFP guidelines, evaluation criteria, hot buttons and distinctive features, and strategic thinking and preproposal contracts. Traveling these

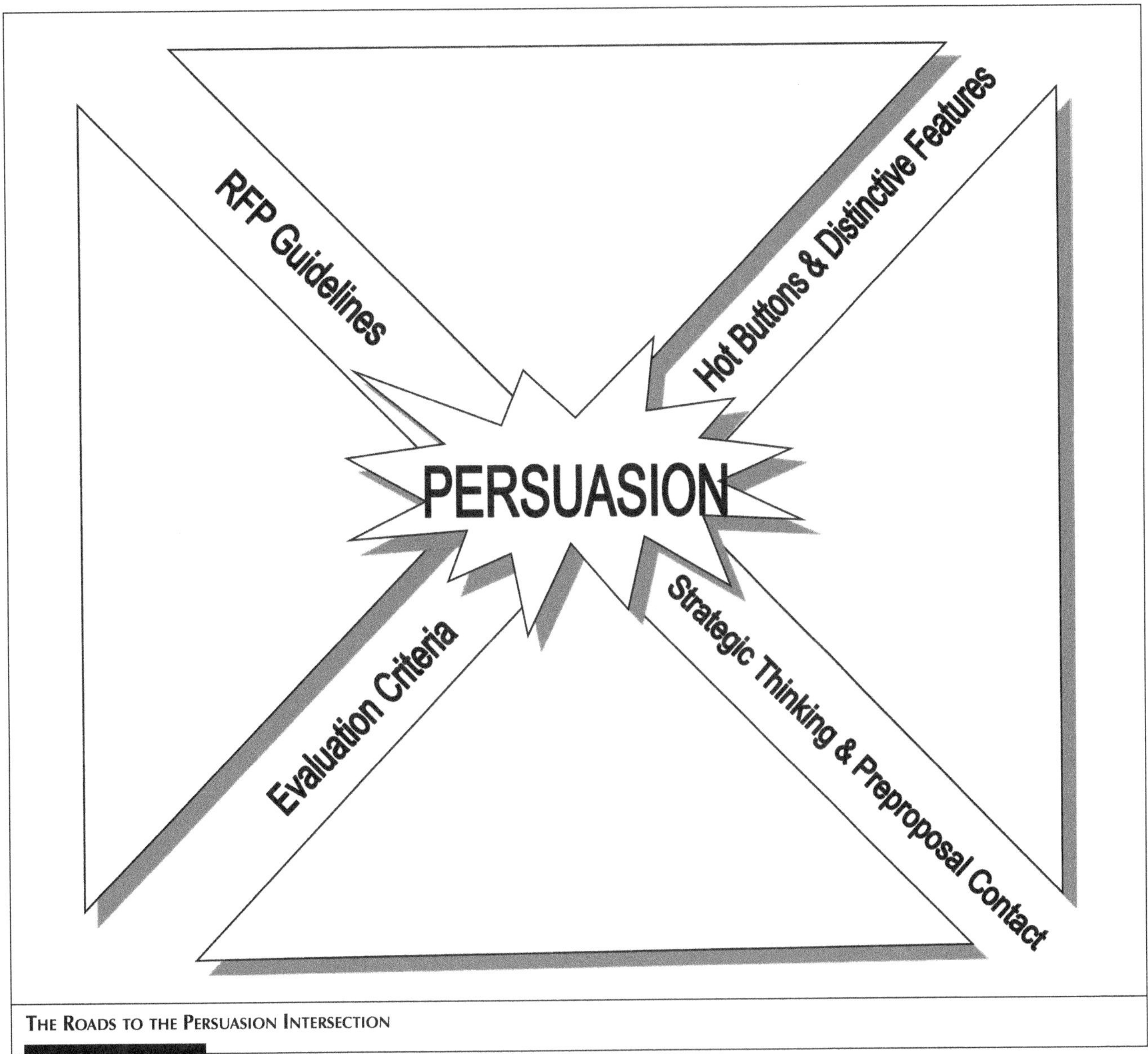

The Roads to the Persuasion Intersection

FIGURE 2

four roads will deepen your understanding of the values of sponsors and will help you to persuade them that you can satisfy their needs.

RFP Guidelines

A Request for Proposal (RFP) is an invitation by a sponsor to submit a grant application. While some sponsors use other terms such as Funding Opportunity Announcement (FOA), Grant Announcement (GA), Request for Application (RFA), Program Announcement (PA), Broad Agency Announcement (BAA), Notice of Funding Availability (NOFA), or Solicitation for Grant Application (SGA), the invitations all spell out the details you need in order to develop a proposal. RFP guidelines generally provide an overview of what the funding announcement is all about, the background or problem that led to this invitation, priority funding areas, sample methodological approaches, timelines, deadlines, evaluation criteria, funds available, and acceptable uses of grant funds.

RFP guidelines also supply you with a first look at how sponsors view the world: magnitudes and key dimensions of problems they wish to solve. Some sponsors, however, do not issue specific RFP guidelines; rather, they may have broad guidelines that they use in all circumstances. Other sponsors, most notably small foundations, may not have any guidelines at all. In these cases, follow the generic structure described in Chapter 3 under "Developing the Proposal." Chapter 4 examines an RFP from a private, special-purpose foundation that uses a three-stage application process. Chapter 5 interprets the broad instructions provided by a private, national foundation that uses a single-stage application process. Chapter 6 dissects the application guidelines issued by a state grantmaker that uses a two-stage application process. Chapter 7 scrutinizes an RFP from a federal government agency that uses a single-stage application process. And finally, Chapter 8 studies the guidance provided by an independent grantmaker that uses a single-stage application process.

Evaluation Criteria

Sponsors' evaluation criteria describe technical aspects of the application process and proposal review procedures. RFP evaluation criteria help you to understand the logical components that must go into the proposal. These components are the sponsors' minimum performance standards, the yardstick against which your proposal is being measured. Proposals that do not meet these minimum expectations will be rejected. To develop a proposal that meets sponsor expectations, however, you also need to know who is reviewing the proposals and the conditions under which they are being reviewed. You'll write differently for general audiences who skim read compared to technical audiences who critically read proposals. (See Chapter 2, Exhibits 3 and 4 for detailed examples of review conditions and writing techniques.)

Strategic Thinking and Preproposal Contact

Strategic thinking forces you to understand your strengths and weaknesses in relation to the values of the sponsor. Your credibility and uniqueness—organizational, individual, and project—are strengths only to the extent that they fulfill sponsor needs. Contrary to popular belief, sponsors do not give money away. They contract with organizations offering services and programs that are consistent with their needs and interests. Sponsors award funds to make a difference in the lives of people. Strategic thinking demonstrates to sponsors that a good match exists between their priorities and your capabilities. Preproposal contact is a process for gathering supplemental information about sponsors and their values and priorities. Making contact with program officers, past grantees, and past grant reviewers can help fine-tune your proposal, so it mirrors the sponsor's concern about specific problems, injustices, and inequities.

Hot Buttons and Distinctive Features

Hot buttons represent the logical and psychological concerns of the sponsor that have an impact on how the project will be conducted. Hot buttons are emphasized *repeatedly* in the RFP and preproposal contact, and gain force through their repetition. These primary concerns affect the shape of a project's structure and implementation processes. However, hot buttons are not always stated as evaluation criteria; watch for recurring themes such as accountability, collaboration, communication, cost-effectiveness, outcomes, participation, replication, and sustainability.

Sponsors may also have secondary concerns that influence the design of certain aspects of the project. Because secondary concerns do not appear repeatedly, they are not hot buttons; rather, they are distinctive features. Distinctive features appear as *singular* instances identified in the RFP and preproposal contact. They often reflect activities in which you are already engaged, yet the sponsor wants explicit assurance that you will continue to do them, e.g., comply with federal regulations, standardize treatment following national guidelines, be able to recruit and retain project participants. Other times, distinctive features are sponsor-imposed activities necessary to meet the terms of the grant, e.g., submit timely progress reports, participate in annual national project meetings, utilize resources provided by the sponsor.

Addressing hot buttons and distinctive features help you to establish a level of trust and understanding with the sponsor. Failing to attend to hot buttons in your proposal may leave a sponsor wondering whether your project truly has their best interest at heart: a potentially fatal flaw. Failing to acknowledge distinctive features in your proposal may be viewed by the sponsor as a controllable project weakness. As a result, you might miss out on indispensable half points or benefit-of-the-doubt consideration in a tight funding decision. In contrast, fully addressing hot buttons and distinctive features will make your proposal stand out from the competition.

Sponsors receive numerous requests for a limited pool of funding dollars. During the review process they discern among proposals by looking for weaknesses—faults in logic, facts, approaches, or conclusions. But even when the logic is sound, proposals may be rejected because they fail to establish a "connection" with the sponsor. On the other hand, persuasive proposals present a seamless argument that stands the test of reason, addresses psychological concerns, and connects project ideas to the values of the sponsor. In the next chapter we describe a systematic process for moving down the Roads to the Persuasion Intersection.

CHAPTER 2

Analyzing Request for Proposals

Analyzing Request for Proposal (RFP) guidelines means asking a lot of questions: questions to determine if this program is a good match for your organization and how much work will need to go into developing a competitive application. To effectively analyze an RFP, read it in multiple passes with increasing scrutiny. The three-step RFP Analysis Process described below will help your organization to answer questions about relevance, feasibility, and probability:

- Step One: **R**elevance—Do we want to do this?
- Step Two: **F**easibility—Can we do this?
- Step Three: **P**robability—Will we be competitive?

In incremental fashion, this RFP Analysis Process moves you along the Roads to the Persuasion Intersection. Step One navigates through the RFP Guidelines. Step Two proceeds along the paths of Evaluation Criteria and Hot Buttons and Distinctive Features. Step Three examines Strategic Thinking and Preproposal Contact. Together, these steps provide you with the details necessary to develop a persuasive proposal.

STEP ONE: RELEVANCE—DO WE WANT TO DO THIS?

RFP Guidelines

At this most basic level, read the RFP guidelines and develop a short list of bulleted points that summarizes the main ideas. The purpose of this list is twofold: (1) to help you understand exactly what this program is all about, and (2) to quickly assess its relevance, determining whether or not it's a good match for your organization. This process answers the question, "Do we want to do this?"

This bulleted list of main points can also form the basis of an internal communication designed to secure organizational support from key personnel for developing an application. The one-page message informs potential project partners, supervisors, and other administrators that you are interested in pursuing the funding opportunity. Whether in print or electronic format, the message may take on the following structure, which can be skimmed in 30 seconds or less:

> "[Sponsor's] [program] is designed to [program purpose]. An overview of some of the main points:
>
> - [estimated number of awards]
> - [eligibility criteria]

- [funding levels]
- [project timeframes]
- [identified project objectives]
- [specific target population]
- [any known deal breakers for your organization, e.g., ability to provide mandatory matching dollars, to meet the percent effort required for project directors, or to sustain activities beyond the granting period]
- [key dates—for letters of intent, full proposals, conference calls, submitting written questions]

For more information about the program, visit this Web address: [www.sponsor.org/guidelines]. Let's meet this week [day, date, and time] in the conference room to discuss further the possibility of developing an application."

STEP TWO: FEASIBILITY—CAN WE DO THIS?

Evaluation Criteria

Assuming that the RFP appears initially to be a good match for your organization and that you intend to develop a proposal, examine the RFP for technical aspects of the application procedure and for stated evaluation criteria. This analysis will begin to answer the question of feasibility—"Can we do this?"—and give you an indication of how much effort will be necessary to develop a proposal. Ask yourself the following types of questions:

- Is a letter of intent required *prior* to the full proposal?
- What specific information should be included in the narrative?
- Can supplemental information be included in an appendix?
- Are letters of support and commitment encouraged?
- Are there budget restrictions on the use of grant funds?
- How many copies of the narrative and budget should be submitted?
- Are there page limitations, type size, and line spacing recommendations for the narrative?
- Does the sponsor have any specific forms that must be completed and submitted?

Hot Buttons and Distinctive Features

In addition, read between the lines of the RFP for hot buttons and distinctive features that must be addressed. Hot buttons represent the logical and psychological concerns of the sponsor, repeated throughout the RFP, that have an impact on how the project will be conducted. These concerns generally influence the shape of a project's structure and implementation processes. Hot buttons may be stated as evaluation criteria, but often times they are not. Look for recurring themes in the RFP such as accountability, collaboration, communication, cost-effectiveness, outcomes, participation, replication, and sustainability. Distinctive features are secondary concerns raised by the sponsor about the design and implementation of the project, but are not repeated throughout the RFP. Distinctive features vary widely by sponsor, but may include activities such as complying with federal regulations, standardizing treatment following national guidelines, being able to recruit and retain project participants, submitting timely progress reports, participating in annual national project meetings, and utilizing resources provided by the sponsor.

Online tools such as word frequency counters and word cloud generators may help you to identify sponsor hot buttons and distinctive features. The tools are exceptionally easy to use. Block copy the RFP and paste it into the tool. Clicking "submit" will then produce an ordered list or visual representation of the words that appear in the text from most to least frequently occurring. As you review the list, ignore little words like prepositions and articles. Instead, concentrate on nouns, verbs, adjectives, and adverbs. Higher frequency words may form the basis for themes to develop in your proposal that will appeal to sponsor hot buttons. Lower frequency words may flag potential distinctive features. (See Exhibit 2 for an expanded example of using technological tools to help find hot buttons and distinctive features.) In short, competitive proposals do more than speak to the minimum performance standards in the stated evaluation criteria; they address sponsors' subjective and objective needs.

A private foundation issued an eight-page RFP inviting applications for grant projects related to changes in health care financing and organization. To get an initial sense of possible hot buttons and distinctive features, the RFP was copied and pasted into a word cloud generator, such as TagCrowd (www.tagcrowd.com), to produce the following image. Words that occur frequently in the RFP are represented in a larger font, and in this case suggested that research and policy analysis on health care financing and organization might be a sponsor hot button.

academyhealth access activities addition analyses analysis applicants assessed
assistance available awarded brief care changes complete
considered costs criteria current data deadline delivery design develop direct
diverse effects encourage evaluation experience expertise explore financing
findings foundation funding grantees grants hcfo
health impacts improve including individual information initial
interested issues johnson large likely major market meet methodology
months national npo online open org organization particular
periodic please policy policy-makers private process program
projects proposals provide
public quality questions related reports requiring research
responses review selection services significant small solicitation staff strategies
submit support survey system technical topic type used website wood work

The RFP was then copied and pasted into a word frequency counter, such as WriteWords (www.writewords.org.uk), to produce an ordered list. Not surprisingly, the five most frequently appearing words were articles and prepositions, which can be ignored: 131 *the*, 111 *and*, 85 *to*, 66 *of*, and 51 *for*. Next came the words that popped out in the word cloud: 39 *health*, 27 *policy*, 18 *hcfo*, 18 *research*, 13 *financing*, and 9 *organization*. Equally significant, however, are words that seem curious, offer suggestions, and imply commands: 6 *must*, 4 *required*, 3 *expected*, 2 *encourage*, 1 *ensure*, 1 *emphasis*, 1 *emphasizing*, 1 *consideration*, 1 *strong*, 1 *strongly*, 1 *purchasers*, 1 *officials*, and 1 *hallmarks*. These less frequently occurring words may be signposts that point to hot buttons and distinctive features.

Searching for these commands, suggestions, and curious words in the RFP using a word processor's "Find" command identified key sentences such as the following:

- "The program places a *strong emphasis* on disseminating findings through peer-reviewed journals, HCFO publications, the program Web site and other vehicles that reach policy makers," which, in conjunction with the technical assistance provider's core mission to generate new knowledge and move it into action, suggested a potential sponsor hot button of dissemination.
- "We *strongly encourage* applications in support of individual candidates who will help us expand the perspectives and experiences we bring to our work," which, in combination with an entire "diversity statement" paragraph, suggested a potential sponsor hot button of diversity and inclusion.
- "Special *consideration* will be given to project teams emphasizing collaboration among researchers and policy makers, health plan *officials*, *purchasers* or providers, whether in the private or public sectors," which, given the juxtaposition of repeated appearances of *researchers* (seven times) and *policy makers* (six times) and the singular appearance of *officials* and *purchasers*, suggested collaboration with health plan officials and purchasers might be a distinctive feature.
- "One of the *hallmarks* of the HCFO program is its ability to provide guidance and technical assistance to applicants and grantees," which suggested that receptivity to receiving technical assistance might be a distinctive feature.

These technological tools helped to target three hot buttons and two distinctive features that, when addressed, will facilitate connecting with the sponsor logically and psychologically.

EXHIBIT 2

STEP THREE: PROBABILITY—WILL WE BE COMPETITIVE?

To develop a highly competitive proposal, this third level of analysis will force you to examine your individual and organizational strengths and weaknesses in relation to the values of the sponsor. As you begin to prepare a proposal, strategic thinking and preproposal contact attempt to answer the question, "Will we be competitive?" or more bluntly, "Is it *really* worth my time and effort to develop an application?" While there are no ironclad guarantees of funding, strategic thinking and preproposal contact will improve your probabilities for success.

Strategic Thinking

Strategic thinking means systematically and objectively assessing internal and external structures, processes, and characteristics associated with the delivery and receipt of project services. It allows you to build on strengths, minimize weaknesses, and connect with sponsor values.

- Evaluate your individual and organizational credibility and uniqueness—are you the *first*, *only*, *newest*, *oldest*, *largest*, *most comprehensive*, *fastest growing*, or *best* at what you do?
- Identify areas of improvement—do your competitors have more effective infrastructures, systems and procedures, personnel, or environments?

- Prioritize issues and resources—what are the key problems, obstacles, and constraints that need to be addressed to successfully implement this project?
- Compare alternative possibilities—how else could project goals, objectives, and outcomes be achieved?

Although RFP guidelines are intended to answer your questions, they may actually generate more questions for you. You may find yourself getting frustrated as you try to decipher and understand the RFP guidelines. As described in more detail below, three types of challenges include interpreting ambiguities, inconsistencies and discrepancies, and omissions.

Ambiguities. Ambiguities in RFP guidelines are often caused by careless word choices: terms may be inadequately defined, intentionally vague, or have multiple interpretations. For example, you may ask for more clarification from the sponsor:

- Which aspects of "quality of life" do you consider to be the most important?
- How do you define "community," e.g., by zip codes, census tracts, geographic or ethnic boundaries?
- What do you consider to be a "significant" impact on the target population? How much change has to occur to be "significant"?
- What is your capital threshold for classifying items as "equipment" or "supplies"?
- Does funding need to be "spent" locally or simply "benefit" local participants?
- Is there a *preferred* level of in-kind contributions?
- What does it mean that "Other criteria may be considered at the discretion of reviewers"?

Inconsistencies and Discrepancies. Inconsistencies and discrepancies occur due to hurried final editing and proofreading: multiple individuals responsible for developing the RFP may use different terminology to describe the same concept; last minute changes to one section may not be carried throughout the RFP. For instance, you may have questions like:

- The term "project coordinator" is used only once in the RFP whereas the term "project manager" is used throughout. Is the project coordinator the same as the project manager? Or are these two different individuals?
- Why does the Program Description specify the target population as "children under age 18" whereas Appendix B of the RFP says "children ages 5–18"?
- The RFP indicates that grantees must participate in an annual conference in Washington, DC, yet it also specifies that "grant funds may not be used for travel expenses." Are grantees expected to cover these costs with internal dollars or will other sponsor funds be made available to fund airfare, hotel accommodations, ground transportation, and meals?
- Section Four of the RFP asks for a description of project methods and Section Five requests a detailed workplan. What's the difference between the "project methods" and "workplan"?
- Why does the section on goals and objectives describe four project outcomes whereas the section on evaluation identifies five key outcomes?
- The submission checklist lists the logic model under required documents but the RFP describes the logic model under the category of optional materials. So is the logic model required or optional?
- The RFP indicates that grant applications are due on Friday, December 29 but since December 29 is actually a Thursday, does that mean the due date is really Friday, December 30?

Omissions. Omissions occur both unintentionally and intentionally. The RFP may intentionally remain silent on some program aspects to avoid inhibiting the creativity of applicants in addressing the problem. On the other hand, sponsors may unintentionally omit information because they did not consider the full implications of their own guidelines. Or, under the crunch of a deadline for releasing the RFP, sponsors may not have all of the final program details worked out. As an illustration, does the RFP leave out particulars such as the following:

- Are principal investigators required to be U.S. citizens or are permanent residents equally eligible to apply?
- Who owns data once it is collected—the applicant or the sponsor?
- Should stipends for meeting attendees be budgeted as participant support costs or as wages, which would have a corresponding impact on fringe benefits and indirect costs?
- Are indirect costs allowed as a budget item? At what level?
- Does the references page count toward the overall page limit?
- At what time on August 6 are electronic submissions due—close of business? 4:30 pm EST? 11:59:59 pm locally?
- Under what conditions will proposals be reviewed—mail, panel, or electronic reviews?

In addition to questions raised by ambiguities, inconsistencies and discrepancies, and omissions in the RFP, you need to ask probing questions about the capacity of your organization to carry out the project, if awarded. Being good at what you do usually isn't good enough in the highly competitive world of grants; you have to be among the best. What makes your organization unique? What is your special niche? What do you do better than others? Establishing your uniqueness enhances your credibility, both for your organization and for your project. Answering the following types of questions will convey to sponsors that you are capable of doing the things that you say you'll do, and justifies why they should fund you:

- What data documents the extent of the problem in the community, especially compared to other known areas?
- How can we illustrate that we have ready access to the target population?
- Is our proposed solution to the problem realistic and cost-effective?
- Why did we select this methodology over other possible methodologies?
- Do we have the individual expertise and organizational capability to implement a quality action plan?
- Is our mixture of collaborative partners appropriate to the needs of the project and the target population?
- Are adequate infrastructure, systems and procedures, and resources in place to effectively carry out the project?
- Which current programs demonstrate our experience with projects of this size and budget?
- Do we have the organizational and fiscal capabilities to manage and report on the award?
- How will we evaluate the project's impact in the community?
- What will be the specific benefits of this program to the target population?
- Do we have experience sustaining project activities beyond an initial granting period?

This iterative analysis process systematically guides you through the types of questions that you'll need to address to develop a highly competitive proposal.

Preproposal Contact

To increase your chances of getting funded, engage in preproposal contacts. Preproposal contact can help fine-tune your proposal so it more closely matches the sponsor's priorities, thereby helping you gain a competitive funding edge. Experienced grantseekers triangulate preproposal contact information from three sources:

1. Call past grant winners to learn secrets of success.
2. Call past grant reviewers to learn about proposal evaluation policies and procedures.
3. Call program officers to validate information and seek further clarifications.

Beginning grantseekers often wonder, "Will these people really talk to me?" The answer is "Yes," and even more so when you have something of value to offer in return. A remarkable level of collegiality exists among grantseekers. Grant winners are willing to talk freely about their experiences with a sponsor when they see potential for long-term networking, information exchanges, collaborative possibilities, and proposal swaps. Past grant reviewers gladly share their experiences when they know that the sponsor referred you to them. Most federal program officers welcome preproposal contact. It saves them—and you—time. Private foundations vary in their receptivity to preproposal contact, a point they usually make in their RFP guidelines.

The list of preproposal contact questions that you could pose is theoretically endless. Nevertheless, experienced grantseekers know that in order to write a successful proposal they must PREP first. PREP is an acronym by which to remember four basic types of questions to ask:

1. **P**osition: what are the baseline situations, present circumstances, and basic facts?
2. **R**ationale: what are the problems, needs, and injustices that exist today?
3. **E**xpectation: what are the implications for addressing these problems?
4. **P**riority: what approaches are most likely to lead to an improved situation now?

Collectively, PREP questions span a continuum of time, from past action to future intentions. Position questions explore baseline information and relationships with the sponsor, and lay the foundation for more probing types of questions. Rationale questions go to the heart of sponsor giving, exploring motivations behind funding projects. Expectation questions identify the sponsor's outlook for changing the problem situation. Priority questions concentrate on identifying the top activities that will effectively and efficiently improve the conditions surrounding the identified problems, needs, and injustices that exist today. Beginning grantseekers often make the mistake of asking too many Position questions and too few Rationale, Expectation, and Priority questions. The appendix presents 124 examples of preproposal contact questions, of which about one third are Position questions and two thirds are Rationale, Expectation, and Priority questions.

At a minimum, use preproposal contacts to learn more about the proposal review process. Your goal is to understand the actual process followed when your proposal is reviewed. In particular, you will want to know:

- Who will be reviewing proposals?
- How will proposals be reviewed?
- Against what yardstick are proposals measured?

By learning about who will be reviewing proposals and their qualifications (e.g., reviewer ages, background, and formal education; sponsor criteria for selecting and training a specific number of reviewers), you can tailor the language of your proposal to meet their expertise. Knowing how proposals will be reviewed (e.g., type of review—mail, panel, and/or electronic; use of a specific reviewer's evaluation form; time allocated to each proposal) enables you to customize your writing style to meet their needs. Understanding the yardstick against which proposals are measured (e.g., scored independently against the guidelines; ranked against each other; prioritized within sponsor funding categories; ordered to special criteria such as geographic distribution of awards; first come, first funded) allows you to emphasize hot buttons and distinctive features, incorporate counters to your competition, and make timely proposal submissions.

For example, Exhibit 3 presents a hypothetical scenario whereby two reviewers each spend a total of 15 hours reviewing a sample of 20-page proposals on a health-related topic. The first is serving as a reviewer for a federal program. The second is a reviewer for a private foundation. Because their situations and review conditions are very different, proposal writers will utilize distinct writing strategies to accommodate critical reading, search reading, and skim reading styles.

	Federal Reviewer	Foundation Reviewer
Review Conditions	The sponsor received 500 proposals for projects designed to address the health of children with special needs. To distribute the workload, multiple concurrent mail reviews were utilized to solicit comments from seven practicing physicians about five proposals. Each physician spends a total of two hours reviewing each 20-page proposal and one hour writing a 10-page analysis. Proposals are scored independently against the application guidelines with the help of a reviewer's evaluation form. Reviewers recommend funding levels to the sponsor for "approved" proposals, but do not actually award or disperse grant dollars.	The sponsor received 60 proposals for projects designed to address the health of children with special needs. A single panel review session was utilized to solicit comments from seven parents of children with special needs about all 60 proposals. Three parents have bachelor's degrees, and four have high school diplomas. The panel spends a total of 10 minutes reviewing each 20-page proposal and five minutes discussing its merits before voting to approve or reject the proposal. The "approved" proposals are subsequently ranked against each other and awarded funding until all of the grant dollars are dispersed.
Writing Strategies	Proposal writers should organize their proposals following the structure of the reviewer's evaluation form. Use the same headings and subheadings so reviewers can quickly and easily locate your answers. Because reviewers are educated experts, include pertinent literature citations to demonstrate your familiarity with current research. Make effective use of transitional paragraphs to show logical connections between each section of the proposal; reviewers may use these interim summary statements verbatim in their written analysis of your proposal.	Proposal writers should organize their proposals to be highly skimmable. Given 10 minutes to read a 20-page proposal, reviewers will spend approximately 30 seconds per page on your proposal. Begin the narrative with a one-sentence summary of the entire proposal. Write in short and simple sentences, no more than 20 words per sentence. Include boldface headings to identify major sections of the proposal. Use bulleted lists to highlight key points. Make judicious use of white space to visually break up long copy. Because reviewers are educated nonexperts, avoid professional jargon. Balance the logical presentation of statistics with the emotional significance of the numbers.

EXHIBIT 3

And in the scenario presented in Exhibit 4, two reviewers each spend a total of 24 hours reading and discussing a sample of short four- to six-page proposals on an education-related topic. The first is serving as a reviewer for a federal program. The second is a reviewer for a private foundation. Though their review conditions are similar, their situations are not. As a result, proposal writers will adopt different writing strategies to effectively engage readers.

Preproposal contact has two main benefits. First, you can get additional information that will help sharpen the focus of your proposal so that it matches closely with the sponsor's priorities and application guidelines. Second, it gives you an opportunity to establish your credibility, which is particularly important if your organization is unknown to the sponsor.

	Federal Reviewer	Foundation Reviewer
Review Conditions	The sponsor received 1,600 proposals for projects designed to support research at institutions of higher education. A two-stage review was organized to solicit comments. First, each reviewer receives 15 proposals electronically and has three weeks to score them independently against the RFP guidelines with the help of a reviewer's evaluation form; each reviewer spends one hour reading each four-page proposal and writing a two-page analysis. Second, reviewers convene face-to-face in five-person panels to discuss each application, update written comments as appropriate, and assign a final rating on a five-point scale; reviewers are not expected to reach consensus as a panel on final ratings. Reviewers do not have a history of working together on panels; reviewers serve for one year only and then must wait at least two more years before volunteering to serve again. Reviewers have a breadth of knowledge in the disciplinary field and relevant expertise in specific topics, geographic areas, and target populations. Based on reviewer feedback, program officers assemble a slate of applications from across all panels that are recommended for funding.	The sponsor received 30 proposals for projects designed to support research at institutions of higher education. A two-stage review was organized to solicit feedback. First, each reviewer receives all 30 proposals electronically and has three weeks to read them independently; each reviewer spends approximately 30 minutes reading each six-page proposal and making personal notes. Second, reviewers convene face-to-face as a 14-person panel and spend a total of 20 minutes considering the merits of each proposal. The sponsor does not have a standardized reviewer's evaluation form and reviewers are not required to prepare written critiques for applicants. Reviewers have a history of working together as a panel; greater than 90 percent of reviewers are the same year-to-year. Reviewers are nationally and internationally recognized disciplinary experts. Proposals are ranked against each other and the panel looks for a drop in proposal quality to establish the cut line for funding awards. With few exceptions, the sponsor accepts the funding recommendations of the panel.

Writing Strategies	Proposal writers should use the reviewer's evaluation form to organize the structure of their proposals, following key headings and subheadings. Use the same vocabulary in the proposal as in the RFP guidelines and reviewer's evaluation form; reviewers may take advantage of electronic tools and conduct keyword searches to find details in your proposal. Make the proposal—and its significance—clear to broad audiences as well as disciplinary scholars. Because the majority of panelists will be branch generalists rather than subject matter specialists, the proposal needs to define terms and limit jargon in order to establish a level of shared understanding. In instances when an application is a resubmission, because 100 percent of reviewers turn over annually, it may not be necessary to acknowledge that the proposal has been revised; calling attention to proposal revisions may increase reviewer scrutiny on details that would have otherwise been accepted at face value.	Proposal writers should follow the RFP guidelines to organize the structure of their proposals; include boldface headings to identify major sections. As subject matter experts themselves, reviewers will expect a great level of detail about methodological approaches and a deep knowledge of the literature in the field. Charts, graphs, and tables allow complex information to be presented in a simple, understandable format. Resist the temptation to use color visuals, which do not show up if proposals are printed in grayscale. Strategically place overview statements at the beginning of sections and paragraphs that call attention to project significance and innovation; reviewers might refer back to these highlights during the panel discussion. In instances when an application is a resubmission, modest tinkering changes may not be enough. Because the annual pool of reviewers is small and mostly constant, they will know almost immediately whether a proposal is a first-time application or a revision of a previously declined idea. The opening one to two pages of the proposal should be rewritten significantly, giving the application a fundamentally fresh feel.

EXHIBIT 4

Using the RFP Analysis Process allows you to answer questions about relevance, feasibility, and probability for funding success. In the next chapter we describe the steps for preparing a complete grant application.

CHAPTER 3
The Complete Grant Application

A complete grant application generally includes six basic components. The following table lists these components in the sequence in which proposal reviewers typically read them as well as the sequence in which proposal writers usually write them; they are not the same.

Proposal Reviewer Sequence	Proposal Writer Sequence
• Cover Letter	• Proposal
• Application Forms	• Budget and Budget Narrative
• Project Summary	• Appendixes
• Proposal	• Project Summary
• Budget and Budget Narrative	• Application Forms
• Appendixes	• Cover Letter

The reviewer sequence shows the way in which most grant applications are assembled for submission; the writer sequence shows the progression followed when preparing a complete grant application. Each section is described below.

DEVELOPING THE PROPOSAL

Analyzing the Request for Proposal (RFP) guidelines was the first step in developing a proposal. Through this iterative analysis process, you quickly determined whether the program is a good match for your organization. And once you secured organizational support for pursuing the grant opportunity, you examined RFP evaluation criteria and identified hot buttons and distinctive features. Evaluation criteria, hot buttons, and distinctive features dictate the form and structure of your proposal as well as aspects of the project. Strategic thinking and preproposal contact supply additional information so that you can fill in the details of the proposal, fine-tuning it to closely match the sponsor's priorities. In their generic structure, proposals include seven categories of information.

- **Problems.** Problems represent gaps between what exists today and what could exist tomorrow. This section of the proposal justifies *why* your project is needed.

- **Objectives.** Objectives are the specific, measurable activities that will help solve the problem. They describe *what* the project will do.
- **Methods.** Methods communicate the plan of action, the steps necessary to implement the objectives. The methodology section explains *how* the project will be conducted.
- **Qualifications.** Qualifications describes individual and organizational resources required to carry out the methods. This section identifies *who* will implement the project and their capabilities to do so.
- **Evaluations.** Evaluations assess the overall worth and success of the project, the extent to which the objectives were realized. They describe *how* project effectiveness will be determined.
- **Budgets.** Budgets identify the cost to fulfill the objectives with the identified methods and qualifications. Budgets explain *how much* the project will cost.
- **Benefits.** Benefits represent the good things that will occur by achieving the objectives. This section of the proposal describes *who will benefit* and specifies the intended outcomes of the project.

As you develop the proposal, your job is to anticipate and answer the critical questions that sponsors will be asking as they read your narrative. Your proposal must convince the sponsor, both logically and psychologically, that you can solve the identified problems and produce specific benefits. Addressing evaluation criteria, hot buttons, and distinctive features enables you to communicate this message in one seamless argument.

Just as analyzing the RFP guidelines was an iterative process, so too is the process for developing the proposal. In fact, this iterative process works for letters of intent as well as full proposals. Some sponsors require a short letter of intent prior to proposal submission. Letters of intent are used on a competing and noncompeting basis. On a competitive basis, sponsors use letters of intent as a screening device before inviting a select number of applicants to submit full proposals. In this case, letters of intent represent a "conceptual shell" of your proposed project. On a noncompetitive basis, sponsors use letters of intent to get an estimate of how many proposals they will receive in which topic areas. These letters help sponsors to better prepare for the review process, e.g., allow enough time to identify a sufficient number of qualified reviewers.

As you develop your proposal, or letter of intent, do so in passes. The beginning admonition from experienced writers is this: "The first draft is for getting down, not for getting good." Rewriting is easier than original writing. On each pass, address a different feature.

1. *Content and Organization*. Does your proposal respond to evaluation criteria? Does it have enough substance? Are your ideas complete? Is your organization logical? Are hot buttons addressed repeatedly throughout the proposal?
2. *Clarity*. Have you expressed your ideas clearly? Are there smooth transitions between proposal sections? Are all acronyms defined?
3. *Mechanics*. Are words spelled correctly, especially proper names? Are all numbers and computations accurate? Are sentences grammatically correct? Are sentences punctuated properly?
4. *Design*. Is the proposal design visually appealing? Did you include ample white space? Are headings specific to your project?

PROPOSAL DESIGN

While you will obviously spend much time working on the content of your proposal, you should also pay attention to its appearance or design. A well-designed proposal makes even complex information look accessible and simplifies the reviewers' jobs. That is, a good proposal design highlights the proposal's structure, hierarchy, and order, helping reviewers find the information that they need.

Some RFP guidelines, more so at the public than private level, stipulate proposal design formats that you must use. If so, follow them! At one federal agency, for instance, the consequence of not adhering to established guidance on using one of five approved type styles is that proposals will be returned without review. On the other hand, if the RFP does not specify formatting details, follow these practical tips, which are used by experienced proposal writers.

Charts and Tables

Include charts and tables selectively in the narrative. The information presented should be central for understanding the proposal. Keep charts and tables simple; complicated displays disrupt the reader's fluency.

Headings

Headings act like a table of contents placed directly in your proposal text; at a glance they reveal the organization of your proposal to the reader. Use headings specific to the RFP. Do not use more than three levels of headings because you may lose readers in the structural detail of your proposal. Effective use of white space sets off headings and enhances readability.

Lists

Lists help to get the message to the reader with a sense of immediacy, without being wordy. Lists help to visually break up long blocks of text. They are easy for reviewers to skim because they convey chunks of information quickly. Use numbered lists when items need to be examined in a specific sequence. Use bulleted lists, rather than writing in long prose, to summarize clearly a series of facts or conclusions.

Margins

A proposal with ragged right margins is easier to read than one that is fully justified because the proportional spacing slows down readability. Unless guidelines indicate otherwise, use standard one-inch margins all around.

Page Numbers

Place page numbers in the top right or bottom center of the proposal. In addition, in the left-hand corner of the page include the name of the project director and applicant organization. In a stack of proposals, this added detail facilitates reassembly if proposal pages become separated. Some sponsor electronic submission programs automatically superimpose their page numbers, usually at the bottom of the page. Posting your page numbers in the upper-right corner will prevent them from being "stamped over" by sponsor software programs.

Type Style

Unless RFP guidelines recommend a particular type style, consider using a serif typeface, e.g., Times New Roman, for the text of your proposal and a sans serif typeface, e.g., Arial, for headings. This contrast in type styles makes headings stand off from the body of the text. For the proposal narrative use 12 point type size.

White Space

Use white space to break up long copy. Ample white space makes your proposal appear inviting and user-friendly. White space gives readers a visual clue to the structure of your proposal. In a page full of print, a block of unprinted lines, or white space, stands out immediately, often indicating that one section is ending and another is beginning. When text is single spaced, double space between minor paragraphs and triple space between major proposal sections. When text is double spaced, indent five spaces at the beginning of minor paragraphs, and insert a full line of white space between major proposal sections.

DEVELOPING THE BUDGET AND BUDGET NARRATIVE

A project budget is more than a statement of proposed expenditures. It is an alternate way to express your project, establish its credibility, and communicate your project's value. Reviewers will scrutinize your budget to see how well it fits your proposed activities. They will consider whether proposed expenses are reasonable, allowable, allocable, and treated consistently. Incomplete budgets are examples of sloppy preparation. Inflated budgets are signals of waste. Insufficient budgets cast doubt on your planning ability. In essence, your budget is as much a credibility statement as your project narrative.

In addition to preparing a budget, you should develop a budget narrative. The budget narrative serves as a bridge between the proposal and the budget. It explains the basis of budget calculations and is meant to persuade reviewers that sufficient funds are requested to achieve project goals and objectives in a cost-effective manner. The budget narrative should include an explanation for every budget line item, which describes: (1) the specific item, (2) the item's relevance to the project, and (3) the basis of cost calculations for the item. Reviewers are subject to eliminating or supporting only a percentage of line items that are not well justified.

Three broad categories of information that should go into your budget narrative include:

- *Personnel.* Personnel costs include items such as salaries, wages, consultant fees, and fringe benefits. Whether you are using internal staff or external consultants, describe their roles, responsibilities, and levels of effort as related to the project's objectives and activities. Indicate the rate and elements of your institution's fringe benefit package. For contractual agreements, identify key dates, dollars, and deliverables for services to be provided.
- *Nonpersonnel.* Nonpersonnel costs include such items as equipment, supplies, and travel. For equipment and supplies, describe how items will be used to fulfill project goals and how estimates for each item were determined. For any travel by internal staff and external consultants, outline who is traveling, the purpose, the destination, the duration, and rates for airfare, ground transportation, per diem, and lodging.
- *Indirect Costs.* Indirect costs are expenses that are necessary to conduct the grant, but are not easily identified, e.g., utilities, space, library usage, payroll processing, and general project administration. Organizations regularly receiving government grants have an approved federal indirect cost rate that is included in the budget and budget narrative of federal proposals. Foundations vary considerably in their policies regarding indirect costs. Some allow indirect costs. Others allow only a fixed percentage. Some do not fund indirect costs. Check with your program officers to determine their stance.

Prepare a line item budget and budget narrative for each year of funding support requested. In addition, prepare a consolidated line item budget for the entire proposed granting period. If you are cost sharing a portion of the project budget, be sure to explain the amount and source of matching support. Include a budget narrative with your proposal immediately following your budget to explain or justify any unusual expenditure items, even if it is not specifically requested in the RFP guidelines. Experienced proposal writers find this practice of always including a budget narrative particularly helpful in preventing a sponsor from recommending a haphazard budget reduction as a condition of an award and in remembering the basis of cost calculations should the program officer encourage revisions and a resubmission in a future grant cycle.

DEVELOPING THE APPENDIXES

Proposal appendixes contain supportive secondary information that will further strengthen your proposal narrative. They can demonstrate that you have logically and systematically documented and addressed all of the essential elements that will contribute to project success. As a writer, you may need to include appendix items such as:

- Agency awards and honors
- Agency publications
- Audit statements
- Bibliography
- Certifications
- Consortia agreements
- Curricula vitae
- Definitions of terms
- Diagrams
- Letters of support and commitment
- Lists of board officials
- Maps of service areas
- Memoranda of understanding
- Needs assessments
- Newsletters
- Organizational charts
- Organizational fiscal reports
- Organizational policies and procedures
- Past success stories
- Photographs
- Publicity material
- Recent annual reports
- References cited
- Reprints of articles
- Résumés
- Significant case histories
- Subcontract agreements
- Tabular data
- Tax exempt status
- Technical specifications
- Testimonials
- Vendor quotes

Some sponsors count appendixes against page limits, a practice you should clarify with your program officer. Other sponsors do not circulate copies of appendixes when transmitting proposals to reviewers; thus, essential proposal information should go in the narrative. Nevertheless, the use of appendixes is recommended, especially when sponsor page limits are constraining.

DEVELOPING THE PROJECT SUMMARY

The project summary, or abstract, serves as a condensed substitute for the entire proposal. It should be carefully written, providing a cogent synopsis of your proposed project. It should provide a quick overview of what you propose to do and rapid understanding of the project's significance, generalizability, and potential contribution. Project deliverables should also be clearly identified. Unless otherwise indicated, limit your summary to between 250 and 500 words. Addressing the project's main points in such a limited space is not easy. Project summaries require exceptional conciseness and clarity of expression.

To ensure consistency of presentation, write the project summary *after* you have completed the proposal. The project summary should adhere to the order of the proposal, maintaining the same overall style and tone. Use major section headings in the project summary and include at least one sentence each on problems, objectives, methods, and benefits (outcomes). Although brevity is of the utmost concern, write in complete sentences, include necessary transitional expressions, and spell out all acronyms. In many cases, 50–90 percent of your project summary may reflect sentences lifted directly from your proposal narrative.

Often, proposal reviewers must write up a summary of your project for presentation to a larger review panel. If you do a thorough job on your project summary, program officers may use it as a basis for their proposal review. A quality abstract simplifies the job of your reviewers. Poorly written summaries make reviewers' jobs more difficult and diminish your funding chances.

COMPLETING THE APPLICATION FORMS

Some sponsors require you to submit an application form along with your proposal. The elements and formats of application forms vary widely within and among public and private sponsors. Nevertheless, sponsor application forms often request a few precise details from five categories of information: you must describe your organization, project director, project, and budget, and provide assurances that you will comply with the terms and conditions of grant awards.

At first blush, completing application forms may seem to be a relatively unimportant step in a bureaucratic paperwork process. The reality is that application forms establish and present your credibility in a condensed format. They reveal to sponsors both logical and psychological dimensions of your organization, key individuals, and the project. For instance, if you don't follow basic instructions when filling out an application form, the sponsor may wonder if you will also be as inattentive when implementing project activities and filing progress reports. Inaccuracies or inconsistencies in budget calculations may suggest to the sponsor that your project is apt to have significant over- or underexpenditures, signs of waste. On the other hand, a neat, clear, and concise application form can indicate that you are careful, efficient, and passionate about your project. Hence, it's essential that you take the time necessary to complete the application forms thoroughly and accurately.

Organization

When you provide sponsors with the information listed below, at a glance they can assess the legal status of your organization to receive funding and identify any existing networking relationships with your organization. In the case where top administrators at your institution have a prior history with a sponsor, your organizational reputation may precede your current project request.

- Organization name
- Address
- Chairperson of governing body
- Institutional chief executive official
- Institutional chief financial officer
- Institutional authorized representative
- Employer Identification Number (EIN)
- Taxpayer Identification Number (TIN)
- Data Universal Numbering System (DUNS #)
- Organization type (state, county, municipal, township, interstate, intermunicipal, special district, independent school district, state controlled institution of higher learning, private university, Indian tribe, individual, profit organization, hospital, private nonprofit)

- Date of establishment
- Number of full-time and volunteer employees
- Congressional district

Project Director

In addition to providing basic contact information, sponsors may wish for you to supply a few pieces of confidential demographic information, which will facilitate their efforts to ensure that traditionally underrepresented groups have equitable access to and involvement in grant programs.

- Name
- Title
- Address
- Contact information (telephone, fax, e-mail)
- Gender
- Race/ethnicity
- Disability status (hearing impairment, visual impairment, mobility/orthopedic impairment, other)
- Citizenship (U.S., permanent resident, other non-U.S. citizen)
- Social security number
- Highest degree and year obtained
- Grant experience (no previous support, prior support only, current support only, current and prior support)

Project

With the following types of summary details, sponsors can quickly understand what your project is all about: *what* you will be doing, *when* it will take place, and *who will benefit*.

- Title
- Purpose
- Summary
- Principal geographic area served
- Type of grant (construction, nonconstruction, capital, project, operating)
- Type of application (new, renewal, continuation)
- Catalog of Federal Domestic Assistance number
- Date submitted
- Duration
- Starting and ending dates

Budget

Before sponsors will invest in your project, they must trust that you will be a good steward of their funds. The following types of details illustrate that your project budget is realistic within sponsor-defined grant award limits, and that your organization has the capacity and experience to successfully administer a grant award of this size.

- Organizational budget (past and current year)
- Dates of organizational fiscal year
- Project direct costs
- Project indirect costs
- Total project cost

- Amount requested from sponsor
- Estimated funding from other sources (federal, state, local, applicant, other, program income)

Assurance and Compliance

Sponsors may want to know that your organization has policies and procedures in place to ensure that project activities, and individuals involved in them, meet ethical standards and comply with all applicable laws and regulations. For instance:

- Drug-free workplace requirements
- Environmental tobacco smoke
- Age Discrimination Act of 1975
- Civil Rights Act of 1964
- Conflict of interest
- Responsible conduct of research
- Fair use of human subjects (Institutional Review Board approval date and assurance of compliance number)
- Fair use of animal subjects (Institutional Animal Care and Use Committee approval date and animal welfare assurance number)
- Assurances for construction programs
- Assurances for nonconstruction programs
- Debarment and suspension
- Disclosure of lobbying
- Proprietary and privileged information
- Inventions and patents
- Executive Order 12372 (Intergovernmental review of federal programs)
- Program Fraud Civil Remedies Act
- Signature of institutional authorized representative

DEVELOPING THE COVER LETTER

The cover letter is usually the first read and one of the last written sections of your grant application. Although cover letters are generally short in length—one to two pages—they should be written carefully because they must highlight a lot of information in a brief space. They should:

- identify the program to which the proposal is being submitted;
- overview the proposal;
- provide an understanding of the project's significance;
- highlight organizational and individual uniqueness, qualifications, and capabilities to conduct the project;
- reflect the project's consistency with sponsor values, funding priorities, evaluation criteria, and hot buttons;
- name a key individual who can be contacted for more information.

Some private sponsors have rather restrictive application forms and guidelines; that is, their forms do not always let you include all of the information that you regard as critical. In such instances, use the cover letter as a transmittal letter (or e-mail) for their completed application forms, and include the details that you weren't able to include in the proposal. This allows you to build a stronger case for securing funding support.

The following is an example of the operative opening paragraph in a cover letter to a private foundation. Notice how the first two sentences set the stage for transmitting the required application materials, and the last two sentences slip in information that was not requested by the RFP guidelines.

> The Care for Children Hospital (CCH) is pleased to submit an application to the Lotsa BigDollars Foundation for a "Health Intervention for Inner-City Children." As required by the guidelines, enclosed are an original and five copies of our completed application forms. Of particular note, the goal of this project is to reduce health disparities among urban and minority children. Given a 62% prevalence rate of moderate-to-severe chronic health conditions among targeted children in our community, our proposal emphasizes a multidisciplinary approach to intervention activities.

Cover letters are not usually included with applications to public sponsors. More often than not, federal grant-making agencies that require use of the Grants.gov electronic submission system do not include a field where a transmittal letter can be attached. The National Institutes of Health does allow an optional cover letter to accompany an application in some cases; only the program officer sees the cover letter, not grant reviewers.

PUTTING IT ALL TOGETHER

After analyzing the Request for Proposal, developing the cover letter, application forms, project summary, proposal, budget narrative, and appendixes, your application is now ready to be assembled and submitted. The entire grant application may range from 5 to 250 pages. In certain respects, a short proposal is more challenging to write than a long proposal. Each sentence must carry a heavy information load. What's more, there is very little relation between proposal length and the amount of money requested. You may write 100 pages of detail for a $10,000 grant from one sponsor and 5 pages of detail for a $1 million grant from another sponsor.

Whether you are a novice or experienced grantseeker, it is often helpful to study samples of winning proposals. Examining previously funded applications shows you how experienced grantees have responded to specific sponsors and RFPs. They help you see how a persuasive argument is developed and what levels of detail sponsors require. Samples may even provide inspiration to overcome writer's block. Models of successful proposals illustrate what constitutes compelling content, effective organization, and forceful style.

The next five chapters contain complete, successful models of proposal planning and writing. Chapter 4 analyzes a community health project funded by a special purpose foundation. Chapter 5 examines a gerontology research project funded by a private, national foundation. Chapter 6 dissects a community-academic partnership development project focusing on food insecurity funded by a state grantmaker. Chapter 7 scrutinizes a library special collections preservation project funded by a federal agency. Chapter 8 studies an international teaching and research fellowship funded by an independent grantmaker. Chapters present the actual RFP, complete grant application (except for appendixes), and correspondence with the sponsor. Accompanying callout thought bubbles interpret and explain subtle nuances of the RFP, complete grant application, and correspondence with the sponsor. In other words, you can see the finished written products and understand the planning and writing process step-by-step.

After the grant award notification arrives, there are steps you should take internally at your organization and externally with the program officer to promote open trust and communication. Chapter 9 shares thoughts about grant stewardship, ways to position your project for success as you prepare to implement planned activities. Responsible stewardship can also help move you toward the Persuasion Intersection when you submit future grant applications to the same and other sponsors.

From RFP to full proposal to grant award notification, the examples presented in the remaining chapters provide an in-depth analysis of salient features that help connect project ideas to the values of the sponsor. They identify the location and interaction of key elements—logic, emotion, and relationships—that make the proposal persuasive. These examples are models that you can follow for planning and writing persuasive proposals of your own.

CHAPTER 4

The Robert Wood Johnson Foundation

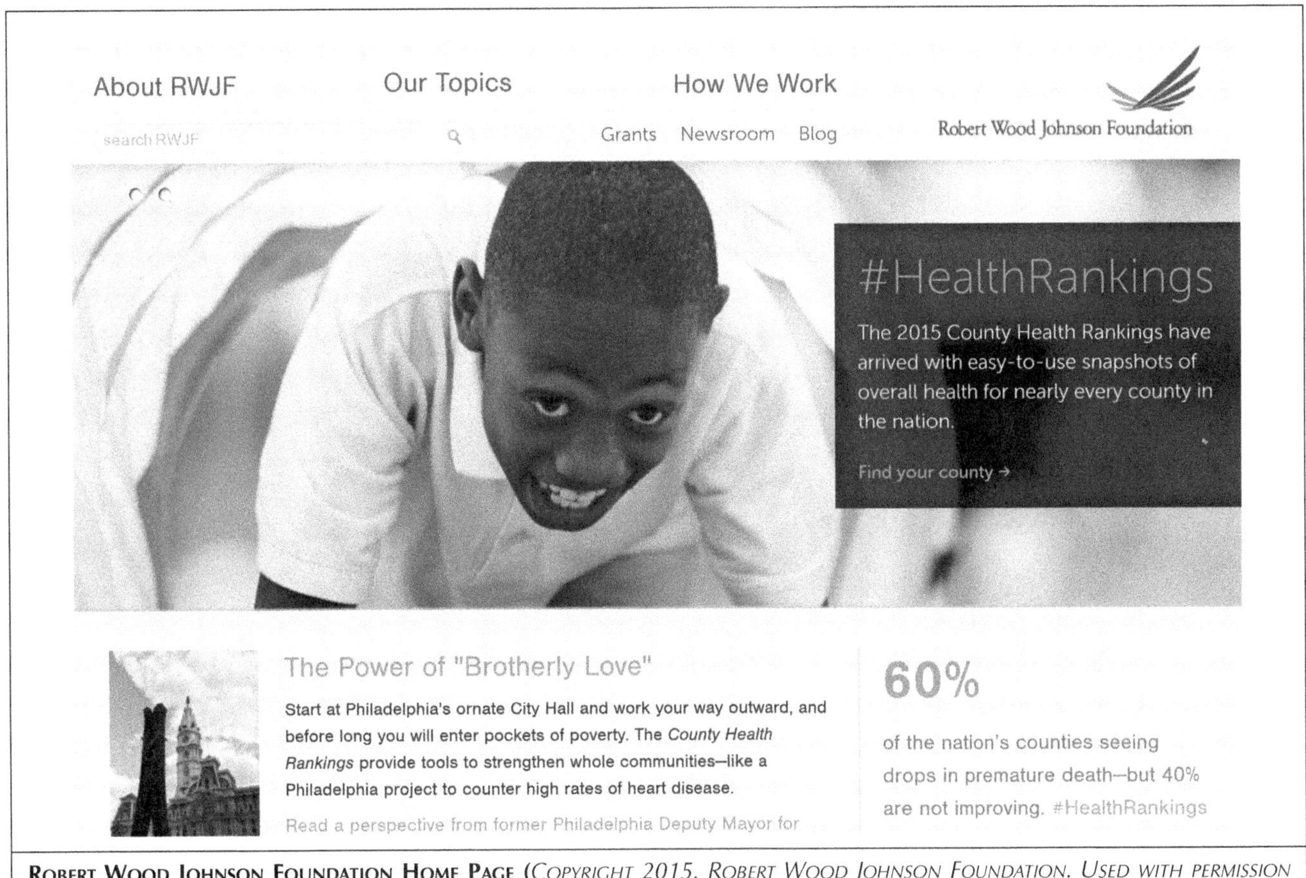

ROBERT WOOD JOHNSON FOUNDATION HOME PAGE (*COPYRIGHT 2015. ROBERT WOOD JOHNSON FOUNDATION. USED WITH PERMISSION FROM THE ROBERT WOOD JOHNSON FOUNDATION.*)

Perhaps the best known special-purpose foundation in the United States is the Robert Wood Johnson Foundation. The foundation specializes in funding health and health care issues. Nearly $400 million in annual grantmaking (2014 figure) is awarded to support topical areas such as healthy communities, violence prevention, health insurance enrollment, early childhood development, nurses and nursing, health care costs, payment reform, and community development and health. The vast majority of grant funding is invested in national programs—organized, multisite efforts to implement a proven strategy or develop new approaches to a problem. A limited number of grants are awarded to single sites in response to an unsolicited proposal or at the foundation's initiative.

The Robert Wood Johnson Foundation supports research, policy analysis, training, and service demonstrations. They like to field-test promising ideas and evaluate the results; take proven ideas and approaches to scale; give heightened visibility to an issue, idea, or intervention; cause coalitions of like-minded or disparate individuals and groups to form and act around a problem or issue; and research and engage organizations and institutions that would not otherwise seek philanthropic support. They provide a wealth of information about their history, mission, grantmaking priorities, award recipients, and application processes online at http://www.rwjf.org.

In this chapter we will take an in-depth look at a successful application to the Robert Wood Johnson's "Allies Against Asthma" initiative, a national demonstration program to support coalition-based efforts to improve asthma care for children and adolescents. Coalitions can apply for a one-year planning grant in order to develop an overall framework and strategy for addressing pediatric asthma in their communities. Upon successful completion of the planning period, coalitions may apply for a three-year implementation grant to support the coalition, targeted activities, and program evaluation.

For this national demonstration program, the Robert Wood Johnson Foundation uses a three-stage application process. In the first stage, applicants submit a five-page letter of intent that responds to the Foundation's Request for Proposal (RFP). In the second stage, the foundation will invite select applicants to submit a 15-page full proposal. In the third stage, the foundation will conduct site visits with select applicants. Accordingly, this chapter is divided into three sections, one for each stage of the application process.

Stage One: Letter of Intent

- The Request for Proposal
- The Cover Letter
- The Letter of Intent

Stage Two: Full Proposal

- The Request for Proposal
- The Cover Letter
- The Application Form
- The Cross-Walk
- The Project Summary
- The Full Proposal
- The Budget and Budget Narrative

Stage Three: Site Visit

- The Site Visit
- The Grant Award Notification

This application is a model of persuasive proposal writing; it presents the right balance of logic, emotion, and relationships to connect with the values of the sponsor. Figure 3 overviews the key elements that we brought together to reach the Persuasion Intersection.

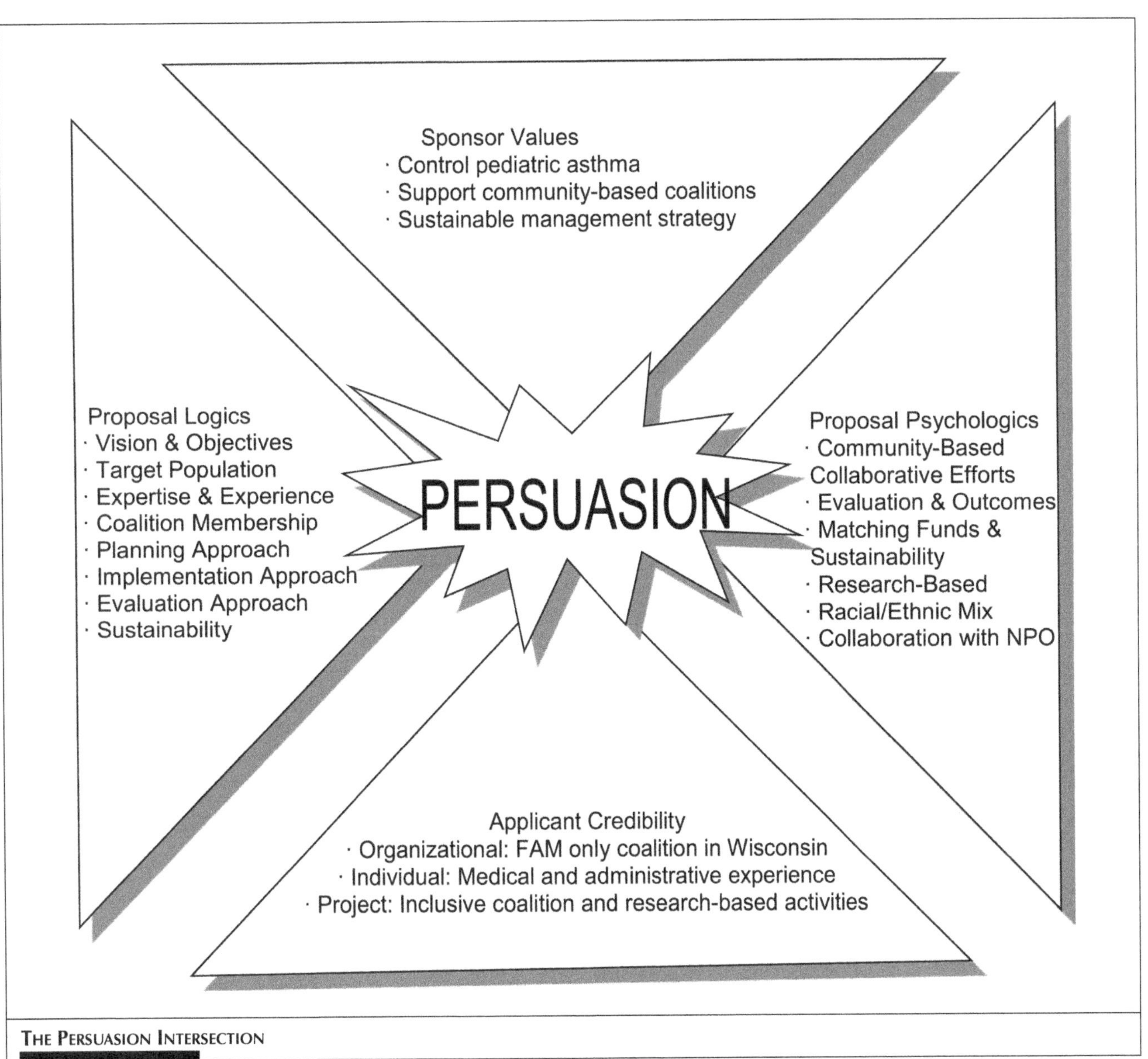

THE PERSUASION INTERSECTION

FIGURE 3

ALLIES AGAINST ASTHMA

The Robert Wood Johnson Foundation

Purpose

Allies Against Asthma is designed to improve efforts to control pediatric asthma. This national program will provide support to community-based coalitions to develop and implement comprehensive asthma management programs that include improved access to and quality of medical services, education, family and community support, and environmental and policy initiatives. The primary aims of the program are to reduce hospital admissions, emergency room visits, and missed school days, to enhance the quality of life of children with asthma and to develop a sustainable strategy for asthma management in the community.

Under this program, $12.5 million was authorized in 1999 to be awarded over a four-year period for up to eight community-based coalitions. Grants will be awarded in two stages. One-year organization and planning grants of up to $150,000 will be awarded to up to eight communities. Sites that successfully complete the planning process will be eligible to apply for the implementation grants of up to $450,000 a year for up to three years to support the coalition, targeted activities, and evaluation.

STAGE ONE: LETTER OF INTENT

Analyzing the RFP.
Analyzing Request for Proposal (RFP) guidelines means asking a lot of questions. The aim is to determine if this program is a good match for our organization and how much work will need to go into developing a competitive application. To effectively analyze the RFP, read it in multiple passes with increasing scrutiny, answering questions about *relevance, feasibility*, and *probability*.

The following call-out thought bubbles provide insight into the process of planning and writing a successful proposal. Because the RFP Analysis Process is iterative by nature, the three steps may not always appear sequentially.

Step One: Relevance.
The Robert Wood Johnson Foundation's "Allies Against Asthma" program is designed to improve efforts to control pediatric asthma. Eight community-based coalitions will be awarded funding: $150,000 for one year for organization and planning and $450,000 per year for three years for project implementation; $150,000 in matching funds is required per year during project implementation.

The program's primary aims are: to reduce hospital admissions, emergency room visits, and missed school days; to enhance the quality of life of children with asthma; and to develop a sustainable strategy for asthma management in the community. The target population is children under the age of 18, especially inner-city children.

Only one application per community will be accepted. A five-page letter of intent is due January 14. A full proposal from those invited to apply is due June 2.

Background

Asthma is a chronic inflammatory disease of the airways. It affects some 15 million Americans and is the most common chronic disease of childhood, affecting an estimated 5 million children. The total number of new cases of children and adults with asthma has more than doubled in the past two decades increasing from 7 million to 15 million today. Asthma prevalence rates have been increasing for all age groups. However, rates remain the highest for children, increasing by 92% over the past decade. Asthma occurs in all social classes, racial and ethnic groups, yet the greatest burden is among children from poor, urban, and minority communities. The economic costs associated with asthma are substantial. Annually the disease accounts for about 15 million outpatient visits, over 445,000 hospitalizations, 1.2 million emergency room visits, and 10 million missed school days. The estimated health care costs of asthma in 1996 were $14 billion.

In the past decade there have been significant advances in asthma management, so that most people with asthma can live active and healthy lives. Recommendations for diagnosing and treating asthma have been translated by the National Asthma Education and Prevention Program (NAEPP) of the National Heart, Lung and Blood Institute (NHLBI) into guidelines for patient care and have been distributed widely. Health care providers, caregivers, patients and their families need to work together to manage the disease. Quality medical care, self-management of symptoms, and a reduction in exposure to allergens such as house dust-mites, cockroaches, animal dander, tobacco smoke, and mold can reduce the frequency and severity of asthma attacks.

Yet, many children continue to suffer with asthma due to a complex set of factors. Despite the use of practice guidelines, there are still large variations in recommendations and practices of many health care providers and in treatment adherence by patients and their families. Furthermore, often children living in poverty lack access to quality health services and are exposed to high levels of environmental allergens and irritants. Schools and childcare providers may limit access to medications, and families may lack resources to purchase medications and necessary equipment for effective self-monitoring of symptoms, or social support to manage the disease on a long-term basis.

Communities are mobilizing to address asthma among children and adolescents. Schools, parents and caregivers of children with asthma, medical providers, public health and environmental agencies, housing professionals, community organizations, local officials, and grassroots advocacy groups are joining forces to develop innovative approaches to manage asthma. If these coalitions are successful in improving asthma management, this approach can be replicated and potentially serve as a model for other conditions.

Step Two: Feasibility.
The RFP uses more than two dozen different words and phrases to emphasize the importance of project efforts being "community-based" and "collaborative." Broad descriptive words for the hot button of community-based collaborative efforts include: *community, community-based, coalitions, broad-based efforts, families, linkages, partnerships,* and *joining forces*.

Step Three: Probability.
Strategic thinking questions might include "Can our community-based coalition compete in a national program and, if so, are we prepared to help set the national standard for improving asthma management?" and "Do we have experience designing models of care for other chronic health conditions that could apply to improving asthma management or models of care that have been replicated by others?"

Step Three: Probability.
Preproposal contact questions might include "Although it is not requested in the RFP, should we describe the magnitude and severity of the asthma problem in our community compared to the national asthma data provided?" and "Are there specific outcomes that are expected of grantees?"

Step Two: Feasibility.
A distinctive feature noted in the RFP is subscribing to national asthma guidelines. Specifically, the sponsor endorses the guidelines established by the National Asthma Education and Prevention Program. Implied in this endorsement is that successful applicants will also subscribe to these guidelines.

Step Three: Probability.
Strategic thinking questions might include "Can we realistically accomplish all eight of the stated program objectives—provide community-based health education, develop and implement provider education, develop and implement targeted communication strategies, provide access to asthma-related medical services in community sites, establish linkages with surveillance systems, establish policies to support self-management, reduce exposure to environmental precipitants, and assess coalition activities?" and "Are there barriers that might prevent the coalition from addressing these eight objectives effectively?"

Step Three: Probability.
Preproposal contact questions might include "Are applicants expected to fulfill all eight of the stated program objectives or would it be appropriate to prioritize the objectives and concentrate on realizing just a few of them?" and "Which measures of children's quality of life do you prefer to evaluate?"

Step Two: Feasibility.
The eighth bulleted item calls attention to the Robert Wood Johnson Foundation's concern for evaluation and outcomes. Five key words appear approximately 20 times throughout the RFP, emphasizing this hot button: *evaluation, outcomes, impacts, assessing,* and *monitoring.*

As grant dollars have become increasingly competitive, comprehensive program evaluations ensure a measure of accountability—that project funds are being spent wisely, that the project is making a difference, and that project benefits are being distributed across the target population or community.

The Program

The Allies Against Asthma program seeks to support community-based coalitions working to control asthma, which are organized to achieve specific outcomes for children such as fewer episodes of wheezing, decreases in emergency department and hospital admissions, fewer missed days of school for children, and greater quality of life for child and family. The coalition is expected to be a broad-based effort designed to:

- Improve the quality of or provide new access to asthma-related medical services in clinic, school, or community sites;
- Develop and implement provider education and other strategies based on existing national guidelines to ensure standard and appropriate treatment of children;
- Develop or improve tracking systems to identify and follow patients and families;
- Develop and implement targeted communication strategies to build awareness, support, and involvement of professionals, patients, families, and community;
- Provide community-based health education to improve identification and self-management of asthma and involvement in coalition activities; undertake prevention efforts to reduce exposure to environmental precipitants (e.g. tobacco smoke, allergens etc.);
- Establish policies to support self-management, enhance services, and provide resources to foster self-management and control asthma (e.g. coverage of appropriate equipment; access to medication in schools and childcare settings);
- Establish linkages with existing asthma or other relevant surveillance systems; and
- Conduct an evaluation to assess the coalition activities including the extent to which they strengthen the coalition's capacity to be effective and achieve asthma control outcomes.

Target Populations: The intent of the coalition is to reach children under the age of 18, especially those seen under publicly financed systems of care; those targeted by safety net providers (e.g. WIC, Early Intervention, Immunization Services, Community and School-Based Health Centers); and by other systems designed to serve inner city or other populations that experience difficulties in securing care.

Constituents of the Coalition: It is expected that there will be active engagement and participation of core representatives on the coalition, including such groups as: community-based organizations, schools, medical service providers, public health and environmental agencies, managed care organizations, housing organizations, academic institutions, childcare providers, businesses, religious organizations, media, voluntary health agencies, grassroots groups, children with asthma, parents of children with asthma, and other community residents.

Organization and Planning Phase: Coalitions awarded the one-year planning grants of up to $150,000 will be expected to develop an overall framework and strategy for addressing pediatric asthma in their communities. The steps would include: developing a structure to ensure an inclusive but manageable planning process; assessing the scope of the asthma problem to identify opportunities for intervention and resources available; and developing a plan with strategic and targeted interventions with specific outcomes and articulated coalition member roles and responsibilities. The plan should identify specific initial outcomes and long-term impacts and efforts to sustain and institutionalize the changes. Successful applicants also must secure a commitment for matching funds totaling one-third of each year's budget (for three years) to qualify for funding for the implementation phase of the project. Planning grant applicants who have secured a commitment for matching funds for the implementation phase, will be considered to be more competitive.

Step Two: Feasibility.
Community-based collaborative efforts is a hot button repeated throughout the RFP and in the "Constituents of the Coalition" section, the sponsor articulates specific examples of community partners: *schools, medical service providers, public health and environmental agencies, managed care organizations, housing organizations, academic institutions, childcare providers, businesses, religious organizations, media, voluntary health agencies, grassroots groups, children with asthma, parents of children with asthma,* and *other community residents.*

Step Two: Feasibility.
The RFP outlines the expectation that applicants will contribute to the costs of implementing the project and continue to fund it even after grant dollars expire. Hot button phrases repeated over a dozen times throughout the application include *matching funds, direct and in-kind contributions, innovative funding mechanisms, sustain and institutionalize, sustainable strategy,* and *coalition will continue.* More significantly, rather than inviting applicants to cost share voluntarily, matching funds are mandatory and the level of matching is quantified: "Successful applicants also must secure a commitment for matching funds totaling one-third of each years' budget (for three years) to qualify for funding for the implementation phase of the project."

Step Three: Probability.
Strategic thinking questions might include "What structure and process changes might be necessary to maintain the manageability of a larger and more inclusive coalition?" and "What levels of cash and in-kind support can realistically be expected from community partners?"

Step Three: Probability.
Strategic thinking questions might include "Does the coalition have experience with the identified implementation strategies?" and "What does the current literature say about the effectiveness of each of these strategies and how does that compare to coalition data and results?"

Step Two: Feasibility.
The hot button of community-based collaborative efforts is punctuated further by the sponsor's stated preference that this initiative "seeks a single application per community."

Step Three: Probability.
Strategic thinking questions might include "Who in the community is best suited to serve as lead applicant?" and "Who else statewide and regionally might submit an application?"

Step Two: Feasibility.
The RFP identifies 15 evaluation criteria by which applications will be judged, including potential for substantially changing systems for asthma control, coalition sustainability, a broad-based coalition, inclusive engagement in planning and implementation, participation by the target population, salience of coalition, leadership experience and qualifications, partner capacity and commitment to success, strength of planning process, support from government officials, clinical knowledge and

Implementation Phase: Implementation grants of up to $450,000 a year for up to three years will support the coalition, targeted activities, and evaluation. Communities completing the organization and planning phase will be eligible to apply for the implementation grants. Types of strategies that would be of interest include: community-based health worker/liaison approaches to asthma management; asthma management systems in schools; safe home and housing initiatives; clinical care in non-traditional settings; organized clinician referral systems to assist families in obtaining medical care; innovative means to identify children with undiagnosed and/or undertreated asthma; ways to ensure that patients receive adequate therapeutic recommendations from clinicians combined with strategies to enhance compliance of patients with therapeutic plans, including avoidance of asthma triggers; ways to improve provider and patient communication and interaction; and adaptation of evaluated effective models for provider, patient, school, family, and community education, and/or comprehensive service delivery. A commitment of matching funds totaling one-third of the annual budget (both direct and in-kind contributions) each year for three years is required. It is anticipated that implementation grant proposals will be due nine months subsequent to the award of the planning grant.

Eligibility and Selection Criteria

The initiative seeks a single application per community. Both public and private organizations are eligible to apply on behalf of the coalition under this program. Preference will be given to applicants that are public agencies or are tax exempt under Section 501(c)(3) of the Internal Revenue Code. Private foundations, as defined under Section 509(a), are ineligible. Public-private partnerships are encouraged. The following selection criteria will be used in evaluating proposals:

- Potential for substantially changing systems for asthma control;
- The use of innovative funding mechanisms to ensure that the coalition is sustainable;
- Evidence of a strong, broad-based coalition that is poised to develop and implement multi-component approaches;
- Evidence of participation by community-based organizations in the coalition and involvement in planning and implementation of coalition plans;
- Representation and involvement of the target population in the coalition;
- Salience of the coalition and its activities;
- Applicant's experience and qualifications for providing leadership, mobilizing key constituents and facilitating the planning process;

- Commitment of the coalition collaborators including their acceptance of significant roles, the amount of their direct financial support and in-kind contributions, and evidence of their institutional capacity to contribute to coalition success;
- Strength of the planning process and proposed activities grounded in science and field experience;
- Evidence of government commitment to the effort including support from key state and local government officials;
- Evidence of knowledge of the clinical aspects of asthma and science base for asthma control;
- The technical and political feasibility of the project;
- Likelihood that the coalition will continue after the grant period and that lasting changes will be made in community capacity to control asthma;
- Commitment of matching funds, including both direct and in-kind contributions; and
- Strength of the proposed evaluation plan, including the quality and availability of data to be used.

science base for asthma control, technical and political feasibility of the project, likelihood for producing lasting change, commitment of matching funds, and strength of evaluation plan. More broadly, the evaluation criteria address all three hot buttons—community-based collaborative efforts, matching funds and sustainability, and evaluation and outcomes.

Step Three: Probability.
Preproposal contact questions might include "How much change has to occur to be considered having potential to 'substantially' change systems for asthma control?" and "Who owns evaluation data once it is collected?"

Step Two: Feasibility.
While community-based collaborative efforts is a hot button, coalition support from government officials is a distinctive feature. The sponsor does not include government officials in the list of "Constituents of the Coalition" but does include them in the tenth bulleted item in the "Eligibility and Selection Criteria." Coalitions with representation from government officials may be perceived as being more competitive than those without. Although not explicitly stated, the sponsor may view state and local government participation as a crucial factor for shaping public policy and securing long-term funding support.

Program Evaluation and Monitoring

The Foundation may undertake an overall evaluation of this program. Such an evaluation would be conducted by an independent research group and would focus on key questions about the program's impact on improving care for children with asthma. All grantees, as a condition of accepting grant funds, will be required to participate in such an evaluation.

Step Three: Probability.
Preproposal contact questions might include "Should evaluations be conducted internally, externally, or both?" and "What types of evaluations are most appropriate for this project—structure, process, outcome, cost-effectiveness, return-on-investment analyses—balancing breadth, depth, and financial resources available?"

Step Two: Feasibility.
The importance of the evaluation and outcomes hot button is emphasized further in the final sentence of the "Program Evaluation and Monitoring" section: "All grantees, as a condition of accepting grant funds, will be required to participate in such an [independent] evaluation."

Use of Funds

Grant funds may be used for project staff salaries, consultant fees, data processing, supplies, a limited amount of equipment, and other direct expenses essential to the proposed project. Funds may not be used to pay for patient care, support clinical trials or approved drugs or devices, for personnel providing patient service, or for the construction or renovation of facilities.

Grantees will be expected to meet Foundation requirements for the submission of annual and final progress and financial reports. Project directors will be expected to provide a written report on the project and its findings, suitable for wide dissemination.

Step Three: Probability.
Preproposal contact questions might include "Are 'supplies' considered to be office supplies or do they include medical supplies such as spacers and allergy screenings?" and "Are these items allowable direct project costs: incentives for community participants, meeting refreshments, postage, telephone, and travel?"

Step Three: Probability.
Strategic thinking questions might include "Are systems and procedures in place so that annual and final progress and financial reports can be submitted in a timely manner?" and "Will this project cost money beyond the matching requirement?"

Direction and Technical Assistance

Direction and technical assistance for the program will be provided by a National Program Office headed by Noreen M. Clark, PhD, program director, and Linda Jo Doctor, deputy director from the University of Michigan, School of Public Health. At the Robert Wood Johnson Foundation, responsible staff are Seth Emont, PhD, senior program officer; Doriane Miller, MD, vice president; Phyllis Kane, program assistant; and Liisa Rand, financial analyst.

A National Advisory Committee will assist in the evaluation of proposals, participate in site visits, and make recommendations to Foundation staff regarding funding.

Step Two: Feasibility.
In addition to community-based collaborative efforts, the sponsor expects coalitions to collaborate with the National Program Office. This distinctive feature emerges in the first sentence in the "Direction and Technical Assistance" section: "Direction and technical assistance for the program *will be provided* by a National Program Office" (emphasis added). Applicants who reassure the sponsor that they will actively collaborate with the National Program Office may be received more favorably than those who remain silent on this point.

Step Three: Probability.
Preproposal contact questions might include "Who are the National Advisory Committee members that will assist in evaluation of proposals?" and "Is there an anticipated number of site visits that will occur?"

How to Apply

Those wishing to apply for funds under this program should first submit ten copies of a letter of intent (an original and nine copies), rather than a fully developed proposal, not to exceed five pages. They should be provided in 12 point or larger font per single line of text. Letters of intent more than five pages will not be accepted. The letter of intent should include the following:

- Brief statement of the proposed project's principal objectives;
- Its target population;
- Expertise, experience, and demonstrated commitment to asthma control and coalition approaches;
- Indication of diverse and broad-based support and commitment of coalition members;

Step Two: Feasibility.
The Robert Wood Johnson Foundation will use the following stated evaluation criteria in their selection process: a five-page letter of interest should include the project's principal objectives, target population, expertise and experience, broad-based support and commitment of coalition members, framework for planning and developing targeted activities, evaluation approach and data to be used, coalition sustainability, task and timetable, budget, and contact information.

Step Three: Probability.
Strategic thinking questions might include "If potential implementation activities are identified now, does that necessitate they be conducted even if the coalition determines at the conclusion of the organization and planning phase that a different course of action is more appropriate?" and "Should the evaluation approach assess the organization and planning period, the proposed implementation activities, or both?"

Step Three: Probability.
Preproposal contact questions might include "What can you tell us about the review process, such as how many reviewers will be assigned to each proposal, how much time will reviewers have to read proposals, and will they be using a specific reviewer's evaluation form?" and "Will awards be made on the basis of any special criteria, such as geography, size of target population, or size of the coalition?"

Step Three: Probability.
Preproposal contact questions might include "For budget development purposes, would it be appropriate to estimate an October 1 start date?" and "Do you anticipate any modifications to the timetable of when proposals will be due, reviewed, and announced?"

Step Three: Probability.
Strategic thinking questions might include "If selected to submit a full proposal, is it feasible to do so during the sponsor's scheduled timeframe?" and "Is the sponsor's projected timetable consistent with our strategic plan for coalition and program development?"

- Proposed framework(s) for planning and developing targeted activities for asthma control;
- Evaluation approach, including quality and availability of data to be used;
- Potential for sustaining the coalition efforts over time;
- An estimated task and timetable, and budget for the planning grant; and
- The name, address, and telephone number of the individual who is to act as the primary contact during the application process.

Full proposals will be requested only from applicants whose letters of intent best meet the program's criteria. Full proposals will be reviewed by the National Advisory Committee, and site visits will be made as needed. The Foundation does not provide individual critiques of letters of intent or proposals submitted.

Letters of intent and all inquiries should be addressed to:

Linda Jo Doctor, Deputy Director
Allies Against Asthma
University of Michigan, School of Public Health
109 South Observatory Street
Ann Arbor, Michigan 48109
Phone: 734-615-3312
Fax: 734-763-7379
Email: asthma@umich.edu

Please Note: All letters of intent must be received at the above address by January 14, 2000. Faxed or emailed letters of intent will NOT be accepted or reviewed.

For more information about the program, consult the Allies Against Asthma Web site: www.sph.umich.edu/aaa

Timetable

Letters of intent and applications will be reviewed according to the following timetable:

January 14, 2000	Deadline for receipt of letters of intent.
March 15, 2000	Notification of applicants selected to submit full proposals.
June 2, 2000	Deadline for receipt of full proposals from those invited to apply.
Fall, 2000	Grant Recipients announced.
July, 2001	Estimated deadline for implementation grant proposals.

About RWJF

The Robert Wood Johnson Foundation® was established as a national philanthropy in 1972 and today is the largest U.S. foundation devoted to health care. The Foundation concentrates its grantmaking toward three goal areas:

- To assure that all Americans have access to basic health care at reasonable cost;
- To improve the care and support for people with chronic health conditions; and
- To promote health and reduce the personal, social, and economic harm caused by substance abuse—tobacco, alcohol, and illicit drugs.

This document, as well as many other Foundation publications and resources, is available on the Foundation's World Wide Web site: www.rwjf.org.

The Robert Wood Johnson Foundation
Route 1 and College Road East
Post Office Box 2316
Princeton, New Jersey 08543-2316

* * *

Step Three: Probability.
Strategic thinking questions might include "What else can be learned from the Robert Wood Johnson Foundation and 'Allies Against Asthma' program Web sites?" and "Do we know others who might have received funding from the sponsor and can share insights on their experiences?

STAGE ONE: LETTER OF INTENT

Developing the Cover Letter. The cover letter is the first section of the complete grant application to be read, yet it is the last one to be written. Developing the cover letter *after* completing the letter of intent ensures consistency in the presentation of our main ideas.

The boldface heading centered at the top of the page identifies that this is a cover letter and *not* the first page of the letter of intent. The heading names the applicant organization and the project title.

The first paragraph is an overview of the entire grant application. It names the applicant organization, relates to the sponsor eligibility criteria for supporting community-based coalitions, names the specific program to which the letter of intent is being submitted, and reiterates the goal of the program.

The second paragraph begins to establish our organizational uniqueness and credibility—the only community-based asthma coalition in the state and one of the first established in the country. The paragraph also foreshadows our approach to one of the sponsor's hot buttons: community-based collaborative efforts. Namely, partnerships are essential to addressing community health problems. In the last sentence of the paragraph we attempt to align ourselves with the sponsor, reiterating a quote that was presented in a journal article about community, practice, and academic partnerships written by the director of the sponsor's National Program Office.

▪ Cover Letter ▪

Children's Health System: Milwaukee
Allies Against Asthma

January 10, 2000

Linda Jo Doctor
Deputy Director
Allies Against Asthma
University of Michigan, School of Public Health
109 South Observatory Street
Ann Arbor, MI 48109

Dear Ms. Doctor:

Children's Health System (CHS), on behalf of our Fight Asthma Milwaukee coalition, is pleased to submit a letter of intent to the Robert Wood Johnson Foundation's "Allies Against Asthma" program to improve efforts to control pediatric asthma. As your guidelines request, we've enclosed ten total copies of our letter of intent.

As you read our letter of intent, you'll note that CHS' Fight Asthma Milwaukee is the only community-based asthma coalition in Wisconsin, and was one of the first established in the country. Partnerships between community-based organizations, public health practice, and academia are an invaluable means to enhancing our community's capacity to address health problems. After all, as we learned from an Ashanti folk tale, "No one person has all the world's wisdom. People everywhere share small pieces of it whenever they exchange ideas."

Fight Asthma Milwaukee was formed in 1994 in response to state health department data showing that parts of Milwaukee's inner city had the highest asthma hospitalization rates in the state: 20 per 1000 residents—ten times the federal Healthy People 2000 goal! Accordingly, this project aims to reduce hospital admissions and emergency department visits, reduce missed school days, enhance quality of life of asthmatic children, and develop a sustainable strategy for asthma management in the community.

Thank you for your consideration of our letter of intent. Please contact John R. Meurer, MD, MBA, to answer questions or provide further information—phone: (414) 456-4116 or email: jmeurer@mcw.edu. We look forward to submitting a full proposal to the Robert Wood Johnson Foundation for this important health initiative.

Sincerely,
Jon E. Vice
President

* * *

In the third paragraph, we articulate the extent of the asthma problem, identify the primary aims of the project, and appeal to two more sponsor hot buttons—matching funds and sustainability, and evaluation and outcomes.

The last paragraph provides phone and e-mail contact information for the project director and ends on a positive note reflecting our mutual interest in improving pediatric health in the community.

The highest ranking organizational official signs the letter of intent to show this application has full institutional support.

STAGE ONE: LETTER OF INTENT

Developing the Letter of Intent.

Analyzing the Request for Proposal (RFP) was the first step in developing a letter of intent. It helped to establish the form and structure of the application as well as identify additional information to fill in the details of the proposal.

The boldface heading at the top of the page identifies the applicant and project title. The project title, "Milwaukee Allies Against Asthma," reflects that of the sponsor's program yet it is customized to our community. Equally important, the title will be appropriate even after sponsor grant funding ends.

The opening paragraph summarizes the entire letter of intent and carries a heavy information load. The first sentence identifies the applicant organization and uniqueness and sets up a shared desire for achieving the overall project goal. The second sentence briefly quantifies the extent of the problem in our community and begins to create a sense of urgency for addressing the problem now. Subsequent sentences spell out how we meet sponsor eligibility criteria. The paragraph also foreshadows the three hot buttons that will be reiterated throughout the letter of intent: (1) community-based collaborative efforts; (2) evaluation and outcomes; and (3) matching funds and sustainability.

Although the evaluation criteria in the RFP do not specifically request data that describes the extent of the problem, research suggests that the problem statement is a key proposal component that influences funding success. The problem statement justifies to the sponsor *why* this project is needed.

Because one of the stated project aims in "The Program" section of

Children's Health System: Milwaukee *Allies Against Asthma*

Children's Health System (CHS), Wisconsin's only independent nonprofit health care system dedicated solely to the health and well-being of children, is deeply concerned about controlling pediatric asthma. Asthma is the number one reason for hospitalization at CHS—nearly 1,000 admissions per year. But our concern for children extends beyond the walls of our hospital. Our Fight Asthma Milwaukee coalition provides quality asthma education, outreach, and referral services that enable children, families, and the community to maintain healthy lifestyles. Coalition constituents include medical service and managed care providers, schools, academic institutions, community-based organizations, childcare providers, and parents and children with asthma. The "Allies Against Asthma" grant opportunity will help to develop a sustainable strategy for asthma management that will improve the health status of vulnerable urban youth.

Asthma is the most common chronic illnesses of childhood, affecting an estimated 100,000 of the state's children under age 18, a majority of whom live in southeastern Wisconsin. Asthma is the leading cause of health-related school absenteeism in Milwaukee; preliminary research suggests that asthma affects 10% of urban school-age children. Between 1997–1999, CHS' Health Education Center, through their "Awesome Asthma School Days" program, surveyed more than 2,000 children with asthma from Milwaukee Public Schools. Most recent survey results illustrate the vulnerability of inner city school children:

- 72% lack spacers for inhalers at school
- 69% do not have a written asthma self-care plan
- 66% with persistent symptoms do not use an anti-inflammatory control medicine
- 59% report smoke exposure in their home (JR Meurer, J School Health, 1999).

More significantly, children who do not receive adequate asthma care have poorer development of lung function and more rapid decline in adult lung function than children who received appropriate primary medical and specialty care. CHS' Fight Asthma Milwaukee coalition can help address these needs to reduce the adverse impact of pediatric asthma in the community.

Project Aims & Objectives. Education, early diagnosis and treatment hold the promise for children with asthma to lead full, active lives. Aggressive identification of children who are at risk can prevent irreversible injury to lungs, improve school performance, and promote healthy lifestyles. The primary aims of this Milwaukee project are to reduce hospital admissions, reduce emergency department visits, reduce missed school days, enhance quality of life of children with asthma, and develop a sustainable strategy for asthma management in the community.

To achieve these aims, our coalition identified eight objectives that cover asthma education, referral, outreach, and reflect the goals of the National Asthma Education & Prevention Program:

- Provide community-based health education to improve identification and self-management of asthma and involvement in coalition activities.
- Develop and implement provider education and other strategies based on existing national guidelines to ensure appropriate treatment of children.
- Develop and implement targeted communication strategies to build asthma awareness, support, and involvement of professionals, children, families, and community.
- Improve the quality of and provide new access to asthma-related medical services in clinic, school, and community sites.
- Establish linkages with existing asthma or other relevant surveillance systems.
- Establish policies to support self-management, enhance services, provide resources, and build capacity of families and communities to control asthma.
- Undertake prevention efforts to reduce exposure to environmental precipitants.
- Conduct evaluations to assess coalition activities including the extent to which they strengthen the coalition's capacity to be effective and achieve asthma control outcomes.

the RFP is to reduce missed school days, we selected pertinent research conducted by our project director to illustrate the vulnerability of children in local schools. Simultaneously, this published research begins to establish the credibility of our project director. The final sentences of the paragraph discuss the adverse consequences of not addressing the asthma problem and emphasize the coalition's ability to reduce the impact of pediatric asthma in the community. Note that this final paragraph addresses the hot button of community-based collaborative efforts: The project director is already collaborating with local schools to educate children about asthma and assess its prevalence and impact.

From this point forward, the letter of intent follows the format and structure established by the evaluation criteria described in the RFP on "How to Apply." Boldface headings reflect key words from each of the nine bulleted points. "Project Aims & Objectives" tell the sponsor exactly *what* we are going to do to solve the identified problem. The primary aims of the project—taken directly from the RFP—are detailed here as the "big picture" approach to solving the problem.

To achieve the primary aims, the coalition will need to take specific measurable steps. Thus, the coalition customized and prioritized the eight project objectives identified in the RFP and presented them as bulleted points in decreasing order of importance. Equally important for the sponsor, our coalition subscribes to the National Asthma Education and Prevention Program, a distinctive feature raised in the RFP.

As a whole, this section touches on all three sponsor hot buttons. Note the use of key words, such as *coalition, community, community-based, evaluation, assess, outcomes,* and *sustainable strategy*.

This section of the letter of intent tells the sponsor *where* the project is taking place and *who will benefit* from targeted activities. These paragraphs on "Target Population" serve two roles. First, they describe the racial/ethnic and socioeconomic status of inner-city children. Second, they document further the extent of the asthma problem in the community.

These paragraphs appeal to the details presented in the "Background" and "Target Populations" portions of the RFP: disparities of asthma prevalence among children and minorities, hospitalizations and emergency department visits, national goals and guidelines, economic costs, uninsured, publicly financed systems of care, and safety net providers. For instance, the second sentence quantifies the needs of the community and relates them to a federally established Healthy People standard. The third sentence emphasizes our organizational credibility and uniqueness and describes our access to the target population; in essence, this answers the question "Why should the sponsor fund you?" *Because we are already treating the vast majority of the community's children who seek emergency care or are hospitalized for asthma.*

The final paragraph emphasizes that the project will serve the children targeted by the RFP, but more importantly, it goes a step further in bulleted list fashion to describe prevention efforts for specific age groups. These prevention efforts relate to the project objectives described in the previous section, and echo the sponsor's hot button for evaluation and outcomes: Assorted evaluation strategies will be necessary to measure the effectiveness of activities serving different age groups.

Target Population. Asthma disproportionately affects children and minorities. The asthma hospitalization rate for children in Milwaukee County is 4.9 per 1000, nearly five times the draft federal Healthy People 2010 goal of 1.0 per 1000. In 1997, there were 1,312 asthma inpatient hospitalizations for children in Milwaukee County, 56% of whom had Medicaid as their primary payer. CHS is uniquely suited to lead this project because we treat greater than 90% of children in Milwaukee seeking emergency care or hospitalization for asthma. The table below compares the ethnic composition of children ages 0–17 in Milwaukee County and CHS asthma emergency department visits in 1998. Although African Americans make up less than one-third of the County's population, they account for over half of emergency department visits for asthma!

Ethnicity of:	*Milwaukee County Children*		CHS Asthma Emergency Visits	
Race	Number	Percent of Total	Number	Percent of Total
African American	78,680	31%	1,896	56%
White	141,390	57%	1,156	34%
Hispanic	19,120	8%	274	8%
Asian	5,830	3%	29	1%
Native American	2,220	1%	5	1%
Totals	247,240	100%	3,400	100%

This project targets children under age 18, especially those residing in the inner city, uninsured or eligible for publicly financed systems, and receiving care from safety net providers. More concretely, project activities will reach four age-specific groups with tailored prevention foci:

- Under age 2: early detection and diagnosis
- Age 2–5: preventing emergency department visits for asthma
- Age 6–12: asthma screening, education, and treatment in school settings
- Age 13–18: preventing ongoing asthma-related problems, including tobacco use

These activities will help reduce health disparities among urban and minority children.

Expertise & Experience. Children's Health System, as lead applicant in a multidisciplinary collaboration of local and state organizations, has the experience and expertise to develop and implement comprehensive asthma management programs that improve access to and quality of medical services, education, family and community support, and environmental initiatives. For over a century, CHS and affiliates have supplied comprehensive medical treatment to children throughout the state and region; in 1998 alone, CHS admitted more than 18,000 children.

CHS' Fight Asthma Milwaukee (FAM) is the only community-based asthma coalition in Wisconsin, and was one of the first established in the country. For half a decade, project partners have worked together on a variety of asthma education, intervention, and research initiatives in the state, including participating in two Centers for Disease Control & Prevention cooperative agreements—Wisconsin's Community-Based Asthma Intervention Project and Wisconsin's Asthma Education Program for Welfare-to-Work Families. These programs demonstrate that the FAM coalition is a powerful and effective mechanism for realizing change at the local level. Quite simply, the best way to reinforce health education is to involve the community so they can advocate for themselves. FAM's parent advisory group ensures appropriate representation and involvement of the target population in the coalition. Creating a sense of community ownership facilitates FAM's vision to be a leading resource for asthma education, outreach, and referrals.

John R. Meurer, MD, MBA, Project Director, has the expertise to make this project succeed. Dr. Meurer is Assistant Professor of Community Pediatrics in the Center for the Advancement of Urban Children at CHS and the Medical College of Wisconsin. He has received federal funding for research on childhood asthma, and has published findings about school-based asthma education, costs of inpatient services for pediatric asthma, trends in the severity of childhood asthma, and risk factors for pediatric emergency visits. Dr. Meurer has collaborated extensively with FAM, coalition members, and the Community Collaboration for Healthcare Quality.

This section on "Expertise & Experience" and the subsequent section on "Broad-Based Support" let the sponsor know *who* is responsible for and *who* is participating in the project. In three paragraphs we establish the credibility of the organization, the coalition, and the project director. These paragraphs also address all three hot buttons: community-based collaborative efforts, evaluation and outcomes, and matching funds and sustainability.

In addition to describing a century's worth of organizational history and experience, the first paragraph emphasizes collaborative relationships with local and state organizations, a distinctive feature raised in the RFP. The second paragraph conveys that our community-based coalition existed long before this grant opportunity appeared and will continue to serve the community until their needs are met. Participating in two federally sponsored statewide grant initiatives demonstrates the coalition's credibility to the sponsor, saying in essence, "We have a history of good stewardship and affecting change in the community. We can do it again."

The final paragraph describes the qualifications of the project director to lead this initiative. His credentials include dual academic degrees (MD and MBA), which address the medical and administrative aspects of project management. Moreover, he has a history of extensive collaborative relationships with community-based agencies and myriad academic publications stemming from federal grant-funded asthma outcomes research. Collectively, these paragraphs express the idea that this project is a systematic continuation of prior community efforts where we have turned vision into success.

Broad-Based Support. Fight Asthma Milwaukee has broad-based support from community agencies, education and service providers, and concerned parents who have access to children with asthma in our four targeted age groups. FAM will provide leadership, facilitate the planning process, and mobilize key constituents to address pediatric asthma in Milwaukee:

- Medical College of Wisconsin
- The Health Education Center
- American Lung Association-Wisconsin
- Black Health Coalition
- La Causa Inc.
- 16th Street Community Health Center
- Childcare Advisory Committee
- Community Collaboration for Healthcare Quality
- City of Milwaukee Health Department
- WI Dept. of Health and Family Services
- Children's Health Alliance of Wisconsin
- PrimeCare, CompCare, Humana, and Managed Health Services health plans
- Children's, Aurora, Covenant, and Horizon health systems
- Milwaukee Public Schools and their School-Based Health Centers

A sample of coalition strengths: the American Lung Association-Wisconsin developed award-winning asthma management training curricula for childcare providers and school teachers; 16th Street Community Health Center, with US Environmental Protection Agency funding, distributed 15,000 asthma self-care plans in English and Spanish to children in Milwaukee Public Schools through the Child Health Champion Campaign; the Community Collaboration for Healthcare Quality, a coalition of health care systems, health plans, and public health agencies distributed asthma practice guidelines to more than 2,000 physicians in Milwaukee County.

Project Framework. The project design will take a multifactorial approach to accomplishing aims and objectives. Specifically, the FAM coalition will adapt a conceptual framework from the dominant health education planning and community health promotion model, *PRECEDE/PROCEED*. This framework will facilitate assessing administrative, educational, behavioral, epidemiologic, and social "diagnoses." Equally important, this model focuses on improving health outcomes for individuals, families, and the community as a whole. Research suggests that by addressing the individual within this larger context, programs are more likely to see positive, long-term changes in the populations they serve.

To illustrate broad-based member support, representative coalition constituents listed were selected carefully so that their organization names were self-explanatory relative to the type of service they provided, e.g., community health center, or to the population they served, e.g., African-Americans, or to their geographic emphasis, e.g., state department of health and family services. Moreover, two coalition members also reflect a distinctive feature: support from local and state government officials.

The sample of intervention activities illustrates coalition successes in collaborating with diverse organizations serving quantified numbers of children, families, and professionals. In fact, the second example demonstrates that individual coalition members have the ability to secure federal grant funding for asthma-related projects. A history of successful grant-seeking reinforces the hot button concept of project sustainability and shows a long-term commitment to serving the needs of the community.

Whereas project objectives tell the sponsor exactly *what* we plan to do, the "Project Framework" describes *how* we plan to accomplish those objectives. In particular, this section: (1) identifies the theoretical model that will guide planning and implementation activities; (2) describes key ingredients for a successful planning phase; (3) describes a multifactorial approach to the project's implementation phase; and (4) justifies this methodological approach to controlling pediatric asthma.

These paragraphs appeal to each of the sponsor's three hot buttons. Notice the strategic repetition of terms such as: *coalition, community, inclusive plan, measurable outcomes, evaluation, outcomes-based framework, long-term changes, matching funds,* and *sustainable structure*.

The key factors in community change are a clear vision and mission, an action plan, quality leadership, resources for community mobilizers, documentation and feedback on changes, technical assistance, and measurable outcomes. Accordingly, during the organization and planning phase, coalition members will produce an inclusive plan that will direct asthma prevention and intervention activities. In particular, the coalition will review the specific needs of the community, define members' roles and responsibilities, identify measurable objectives, assess organizational and administrative capacities, plan systematic and sustainable change in the community, and assess risk and cost factors. In the implementation phase, education and service delivery activities will target four areas:

Coalition Policy Initiatives	Community Education
• Asthma management systems in schools and childcare settings, including access to medication and equipment • Safe housing initiatives to protect children from allergens • Payer coverage of appropriate equipment	• Open communication among professionals, children, families, and community • Community-based health education and case management • Access to medical services in clinic, school, and community sites
Parent & Child Education	**Provider Education**
• Enhance patients' adherence to therapeutic plans and avoidance of triggers, especially tobacco • Adapt asthma education curriculums for school and childcare settings • Identify children with undiagnosed and undertreated asthma	• Improve provider/patient communication • Ensure clinician compliance with asthma guidelines based on self-regulation theory • Implement guidelines for clinician referral systems to asthma specialists • Provide effective clinical care in non-traditional settings

Recognized and respected asthma specialists Kevin J. Kelly, MD, and John Clare, MD, will lend their expertise to project design and evaluation. Further, coalition members have verbally committed matching funds totaling one-third of each year's budget for three years—$150,000 per year. In short, our methodology has all the critical elements for a successful planning year: a broad-based asthma coalition, a resource-rich environment, highly trained professionals, and a theoretical model to guide activities. This outcomes-based framework represents a clinically effective and fiscally responsible way to establish a sustainable structure that addresses pediatric asthma, one that can be replicated and potentially serve as a model for other health conditions.

The second and third paragraphs detail the activities that will occur in the organization and planning phase and the implementation phase. These paragraphs were tailored to reflect the language and ideas presented in the RFP "Organization and Planning Phase" and "Implementation Phase" sections. For instance, we categorized the RFP listing of potential implementation strategies into four types: coalition policy initiatives, community education, parent and child education, and provider education. The four types emphasize a multifactorial and multidisciplinary approach to accomplishing project aims and objectives.

The fourth paragraph justifies the coalition's methodological approach, relating to sponsor hot buttons. Namely, all of the critical elements are in place: a broad-based asthma coalition, a resource-rich environment with verbally committed matching funds, and an outcomes-based theoretical framework to guide activities. The last sentence of this section takes the next step, looking at the long-term significance of this project framework and echoing the last sentence of the "Background" section of the RFP: this approach "can be replicated and potentially serve as a model for other conditions."

The "Evaluation" section, similar to "Project Framework," answers *how*—how project effectiveness will be determined. Because this entire section is a hot button, it is essential that we provide more persuasive detail than the RFP's minimum expectation of describing the "evaluation approach, including quality and availability of data to be used." This means: (1) identifying and justifying the theoretical model that will guide evaluation activities; (2) describing the types of evaluations that will be conducted and sources of data; (3) establishing the credibility and capabilities of internal evaluators; and (4) indicating the coalition's willingness to participate in a national cross-site evaluation.

Evaluation. Performance monitoring, evaluation, and dissemination are essential components for achieving objectives. FAM will use the Institute of Medicine's *Community Health Improvement Process* to develop a pediatric asthma community health profile based on sociodemographic characteristics, health and functional status, risk factors, resource consumption, and quality of life. The iterative process of problem identification, prioritization, analysis, and implementation will be integrated with the *PRECEDE* framework to meet community needs.

Assessing the effectiveness of FAM coalition efforts and activities means conducting process and outcome evaluations. Process evaluations improve project efficacy during the granting period, and outcome evaluations document the extent to which project objectives were achieved:

The bulleted list verifies that evaluation is an inclusive process: parents, community members, and professionals from local and state, traditional and nontraditional settings will provide access to primary and secondary data that will demonstrate the effectiveness of the coalition and asthma intervention activities. Moreover, the first bulleted point addresses a distinctive feature: support from government officials.

- Establish linkages with relevant surveillance systems and access valid and reliable data available from the Wisconsin Bureau of Health Information as well as from members of the Community Collaboration for Healthcare Quality, specifically the Milwaukee Health Department, four major health delivery systems, and four major health plans.
- Improve tracking systems to identify and follow patients and families in both clinical and non-traditional settings.
- Assess coalition activities, overall effectiveness, and capacity to achieve asthma control outcomes by engaging stakeholders, describing the program, focusing the evaluation design, justifying our conclusions, ensuring useful information, and sharing lessons learned.

To make certain that the evaluation of community interventions is objective, meets rigorous standards of research, and is sensitive to ethnic and cultural difference, the FAM coalition will team up with CHS' Center for Outcomes Research and Quality Management, one of only a few centers of its kind in the country. Ramesh Sachdeva, MD, PhD, MBA, Center Director will ensure that studies are high quality and statistically valid. Further, FAM will benefit from the direction and technical assistance of the National Program Office and Advisory Committee, and will participate in the overall evaluation of the program. Coalition members will contribute to and use tools developed by the "Allies Against Asthma" program for planning, implementing, and evaluating pediatric asthma management programs and systems of care.

Sustaining Efforts. While many community-based organizations have high personnel turnover, CHS' FAM coalition is engrained in an organizational structure that offers long-term stability and sustainability. Accordingly, FAM has the potential for substantially changing systems for pediatric asthma control beyond the granting period. With initial CDC grant support, Milwaukee has sustained an effective environmental lead prevention coalition. We anticipate that generous RWJF support will have a similar impact on asthma in our community.

The first two sentences of the final paragraph identify personnel responsible for conducting the evaluation, establish their credibility through their individual and organizational uniqueness, and describe their contributions to the project, e.g., maintain objectivity, rigorous standards of research, and cultural sensitivity. The third sentence addresses a distinctive feature raised in the RFP: collaboration with the National Program Office. Their third and fourth sentences together reassure the sponsor that the coalition will receive direction and actively participate in the national program evaluation. National evaluation is particularly important to the sponsor because if coalitions are successful in implementing asthma management strategies, these approaches can be replicated and serve as models for other chronic health care conditions.

Although this section is considerably shorter than previous sections, its significance and information load are quite high; after all, this entire section is a hot button. The first part of the first sentence identifies high personnel turnover as a widespread problem for many community-based organizations; the second part of this sentence serves to differentiate our coalition from other potential applicants: our "coalition is engrained in an organizational structure that offers long-term stability and sustainability."

The second sentence explicitly answers the RFP's question about potential for sustaining the coalition efforts over time: We can do it. The final two sentences of the paragraph justify our belief that the project efforts can be sustained beyond the initial granting period by giving a concrete example of another local community coalition that was started with federal funding and continued after grant dollars ended. This history of successful grantseeking and coalition sustainability strengthens the argument that we can do it again.

This section of the letter of intent describes *when* project activities will occur and *how much* the project will cost. The first paragraph overviews the time frames for key tasks to be accomplished during the project period. In essence, this paragraph is a synthesis of the main ideas presented in the "Timetable," "Organizational and Planning Phase," and "Implementation Phase" sections of the RFP. Once again, we appeal to sponsor hot buttons using key words such as *coalition member roles, inclusive, specific outcomes, long-term impacts, sustain and institutionalize changes, available resources,* and *matching funds totaling $150,000 annually.*

The second paragraph briefly sketches out our budget request. The first sentence requests the full amount for the organization and planning grant; subsequent sentences give a breakdown of how funds will be spent within the given "Use of Funds" parameters outline in the RFP. Budget line items also reflect that funding will go to support all parts of the coalition: community leaders, families, and local agencies. Distributing grant dollars across the coalition demonstrates to the sponsor that this truly is a collaborative project with inclusive participation.

The final paragraph provides the requested contact information for the project director, who is serving as the primary contact.

Although space did not permit, ideally we should have included a concluding paragraph to this letter of intent that tied together our main points and hot buttons, maintaining a focus on the impact that this project will have on the target population and community.

Task & Timetable & Budget. With respect to the "Allies Against Asthma" initiative, in October 2000, the FAM coalition will develop a structure to ensure an inclusive but manageable planning process. In Fall 2000, we will assess the scope of the asthma problem and identify available resources. In Winter 2000–01, we will develop a plan with strategic and targeted interventions, specific outcomes and long-term impacts, and articulated coalition member roles and responsibilities. In Spring 2001, we will identify efforts to sustain and institutionalize changes and will secure a written commitment for matching funds totaling $150,000 annually for three years. By July 2001, we will submit an implementation grant proposal to RWJF.

With the demonstrated concern that you have shown for addressing pediatric asthma, we request an organization and planning grant of $150,000. Funds will support: salaries and fringe benefits for the .25 FTE project director ($22,900) and 1.0 FTE project coordinator ($37,200); consultant fees for community leaders and mobilizers ($20,000); incentives for asthmatic children and their families to participate in planning activities ($25,000); data processing by delivery systems, health plans, and public health agencies ($20,000); data analysis by the CHS Outcomes Research Center ($20,000); office supplies ($900); and spirometers for screening children in the community and school-based health centers ($4,000).

Contact Person. To answer questions or provide further information, please contact:

Dr. John R. Meurer, Center for the Advancement of Urban Children, Medical College of Wisconsin, 8701 Watertown Plank Road, Milwaukee, WI 53226. Phone: (414) 456-4116;

Fax: (414) 456-6539; Email: jmeurer@mcw.edu

* * *

Issues to be Addressed by Applicant in Full Grant Application

ID Number: 36

Coalition: Fight Asthma Milwaukee Coalition

Please include responses to the following issues in your application narrative:

1. Describe plans for evaluation and specify particular outcomes of interest.
2. Describe the staff and personnel who will lead/oversee the Coalition and manage Coalition efforts over time.

STAGE TWO: FULL PROPOSAL

Analyzing the RFP.
Our letter of intent to the "Allies Against Asthma" program received a favorable review, and we were invited to submit a full proposal.

The following call-out thought bubbles provide insight into the process of planning and writing the full proposal. Because the RFP Analysis Process is iterative by nature, the three steps may not always appear sequentially.

Step One: Relevance.
We had already determined that this program was indeed relevant to our organization. Thus, this time in step one of our RFP Analysis Process we simply summarized main points:

- 26 of 253 applicants were selected to submit a full proposal.
- 8 applicants will be awarded funding.
- $150,000 is available for one year for organization and planning.
- A full 15-page proposal is due June 2 and must address questions raised by reviewers.
- Site visits will occur in July through September.
- Funding decisions will be made in November.

Step Two: Feasibility.
In step two of the RFP Analysis Process, we examined the "Issues to be Addressed by Applicant in Full Proposal" and RFP for evaluation criteria, hot buttons, and distinctive features.

The three hot buttons identified during the development of the letter of intent are once again repeated throughout the application materials: community-based collaborative efforts, evaluation and outcomes, and matching funds and sustainability.

All five of the "Issues to be Addressed" relate to these hot buttons. The first three issues—evaluation plans, coalition leadership and management, and sustainability plans—match up explicitly with hot buttons. The fourth and fifth issues are more subtle versions of these hot buttons. Specifically, the issue of organizational "weaknesses and challenges" relates to community-based collaborative efforts and outcomes. And the issue of "potential approaches for system-wide change" relates to project sustainability. In other words, the question we must be able to answer is, "When a diverse mix of organizations come together around a single topic, can they agree to implement and institutionalize changes that will impact systems of care over the long term?"

3. Discuss the potential for sustaining Coalition efforts following the end of the grant period.
4. What component or efforts of the Coalition will address health system weaknesses and challenges?
5. What potential approaches hold most promising for system-wide change?

PROPOSAL FORMAT

A. REQUIRED CONTENTS OF THE APPLICATION

A checklist for use in preparing your proposal is included in Appendix I. Each proposal should include the following items:

1. Cover Letter

2. Table of Contents

3. The Robert Wood Johnson Foundation "Request for Project Support and Conditions of Grant" Form

4. One-page Project Summary

5. Proposal Narrative (Section B provides detailed guidance)

This section is the heart of the proposal. It should describe the vision for the project and the proposed approach. Taken as a whole, information in this section should convey to the reader a clear sense that (1) there is a need for improving systems of care for children with asthma, (2) the proposed approach is comprehensive, feasible, and likely to improve the health and quality of life of a significant number of children with asthma; and (3) the outcomes specified are reasonable and the applicant has the capability to measure the effects of coalition efforts on these outcomes.

The narrative should address the following 8 areas (described further in Section B):

Step Two: Feasibility.
The Robert Wood Johnson Foundation will use the following stated evaluation criteria in their selection process. Proposals should include:

- A one-page cover letter
- A table of contents
- An application form
- A one-page project summary
- A 15-page proposal narrative that describes:
  Vision and principal objectives
  Target population and level of need
  Expertise and experience in asthma control
  Coalition membership, infrastructure, and capacity
  Planning approach and timeline
  Preliminary implementation approach
  Evaluation approach
  Sustaining coalition efforts over time
- A budget and budget narrative
- Attachments:
  Résumés of key project personnel
  Description of the application process
  Letters of support
- Issues to be Addressed by Application in the Full Proposal:
  Plans for evaluation and outcomes
  Coalition leaders and staff
  Potential for sustaining coalition efforts
  Efforts to address health system weaknesses and challenges
  Potential approaches for system-wide change
- Use 12-point font
- Due date: June 2

a. Vision and principal objectives
b. Target population and level of need
c. Expertise and experience in asthma control
d. Coalition membership, infrastructure, and capacity
e. Planning approach and timeline
f. Preliminary implementation approach
g. Evaluation approach
h. Sustaining coalition efforts over time;

It is recognized that specifics in some of these areas will be refined during the planning process. Applicants should, however, at least demonstrate a grasp of the issues involved and options that should be considered. In general, it is better to be explicit about areas of uncertainty and speak to how this will be dealt with rather than making definitive statements based on weak information.

Applicants are encouraged to limit the narrative section to 15 pages. Reviewers will consider favorably proposals that are organized well and that address each area completely and concisely.

6. Proposed Budget and Budget Narrative

Applications must include a detailed budget and accompanying budget narrative for the one-year planning phase. The budget documents will allow reviewers to cross-walk budget items with the proposed approach to ensure consistency and compatibility. The budget submitted should project accurately the expenses anticipated and delineate how Foundation funds would be used. It must also specify other sources of direct and in-kind support for coalition efforts.

Applicants are strongly encouraged to pay close attention to the Foundation's guidelines for allowable uses of grant funds when preparing their budgets. Applicants are also reminded that the maximum award for the planning period is $150,000; the Foundation's contribution can be lower than but cannot exceed this maximum amount.

A copy of the Robert Wood Johnson Foundation "National Program Site Budget Preparation Guidelines" is included in Appendix IV. To be eligible for an award, applications must include budgets that comply with Foundation policies and guidelines. The proposed budget will be reviewed carefully, and negotiations may be held with the applicant lead agency to identify areas requiring change or clarification to comply with Foundation policies.

7. Key Staff and Leadership

In an attachment to the proposal, provide a resume or a summary of experience for key project staff (hired directly or through a subcontract) and individuals who will serve in a leadership/governance capacity. Include individuals responsible for managing the daily operations of the coalition and planning efforts, and individuals responsible for evaluation activities.

Step Two: Feasibility.
Hot buttons appear early in the RFP and are repeated throughout the application materials.

Two dozen different words and phrases are used to emphasize the importance of project efforts being "community-based" and "collaborative." Broad descriptive hot button words include: *community, community-based, coalitions, coalition-based, families, linkages, meaningful involvement,* and *sufficiently inclusive.*

Ten key words and phrases appear approximately 35 times throughout the RFP, highlighting the foundation's hot button concern for systematic evaluation and measurable outcomes: *evaluation, cross-site evaluation, evaluation efforts, outcomes, asthma control, assess, data, baseline data, data collection,* and *analysis.*

The RFP outlines the expectation that applicants contribute to the costs of implementing this project and continue to fund it even after grant dollars expire. Hot button phrases for matching funds and sustainability are repeated a dozen times throughout the application and include *matching contributions, direct and in-kind support, resources, sustain coalition efforts, institutionalize effective strategies,* and *continue beyond the time period funded.*

Step Three: Probability.
Preproposal contact questions might include "To what degree does flexibility exist to rebudget funds as necessary during the project period?" and "What are the most common budget challenges faced by grantees?"

Step Three: Probability.
Preproposal contact questions might include "Is there a preferred format and length for résumés of key project staff?" and "Are there any expected categories of information to be

In addition, for each key staff position provide the following:

A description of the position (duties and qualifications)
A description of the hiring process and the individuals or organizations responsible for making hiring decisions

8. Description of the Application Process

Provide a description of the process involved in preparing the planning grant application, and provide documentation to characterize the effort involved (meetings, individuals involved, etc.).

B. DETAILED INSTRUCTIONS FOR NARRATIVE SECTION

The narrative section of the proposal should be organized into the following areas, and applicants should follow the guidelines outlined below in preparing each section. This portion of the proposal will receive the greatest attention by the review committee, and applicants are encouraged to pay close attention to the content and organization of each section. ***In preparing these sections, applicants should also ensure that any specific areas or items noted in the letter from the National Program Office (items identified during the letter of intent review process) are addressed completely.***

1. Vision and Principal Objectives

This section should begin by describing the overall vision for the proposed effort, including: why the effort is needed and the types of changes envisioned. Applicants may provide a diagram or a flow chart if it will help in conveying this vision clearly.

Proposals should also include a brief and specific statement of the project's overall goals and objectives. Include and differentiate as relevant goals and objectives for the (1) organization and planning phase, and the (2) implementation phase. Discuss why the community is applying for the grant, and what is hoped that the project will accomplish. Ensure that stated goals and objectives are realistic, give the time frame and magnitude of project efforts.

Applicants should demonstrate an understanding of the various factors and sub-systems (i.e., families, health care settings, schools, housing) that influence asthma control and quality of life for children with asthma within a community. Consideration should be given to changes at the organizational and sub-system levels and their relationships that are needed to promote stronger community-wide systems of care.

included on résumés beyond the standard: education, positions held, publications and presentations, professional activities, association memberships, and honors and awards?"

Step Three: Probability.
Preproposal contact questions might include "What level of documentation is expected for the 'Description of the Application Process'—a brief summary or complete meeting minutes, reports, and correspondence?" and "Is there a preferred page length for the 'Description of the Application Process'?"

Step Three: Probability.
Preproposal contact questions might include "Why does the RFP ask applicants to 'include and differentiate as relevant goals and objectives for the (1) organization and planning phase, and the (2) implementation phase' when the purpose of the planning phase is to prepare for an effective implementation phase?" and "Which survey tools do you recommend that coalitions use to evaluate which specific measures of children's quality of life?"

Step Three: Probability.
Strategic thinking questions might include "Which factors pose the greatest challenges to asthma control within our community?" and "Which factors hold the greatest potential for immediate success and long-term improvement?"

Step Three: Probability.
Preproposal contact questions might include "What do you see as essential to improving systems of care for children with asthma that isn't happening now?" and "One selection criterion used in evaluating proposals is the 'potential for substantially changing systems for asthma control.' What is considered 'substantial' change?"

Step Three: Probability.
Strategic thinking questions might include "What specific geographic areas will be served—county, city, inner city, census tracts, zip codes, neighborhood strategic planning areas?" and "What gaps in data exist about the prevalence of pediatric asthma in the community?"

Step Three: Probability.
Strategic thinking questions might include "Are there any key members who need to be added to the coalition?" and "Have we identified the core individuals, their degrees, areas of expertise, and organizations?"

Step Two: Feasibility.
Community-based collaborative efforts is a sponsor hot button, and in the "Coalition Membership" section, the RFP provides 14 specific categories of partners to be included in organization and planning and implementation activities. The RFP stresses that coalitions should have comprehensive membership and inclusive participation. Applicants must provide a complete list of coalition members, their organizational affiliations, and the sector they represent. The RFP even states, "Reviewers will look for evidence that the planning process was comprehensive, that it included meaningful level of involvement from key stakeholder groups."

2. Target Population and Level of Need

As outlined earlier, the intent of the Allies Against Asthma program is to improve systems of care for children with asthma, especially those facing greater risks and barriers to care because of their socioeconomic status. Applicants must provide a clear description of the geographic area(s) and population(s) targeted by the proposed project. The description must include information sufficient to characterize the number of children with asthma likely to be affected (estimates are acceptable), where they are located, and the level of need within their families and communities. In addition, information contained in this section should demonstrate the applicant's working knowledge of populations targeted by the project.

It is recognized that many communities lack complete data on pediatric asthma prevalence. Applicants are expected to make the best use of available data, and to outline clearly important gaps and how these will be addressed by the project.

3. Asthma Control Expertise and Experience

It is essential that the coalition have within its membership sufficient expertise in the clinical aspects of pediatric asthma and in the scientific foundation for asthma control. This section should identify the individuals and organizations that will contribute this type of expertise, describe their background/nature of their expertise in pediatric asthma and its control, and discuss how this expertise will be tapped during the planning process.

4. Coalition Membership, Infrastructure, and Capacity

The purpose of the coalition is to ensure that efforts during the planning and implementation phase will be shaped and guided by representatives from the various sub-systems influencing asthma control and quality of care for children with asthma. This section of the proposal must describe the coalition membership, the staff and infrastructure for supporting coalition activities, and the applicant's expertise and experience with coalition approaches.

Coalition membership. Applicants are strongly encouraged to include in the coalition representatives from the following sectors:

a. Parents and other family members of children with asthma

b. Children with asthma

c. Medical/clinical providers (physicians, nurses, other health care professionals)

d. Health care delivery system entities (hospitals, school-based health clinics, safety net clinics, other)

e. Schools and childcare providers

f. Public health and environmental agencies

g. State and local government

h. Housing organizations

i. Payers or insurers and managed care organizations for low-income and uninsured populations

j. Voluntary health organizations

k. Community-based organizations such as churches and other religious organizations, grassroots groups, and others representing the proposed target population

l. Academic institutions and individuals with expertise in evaluation

m. Media

n. Business and industry

In table format, applicants should provide a complete list of coalition members that indicates:

(1) the name of each individual involved

(2) their organizational affiliation (if applicable)

(3) the sector they represent (defined using categories a through n outlined above)

(4) whether they are already committed, or their involvement needs to be secured

(5) a brief description of their role

Applicants should also describe the extent to which the coalition as proposed reflects the racial and ethnic composition of the target community(ies).

If new members will be added to the coalition, applicants should discuss how these individuals will be identified and recruited.

In an attachment to the proposal, the applicant should include memoranda of understanding and letters of support for those members/groups already committed to the coalition.

Coalition Infrastructure. Applicants must describe how the coalition will be structured and supported. Descriptions should address the following areas:

Step Two: Feasibility.
In both the first and second stage of the application procedure, the RFP articulates a distinctive feature that relates to the hot button of community-based collaborative efforts. Support from government officials caught our attention as a distinctive feature because of an inconsistency in the RFP for the letter of intent: government officials were not required constituents of the coalition, yet evidence of their participation was essential to satisfy the sponsor's eligibility and selection criteria.

The RFP for the full proposal clarifies this inconsistency, specifically listing state and local government among required coalition constituents and includes a new distinctive feature: racial/ethnic composition of the coalition. In the "Coalition Membership" section, the guidelines request a table that provides a complete list of member representatives and, almost in passing, state, "Applicants should also describe the extent to which the coalition as proposed reflects the racial and ethnic composition of the community." Because asthma disproportionately affects minority groups, the sponsor recognizes that their participation in the organization and planning phase will improve the likelihood of success during the project's implementation phase.

Step Three: Probability.
Preproposal contact questions might include "How many letters of support and commitment from collaborating agencies would be appropriate to include as attachments to our application?" and "What's the desired local impact you'd like to see, while maintaining a balance across project breadth, depth, and financial resources available?"

Step Three: Probability.
Strategic thinking questions might include "How will committees be organized to accommodate inclusive participation?" and "How will committee appointments, reappointments, and term limits be handled?"

Leadership/governance: organization(s) and individuals who will play leadership roles in the coalition and a discussion of their expertise in this capacity. Description of governance or leadership committees, if any, for the proposed or existing coalition;

Committee structure, including a description of key committees and subcommittees already identified, and how important committee positions will be filled;

In cases where the proposed coalition builds on one or more existing coalition(s), applicants must clarify whether or not these other coalitions will continue to function and, if so, how the proposed coalition will differ from and/or relate to these other groups.

Step Three: Probability.
Strategic thinking questions might include "What structure and process changes might be necessary to maintain the manageability of a larger, more inclusive coalition?" and "How will we ensure that communications are culturally sensitive?"

Coalition Capacity. Provide evidence of the capacity of the proposed coalition to function successfully to improve asthma control outcomes. Focus on the following two areas when describing the capacity of the proposed coalition:

- Past experience with coalition-based approaches to improving health outcomes
- Approach for managing and supporting the coalition

Administrative support: the person(s) responsible for organizing meetings and handling administrative functions such as preparing agendas, arranging for meeting times and locations, and facilitating meeting activities;

Management approach: the process of coordinating and facilitating consensus-building, establishing and maintaining linkages among relevant organizations and individuals, and ensuring that the role played by the coalition is appropriate and reflects the changing needs of the project over time. Clarify the role of the coalition and membership in the planning process, and the role envisioned for the implementation phase.

Step Three: Probability.
Preproposal contact questions might include "Is there a preferred theoretical model for managing a large coalition?" and "How many committees are realistic?"

Communication strategy: the methods the coalition will use to promote community awareness of the initiative, secure involvement of a wide group of people, and disseminate findings of its accomplishments.

5. Planning Approach and Timetable

Step Three: Probability.
Strategic thinking questions might include "How does the planning approach fit into the project's overarching theoretical model and relate to the overall project vision?" and "How do we ensure that project planning activities are manageable and outcomes are specific?"

The purpose of the planning phase is to prepare for an effective implementation phase and to strengthen local capacity for sustaining over time a coalition-based approach to asthma control. To that end, the proposed planning process should demonstrate the following:

- A logical and feasible process for assessing asthma-related needs and resources, identifying gaps, and developing goals and objectives for improving community-wide systems of care
- Adequate focus on building assessment and planning capacity at the community level

- Meaningful involvement of the many individuals and organizations with a role in asthma control (health systems and health care professionals, payers and policy leaders, school administrators and teachers, parents and patients, etc.)
- Consideration of the full gamut of potential strategies and settings for asthma control
- Evidence that the approach will gain the acceptance of families and other community members targeted by the proposed interventions
- A resulting plan that specifies strategies and interventions, coalition member roles and responsibilities, and measurable intermediate and longer-term outcomes
- Integration with existing community health improvement efforts.

It is expected that this section of the proposal will be very concrete. Specific activities and tasks should be described clearly, along with how these activities relate to each other and to an overall strategy or vision. Applicants should include a timeline that depicts that order, frequency and duration of specific activities during the planning phase.

Some communities and coalitions will be starting the planning process from scratch while others will be further along. In cases where the coalition will build on previous efforts (for example, to assess needs and resources and/or to identify strategies and interventions), applicants must describe the planning process that was involved. Reviewers will look for evidence that the planning process was comprehensive, that it included a meaningful level of involvement from key stakeholder groups, and that the resulting goals and strategies have been shaped and understood by those groups most affected within the community. To the extent that the planning approach was not comprehensive or sufficiently inclusive, applicants should take steps during the planning phase to expand on and refine previous planning efforts.

6. Preliminary Implementation Approach

Although we expect the planning process to influence coalition decisions about specific strategies and interventions during the implementation phase, applicants should provide a preliminary sketch or vision of the types of interventions the coalition would consider employing during the implementation phase. In addition to identifying the types of strategies and interventions the coalition may employ, discuss the relationship or linkages among the different interventions and strategies. This discussion should complement yet go one step further than the discussion in the section on "Vision and Objectives."

Step Three: Probability.
Preproposal contact questions might include "What timeframes are appropriate for 'intermediate' and 'longer-term' outcomes?" and "Is it expected that an implementation plan must be submitted prior to the release of subsequent funding for implementation activities?"

Step Three: Probability.
Strategic thinking questions might include "Have the National Advisory Committee members published research about potential implementation strategies?" and "Do implementation strategies address environmental issues as well as the needs of children, parents, families, providers, health professionals, and the community as a whole?"

Step Two: Feasibility.
A research-based approach to asthma control is a modified version of a distinctive feature noted in the first stage of the application procedure: subscribing to national asthma guidelines. In the first stage, the sponsor specifically endorses the recommendations for diagnosing and treating asthma translated by the National Asthma Education and Prevention Program (NAEPP). In the second stage, the RFP does not mention the NAEPP guidelines; rather, the "Preliminary Implementation Approach" section states that intervention strategies should be "grounded in sound and relevant research and practice."

In reality, the two versions of this distinctive feature are complementary. That is, the national asthma guidelines are based on the most recent scientific literature and treatment methods. Said differently, rather than inventing new strategies for asthma control, the sponsor values using approaches that have already been researched and demonstrated to be effective.

Reviewers will consider the extent to which the proposed approach: is innovative, comprehensive and oriented toward systems change; is grounded in sound and relevant research and practice; and reflects an understanding of the interplay among various approaches, settings and systems. Even more important than the specific interventions and strategies is the way in which the proposal makes clear the relationships between the different pieces, and how together they are likely to result in meaningful improvements in systems of care for children with asthma.

7. Evaluation Approach

Each project is expected to conduct an evaluation to assess the effectiveness of coalition efforts during both the planning phase and the implementation phase. Projects will also collaborate in and contribute to a cross-site evaluation of the Allies Against Asthma Initiative that will be directed out of the National Program Office. The Foundation may also undertake an evaluation of its multi-pronged Pediatric Asthma Initiative, which would be conducted by an independent research group, and grantees would also be expected to participate in such an evaluation as well. The evaluation section of the proposal should address project-specific evaluation activities, and include the following:

Step Two: Feasibility.
Collaboration with the National Program Office is a distinctive feature that is consistent in both the first and second stages of the application procedure. For the full proposal, this distinctive feature appears twice in the "Evaluation Approach" section of the RFP: "Projects will be expected to participate in periodic meetings with other projects and the NPO designed to coordinate, streamline, and enhance the value of local evaluation efforts" and "Projects will also collaborate in and contribute to a cross-site evaluation of the Allies Against Asthma Initiative that will be directed out of the National Program Office."

Clearly, the sponsor views this grant initiative as a shared partnership. That is, in addition to providing financial support, the sponsor is participating in the design and conduct of the program. Applicants may be

- Identification of specific outcomes relevant to both the planning and implementation phases (recognizing that these will be refined further during the planning phase). Outcomes must adequately capture the impact of coalition efforts on pediatric asthma morbidity, including measures of health care use, symptom/disease status, mortality, and the quality of life of children with asthma. In addition, it is expected that projects will include outcome measures that relate to system-level change and to the composition and strength of coalition and planning efforts.
- Discussion of available data sources, including sources of baseline data and limitations or gaps in available data sources and how these will be addressed.
- Discussion of how the coalition will secure access to data from secondary sources, such as hospitals and schools, including any issues related to confidentiality.
- Discussion of methods for measuring changes in outcomes due to coalition efforts.
- Discussion of how the coalition plans to obtain and use input from a broad range of coalition members in the design and implementation of the evaluation.
- A brief outline of the timing of design, data collection and analysis activities.
- Identification of the individual(s) with primary responsibility for evaluation activities.

Projects will be expected to participate in periodic meetings with other projects and the NPO designed to coordinate, streamline and enhance the value of local evaluation efforts. In addition, projects will be expected to submit periodic program updates that include information about the evaluation, and to prepare a final evaluation report, suitable for wide dissemination.

received more favorably when they explicitly acknowledge and assure the sponsor that they will actively collaborate with the National Program Office. In particular, this means submitting timely progress and final reports, sharing "lessons learned," and contributing to the development of best practice standards that can be replicated in other communities.

Step Two: Feasibility.
The hot button of evaluation and outcomes is consistent across stage one and stage two of the application procedures. In this second stage, the RFP identifies specific examples of outcome measures to be collected, including: *pediatric asthma morbidity, including measures of health care use, symptom/disease status, mortality, and the quality of life of children with asthma*. Projects must also include outcome measures that relate to system-level change and to the composition and strength of coalition and planning efforts.

Furthermore, the "Evaluation Approach" section of the RFP also has an emphasis on evaluation data—availability of baseline data, access to primary and secondary data sources, and timing of data collection and analysis. In other words, the sponsor is looking for a considerable amount of detail: *Who* will be collecting and evaluating *what* data, *when*, and *how*.

Step Three: Probability.
Strategic thinking questions might include "Are tracking systems at partner agencies compatible for sharing data?" and "How will evaluation feedback be used?"

Step Two: Feasibility.
The entire "Sustaining and Institutionalizing Coalition Efforts" section is a hot button for matching funds and sustainability. Further, the RFP quantifies the required level of matching funds: "Applicants must secure matching contributions for the implementation phase that total at least one-third of the applicant's total annual budget (or roughly $150,000)." Quite simply, matching funds encourage project sustainability. Supervisors and administrators who buy into a project conceptually and financially are more likely to provide future funding support and institutionalize effective strategies after the initial granting period ends. The RFP is looking for evidence of a sustainability plan, not an absolute guarantee of future project funding.

Step Three: Probability.
Preproposal contact questions might include "What level of documentation is expected as evidence of cash and in-kind support?" and "The RFP indicates that model programs must be sustainable. Does that mean activities must be institutionalized, or are there other strategies for supporting project continuation that applicants typically include in their proposals?"

Step Three: Probability.
Preproposal contact questions might include "Will each proposal be reviewed by a panel of 10 National Advisory Committee members?" and "As part of the review process, how much time will reviewers have to read proposals and will they be using a specific reviewer's evaluation form?"

8. Sustaining and Institutionalizing Coalition Efforts

It is expected that coalition efforts will continue beyond the time period funded by the Foundation, and to this end applicants must secure matching contributions for the implementation phase that total at least one-third of the applicant's total annual budget (or roughly $150,000). Beyond this support, sustaining coalition efforts will require changes at the provider, policy and system level to institutionalize effective strategies and approaches. This section of the application should discuss how the coalition plans to secure other sources of in-kind and financial support to sustain coalition efforts, and other ways in which the coalition will ensure that effective strategies become institutionalized within the community.

C. PROPOSAL SUBMISSION DETAILS

Applicants should submit one (1) original signed proposal and nine (9) copies. Applications must be received by the Allies Against Asthma National Program Office before 5:00 p.m. (Eastern Time) on Friday, June 2, 2000. Applications should be mailed to the following address:

Linda Jo Doctor, Deputy Director
Allies Against Asthma
University of Michigan, School of Public Health
109 South Observatory Street
Ann Arbor, Michigan 48109

Please note that FAX copies will not be accepted. The application should be prepared with a font size of at least 12 point and with one-inch margins.

D. PROPOSAL REVIEW

After an initial review of the applications, communities may be asked to respond to questions or to provide further clarification on some aspect(s) of their proposal. Site visits will be conducted to selected applicants during the months of June through September. The Foundation expects to announce grant awards in November, 2000.

E. APPENDIXES

Appendix I: Proposal Preparation Checklist
Appendix II: Sample Cover Letter
Appendix III: The Robert Wood Johnson Foundation "Request for Project Support and Conditions of Grant" Form and Tax Documentation Submission Requirements
Appendix IV: The Robert Wood Johnson Foundation National Program Site Budget Preparation Guidelines

* * *

Linda Jo Doctor, MPH May 31, 2000
Deputy Director
Allies Against Asthma National Program Office
at The University of Michigan
School of Public Health
109 S. Observatory, Room M5318 SPH II
Ann Arbor, MI 48109-2029

Reference: Fight Asthma Milwaukee Coalition (ID #36)

Dear Ms. Doctor:

On behalf of the Fight Asthma Milwaukee coalition, Children's Health System is submitting a proposal under the *Allies Against Asthma* initiative. Fight Asthma Milwaukee is the only community-based asthma coalition in Wisconsin, and was one of the first established in the country. We are requesting $150,000 to fund the planning phase of this effort between November 1, 2000, and October 31, 2001.

The attached copies of our tax documentation are true and current copies of the originals are on file with Children's Health System and they remain in full force and effect.

The President of our organization is:

Jon E. Vice, President
Children's Health System
9000 W. Wisconsin Avenue
P.O. Box 1997
Milwaukee, WI 53201

To answer questions or provide further information, please contact me directly by—phone: (414) 456-4116; fax: (414) 456-6539; or, email: jmeurer@mcw.edu

Step Three: Probability.
Preproposal contact questions might include "Will applicants be expected to respond to additional questions and provide further clarification in advance of or during a site visit?" and "What can you tell us about the site visit process, such as how many National Program Office representatives will participate and is there a preset agenda of items for exploration?"

STAGE TWO: FULL PROPOSAL

Developing the Cover Letter.
Developing the cover letter for our full proposal was quite easy because we followed the model established by the sponsor in Appendix II of the RFP. Although the cover letter is short in length, it carries a heavy information load. The first paragraph:

- identifies the coalition;
- specifies the lead organization submitting the application;
- names the program to which the proposal is being submitted;
- highlights the coalition's uniqueness and credibility;
- stipulates the amount of grant funds requested and the time period.

The remainder of the cover letter:

- includes a statement about the current legal and organizational status of the lead organization;
- identifies the name and address of the president of the organization;
- provides contact information for the project director;
- includes the signature of the project director, the individual authorized to negotiate on behalf of the coalition.

This model cover letter, however, does not allow us to present an overview of the proposal, describe the project's significance, or reflect the project's consistency with sponsor values, funding priorities, evaluation criteria, and hot buttons. Thus, it is essential that we incorporate these ideas into the project summary and the first paragraph of the full proposal.

Because we do not want our proposal to be rejected on a technicality, we adhere to the format of the sponsor's sample cover letter. Working within the RFP can sometimes be a challenge, yet we find creative ways to tell the sponsor both what they want to know and what we want them to know. Addressing logical and psychological needs in one seamless argument throughout our complete grant application will increase our chances for funding success.

Sincerely,

John R. Meurer, MD, MBA, Project Director
Assistant Professor of Community Pediatrics and Health Policy,
Center for the Advancement of Urban Children,
Medical College of Wisconsin and Children's Health System

* * *

The Robert Wood Johnson Foundation
Route 1 and College Road East
Princeton, NJ 08543-2316

Request for Project Support

Title of Project: Milwaukee Allies Against Asthma	
Purpose of Project: To improve efforts to control pediatric asthma in Milwaukee through a community-based coalition	
Applicant Institution (name and address): Children's Health System, Inc. 9000 W. Wisconsin Avenue Milwaukee, WI 53201	**Check to be Made Payable to:** Children's Health System, Inc.

STAGE TWO: FULL PROPOSAL

Developing the Application Form.
The Robert Wood Johnson Foundation requires a completed "Request for Project Support" application form to be submitted with the full proposal. This form helps establish our credibility in a condensed format. In 10 line elements, we present information about our organization, institutional officials, project director, project, and budget.

Title of Project.
Our project title is short and descriptive, "Milwaukee Allies Against Asthma." It reflects the collaborative nature of our project and connects us to the priorities and values of the sponsor.

Purpose of Project.
The application form limits the purpose statement to one sentence. In a 13-word telegraphic phrase, we describe both our overarching goal, i.e., "To improve efforts to control pediatric asthma," and methodological approach, i.e., "through a community-based coalition." These two concepts were taken directly from the first two sentences of the RFP.

Applicant Institution.
Grant awards are made to organizations, not individuals. Thus, Children's Health System, Inc., is the legal applicant. Our asthma coalition is a subsidiary under this parent entity.

Check to be Made Payable to.
The sponsor includes this line item in case the applicant institution and fiscal agent are not one in the same.

Amount of Support Requested.
At a glance, reviewers can determine that our request adheres to the imposed limit of $150,000 for a one-year planning grant.

Period for Which Support is Requested.
Following the RFP, we enter November 1 as the starting date for the 12-month organization and planning period.

Institutional Financial Officer.
We enter the name and title of the official who has responsibility for all financial matters for the institution, including management, reporting, and audits.

Project Director.
The project director is the individual ultimately responsible for all programmatic aspects of this initiative. Reviewers will recognize that the project director is well qualified to lead the coalition. He has advanced academic degrees that address both the medical side (MD) and the administrative side (MBA).

Amount of Support Requested: $150,000 **Period for Which Support is Requested:** from 11/01/2000 through 10/31/2001	**Institutional Financial Officer (name, title, telephone):** Timothy L. Birkenstock Treasurer/ CFO Children's Health System, Inc. (414) 266-6220; (414) 266-6409 FAX
***Project Director (name, title, telephone):** John R. Meurer, MD, MBA Assistant Professor of Pediatrics Medical College of Wisconsin (414) 456-4116; (414) 456-6539 FAX	**Applicant Institutional Approval:** Jon E. Vice President Children's Health System, Inc.

Please provide the following evidence of your institution's tax status:

If your institution is a tax-exempt organization described in Section 501(c)3 of the Internal Revenue Code. (i) a copy of the letter of your institution received from the Internal Revenue Service stating that your institution is exempt from taxation by virtue of being described in Section 501(c)3; (ii) a copy of the letter your institution received from the Internal Revenue Service stating that your institution is not a private foundation described in Section 509(a) or stating that your institution is an exempt operating foundation described in Section 4940(d)2; and (iii) a copy of Form 4653 or Form 1023 and other data, if any, your institution has filed with or received from the Internal Revenue Service concerning your tax status.

In your institution is an organization described in Section 170(c)1 or Section 511(a)2B of the Internal Revenue Code. (i) a copy of the correspondence, if any, from the Internal Revenue Service stating that fact; or (ii) a copy of the legislation establishing your institution.

These documents must be accompanied by a letter signed by a responsible officer of your institution certifying that the copies so provided are true and correct copies of the originals on file with your institution and that they remain in full force and effect.

Any questions you may have about your tax-exempt status should be directed to the Office of the Vice President, General Counsel and Secretary (609) 243-5908.

* The project director is the individual directly responsible for developing the proposed activity, its implementation, and day-to-day direct supervision of the project should funds be made available.

* * *

Applicant Institutional Approval.
We enter the name and title of the official who has the authority to accept grant funding and commit the institution to executing the proposed project.

Evidence of Tax-Exempt Status.
Under federal law, most grant awards made by private foundations are to tax-exempt nonprofit organizations. Children's Health System, Inc., is such an organization under Section 501(c)(3) of the Internal Revenue Code.

STAGE TWO: FULL PROPOSAL

Developing the Cross-Walk. Although the Request for Proposal (RFP) did not specifically ask for it, we included a one-page "cross-walk" to the location of responses to specific reviewer questions. The cross-walk restates each of the five questions presented in the "Issues to be Addressed by Applicants in Full Grant Application" and presents in bulleted list fashion the page number, proposal section, and an overview of the answers. Because all five of the "Issues to be Addressed" relate to hot buttons, the answers to these questions are emphasized throughout the proposal.

The cross-walk, similar to the project summary, previews the proposal and is a useful tool for reviewers when writing up an analysis of our project. Although the proposal answers all five specific "Issues to be Addressed," it was a challenge to provide succinct answers within the context of the prescriptive structure and page limits of the proposal narrative. The cross-walk is a surreptitious way to circumvent space restrictions yet do so in a way that simplifies the jobs of reviewers. The stimulus idea for including a cross-walk came from the "Proposed Budget and Budget Narrative" section of the RFP, which suggested "the budget documents will allow reviewers to cross-walk budget items with the proposed approach to ensure consistency and compatibility."

The first three "Issues to be Addressed" match up directly with hot buttons and relate to specific sections of the RFP, e.g., "Evaluation Approach," "Expertise and Experience in Asthma Control," and "Sustaining Coalition Efforts over Time." The fourth and fifth issues are more subtle versions of hot buttons and relate to multiple sections of the RFP.

Cross-Walk to Specific Reviewer Questions

1. Describe plans for evaluation and specify particular outcomes of interest.

- Pages 13–15, "Evaluation Approach" describe relevant outcomes, sources of primary and secondary data, methodology for measuring change, and key evaluation personnel.

2. Describe the staff and personnel who will lead/oversee the Coalition and manage Coalition efforts over time.

- Page 5, "Asthma Control Expertise & Experience" provides detail about the Project Director and Committee Chairs and Coordinators.
- The Attachment, "Key Staff & Leadership" contains curriculum vitae for key individuals who will serve in a leadership/governance capacity.

3. Discuss the potential for sustaining Coalition efforts following the end of the grant period.

- Page 15, "Sustaining & Institutionalizing Coalition Efforts" describes coalition contributions during planning and implementation years, and strategies for long-term sustainability.
- The Attachment, "Description of the Application Process" includes a coalition-generated list of potential sources of support beyond the granting period.

4. What component or efforts of the Coalition will address health system weaknesses and challenges?

- Pages 5–10, "Coalition Membership, Infrastructure, & Capacity" describe how MAAA will become more inclusive by broadening the mission of member agencies, developing more comprehensive strategies, and recruiting new members annually; will have a multi-disciplinary committee structure to address family, community, provider, environmental, surveillance, and evaluation issues through multiple communication mechanisms. The Budget Narrative contains a table illustrating MAAA Coalition expanded roles.
- Pages 10–11, "Planning Approach & Timetable" articulate how strategic plans will be based on psychosocial theory and scientific evidence and have an on-going evaluation of processes and outcomes of asthma care from primary and secondary sources.
- Pages 12–13, "Preliminary Implementation Approach" describe effective interventions to promote physician adoption of national asthma practice guidelines.

5. What potential approaches hold most promising for system-wide change?

- Pages 10–12, "Planning Approach & Timetable" outlines a planning process that is inclusive, manageable, and has specific outcomes; and contains a coalition-generated list of problems facing children with asthma and potential approaches for implementing change.
- Pages 12–13, "Preliminary Implementation Approach" details a mixture of strategies to produce system-wide change: family & community advocacy, provider quality improvement, and environmental risk reduction.

* * *

The fourth issue, "health system weaknesses and challenges," relates to the hot buttons of community-based collaborative efforts and outcomes. That is, one challenge for our coalition is to broaden its community-based membership. The RFP guidelines "strongly encourage" coalitions to include representatives from 14 different public and private sectors, and at the same time, membership should reflect the racial and ethnic diversity of the community. A second challenge for our coalition will be to effectively implement research-based strategies that improve asthma control outcomes. Although coalition members know and subscribe to national asthma guidelines, large variations still exist in the recommendations and practices of some health care providers. In short, addressing challenges at the system level is necessary to affect long-term outcomes.

The fifth issue, "potential approaches for system-wide change," relates to the hot button of project sustainability. The RFP is clear that to sustain over time a coalition-based approach to asthma control, we must have meaningful involvement of the many individuals and organizations with a role in asthma control; consider the full gamut of potential strategies and settings for asthma control; and develop a plan that specifies strategies and interventions, coalition member roles and responsibilities, and measurable intermediate and longer-term outcomes. Said differently, when diverse organizations plan, implement, and institutionalize effective strategies for asthma control, they will be able to produce system-wide change.

As a whole, the cross-walk illustrates how these issues, which are also sponsor hot buttons, are addressed throughout the proposal. Further, it foreshadows how our project design will satisfy the logical and psychological needs of the sponsor.

STAGE TWO: FULL PROPOSAL

Developing the Project Summary.
The project summary serves as a condensed 500-word substitute for our entire proposal. It provides a quick overview of what we propose to do and a rapid understanding of the project's significance, generalizability, and potential contribution. To ensure consistency of presentation, the project summary was written *after* the proposal was completed. The project summary adheres to the order of the proposal, uses major section headings, and maintains the same overall style and tone.

The first paragraph identifies the applicant organization, describes our organizational uniqueness, establishes coalition credibility, and defines the significance of the project in terms of *what* we will accomplish—developing a sustainable strategy for asthma management that will improve health outcomes for the target population. This paragraph is quite similar to the first paragraph of the full proposal. The first and last sentences, in fact, are identical.

Key acronyms for our organization, coalition, and project are spelled out in full. This paragraph also introduces the three hot buttons that will be reiterated throughout the proposal: community-based collaborative efforts, evaluation and outcomes, and matching funds and sustainability. Notice the use of key phrases such as *coalition*, *improved health status*, and *sustainable strategy*. Finally, articulating the benefit of the project to the target population in the last sentence provides a smooth transition to the next paragraph.

"Target Community & Population" quantifies the extent of the asthma problem among targeted community members. That is, this paragraph

Project Summary

Children's Health System (CHS), Wisconsin's only independent nonprofit health system dedicated solely to the well-being of children, is deeply concerned about controlling pediatric asthma. Our Fight Asthma Milwaukee (FAM) coalition is the only community-based asthma coalition in the state, and was one of the first established in the country. Building on the strengths of FAM, this project will create a new, more inclusive *Milwaukee Allies Against Asthma (MAAA)* coalition. MAAA will develop a sustainable strategy for asthma management that will improve the health status of vulnerable urban youth.

Target Community & Population. Although asthma affects people of all ages, races, and ethnic groups, low-income and minority populations experience substantially higher rates of fatalities, hospital admissions, and emergency department visits due to asthma. Nearly half of Wisconsin's total asthma inpatient hospitalizations of children ages 0–17 occur in Milwaukee County. The asthma hospitalization rate for children in Milwaukee County is 4.49 per 1000, over four times the Healthy People 2010 goal of 1.0 per 1000. Although African Americans make up less than one-third of the County's population, they account for over two-thirds of asthma hospitalizations. Children's Health System is uniquely suited to lead this project because we treat greater than 95% of children admitted for asthma care in Milwaukee.

MAAA Coalition. Coalitions are powerful and effective mechanisms for realizing change at the local level. Dr. John Meurer, Project Director, has the expertise and collaborative history with coalition partners to make this project succeed. MAAA is driven by three key principles:

- ***Inclusive Participation***—the coalition includes diverse health-related agencies, community-based organizations, educational institutions, and concerned parents of children with asthma.
- ***Expert Leadership***—a core group of respected asthma specialists and dedicated parents lend their expertise to designing effective community projects and maintaining the coalition.
- ***Shared Vision***—coalition participants accept the shared responsibility and decision-making for improving the quality of life for children with asthma and their families.

Planning Approach. MAAA's planning approach is driven by and directly responsive to community needs. Programs and evaluations will reflect a theoretical understanding of behavior change. Our application of social learning theory will address both the psychosocial dynamics underlying health behavior and the methods of promoting behavior change, while emphasizing cognitive processes and their effect on behavior. MAAA will promote stronger community-wide systems of care by integrating two conceptual models into planning and implementation: *PRECEDE/PROCEED*, the dominant health education and community health promotion model, and the Institute of Medicine's *Community Health Improvement Process*, a planned approach for improving health. MAAA will take a multifactorial approach to achieving goals and objectives, enacting a mixture of strategies broadly targeting families, providers, and environmental risks.

identifies *where* the project is taking place, *who will benefit* from targeted activities, and *why* the project is needed. The first sentence recognizes that the asthma problem disproportionately affects children and minorities. The second sentence justifies why the need is greater in our community than in other parts of the state. The third sentence compares our community's asthma hospitalization rate against the federal standard. The final sentence states our credibility to lead this project and effectively segues to the next section.

This "MAAA Coalition" paragraph describes the value of community-based coalitions and identifies exactly *who* is responsible for leading project efforts. In bulleted list fashion we overview three unique features of our coalition that relate to sponsor hot buttons: inclusive participation, expert leadership, and shared vision. These features demonstrate to the sponsor that we've put a considerable amount of thought into developing a manageable project that will have a significant long-term impact in the community.

The "Planning Approach" describes our project methodology—*how* the project will be conducted in order to achieve the desired results. Taken as a whole, this paragraph conveys to the sponsor that our approach is comprehensive, feasible, measurable; based in sound theory and relevant practice; and is likely to improve health outcomes for children with asthma. Notice how the fourth sentence justifies our methodological selections to guide planning and implementation phases; namely, we are using the dominant health education and community health promotion models in the field. The final sentence describes how enacting this combination of approaches will enable us to achieve project goals including affecting system-wide change, which is detailed further in the next paragraph.

This concluding paragraph on "System-Wide Change" ties the whole proposal together. It succinctly summarizes our credibility and capacity to carry out this project, and it highlights the main points and hot buttons repeated throughout the proposal. We have all of the critical elements in place to implement a successful project: highly trained professionals, broad-based support, a resource-rich environment, and a sound approach to realizing lasting change in the community. The summary ends on a humanistic note, articulating the benefit of the project to the target population.

System-Wide Change. MAAA is uniquely positioned to harness and focus collective talents, expertise, and asthma resources to effect lasting change in the community. When properly nurtured, coalitions have tremendous potential to shape public policy, to reach asthma patients with programs and services, and to educate health care providers. Collectively, these approaches hold the most promise for long-term, system-wide change that will enhance the quality of life of children with asthma and their families.

* * *

STAGE TWO: FULL PROPOSAL

Developing the Full Proposal. The invitation to submit a full proposal came as a direct result of our letter of intent. Building on that initial success, the full proposal recaps and expands the letter of intent, thus there is some overlap in the information presented. In this case, select redundancy is a proposal strength. It shows the sponsor a level of consistency in project development, and more importantly, ideas gain strength through repetition. The same three hot buttons identified for the letter of intent are once again addressed repeatedly throughout the full proposal. Distinctive features in the full proposal are similar, but not identical, to those in the letter of intent. Each distinctive feature is addressed twice in the full proposal, thus ensuring that reviewers who skim read do not miss them.

Children's Health System: *Milwaukee Allies Against Asthma*

The opening paragraph summarizes the entire proposal, identifying the applicant organization, the extent of the problem in the community, and the overall project goal. For the purposes of consistency, the opening is quite similar to that used in the letter

Children's Health System (CHS), Wisconsin's only independent nonprofit health system dedicated solely to the well-being of children, is deeply concerned about controlling pediatric asthma. Asthma is the number one reason for hospitalization at CHS—nearly 1,000 admissions per year. But our concern for children extends beyond the walls of our hospital. Our Fight Asthma Milwaukee (FAM) coalition provides quality asthma education, outreach, and referral services that enable children, families, and the community to maintain healthy lifestyles. FAM is the only community-based asthma coalition in Wisconsin, and was one of the first established in the country. Building on the strengths of FAM, this project will create a new, more inclusive *Milwaukee Allies Against Asthma* (MAAA) coalition. MAAA will develop a sustainable strategy for asthma management that will improve the health status of vulnerable urban youth.

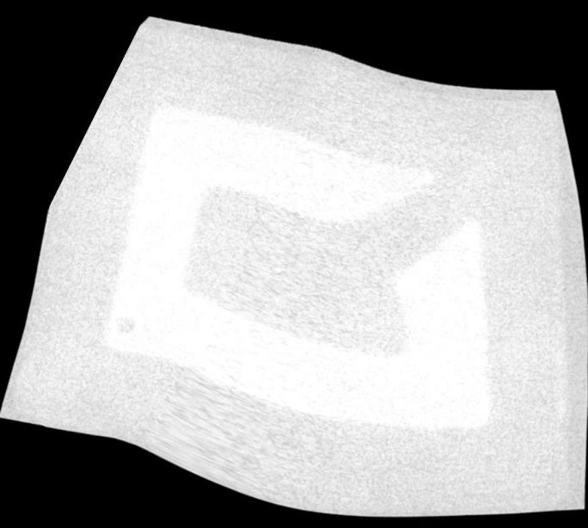

1. Vision & Principal Objectives. An epidemic is underway in the US. The number of people with asthma has more than doubled in the past 15 years. Asthma is the most common chronic childhood illness, affecting nearly 100,000 of Wisconsin's children under age 18, a majority of whom live in southeastern Wisconsin. Children who do not receive adequate asthma care have poorer development of lung function and more rapid decline in adult lung function than children who received appropriate primary medical and specialty care (Pappas 1997). The Milwaukee Allies Against Asthma coalition, using national Healthy People 2010 goals for asthma as targets, aims to reduce the adverse impact of pediatric asthma in the community.

MAAA's vision for the overall project effort is based on Lu Ann Aday's "Framework for Classifying Topics and Issues in Health Services Research" (1998). Project goals and objectives reflect Aday's model for addressing structure, process, and outcomes. More specifically, addressing **structure** goals during the Organization & Planning Phase will allow us to accomplish **process** and **outcomes** goals during the Implementation Phase.

Structure Goal: Develop a sustainable strategy for asthma management in the community

Health Policy Objective: Develop approaches to address barriers to asthma care financing and treatment: establish policies to support self-management, enhance services, provide resources, and build capacity of families and communities to control asthma.

Delivery System Objectives: Develop and implement provider education based on existing national guidelines to ensure standard and appropriate treatment of children. Establish linkages with existing asthma and other relevant surveillance systems.

Population at Risk Objectives: Develop a pediatric community health profile. Decrease racial/ethnic disparities in asthma care. Provide community-based health education to improve asthma identification/self-management and involvement in coalition activities.

Environment Objective: Assess the prevalence of environmental allergens and tobacco smoke. Use *PRECEDE/PROCEED* and *Community Health Improvement Process* models to evaluate physical, social, and economic environments.

Process Goal: Develop and implement targeted communication strategies to build asthma awareness, support, and involvement of professionals, children, families, and community

Realized Access Objectives: Improve the quality of and provide new access to asthma-related medical services in clinic, school, child care, and community sites. Improve access to resources to obtain appropriate asthma medications and asthma equipment.

of intent—the first four sentences, in fact, are identical. Subsequent sentences establish coalition creditability and uniqueness and foreshadow the three hot buttons that will be reiterated throughout the full proposal: (1) community-based collaborative efforts; (2) evaluation and outcomes; and (3) matching funds and sustainability. The paragraph ends on a humanistic note, articulating the benefit of the project to the target population.

The "Vision & Principal Objectives" section establishes the tone for the entire project. It summarizes the asthma problem; describes the project's vision, goals, and objectives based on a theoretical model; and illustrates the project's framework. And when considered in combination with the next section, "Target Population & Need," approximately 25 percent of the narrative is dedicated to *why* we are applying for grant funding and *what* we hope to accomplish in our community.

Our vision statement paints, in broad brushstrokes, the "big picture" or the lay of the land. It shows the sponsor that we know where we are at and where we are going; we have identified the problem, a solution, and the potential benefits to the target population.

The project design is based on a nationally recognized theoretical model for addressing structure, process, and outcomes. Following the model, "Project Aims & Objectives" presented in the letter of intent are recast as project goals and objectives to be accomplished in the organization and planning phase and the implementation phase. The need for these objectives is addressed in the next section of the proposal, "Target Population & Need."

Following the suggestion in the RFP, to help convey our project vision we provided a diagram illustrating the complex relationship between factors and systems that influence asthma control within the community. The added value of the diagram is that it depicts patterns and associations that may otherwise have gone unnoticed in the narrative alone. Our project framework quickly reveals our conceptual approach to addressing structure, process, and outcome goals. This framework also guides our division of organization and planning and implementation activities into structure, process, and outcomes. In other words, "Vision & Principal Objectives" overviews the project in relation to the community, while "Planning Approach & Timetable" and "Preliminary Implementation Approach" detail specific activities that will make the project a success.

Equally significant, this section introduces the three sponsor hot buttons that will be repeatedly addressed throughout the proposal: community-based collaborative efforts, evaluation and outcomes, and matching funds and sustainability. Note the use of key words and phrases such as: *coalition, community, professionals, children, families, linkages, assess, outcomes, evaluate, quality of life, resources,* and *sustainable strategy*. Strategic repetition of ideas that speak to a sponsor's subjective and objective needs increase the competitiveness of our proposal.

Health Risks Objective: Undertake prevention efforts to reduce exposure to environmental precipitants, e.g., tobacco smoke, household dust mites, and cockroaches.

Intermediate Outcome Goal: Reduce hospital admissions, emergency department visits, missed school days, and wheezing episodes

Effectiveness, Equity, & Efficiency Objective: Conduct evaluations to assess coalition activities including the extent to which they strengthen the coalition's capacity to be effective and achieve asthma control outcomes.

Ultimate Outcome Goal: Control pediatric asthma

Health Objective: Enhance the quality of life of children with asthma and their families.

Framework for *Milwaukee Allies Against Asthma.* The following diagram depicts our adaptation of Aday's model to address pediatric asthma, and illustrates the complex relationship between factors and sub-systems that influence asthma control within the community.

Structure Goal: develop a sustainable strategy for asthma management

Process Goal: Implement targeted communication strategies to build asthma awareness

Intermediate Outcome Goal: Reduce hospital admissions, emergency department visits, missed school days, and wheezing episodes

Ultimate Outcome Goal: Control pediatric asthma

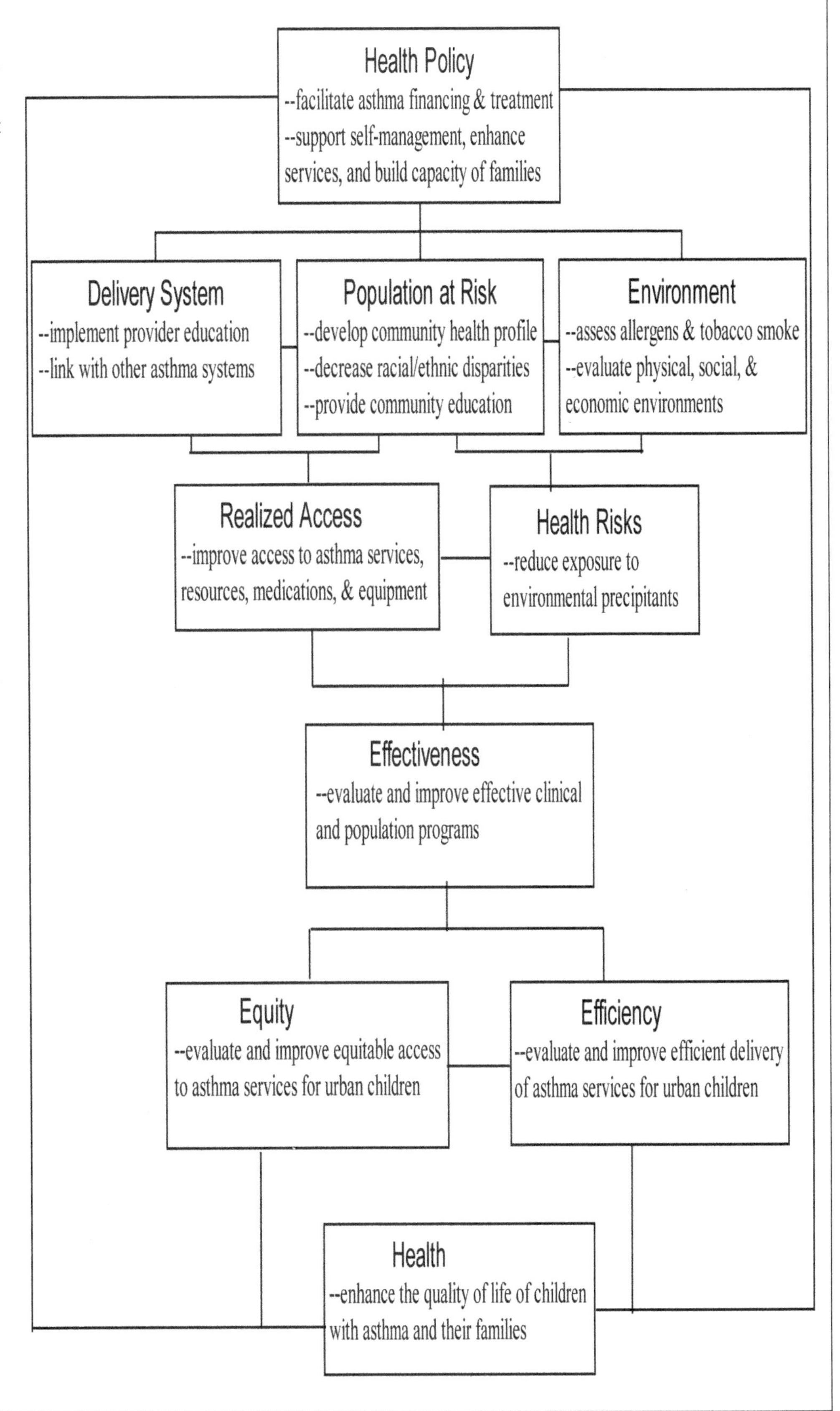

This "Target Population & Need" section tells the sponsor *where* the project is taking place, *who will benefit* from targeted activities, and *why* the project is needed. Although the sponsor did not request details about the statement of the problem—or level of need—in the letter of intent, we included it as a means to make our application stand out from the competition. Documentation of the need is a crucial factor for reviewers because it provides the rationale for our project.

In this full proposal we supplement the letter of intent's presentation of four types of needs: hospitalization rates, poverty, school absenteeism, and smoke exposure. We subsequently expand our discussion of the problem statement to include two additional needs: morbidity and mortality, and gaps in data. The issue of "gaps in data" is specifically identified in the RFP. Gaps in knowledge and supporting data may actually contribute to the pediatric asthma problem. More broadly, repetition of key topics maintains the continuity between our letter of intent and full proposal. Introducing new issues and details shows our comprehensive knowledge and understanding of the needs of the community.

In this subheading on "Hospitalization Rates," we include two paragraphs and a table that provide concrete detail about the number of children affected with asthma and hospitalized in our community as well as the costs for care. Reviewers can see quickly that disparities exist among low-income and minority populations.

The short paragraph after the table reinforces the hot button of community-based collaborative efforts: together, coalition partners have direct access to significant numbers of children in the target population to be served.

2. Target Population & Need. Although asthma affects people of all ages, races, and ethnic groups, low-income and minority populations experience substantially higher rates of fatalities, hospital admissions, and emergency department visits due to asthma (DHHS 2000). The asthma hospitalization rate for children in Milwaukee County is 4.49 per 1000, over four times the Healthy People 2010 goal of 1.0 per 1000. The Wisconsin Office of Health Care Information reports that nearly half of the state's total asthma inpatient hospitalizations of children ages 0–17 occur in Milwaukee County. Children's Health System is uniquely suited to lead this project because we treat greater than 95% of children admitted for asthma care in Milwaukee.

Hospitalization Rates. The table below, "Child Asthma Hospitalization Rates in Milwaukee County, 1998," illustrates asthma rates per thousand. Table cells also show the number of children admitted for asthma divided by the population of children. Of the 638 central city children and the 439 non-central city children, 74% and 48% respectively were enrolled in Medicaid; total Medicaid charges exceeded $1.3 million. And although Blacks make up less than one-third of Milwaukee County's population, they accounted for 68% of asthma hospitalizations.

Description	Central City Milwaukee Rates	Non-central City Milw. County Rates	Healthy People Goals
AGE: 0–4 years	337/31,418 = **10.73**	187/41,908 = **4.46**	**2.50**
AGE: 5–17 years	301/70,050 = **4.30**	252/96,646 = **2.61**	**.80**
RACE: Black	539/66,272 = **8.13**	185/10,807 = **17.12**	**2.65**
RACE: White	49/23,564 = **2.08**	201/122,028 = **1.65**	**NA**
RACE: Hispanic	37/10,934 = **3.38**	46/7,176 = **6.41**	**2.65**

Between 1992–1994, hospitalization rates were highest (> 15/1000 population) in Milwaukee zip codes with high poverty rates (53205-6, 12, 10) (WI OHCI 1996). In 1999, clinics representing four health systems in the Milwaukee Allies Against Asthma coalition—Children's, Aurora, Covenant, and Horizon—collectively served nearly 5,000 children with asthma. And two health plans in MAAA—United Healthcare and Humana—served 2,000 pediatric asthma members.

Poverty. Milwaukee County children, particularly those in the central city, experience compromised access to health services due to economic, structural, and environmental barriers. University of Wisconsin-Milwaukee data (1998) reveal that many families in the County do not earn enough to adequately support their children: 113,000 children were in employed families with income below 185% Federal Poverty Level. Further, research attests that children of low socioeconomic status are subjected to inadequate medical management of their asthma (Togias 1997). Asthma management for children in the central city is characterized by reliance on episodic and emergency care, non-conformance to asthma medication management guidelines, and prevalent school absences and workdays lost due to asthma symptoms (Rand 2000).

This "Poverty" subheading confirms that many children in the central city face greater risks and barriers to care because of their socioeconomic status. Current research documents the number of children in the community who are below the federal poverty level and articulates the consequences of poverty, e.g., inadequate medical management, reliance on emergency care, and missed school days. These examples foreshadow the asthma-related problems in subsequent paragraphs.

Morbidity & Mortality. Asthma morbidity and mortality are disproportionately high in urban centers, and minority children are especially vulnerable. The age-adjusted asthma mortality rate in Milwaukee is 2.3 per 100,000 residents (NHLBI 1999). African American children are over four times as likely to die from asthma than white children (DHHS 2000). Factors that contribute to this disparity include inadequate preventive care for asthma management, inadequate asthma knowledge and management skills among children and their families, psychosocial factors, and environmental exposure to allergens or irritants (Malveaux 1995). Although effective therapy is available, many African Americans and Latino children receive episodic treatment for asthma that does not follow current guidelines for care (Evans 1997). Further, increased asthma morbidity and mortality may be associated with a combination of social, structural, and physical factors in the environment, e.g., inadequate housing, exposure to toxins, unemployment, and the lack of supportive interpersonal relationships (Israel 1994).

Morbidity and mortality is an extension of hospitalization. This subheading provides the asthma morbidity and mortality rate in our community, articulates the extent of disparities between minority and nonminority children, describes factors that contribute to this disparity, and foreshadows additional asthma-related problems, e.g., gaps between theory and practice of asthma guidelines. The literature cited in this paragraph reflects best practices in the field, including articles published by National Advisory Committee members.

School Absenteeism. Asthma is the leading cause of health-related school absenteeism. Nationwide, children with asthma miss an average 7.2 school days per year compared to 3.4 days per year for children without asthma. Locally, preliminary research from clinics and schools suggests that asthma affects 10–16% of Milwaukee's urban school-age children. Among 369 children with asthma served by 12 clinics in metropolitan Milwaukee, risk factors significantly associated with emergency department visits for asthma were age 0–3 years, persistent asthma symptoms, African-American race, and parents without high school diplomas (Meurer, in press). Between 1997–2000, CHS' Health Education Center, through their "Awesome Asthma School Days" program, surveyed 1,579 children with asthma from Milwaukee Public Schools. Most recent survey results illustrate the vulnerability of inner city school children:

- 73% do not have a written asthma self-care plan
- 66% with persistent symptoms do not use an anti-inflammatory control medicine
- 57% report smoke exposure in their home (Meurer 1999, and unpublished).

Asthma-related school absenteeism was introduced as a serious problem in the letter of intent and is supplemented here. For comparison purposes, national and local data are provided about school absenteeism. The literature cited illustrates the vulnerability of local central city school children. Simultaneously, this published literature begins to establish the credibility of our project director, whose expertise and experience are detailed more fully in the next proposal section. This paragraph also touches on sponsor hot buttons of community-based collaborative efforts and evaluation and outcomes.

That is, the project director has already joined forces with local schools to educate children about asthma and assess its prevalence and impact. The last bulleted point, "57% of children report smoke exposure in their home," effectively transitions to the next paragraph on smoke exposure.

This subheading on "Smoke Exposure" documents the statewide increase in smoking, estimates the number of smokers in our community, quantifies the direct health care costs of smoking, articulates the consequences of youth smoking, and ties smoke exposure to two other asthma-related problems: morbidity and mortality, and poverty. The final sentence of the paragraph begins to hint at a solution to these problems—focus on prevention and wellness.

The final subheading in this section reemphasizes that the project will serve the children targeted by the RFP with tailored prevention foci for specific age groups, as described initially in the letter of intent. The RFP also set up the expectation that many communities lack complete data on pediatric asthma prevalence. By acknowledging this "weakness" in the proposal, in effect we turn it into a strength. That is, we know what we do not know. Accordingly, we can address weaknesses in the organization and planning phase. Our community faces two specific gaps: (1) a shortage of data on the number of children under age two with asthma, and (2) a disparity between recommended and actual asthma management practices at both the provider and family levels. The paragraph and section end on a positive note: our coalition can overcome these barriers to improve the quality of life for children.

Smoke Exposure. Wisconsin's incidence of smoking increased from 32% in 1993 to 38% in 1999 (WI Youth Behavior Survey 2000). Nearly 20,000 of 215,000 smokers in Milwaukee County are children ages 14–17; the Wisconsin Department of Health & Family Services determined the direct health care costs of smoking in Milwaukee County to exceed $207 million annually! Exposure to tobacco smoke contributes to onset of asthma earlier in life and is a risk factor for asthma morbidity. Since disparity of asthma mortality and morbidity among minority children in urban centers is closely linked to socioeconomic status and poverty, measures to reduce exposure to environmental allergens/irritants and to eliminate barriers to access to health care are likely to have a major positive impact. Interventions for children in urban Milwaukee must focus on prevention of asthma symptoms and promotion of wellness (Malveaux 1995).

Gaps in Data. This project targets children under age 18, especially those residing in the inner city, uninsured or eligible for publicly financed systems, and receiving care from safety net providers. We will reach four age-specific groups: (1) Under age 2: early detection and diagnosis; (2) Age 2–5: prevent emergency department visits; (3) Age 6–12: educate/screen in schools; (4) Age 13–18: reduce tobacco use. MAAA understands the community's asthma needs; however, a shortage of data exists on the number of children under age two with asthma. And despite the existence of national asthma diagnosis and management guidelines, a substantial gap remains between their recommendations and actual practices (DHHS 2000). According to Cabana (1999), barriers to physician adherence to clinical practice guidelines are related to ***knowledge*** (lack of awareness or familiarity), ***attitudes*** (lack of agreement with guidelines, lack of self-efficacy or outcome expectancy, or inertia of previous practice), and ***behavior*** (external barriers related to guideline, patient, or environmental factors). Likewise, parents may not recognize early signs of asthma or fail to avoid environmental factors that trigger their child's asthma. MAAA activities will help reduce health disparities among urban and minority children.

3. Asthma Control Expertise & Experience.

Children's Health System, as lead applicant in a multidisciplinary collaboration of local and state organizations, has the clinical expertise and research experience to develop and implement comprehensive asthma management programs in Milwaukee. For over a century, CHS has supplied comprehensive medical treatment to children throughout the state and region; in 1999 alone, CHS admitted more than 19,000 children.

Combating increases in asthma morbidity and mortality necessitates an understanding of social and behavioral aspects of the disease. Education for patients, professionals, and the public based on the most current scientific information is required (Clark 1993). Accordingly, MAAA asthma control activities are designed to improve access to and quality of medical services, education, family and community support, and environmental initiatives. MAAA coalition leaders include:

John R. Meurer, MD, MBA, Project Director, has the expertise and collaborative history with coalition partners to make this project succeed. Dr. Meurer is Assistant Professor of Community Pediatrics in the Center for Advancement of Urban Children at CHS and the Medical College of Wisconsin. He has received federal funding for research on childhood asthma, and has published findings about school-based asthma education, costs of inpatient services for pediatric asthma, trends in the severity of childhood asthma, and risk factors for pediatric emergency visits.

Kevin J. Kelly, MD, MAAA Steering Committee Chair, is the Director of CHS' Asthma and Allergy Center and Professor of Pediatrics at Medical College of Wisconsin. A Board Certified allergist and pediatrician with 20 years experience, Dr. Kelly's expertise in allergy is recognized nationally and was instrumental in the State of Wisconsin's asthma surveillance and intervention program funded by the Centers for Disease Control and Prevention from 1996–1999.

Ramesh Sachdeva, MD, PhD, MBA, MAAA Surveillance & Evaluation Committee Chair, is the Director of CHS' Center for Outcomes Research and Quality Management, one of only a handful of centers of its kind in the country. Dr. Sachdeva's PhD in epidemiology focuses on Health Policy/Management and Biometry emphasizing study and survey design, health economics, decision analysis, and statistical modeling. Dr. Sachdeva will ensure that outcome measures and studies are high quality, meet standards of research, and are sensitive to cultural differences.

This section of the proposal establishes our credibility to successfully carry out this project, describing the asthma control expertise and experience of our organization, coalition, and key personnel. These paragraphs let the sponsor know exactly *who* is responsible for and *who* is participating in coalition efforts. Although it is one of the shortest sections of the proposal (only 6 percent of the total), we compensate by including supplemental information in the appendixes, e.g., biosketches and letters of support and commitment. Each paragraph in this section also contributes to the development of sponsor hot buttons: community-based collaborative efforts, evaluation and outcomes, and matching funds and sustainability.

Similar to the letter of intent, the first paragraph describes a century's worth of organizational history and experience and emphasizes collaborative relationships with local and state organizations, a distinctive feature raised in the original RFP. The second paragraph draws on research published by individuals at the National Program Office to support the coalition's multidisciplinary project approach. In other words, we recognize the sponsor's expertise in research-based approaches to asthma control—a distinctive feature raised in the RFP for this second stage of the application procedure—and demonstrate that we share their values.

The third, fourth, and fifth paragraphs establish the expertise and experience of the project director, the coalition steering committee chair, and the coalition surveillance and evaluation committee chair. These paragraphs in particular appeal to the sponsor's hot buttons: Key personnel have a history of participating in collaborative community-based efforts, are recognized nationally as skilled researchers and evaluators, and have successfully secured federal grant dollars to implement and support a variety of asthma-related projects.

The final paragraph illustrates that the coalition has inclusive participation from myriad individuals and organizations, and it suggests that the project will be sustainable beyond the granting period. That is, the sheer diversity of organizations committed to project efforts increases the likelihood that intervention activities will be institutionalized by coalition members. Because our approaches are community centered and community driven, each organization takes responsibility for contributing to a project that is greater than any one partner could manage. The overview of steering committee leadership and the four core project planning committees also provides a smooth transition to the following section on coalition members, infrastructure, and capacity.

To ensure that the project planning and implementation phases will be shaped by representatives from the various subsystems influencing asthma control, the RFP asks for considerable detail about coalition membership, infrastructure, and capacity. Consequently, this is the longest section of narrative, approximately 30 percent of the proposal's length. The first two paragraphs provide the overview of this entire section, accentuating that project efforts are collaborative and community based, a sponsor hot button. They reiterate the overall project goal, i.e., to control pediatric asthma, that we defined in the first section of the proposal; document the elements of a successful coalition; identify the three underlying concepts that drive our coalition; and draw on current research to justify our approach to coalition membership and infrastructure.

To increase the readability and manageability of this lengthy section, we introduced three unifying concepts that relate to hot buttons: inclusive participation, expert leadership, and shared vision. Each paragraph in this section contributes to at least one of these concepts and serves to establish the overall credibility of the coalition and its members to make this project a success. This level of detail

Additional MAAA experts who contribute to project planning as Committee Chairs and Coordinators: **Family & Community Advocacy**—*Aidan Tyler*, American Lung Association-Wisconsin and *Cameron Nicholaus*, Fight Asthma Milwaukee; **Provider Quality Improvement**—*Brychan William*, *MPH*, Community Collaboration for Healthcare Quality, and *John Calder*, Children's Hospital Respiratory Therapist; **Environmental Risk Reduction**—*Dominic Michael*, *MPH*, Milwaukee Health Department, and *Phoebe Ross*, *MPA*, Medical College of Wisconsin; and Advisory consultants to the **Surveillance & Evaluation Committee**—*Patrick Ignatius*, *PhD*, *RN*, Black Health Coalition, and *Sharon Tilly*, *MD*, *MPH*, Director of the Center for Advancement of Urban Children at Medical College of Wisconsin.

4. Coalition Membership, Infrastructure & Capacity.

MAAA members represent mixed organizations and parents working together to achieve a common goal: control pediatric asthma. Researchers are still investigating factors that influence the success of coalitions, yet preliminary findings indicate that the maturation of coalitions requires time, effort, and resources (Institute of Medicine 1997). Accordingly, this Milwaukee Allies Against Asthma coalition expands prior Fight Asthma Milwaukee coalition efforts, and is driven by three underlying principles:

- **Inclusive Participation**—the coalition includes diverse health-related agencies, community-based organizations, educational institutions, and concerned parents of children with asthma.
- **Expert Leadership**—a core group of respected asthma specialists and dedicated parents lend their expertise to designing effective community projects and maintaining the coalition.
- **Shared Vision**—coalition participants accept the shared responsibility and decision-making for improving the quality of life for children with asthma and their families.

Indeed, multiple stakeholders *must* be involved in designing, implementing, and evaluating health education programs (Israel 1995). State of the art community-based health promotion requires explicitly acknowledging the diverse interests of the parties at the earliest stages of program planning; making concerted efforts to bridge cultural gaps; structuring funding to allow lead time for partnerships to develop or using social reconnaissance to identify strong existing partnerships; and integrating evaluation more closely into program development (Cheadle 1997).

Coalition Membership. The following table is a complete list of current coalition members, approximately 20% of whom represent key minority groups. Letters of support from core organizations are attached. During planning and implementation phases, coalition committee members will be required to identify and recruit new members annually. In year one, we will reach out to businesses, housing organizations, media, and elected offices. By participating in the coalition, businesses, for example, may benefit from a more productive workforce if community efforts can improve asthma control among dependents of employees. Demonstrated benefits to target groups will ensure that new members stay active in project activities.

Coalition Infrastructure. MAAA has the necessary infrastructure, systems and procedures to effectively govern and operate coalition activities. As illustrated in an Organization Chart in the attachments, a Steering Committee will assume full authority, oversight, and responsibility for the coalition, and four standing committees ensure that educational, advocacy, environmental, and evaluation activities are consonant with the coalition's overall mission. MAAA's inclusive nature and family-centeredness make it unique, and importantly, responsive to community needs.

also shows the sponsor that we are not simply chasing grant dollars because they are available; rather, we have put a considerable amount of time, effort, and energy into developing a project that will truly make a difference in the community.

The RFP wants to know who is and is not represented in the coalition. Accordingly, we provide a table that illustrates a complete list of coalition members by names, organizational affiliations, sector, and major roles. This "Coalition Membership" subheading also begins to describe the extent to which the coalition reflects the racial and ethnic composition of the community, a distinctive feature raised in the RFP. To further emphasize our inclusiveness and shared vision, we strategically make a cross-reference to the proposal attachments, which contain letters of support and commitment from collation members.

While a majority of the constituents recommended by the RFP already participate in our coalition, not all are represented. We acknowledge this "weakness" and identify four specific groups that will be added to the coalition during the planning and implementation phases. Syntactically, however, we have minimized the effect of this weakness by burying it in the middle of the paragraph. And in the last two sentences we turn this weakness into a relative strength by explaining the benefits of recruiting new constituents to the coalition. Page limitations prohibited an expanded discussion of exactly how individuals will be recruited into the coalition.

In this subheading on "Coalition Infrastructure," three paragraphs describe the coalition's structure, leadership, and responsiveness to community needs. A steering committee provides oversight for the coalition, and four standing committees ensure that the educational, advocacy, environmental, and evaluation activities are consonant with the coalition's overall mission. We identify the number of individuals who will participate on each committee, the frequency of committee meetings, and a summary of committee roles and responsibilities.

This paragraph answers the RFP's question about how this project will build on an existing coalition: The steering committee chair conceptualized, developed, and secured funding for the first coalition; now he is steering efforts to expand the coalition to make it larger and more inclusive.

Leadership/Governance. The coalition will be governed by a 12 member ***Steering Committee,*** who have a cumulative 100 years of experience in pediatric care, management, health education programming, and community leadership. The Steering Committee will convene every two months and integrate coalition activities into existing community health improvement efforts. Steering Committee Chair, Dr. Kevin Kelly, was instrumental to conceptualizing, developing, and securing funding for the Fight Asthma Milwaukee coalition. MAAA member agencies will identify and mobilize parents of children with asthma to participate on the committees and in quarterly Coalition Conferences. Parents will reflect Milwaukee's racial and ethnic diversity, and bring a range of personal expertise to the coalition.

Milwaukee Allies Against Asthma Coalition Partners

Sector	Individuals Involved	Organization Affiliation	Major Roles
Parents of Children with Asthma and Adolescents with Asthma	• Cody Austin, Alejandro Fernandez, Julie Mitchell, Nicole Jordan, Charles Taylor, Lauren Walker, Steve Schneider, Emily Simpson, Sandy Williams, Chelly Matthews, Hannah Stevens • Wayne Allen (16 yrs), Kevin James (14 yrs)	None	Representation on all committees Collect primary survey data from other parents and children with asthma and recruit them to join the coalition Develop a family-focused plan and interventions
Clinical Providers	• Brychan William, John Clare • Michelle Berg, Ron Nextall • Josie Recchi	• Community Collaboration for Healthcare Quality • Downtown Health Center • Children's Medical Group School-Based Health Center	Representation on Provider Quality Improvement Committee. Collect primary survey data from providers Develop provider-focused plan and interventions

Health Care Delivery Systems	• Ron Blake, Erica Jardins, Martha Sorley, Luke Robidall, Jerry Curry, Wayne Gresky • Amy Ryan • Sean Kyle, Jacqueline Bradley • John Calder, Stacey Douglas, Todd Russell, Jon Vice	• Aurora HealthCare • Horizon • Covenant • Children's Hospital of Wisconsin	Representation on all committees Collect primary data from providers and patients Collect secondary data from hospitals, emergency departments, and clinics Develop a community-focused plan and interventions
Schools and Childcare Providers	• Maria Lemieux • Paula Karina • Brett Hall, Mary Proud	• Milwaukee Public Schools • Planning Council • Milw. County Human Services Dept. Child Care Advisory Cmt.	Represent Family & Environ. Cmt. Collect primary survey data Develop a community-focused plan and interventions
Public Health and Environment Agencies	• Dominic Michael, Earl Tucker, Lisa Marcell • Justin Heatley, Wendy Rogers, Megan Roy, Kris Tselios, Tyrone Harris, Grace Barry, Gloria Cesar, Charles Manning • Elizabeth Marie	• Milwaukee Health Department • Wisconsin Division of Public Health • Wisconsin Division of Health Care Financing	Lead Environmental Cmt. or representation on all committees Provide secondary data from hospital, Medicaid, and environmental data bases Develop a community-focused plan and interventions
State/Local Govt.	• Leonard Tyson	• WI Dept. of Health & Family Services-Southeast Region	Provide access to necessary personnel for coalition development

Payers, Insurers, and Managed Care Organizations	• Evelyn Margaret, Jarome Jagger, Terrell Reed, Jamal Demarcus • Orlando Nelson • Hillary Colby, Deb Abrahams • Katrina Nellis	• UnitedHealthcare of WI • Humana • Innovative Resource Group (CompcareBlue) • United Wisconsin Services	Represent Family & Provider Cmts. Provide primary survey data from members and secondary data about pediatric asthma utilization including medications Develop family- and provider-focused plan and interventions
Voluntary Health Agencies	• Aidan Tyler, Javier Sainz, Lindy Ross • Jessica Kwasny	• American Lung Association of Wisconsin • Children's Health Education Center	Lead Family Cmt. And representation on Steering and Evaluation Cmts. Collect primary survey data Develop a family-focused plan and interventions
Community-Based Organizations	• Cameron Nicholaus • Ray Bork, Katy Bourland, Esther Rodriguez, Pilar Witt • Jonathan Christopher • Patrick Ignatius • Margarita Rodriguez • Alfred Morgan	• Fight Asthma Milwaukee • 16th St. Community Health Center • Children's Health Alliance of WI • Black Health Coalition of WI • Bilingual Communications and Consulting • Interfaith Conference of Greater Milwaukee	Representation on all committees Collect primary survey data Develop culturally and linguistically appropriate education, prevention, and intervention strategies Coordinate and integrate asthma activities with existing community health efforts Support coalition's community awareness campaign

Academic Institution	• Kevin Kelly, Ramesh Sachdeva, Sharon Tilly, John Meurer, Phoebe Ross, Griffin Boyes	• Medical College of Wisconsin	Lead Steering and Evaluation Cmts. Communicate to link all Cmts. Develop an integrated plan and sustainable strategy

In case reviewers want more detail, the opening and closing paragraphs in the "Coalition Infrastructure" section make explicit references to two documents in the proposal attachments: an "Organization Chart" and a "List of Committees, Representation, and Key Tasks." The RFP did not specifically request these types of attachments; rather, we took the liberty to include them with the requested résumés, letters of support, and description of the application process. Attachments are a good way to overcome constraints on page limits. However, because some sponsors instruct reviewers not to spend much time reading attachments, we included the most vital information in the proposal narrative.

Committee Structure. The Steering Committee will appoint and oversee ***Family & Community Advocacy, Provider Quality Improvement, and Environmental Risk Reduction Committees***. These committees will meet eight times a year, and consist of 12–15 members, including parents of children with asthma, and health and education experts. These committees will make recommendations to the Steering Committee regarding MAAA's strategic direction and policy such as identifying asthma programming and outreach opportunities; identifying appropriate cultural and linguistic mediums; evaluating asthma education activities; and, adapting to the needs of the community. In addition, a ***Surveillance & Evaluation Committee***, comprised of 12 researchers, academicians, and parents will meet every two months, alternating with the Steering Committee. A list of committees, representation, and key tasks is attached.

Coalition Capacity. Fight Asthma Milwaukee is the only community-based asthma coalition in Wisconsin, and was one of the first established in the country. For half a decade, partners have collaborated on education, intervention, and research initiatives, including participating in two Centers for Disease Control cooperative agreements—Wisconsin's Community-Based Asthma Intervention Project and Wisconsin's Asthma Education Program for Welfare-to-Work Families. Further examples of Milwaukee coalition-based approaches to improving asthma outcomes:

- ***CHS' Health Education Center*** provided asthma education to more than 1,500 Milwaukee Public School children through their "Awesome Asthma School Days" program.
- ***American Lung Association-Wisconsin*** developed award-winning asthma management training curricula for childcare providers and school teachers and coaches.
- ***16th St. Community Health Center*** distributed 15,000 asthma self-care plans in English and Spanish to children in Milwaukee Public Schools through Child Health Champion Campaign.
- ***Community Collaboration for Healthcare Quality*** distributed the National Asthma Education and Prevention Program guidelines to more than 2,000 physicians in Milwaukee.

In this subheading we demonstrate "Coalition Capacity" by providing evidence of our past experience with coalition-based approaches to improving health outcomes and outline our planned approach to managing and supporting the coalition. The first paragraph and subsequent four bulleted points reiterate key ideas from our letter of intent, describing coalition uniqueness, federal funding history, and concrete examples of coalition efforts to improve asthma outcomes. Recapping these main points provides a basis for understanding our vision and approach to expanding the coalition to be more inclusive.

The second paragraph draws on current research to support our emphasis on a community-based collaborative approach to asthma control. Six bulleted points, shown in a two-column format, present specific examples of expanded coalition functions and do so in a manner that conserves space.

The fourth paragraph identifies the particular individuals who will assume managerial responsibilities and the fifth paragraph justifies this approach in terms of published research. Effectively managing a coalition also means recognizing the intangibles: trust, energy, respect, passion, and commitment. With sponsor support, our coalition can systematically build on prior efforts to affect greater change in the community.

The sixth paragraph describes the importance of promoting community awareness of the initiative and disseminating key findings—to affect the knowledge, attitudes, and behaviors of children, parents, and providers relative to asthma principles and practices. This justification of dissemination goes well beyond providing a laundry list of potential strategies. It moves from providing information to persuading the sponsor that we are doing the right things for the right reasons.

These programs demonstrate that coalitions are powerful and effective mechanisms for realizing change at the local level. To make our coalition work, enlightened community leaders will intensify existing dialogues accentuating the benefits of collaboration and disadvantages of division, learning from one another, affirming and respecting each other's unique ethnic and cultural differences, increasing trust, and struggling to remove barriers which impact negatively on participating groups (Torres 2000). With RWJF support, the new MAAA coalition will build on FAM successes and systematically expand its functions (Braithwaite 2000):

- Broaden the mission of member agencies
- Develop more comprehensive strategies
- Develop wider public support for issues
- Increase participation from diverse sectors
- Increase accountability
- Improve capacity to plan and evaluate

Administrative Support. Phoebe Ross, MPA, Research Coordinator in the Center for the Advancement of Urban Children, will serve as MAAA Project Coordinator. She will be responsible for organizing and attending all committee meetings and handling administrative functions such as preparing agendas, arranging for meeting times and locations, and facilitating meeting activities. She will report directly to Dr. John Meurer, Project Director.

Management Approach. Dr. Kelly, Steering Committee Chair, and Dr. Meurer will oversee the process of coordinating and facilitating consensus-building, establishing and maintaining linkages to relevant organizations and individuals, and ensuring that the role played by the coalition is appropriate and reflects the changing needs of the project over time. Steering Committee members will convene every two months to identify asthma problems in the community, prioritize potential approaches that hold the most promise for system-wide change, and identify readily available community resources. Coalition members respect Drs. Kelly and Meurer for their asthma experience, expertise, and enthusiasm to make this coalition succeed.

Drs. Kelly and Meurer will foster a participative management style nurturing the valuable contributions of every coalition member. To optimize collaboration, they will constructively apply basic principles of assertive problem solving and conflict resolution. They will separate people from problems; focus on needs and interests, not positions; invent options for mutual gain; and insist on using objective criteria (Fisher 1983). Further, they will use memorandums of understanding, orient new members, recruit continually, recognize member achievements, conduct training and technical assistance, and plan strategically (Braithwaite 2000).

Communication Strategy. The intended outcomes of dissemination strategies are to affect the knowledge, attitudes, and behaviors of children, parents, and providers relative to asthma principles and practices. Accordingly, MAAA will use a combination of strategies to promote community awareness, secure wide involvement, and disseminate findings, including: (1) newsletters distributed quarterly to providers and parents; (2) press kits for public reporting—newspapers, radio, and television public service announcements; (3) a Web page through CHS: http://www.chw.org; (4) professional forums and manuscripts; (5) annual reports submitted to RWJF and other state and local groups. In sum, MAAA has the membership, infrastructure, and capacity to develop sustainable systems of change that will improve community health.

Because coalition activities target general and professional audiences, we included a variety of dissemination strategies. Notice the level of detail: Newsletters are distributed quarterly; press kits include newspaper, radio, and television announcements; our Web site address is listed. Unfortunately, page limitations prohibited us from including names of professional journals, tentative titles, and submission dates of manuscripts to be published. The section ends on a confident note, echoing a sponsor hot button and focusing on the target population: Our coalition has the capacity to develop sustainable systems of change that will improve community health.

5. Planning Approach & Timetable.

MAAA's planning approach is driven by and directly responsive to community needs. The key factors in community change are a clear vision and mission, an action plan, quality leadership, resources for community mobilizers, feedback on changes, technical assistance, and measurable outcomes. Our methodology for the planning phase follows directly from Aday's model of addressing structure, process, and outcomes:

- **Coalition structure is inclusive**, enjoying meaningful involvement from major private and public community stakeholders and concerned parents with a role in asthma control.
- **Coalition process activities are manageable**, logical, and integrate into existing community health improvement efforts. Theoretical models systematically identify community needs.
- **Coalition outcomes are specific**, thus establishing the groundwork for an effective Implementation Phase. Collectively, structure, process, and outcomes strengthen the coalition's capacity to sustain over time a community-driven approach to asthma control.

This "Planning Approach & Timetable" section comprises 15 percent of the narrative and serves to translate theory into practice: Specific activities in the planning approach fulfill the vision and principal objectives described in the first section of the proposal. The project methodology, derived directly from our theoretical model, describes *how* we will set up appropriate systems and procedures that will produce desired results. Literature citations support our methodological selections.

Collectively, paragraphs in this section appeal to each of the three hot buttons. Notice the strategic repetition of words and phrases such as *community, inclusive, meaningful involvement, coalition, outcomes, quality of life, baseline data, evaluate and assess, resources, matching funds*, and *system-wide change*.

Furthermore, the bulleted points in the first paragraph build on the unifying concepts presented in the previous section and set the stage for illustrating our planning approach in the timetable. The timetable depicts the order, frequency, and duration of specific planning phase activities.

The RFP explicitly states, "It is expected that this section of the proposal be very concrete." Accordingly, the third paragraph starts with the transition, "More concretely, we will . . . ." The rest of the paragraph, similar to the letter of intent, identifies and justifies our selection of conceptual models to guide planning and implementation phases; namely, these are the dominant models in the field. Similar to the project's theoretical model, the timetable is divided into three categories: inclusive structure, manageable process, and specific outcomes.

The timetable reveals which coalition committees will be responsible for ensuring that specific activities occur at key points during the planning year. Activities are presented in bullet point fashion; key phrases start with descriptive verbs. Reviewers can quickly skim read the table and understand the entire planning approach. Bulleted organization and planning activities address sponsor hot buttons, e.g., recruit new coalition members annually, evaluate and assess coalition activities, and secure commitment for annual matching funds.

MAAA will design both programs and evaluations that reflect a theoretical understanding of behavior change (Clark 1994), and project design will take a multifactorial approach to accomplishing goals and objectives. That is, our application of social learning theory will address both the psychosocial dynamics underlying health behavior and the methods of promoting behavior change, while emphasizing cognitive processes and their effect on behavior. An individual's behavior is uniquely determined by a combination of social and environmental factors; thus, these factors become the elements for intervention strategies (Kelder 1996).

More concretely, we will promote stronger community-wide systems of care by integrating two conceptual models into planning and implementation. *PRECEDE/PROCEED*, the dominant health education and community health promotion model, uses an interdisciplinary framework that draws on the fields of epidemiology, social and behavioral science, administration, and education, and emphasizes two core propositions: health and health risks are caused by multiple factors, and efforts to effect change must affect both behavior and environment (Green 1999; Kreuter 1998). The *Community Health Improvement Process* supports the development and implementation of a planned approach for improving health. This means developing a pediatric community health profile based on socio-demographic characteristics, risk factors, health and functional status, resource consumption, and quality of life (Institute of Medicine 1997). The table below illustrates iterative planning activities that will improve community health outcomes.

Organization & Planning Phase Activities	Begin	End Date	Personnel
Inclusive Structure			
• Host quarterly Coalition Conferences	Nov. 2000	Sept. 2001	Entire Coalition
• Recruit parents of children with asthma to participate on the coalition committees	Nov. 2000	Oct. 2001	Entire Coalition
• Establish and convene alternating bimonthly Steering and Evaluation committees; monthly Family, Provider, & Environmental committee	Nov. 2000	Oct. 2001	All Committees
• Recruit new coalition members annually	Nov. 2000	Oct. 2001	Entire Coalition
Manageable Process			
• Evaluate local asthma problems, physical, social, economic environments; develop a community health profile from baseline data	Nov. 2000	Mar. 2001	All Committees
• Conduct a retrospective analysis of community health improvement efforts	Nov. 2000	Mar. 2001	Evaluation, et al., Committees
• Identify opportunities for intervention and assess the quality of available resources	Jan. 2001	Oct. 2001	All Committees
• Link with other asthma systems	Jan. 2001	Oct. 2001	Steering Cmt.
• Coordinate and integrate asthma education activities with current community efforts	Jan. 2001	Oct. 2001	All Committees
• Gather program development information from diverse community stakeholders and families	Jan. 2001	Oct. 2001	Family Committee
• Evaluate and assess coalition activities	Jan. 2001	Oct. 2001	Evaluation Cmt.

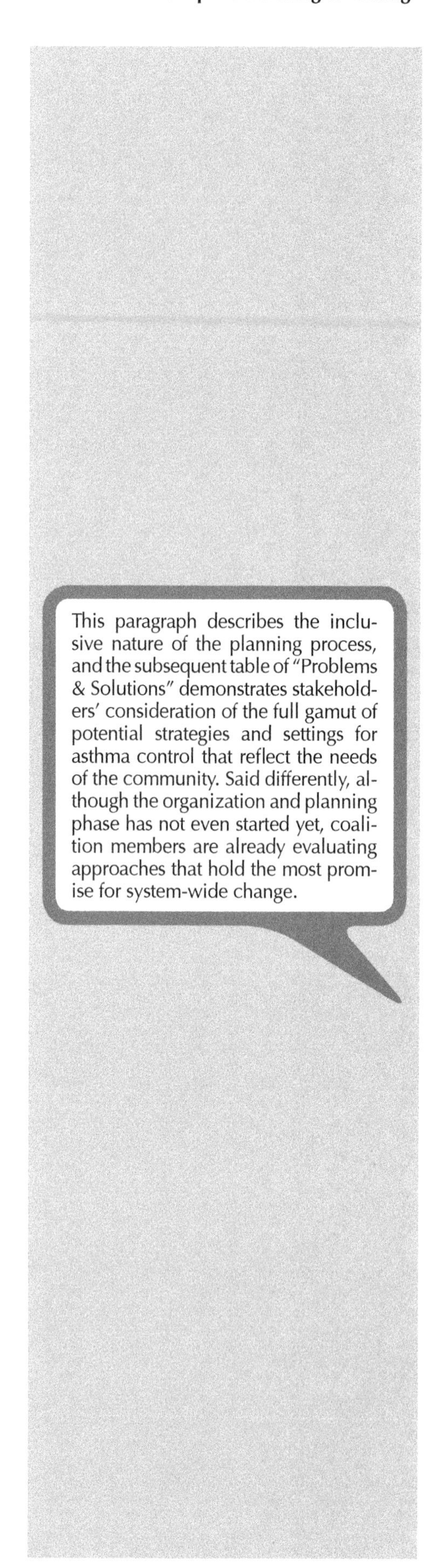

Specific Outcomes			
• Develop an implementation plan with: (1) strategic goals and objectives, (2) targeted interventions, (3) specific outcomes, and (4) articulated coalition roles and responsibilities	Feb. 2001	June 2001	Steering and all Committees
• Secure commitment for annual matching funds	Apr. 2001	June 2001	Steering Cmt.
• Initiate community awareness campaign	May 2001	Oct. 2001	All Committees
• Provide community-based asthma education	July 2001	Oct. 2001	Fam/Env. Cmt.
• Enhance asthma education for providers	July 2001	Oct. 2001	Provider Cmt.
• Develop culturally and linguistically appropriate education and publicity materials	July 2001	Oct. 2001	Family Cmt.
• Submit Implementation grant proposal	July 2001	July 2001	Steering Cmt.

To ensure inclusive participation in coalition planning efforts, Dr. Meurer organized a series of community meetings that brought together major asthma stakeholders, over 30 individuals from 20 different local and state agencies. At these meetings, participants began to identify the key problems facing children with asthma in the community and prioritize potential approaches that hold the most promise for system-wide change. (c.f., Description of the Application Process).

Problems	Solutions
• Asthma management is not coordinated among children, families, schools, day cares, and health care providers.	• Establish comprehensive asthma case management based on the local prenatal care coordination model.
• Health care providers vary widely in their use of asthma practice; parents need more family-centered approaches to education.	• Establish organizational linkages to integrate medical services, provider and family education, & environmental control.
• Families face multiple socioeconomic issues and critical survival needs perceived as more important than asthma.	• Implement media communication strategies uniquely targeting families/ professionals, and to build awareness of the coalition.
• Many children are exposed to high levels of irritants and environmental allergens.	• Reduce exposure to environmental triggers through safe housing initiatives.

This short paragraph and bulleted list address another concern raised in the RFP: demonstrating community acceptance of project efforts. Survey results quantify the concerns of parents of children with asthma and suggest their willingness to participate in interventions that focus on these areas.

A separate survey revealed similar concerns: during FAM's Asthma Wellness Day, 41 parents answered the question "What are the biggest problems in trying to care for your child's asthma?"

- 68% Too many asthma triggers at home (smoke, dust, cockroaches, mold).
- 41% We don't have enough useful asthma education materials.
- 32% Doctors and nurses aren't sensitive to my culture.

MAAA has all the critical elements for a successful planning year: a broad-based and inclusive coalition, a resource-rich environment, highly trained professionals, dedicated parents, and a theoretical model to guide activities. Planning efforts will produce an implementation plan with strategic goals and objectives, targeted interventions, specific outcomes, and articulated coalition member roles and responsibilities. Our approach can be replicated and serve as a model for other conditions because it is based in sound theory, rigorous research, and relevant practice.

The final paragraph summarizes the critical elements that will make our coalition successful, strategically hinting at all three sponsor hot buttons. The second sentence provides a smooth transition to the next section of the proposal, "planning efforts will produce an implementation plan." The last sentence reflects our shared values with the sponsor—our model for planning is based in sound theory, rigorous research, relevant practice, and can be replicated for other health conditions.

The "Preliminary Implementation Approach" tells the sponsor *how* the project plan will be accomplished. Although the purpose of the planning process is to develop an implementation plan, the RFP puts the cart before the horse, asking for a description of the types of interventions that might be employed. Because some of the implementation approaches are yet to be determined, this section is a bit shorter than the previous section on "Planning Approach & Timetable." In total, we dedicate one page of narrative to this section, nearly 8 percent of the proposal's total length.

Our preliminary planning indicated that several categories of problems exist. Accordingly, the first paragraph of this section describes a multidimensional approach to project implementation. Strategic use of journal citations shows our coalition's sensitivity to a distinctive feature raised in the RFP; namely, approaches to asthma control must be research based and reflect an interplay among the various settings and systems.

Paragraphs two, three, and four include specific examples of our comprehensive approach to system change, targeting family and community advocacy, provider quality improvement, and environmental risk reduction. These three categories represent a refinement of the broad implementation areas originally identified in the letter of intent. Note that each paragraph contains at least two citations of published research, which justify our methodological selections to address these particular problems. The asthma intervention strategies identified also represent the currently accepted best practices in the field, many of which have been written about by individuals at the Robert Wood Johnson Foundation, the National Program Office, and the National Advisory Committee. These citations reflect our shared values with the sponsor.

6. Preliminary Implementation Approach.

In the Implementation Phase, we will enact a mixture of strategies to enhance the quality of life of children. MAAA has already identified innovative approaches that are technically, politically, and economically feasible. Initiatives will broadly target families, providers, and environmental risks. Dominant theoretical models used in health education today are based in social psychology, and seek to explain causes of health problems, whereas principles of practice assist intervenors to achieve objectives. By elucidating the relationships between theory and practice, we can develop more effective interventions (Freudenberg 1995). Educational efforts to change policy and behavior of individuals and communities currently constitute our best chance to promote health. Thus, health education programs will be theory-based, multidisciplinary, and outcome-oriented (Clark 1995).

Family & Community Advocacy. Family education programs for asthma self-management will be based on social cognitive theory, targeted behavior capability, self-efficacy, and outcome expectations as integral parts of clinical care (Bartholomew 1997). People are predisposed to take action to manage asthma by virtue of internal (knowledge, attitudes, beliefs) and external (models of behavior, technical advice, money) factors. Through processes of self-regulation, i.e., the ability to observe, make judgments, and react to their own behavior, people learn which management strategies—prevention, symptom management, negotiation, communication—work for them (Clark 1994). Self-regulation behaviors are associated with more frequent use of asthma management strategies by patients; counseling by providers can encourage self-regulation and better at-home management of asthma (Clark 1994 JA). Examples of effective preventive interventions include small-group discussions, outreach to high-risk populations, and training peers and volunteers (Janz 1996).

Provider Quality Improvement. Potentially effective interventions to promote physician adoption of practice guidelines include reminder systems, restructured medical records, academic detailing and educational outreach by educationally influential clinicians, multiple interventions, concurrent audit and feedback targeted to specific providers. Interventions will be delivered by peers or opinion leaders (Davis 1997), physicians (Greco 1993), patient involvement (Grimshaw 1994), interactive seminars based on self-regulation (Clark 1998 P), and interactive educational meetings (Bero 1998). Training will be based on NAEPP guidelines, including screening to identify new cases, health education to improve family management, promotion of written asthma management plans and anti-inflammatory medications for persistent asthma, and strong administrative support to promote provider behavior change (Evans 1997).

Environmental Risk Reduction. Urban minority families with children with asthma often live in homes with high allergen and irritant levels. Decreasing asthma severity in this population means preventing and controlling known risk factors in the home. We will emphasize smoking cessation programs, covering mattresses, and dust and animal dander control (Huss 1994). The Fresno California Asthma Project will serve as a model intervention to control asthma in a low-income, multiethnic, inner city community. In the last few months of the planning phase, we will initiate innovative education for pediatric asthma providers in the central city. Small group education will be provided in age- and culturally-appropriate formats to children and families in convenient settings for them. General and ethnic media and a speaker's bureau will be used to raise public awareness of asthma as a serious but controllable health problem (Wilson 1998).

Because asthma is triggered and exacerbated by a complex mix of medical and social factors, MAAA will triangulate educational, advocacy, and environmental outreach strategies to promote wider use of current knowledge to diagnose and manage asthma. This multifaceted approach reflects a comprehensive understanding of the interplay among multiple audiences, settings, and systems. Most importantly, research shows that effective medical management and patient education reduces the use of emergency services and improves quality of life (DHHS 2000).

The final paragraph summarizes and clarifies the relationships among the different strategies: "because asthma is triggered and exacerbated by a complex mix of medical and social factors, the coalition will triangulate educational, advocacy, and environmental outreach to promote wider use of current knowledge to diagnose and manage asthma." The last sentence of this section goes the next step to describe the significance of this multifaceted approach: it facilitates achieving project goals and objectives, e.g., reduce the use of emergency services and improve quality of life.

7. Evaluation Approach.

Evaluation is integral to ensuring long-term project success. Sound evaluations should have utility, feasibility, propriety, and accuracy. That is, MAAA's evaluation will serve the information needs of intended users; be realistic, prudent, and frugal; be conducted legally, ethically, and with due regard for the welfare of those involved, as well as those affected by its results; and determine the merit of the program being evaluated (Joint Cmt. On Standards for Educational Evaluation 1994). Based on evaluation feedback, the coalition can better allocate resources, improve services, and strengthen overall project performance, thus improving the likelihood of accomplishing ultimate outcome goals—control pediatric asthma.

The "Evaluation Approach" answers *how* project effectiveness will be assessed. Because this entire section is a sponsor hot button, we provide substantial detail to establish our credibility to conduct and participate in local and national evaluations using a variety of tools that are based on recognized scientific models for assessment. In all, this section makes up approximately 10 percent of the total length of the proposal.

The first paragraph defines the characteristics of a quality evaluation approach. By defining the characteristics first, in effect, we create the yardstick against which to measure ourselves and others. Not surprisingly, we measure up. The "Evaluation Approach" goes beyond describing how the project will be evaluated and explains how evaluation feedback will be used to improve the likelihood of achieving the overall project goal. This added detail makes our proposal stand out from other applications.

The remaining seven paragraphs address each of the bulleted points in the RFP; due to page limitations, the bulleted points on soliciting broad coalition input and outlining a brief timeline were combined into one paragraph. The second paragraph in this section describes who will be surveyed by whom to assess relevant outcomes according to national asthma guidelines. At the same time, we strategically appeal to a distinctive feature raised in the RFP—research-based approaches to asthma control.

The third paragraph provides examples of existing protocols that will be adapted to gather baseline and primary data. The fourth paragraph lists collaborative partners who have volunteered access to pediatric asthma data. Equally significant, we describe measures to ensure the confidential and ethical use of data; although the RFP does not address issues of confidentiality, including this persuasive detail shows the sponsor that we have put considerable thought into developing our project.

The fifth paragraph describes types of evaluation and sample methodologies that will be used to assess the coalition, its processes, and resulting outcomes. This builds on the ideas presented in the proposal sections on "Asthma Control Expertise & Experience" and "Coalition Membership, Infrastructure & Capacity."

Relevant Outcomes. Through primary surveys of patients, families, and providers by partner organizations, MAAA will monitor activity limitations and school days missed due to asthma. Further, we will monitor the proportion of children with asthma and their families who receive formal patient education, including information about community and self-help resources as an essential part of the management of their condition. We also will assess the proportion of children who receive appropriate care according to NAEPP guidelines. Finally, we will establish a surveillance system for tracking asthma death, illness, disability, impact of environmental factors on asthma, access to medical care, and asthma management (DHHS 2000).

Data Sources. Elements of the design and methods of the National Cooperative Inner City Asthma Study may be adapted for epidemiological investigation of a cross-sectional sample of accessible children with asthma. The protocol will include an eligibility assessment and a baseline visit, during which symptom data, e.g., wheezing, lost sleep, changes in activities of daily living, inpatient admissions, and emergency department and clinic visits will be collected. Asthma knowledge and attitudes will be assessed. Currently mailed surveys to more than 700 parents of children with asthma at six Medical College of Wisconsin clinics will begin the process of surveillance (Helstad 1999). In addition, access and barriers to the medical system will be addressed by a series of questions including the location, availability, and consistency of treatment for asthma attacks, follow-up care, and primary care. Prior Milwaukee studies will be reviewed of in-home dust sample allergen collection and documentation of home environments.

Secondary Data Sources. Partnering hospital systems, health plans, school-based health centers, and the State have volunteered access to asthma data including deaths, hospitalizations and total charges, emergency department visits, clinic visits, and asthma medication prescriptions by patient age group, race/ethnicity, payer, and zip code of residence. Computer-based prediction models can identify children at high risk for adverse asthma outcomes, and will be used in our population-based efforts to improve asthma management (Lieu 1998). MAAA will apply the ethical standards set forth in the US Department of Health and Human Services policy for the protection of human research subjects. To protect confidentiality, MAAA will not use nor permit others to use data in any way except for research, analysis, and aggregate statistical reporting. MAAA also intends to participate in NAEPP's Asthma Coalition Exchange.

Measuring Change. Formative, process, and summative evaluations will be conducted to assess coalition effectiveness. Formative evaluations will assess coalition formation through a meeting effectiveness inventory, surveys on committee functioning and member satisfaction, and community needs assessments (Butterfoss 1996). Process evaluations will assess project plan implementation, i.e., correlation between activities and plans. Summative evaluations will assess the impact of interventions on key process, intermediate outcome, and ultimate outcome measures (Goodman 1996). Randomized controlled trials or prospective cohort studies will be designed to study the effectiveness of proposed interventions on accessible samples of children.

Coalition Input & Timing. Clearly, for this evaluation to be successful, MAAA must obtain and use input from a broad range of coalition members in project design and implementation. Accordingly, community-based research experts and parents are integral members of the Surveillance & Evaluation Committee chaired by Dr. Ramesh Sachdeva. In November 2000, this committee will begin to design the evaluation; by January 2001 they will begin to collect data, and in March 2001 they will begin data analysis and interpretation.

Drs. Meurer and Sachdeva will also participate in periodic meetings with other projects and the National Program Office to coordinate, streamline, and enhance the value of local evaluation efforts. And, of course, they will submit annual program updates that include information about progress to date, planned action items, project strengths/weaknesses, and process evaluations of the coalition and activities. In Winter 2004–5, a final evaluation suitable for wide dissemination will be prepared and contain a comprehensive analysis of the Milwaukee Allies Against Asthma coalition, including lessons learned and best practices for community-based asthma coalitions.

Key Individuals. To make certain that evaluations of community interventions are objective, meet rigorous standards of research, and are sensitive to ethnic and cultural differences, MAAA will team up with CHS' Center for Outcomes Research and Quality Management. Dr. Sachdeva, Center Director will help design epidemiological and outcome studies, ensure quality control of data and statistical validity of findings, and supervise statistical analysis. Following Aday's research model, Dr. Sachdeva will set up appropriate systems to capture and analyze data that illustrates effectiveness, equity, and efficiency. MAAA will also benefit from the direction and technical assistance of the National Program Office and Advisory Committee, and will participate in and can contribute to the overall cross-site evaluation of the program.

The sixth paragraph emphasizes that a broad range of research experts and coalition members are involved in evaluation planning and implementation, and that they will follow a specific timeline for evaluation design, data collection, and analysis.

Paragraph seven affirms that the coalition will coordinate evaluation activities with the National Program Office and other funded project sites, a distinctive feature raised in the RFP. The purpose of evaluation, as articulated in the last sentence of the paragraph, is to contribute to best practice standards that can be disseminated and replicated.

The final paragraph identifies personnel responsible for conducting the evaluation, establishes their credibility and capabilities, and relates their methodological approaches to the project's overarching theoretical framework. We also engage a distinctive feature raised in the RFP. Specifically, the section ends by affirming the coalition's willingness to collaborate with and take direction and technical assistance from the sponsor; grant dollars represent a shared investment in an improved future.

8. Sustaining & Institutionalizing Coalition Efforts.

MAAA is built on inclusive participation and a shared vision, principles that form the cornerstone of long-term coalition sustainability. MAAA is engrained in an organizational structure that offers stability, and based on expected education, environmental, and community outcomes, provides the basis for many initiatives to be institutionalized by member agencies and the community. In short, MAAA has the potential for changing systems for pediatric asthma control beyond the granting period.

MAAA coalition members have already demonstrated their commitment to success, providing matching funds of $250,000 during the planning year and funds exceeding one-third of each year's budget for three implementation years—$250,000 per year. (c.f., Budget and Letters of Support). Additionally, during community meetings, major asthma stakeholders brainstormed a list of innovative mechanisms to support coalition efforts after RWJF funding is complete:

While "Sustaining & Institutionalizing Coalition Efforts" is a relatively short section (5 percent of the proposal's total length), it is an important one because it addresses a sponsor hot button. In the first paragraph, the first sentence reintroduces two unifying concepts from the "Coalition Membership, Infrastructure, and Capacity" section—inclusive participation and shared vision—and describes how they form the basis of long-term coalition sustainability. The second sentence borrows from the letter of intent to emphasize that because the coalition is engrained in an organizational structure that offers stability, coalition initiatives are more likely to be institutionalized by member agencies. The third sentence stresses the significance of sustainability and institutionalization of coalition efforts; namely, they allow communities to substantially change systems of care for pediatric asthma beyond the granting period.

The second paragraph provides explicit detail about matching contributions and plans to secure other sources of financial support to further coalition efforts. The first sentence describes both mandatory and voluntary cost sharing. As one of the eligibility requirements, the sponsor expects matching dollars totaling at least one third of the total annual budget, roughly $150,000 per year during the project's implementation years. Coalition partners exceeded this mandatory amount: as an additional incentive to the sponsor to select our project for grant funding, coalition members volunteered matching funds totaling $250,000 during the planning year. We refer reviewers to the attached budget and letters of support for documentation and levels of matching support from collaborative partners.

- Obtain support from pharmaceutical firms, e.g., through the Prescription Assistance Program, and from other Milwaukee businesses whose employees are affected by childhood asthma.
- Expand Medicaid coverage and reimbursement and use Title V funds for comprehensive asthma services including multidisciplinary team care, case management, individual and group patient education, and multiple medications/holding chambers for home and school.
- Collaborate with elected State officials to appropriate general purpose revenue for the coalition for the public health agency involvement.
- Apply to the Tobacco Control Board, state and federal government, local and national private foundations for support (c.f., Description of the Application Process).

Milwaukee Allies Against Asthma is uniquely positioned to harness and focus collective talents, expertise, and asthma resources to effect lasting change in the community. When properly nurtured, coalitions have tremendous potential to shape public policy, to reach asthma patients with programs and services, and to educate health care providers (Schmidt 1999). Collectively, these strategies will provide long-term, continuous support to Milwaukee's community-based asthma coalition and enhance the quality of life of children with asthma and their families.

* * *

The bulleted list demonstrates that coalition members are committed to sustaining project efforts and have given extensive thought to securing future sources of financial support. These concrete examples of future funding mechanisms inspire more confidence than a general statement, "We will continue to look for alternative sources of support for this project." More samples are included in the attachment "Description of the Application Process." In short, this combination of mandatory and voluntary cost sharing, and an articulated albeit tentative plan for future project funding, was strategically designed to increase our chances for funding success.

The concluding paragraph ties the whole proposal together. It succinctly summarizes our credibility, uniqueness, and capability to carry out the project, and it highlights the main points and hot buttons repeated throughout the proposal. The final sentence ends on a positive note, maintaining a focus on the impact that this project will have on the target population and touching all three hot buttons: "Collectively, these strategies will provide *long-term* continuous support to our *community-based asthma coalition* and enhance the *quality of life* of children with asthma and their families."

STAGE TWO: FULL PROPOSAL

Developing the Budget and Budget Narrative.
A detailed budget and budget narrative allow the sponsor to examine the relationship between a proposed project approach and associated cost items. Although the budget and budget narrative are frequently developed after the proposal narrative is nearly completed, they should be planned and constructed with the same care that went into writing the narrative. Reviewers will scrutinize the budget and budget narrative to see whether expenses are:

- Realistic projections to accomplish project goals and objectives;
- Consistent with the degree, breadth, and depth of activities described in the narrative;
- Necessary and sufficient to fulfill individual project activities;
- Accurately calculated;
- Compatible with the sponsor's vision, priorities, and program purpose;
- Within sponsor-defined grant award limits;
- Allowable under sponsor's policy guidelines and budgeting practices.

As we developed our budget, we modeled it after the sponsor's sample line item budget, which shows the format for identifying costs associated with the proposed project. Although the budget preparation guidelines offer that we may present the budget using our institution's format instead of the sample line item budget, for the sake of convenience and familiarity for reviewers, we use the style that they are expecting to see—their own.

Milwaukee Allies Against Asthma

Detailed Line Item Project Budget

Grant Period: from 11/1/00 to 10/31/01
Budget Period: from 11/1/00 to 10/31/01
Project Year One (Planning Phase)

I. PERSONNEL (employed by Children's Health System)

Name	Position	Base Salary	% Time	Total	RWJF Support	Other Support	Source of Other
Cameron Nicholaus	Family Advocacy Cmt. Coordinator	40,000	60%	24,000	16,000	8,000	CHEC
Jessica Kwasny	Steering Cmt. Member	55,500	10%	5,500	2,775	2,775	CHEC
TBA Biostats	Evaluation Cmt. Coordinator	47,500	58%	27,500	7,500	20,000	CHW
John Calder	Provider QI Coordinator	47,000	10%	4,700	0	4,700	CHW
Christopher Jonathan	Steering Cmt. Member	85,000	10%	8,500	0	8,500	CHAW
TBA Manager	Family Advocacy Cmt. Member	34,000	10%	3,400	0	3,400	CHAW
Fringe Benefits (28%)				19,670	7,357	12,313	CHS
SUBTOTAL PERSONNEL			158%	93,320	33,632	59,688	

II. OTHER DIRECT COSTS

Description			Total	RWJF	Other	Source
OFFICE OPERATIONS						
Supplies			1,431	1,431	0	
Duplicating			1,300	1,300	0	
Telephone			600	600	0	
Postage			1,500	1,500	0	
Equipment Rental			0	0	0	
Service Agreements			5,000	0	5,000	WI BEH
Training & Tech Support			4,000	4,000	0	
COMMUNICATE/ MARKET			4,000	4,000	0	
SOFTWARE			0	0	0	
COMPUTER TIME			0	0	0	
MEETING COSTS			0	0	0	
TRAVEL			5,060	2,780	2,280	MCW
SUBTOTAL OTHER DIRECT			22,891	15,611	7,280	

III. INDIRECT COSTS (9%)

Description			Total	RWJF	Other	Source
Indirect Costs			4,432	4,432		

IV. EQUIPMENT

Description			Total	RWJF	Other	Source
None			0	0	0	

The budget is divided into five line item categories:

1. Personnel
2. Other Direct Costs
3. Indirect Costs
4. Equipment
5. Consultant/Contractual Agreements

Within these line item categories, to illustrate the basis of budget calculations and to delineate between requested support and matching funds, budget columns identify:

- Name of Personnel
- Position
- Base Salary
- Percent Time
- Total
- RWJF Support
- Other Support
- Source of Other Support

The budget is divided into 12-month project periods. For multiyear requests, a line item budget and budget narrative should be prepared for each year of sponsor support, and a consolidated line item budget should be prepared for the entire proposed grant period. For example, a four-year project would require five budgets: one for each of the four individual project years and one that summarizes the entire four-year project.

Multiyear budgets should also plan for standard cost of living increases for key personnel. Cost of living raises often range from 3 to 5 percent per year and should be explained in the budget narrative. Recognize that these annual adjustments for inflation will have a corresponding impact on the amount of grant funding required for salary-related fringe benefits. Annual budget adjustments for nonpersonnel categories, such as equipment, travel, and materials and supplies, are not based on a fixed percentage; rather, they are realistic estimates based on predicted usage and projected price increases.

As we developed the budget, we kept in mind that the Robert Wood Johnson Foundation "Financial Reporting/ Budgeting Practices and Grant Budget Revision Guidelines" allow for any budget category (Personnel, Other Direct Costs, Equipment, Consultants/ Contractual Arrangements) to be overspent by 5 percent provided that the approved budget total is not exceeded. In other words, the sponsor allows some flexibility to move grant dollars among budget categories in case project expenses are moderately over- or underestimated.

Further, budget revision guidelines also state that unexpended grant funds remain in the grant account and are not automatically carried forward to the next budget year. Grantees may request that funds unexpended from the previous budget periods be used in subsequent budget periods. A revised budget and budget narrative must be submitted that outlines the use of these funds.

Expenses listed in the budget must be incurred during the proposed project period and should relate directly to activities described in the proposal narrative or appendixes. With few exceptions, the costs of developing a grant application may not be included in the project budget because the work was completed prior to the start of the granting period.

V. CONSULTANT/CONTRACTUAL AGREEMENT

Name	Positon	Salary	Time	Total	RWJF	Other	Source
Subcontract with MCW							
John Meurer	Project Director	110,000	40%	44,000	22,000	22,000	MCW
Phoebe Ross	Steering Cmt. Coordinator	45,000	40%	18,000	9,000	9,000	MCW
Ramesh Sachdeva	Evaluation Cmt. Chair	195,000	10%	19,500	9,750	9,750	MCW
Kevin Kelly	Steering Cmt. Chair	205,000	5%	10,250	5,125	5,125	MCW
Sharon Tilly	Family Advocacy Cmt. Member	165,000	5%	8,250	4,125	4,125	MCW
Fringe Benefits (25%)				25,000	12,500	12,500	MCW
Subtotal MCW			100%	125,000	62,500	62,500	

Subcontracts with Other Organizations or Individuals							
10 TBA Parents	Family Advocacy (6); Provider QI (2); Environ (2)			10,560	10,560	0	
3 TBA Parents	Co-Chairs of Family, Provider, Environ Cmt.			3,265	3,265	0	
Aidan Tyler	Family Advocacy Cmt. Co-Chair			15,500	4,000	11,500	ALA
Brychan William	Provider QI Cmt. Co-Chair			4,000	4,000	0	MSMC
Patrick Ignatius	Evaluation Cmt. Consultant			4,000	4,000	0	BHC
Maria Lemieux	Family Advocacy Cmt. Member			2,000	2,000	0	MPS
Paula Karina	Family Advocacy Cmt. Member			2,000	2,000	0	PC
Margarita Rodriguez	Provider QI Cmt. Member			2,000	2,000	0	BCC

Ray Bork	Environment Cmt. Member			2,000	2,000	0	SSCHC
Subtotal Other Organizations				45,325	33,825	11,500	

Organizations Providing In-Kind But Not Requiring Subcontracts							
Justin Heatley	Environment Cmt. Member		30%	29,300	0	29,300	WI BEH
Kris Tselios	Family Advocacy Cmt. Member		10%	10,000	0	10,000	WI BFCH
Peter Berg	Provider QI Cmt. Member		5%	5,000	0	5,000	WI BCD
TBA WI DPH staff	Regional Public Health Coordinator		1%	700	0	700	WI DHFS
TBA Child Care staff	Family Advocacy, Environment Cmt			30,000	0	30,000	MC DHS
Dominic Michael	Environment Cmt. Co-Chair				0		MHD
Ron Blake	Provider QI Cmt. Member			10,000	0	10,000	Aurora
Erica Jardins	Family Advocacy Cmt. Member			6,376	0	6,376	Aurora
Martha Sorley	Provider QI Cmt. Member			14,976	0	14,976	Aurora
TBA Parish Nurse	Environment Cmt. Member			1,145	0	1,145	Aurora
TBA Resp. Therapist	Environment Cmt. Member			6,000	0	6,000	Aurora
Evelyn Margaret	Family Advocacy Cmt. Member			3,800	0	3,800	UHC
Jarome Jagger	Evaluation Cmt. Member			3,000	0	3,000	UHC
Subtotal In-kind Support				120,297	0	120,297	
SUBTOTAL AGREEMENTS				290,622	96,325	194,297	
TOTAL				411,265	150,000	261,265	

In the budget and budget narrative, line item costs must be clearly identified and explained. Any combination of ambiguities, inconsistencies, discrepancies, and omissions between the proposal narrative and the budget and budget narrative may provide reviewers with enough justification to reduce a funding request or reject the grant application. The budget and budget narrative should demonstrate to reviewers that sufficient funds are requested to achieve project goals and objectives in a cost-effective manner.

The budget narrative must include an explanation for every line item, which describes in as much detail as possible:

- The specific item;
- The item's relevance to the project;
- The basis of cost calculation for the item.

This level of detail explains *what* items are needed, *why* they are needed, and *how much* they will cost. In a few cases, to strengthen the budget narrative we make cross-references to information contained on specific pages in our proposal narrative.

Following the sample budget narrative provided in the Robert Wood Johnson Foundation "National Program Site Budget Preparation Guidelines," we use Roman numerals corresponding to the line item budget to organize each category description. In each description we specify the level of funding requested from the sponsor and the level, type (cash or in-kind), and source of matching funds.

Similar to the information required on the sample line item budget form, we include a detailed description of the key personnel's title, name, professional education degree, role in the project, and full-time equivalency (FTE). Specific activities performed by key personnel touch on all three sponsor hot buttons: community-based collaborative efforts, evaluation and outcomes, and matching funds and sustainability. Note the use of phrases such as "identifies, recruits, and retains families, children with asthma, representatives of schools, child care centers, churches, public health agencies, health plan asthma managers, and others"; "supervises collection of secondary data from data managers at hospitals, health plans, and public health agencies"; and "develops a sustainable coalition and an integrated strategic plan and targeted interventions."

Milwaukee Allies Against Asthma

Budget Narrative

I. PERSONNEL

The Family & Community Advocacy Committee Coordinator, Cameron Nicholaus, is Project Coordinator of Fight Asthma Milwaukee. He identifies, recruits, and retains families, children with asthma, representatives of schools, child care centers, churches, public health agencies, health plan asthma managers, and others for Committee meetings and activities. Specific responsibilities include scheduling and recording minutes and communicating information for the Family Committee. He facilitates collection of primary survey data from parents and children with asthma through Committee members and coalition partners. With the Project Director and Family Committee Chair, he establishes the agenda of meetings to develop a family- and community-focused strategic plan and targeted interventions. He also contributes to quarterly conferences. For Mr. Nicholaus' total 60% effort, the requested budget is $16,000 plus an additional $8,000 will be supported in-kind by Children's Health Education Center.

The Surveillance & Coalition Evaluation Committee Coordinator will be professional staff with masters level training in epidemiology and biostatistics in the Center for Outcomes Research and Quality Management at Children's Hospital of Wisconsin. The Coordinator assists the Evaluation Committee Chair in the following specific responsibilities: supervises collection of secondary data from data managers at hospitals, health plans, and public health agencies; controls the quality of primary and secondary data; analyzes primary and secondary data; and schedules meetings, records minutes, and communicates information for the Evaluation Committee. For the Evaluation Coordinator's total 58% effort, the requested budget is $7,500 plus an additional $20,000 will be supported in-kind by Children's Hospital of Wisconsin.

The Provider Quality Improvement Committee Coordinator, John Calder, RRT, is Asthma Program Coordinator for Children's Hospital of Wisconsin. He identifies, recruits, and retains parents, physicians, nurses, pharmacists, and others for Committee meetings and activities. Specific responsibilities include scheduling and recording minutes and communicating information for the Provider QI Committee. He facilitates collection of primary survey data from providers through Committee members and coalition partners. With the Project Director and Family Committee Coordinator, he establishes the agenda of meetings to develop a provider-focused strategic plan and targeted interventions. He also contributes to quarterly conferences. For Mr. Calder's total 10% effort, the requested budget is $0 with $4,700 supported in-kind by Children's Hospital of Wisconsin.

Paragraphs are strategically designed to facilitate the skim-reading process. In each case, the first sentence identifies the key personnel by title and the last sentence indicates the amount of funding requested form the sponsor and the amount contributed by other sources. This presentation allows reviewers who are programmatically oriented to glance at topic sentences to find relevant information, and it allows reviewers who are financially oriented to scan concluding sentences to find specific budget details.

Although this is only a one-year grant, it poses a common budgeting challenge: The award period crosses over two fiscal years. This is to say, during a 12-month timeframe, key personnel will receive their present base salary from only a portion of the institution's current fiscal year before they are given a cost of living increase that will raise their base salary during the institution's next fiscal year.

For example, a committee coordinator with a base salary of $39,604 who dedicates 60 percent effort to the program for a full year, at first blush, would require $23,762 in grant support: ($39,604/yr * .60 FTE * 1 yr) = $23,762. In reality, however, the committee coordinator will work only nine months at a base salary of $39,604 before receiving a 4 percent cost of living raise and then work the remaining three months at a base salary of $41,188. This means that the committee coordinator would require $24,000 in grant support: [($39,604/yr * .60 FTE * .75 yr) + ($41,188/yr * .60 FTE * .25 yr)] = $24,000. While the difference between these two amounts, a total of $238, is a rather modest sum, it represents a real cost borne by grant funds.

More broadly, from the beginning, personnel costs must be planned carefully. Otherwise grant funds will need to be rebudgeted later from other categories (e.g., direct costs for Office Operations) to cover any shortfalls. The simple solution is to start the budget planning process by prorating the base salaries of key personnel to match the award period. This will help ensure that sufficient funds are requested to cover staffing costs.

Steering Committee Members who are Children's Health System personnel include **Jessica Kwasny, MS,** Education Director of Children's Health Education Center, and **Christopher Jonathan, MBA,** Executive Director of Children's Health Alliance of Wisconsin (CHAW). They will communicate with their constituencies to foster linkages with the coalition. They will contribute to the development of a sustainable coalition and an integrated strategic plan and targeted interventions. They will also contribute to quarterly coalition conferences. Ms. Kwasny directly supervises the Family Committee Coordinator and Mr. Jonathan directly supervises the CHAW Project Manager serving on the Family Committee. For Ms. Kwasny's total 10% effort, the requested budget is $2,775 plus and additional $2,775 will be supported in-kind by Children's Health Education Center. For Mr. Jonathan's total 10% effort, the requested budget is $0 with $8,500 supported in-kind by Children's Health Alliance of Wisconsin through a sub-contract with the Wisconsin Department of Health and Family Services.

We list the fringe benefits that will be provided and how the amount was calculated. When different benefit rates are used for different individuals, the budget narrative should contain a table that summarizes the calculation for each individual. Depending on the type of individual position or appointment held, specific fringe benefits may include vacation, holidays, sick leave, short-term and long-term disability, Family Medical Leave Act, leave of absence, life insurance, health insurance, dental insurance, retirement contribution, dependent care reimbursement plan, education, child care, professional liability, and unemployment compensation.

Fringe Benefits: Fringe benefits may include vacation, holidays, sick leave, short-term and long-term disability, Family Medical Leave Act, leave of absence, life insurance, health insurance, dental insurance, retirement plan, dependent care reimbursement plan, education, child care, and professional liability, depending upon the type of individual position or appointment held. The fringe benefit rate is 28% for personnel at Children's Health System.

II. TOTAL DIRECT COSTS

Office Operations:

Supplies: The requested supply budget is $1,431. This includes office supplies such as paper, pens, staples, paper clips, diskettes, ink cartridges, overhead paper, and slide film. Additional supply expenses will be supported in-kind at no cost by partner organizations in the coalition.

Duplicating: The requested duplicating budget is $1,300. This includes photocopying project correspondence and reference material for all committee meetings, conferences, and reports.

Telephone: The requested telephone budget is $600. This includes local calls by Children's Health System personnel and Medical College of Wisconsin sub-contracted partners. It also includes long-distance calls and faxes from the Project Director and Project Coordinator to the National Program Office and other coalition sites. Additional telephone and fax expenses will be supported in-kind at no cost by partner organizations in the coalition.

Postage: The requested postage budget is $1,500. This includes mailing routine correspondence as well as mailing and self-addressed return postage paid envelopes for a limited number of primary surveys of parents, providers, and coalition partners. Most surveys will be administered and collected by coalition partners at meetings, in their organizations, or in their community sites. Additional postage expenses will be supported in-kind at no cost by partner organizations in the coalition.

Equipment Rental: None.

Service Agreement: The requested service agreement budget is $0. However, the Wisconsin Bureau of Environmental Health will provide $5,000 of in-kind support for laboratory analysis of molds and other allergens found in specimens from selected homes, schools, and child care centers.

Training & Technical Support for Parents: The requested training and technical support for parents budget is $4,000. This includes $400 per parent for continuing education regarding effective participation in coalition efforts and information on asthma diagnosis and management from the NAEPP guidelines. Training and technical support primarily will be provided by Black Health Coalition of Wisconsin with assistance from Children's Health System, the Medical College of Wisconsin, and the American Lung Association of Wisconsin, among other coalition partners.

The projected expenditures for supplies, duplicating, telephone, postage, equipment rental, and service agreements are listed separately along with a description of how estimates for each were determined. Elements such as duplicating, telephone, and postage can be treated as direct or indirect cost items depending on their usage. For the purpose of this project we included them as direct costs because we will exceed their "normal" use, i.e., making long-distance phone calls to the National Program Office and other coalition sties, photocopying materials to distribute at coalition meetings, and mailing surveys to parents of children with asthma. Budget elements such as training and technical support for parents are also classified under this line item category of Office Operations. We identify who will be providing the training and technical support and explain its significance in fulfilling project objectives.

Funds allocated to increasing awareness and visibility as well as promoting our project include billboard advertising, public service announcements, and printing of brochures, newsletters, and press kits. Along with a brief description here, we make a strategic cross-reference to the "Communication Strategy" section of the proposal narrative for more detail. We also confirm that we will comply with the sponsor's public reporting expectations.

We did not request any sponsor funds for software and computer time; nonetheless, we justify to the sponsor why we do not need funding for this category: all partner organizations have personal computers with relevant software for written and electronic communications. If we would have required special technology or computer processing, we would have identified the software or service necessary and explained how it related to achieving project objectives.

After much discussion among coalition members, meeting space and supplies were offered as in-kind costs supported by partner organizations. This includes such expenses as meeting room rental, audiovisual equipment rental, slide presentation costs, child care, and meals. Because some coalition partners had never calculated the costs of hosting an individual meeting, we did not attempt to quantify the value of this matching support. We do, however, make a strategic cross-reference to the "Coalition Infrastructure" section of the proposal narrative for more detail about the purpose of various meetings.

Communications/Marketing: The requested communications/marketing budget is $4,000 with additional contributions supported in-kind at no cost from partner organizations in the coalition. Funds will be allocated to increase awareness and visibility as well as to promote our project. This includes billboard advertising and public service announcements on local radio and television stations, brochures, newsletters, press releases, annual reports, and other media communications noted in the Proposal (see "Communication Strategy"). We will comply with public reporting expectations as identified in Section 7 of the Conditions of the Grant.

Software and Computer Time: The requested software and computer time budget is $0 with additional contributions supported in-kind at no cost from partner organizations in the coalition. All partner organizations have personal computers with Microsoft Office, printers, electronic mail, and Internet access. For parents and older children with asthma who lack personal computers, written information will be mailed and urgent communications will be telephoned.

Meeting Costs: The requested meeting costs budget is $0 with additional contributions supported in-kind at no cost from partner organizations in the coalition. This includes meeting room and audiovisual equipment rental. Meals and child care will be provided by volunteers with the coalition. The purpose of meetings is noted in the Proposal (see "Coalition Infrastructure") and in the table of Committees at the end of the Budget Narrative. Committee meetings may be held at any partner organization with adequate space, parking, and audiovisual equipment. Conferences will be held at the Children's Health Education Center, Children's Hospital of Wisconsin, or the Medical College of Wisconsin.

Travel:

Project Staff Travel:

Local Travel – The requested travel budget is $2,880 for local travel by parents = (10 parents x $20/meeting x one meeting or conference/month x 12 months) + (3 Co-Chair parents on Steering and Evaluation Committees too x $20/meeting x 2meetings/month x 8 months). The $20 is the estimated average cost of taxi fare plus tip round trip from homes to the meeting or conference location.

Non-Local Travel – None.

Annual Meeting Travel: The Medical College of Wisconsin Department of Pediatrics Academic Development Funds for Dr. Meurer and Ms. Ross will be used to provide in-kind support for a two-night stay ($1,140) for the Project Director and Project Coordinator to attend the National Allies Against Asthma Program's annual meeting involving all grantees, Foundation representatives, and the National Program Office, to exchange information and provide mutual assistance (total $2,280).

Consultant Travel: None.

Projected travel expenditures for Project Staff and Consultant/Contractual Agreements outline the destination, purpose, and the basis of calculations. Estimates for local travel are consistent with our organization's current policies. In order to maximize the impact of sponsor funds, and to ensure that transportation is not a barrier to inclusive participation, we opted to request local travel funds only for parent representatives to the coalition.

Following the RFP, we budgeted a two-night stay for two project staff to attend the National Program's annual meeting each year. Budget figures include airfare, lodging, meals, and ground transportation. Because we did not use any consultants, we did not need to budget any additional local or nonlocal travel costs.

III. INDIRECT COSTS:

The requested indirect cost budget of $4,432 is 9% of Children's Health System personnel and other direct costs only. Indirect costs cover grant-related costs that are not easily identified but are necessary to conduct the grant, i.e., accounting and reporting costs, payroll processing, space rental costs, legal counsel for sub-contract development, etc.

According to budget preparation guidelines, indirect costs may be calculated up to 9 percent on budget categories I and II, Personnel and Other Direct Costs. Indirect costs are not calculated on the amounts budgeted for categories IV and V, Equipment and Consultant/Contractual Agreements. This indirect costs line item is intended to cover grant-related expenses that are not easily identified but are necessary to conduct the grant, i.e., reporting costs, payroll processing, utilities, space rental costs, and legal counsel for subcontract development.

Interestingly, the sponsor did not ask for evidence of our actual indirect cost rate. Organizations regularly receiving federal grants often have an approved federal indirect cost rate that they use in calculating budgets and include as an appendix item in their compete grant application. The budget narrative frequently includes a summary statement such as the following: "Indirect costs are calculated on the basis of 26 percent of modified total direct costs, a rate approved by the Department of Health and Human Services, effective January 1, 2000 to December 31, 2002."

The purpose of this one-year grant is to develop an overall plan and strategy for addressing pediatric asthma in the community. We do not require any specific equipment to achieve project goals and objectives. In fact, nearly 87 percent of funds are dedicated to supporting the salaries, wages, and benefits of many individuals participating in the coalition's planning process. During this planning phase, we will need to consider interventions carefully because the sponsor will not support large amounts of equipment in the budget request for the implementation years.

Consultants are individuals who are brought into grant projects to add expertise in specific areas of professional activity. When these individuals are employed by and represent other organizations, contractual agreements are used to describe the collaborative arrangements between multiple organizations. Whether serving as individuals or part of a consortium, consultants often have great intuitive knowledge of problems and issues and can communicate that information in an immediately usable form. They can act as strong advocates for planned and systematic change.

We did not require any individual consultants for this project; all of our outside expertise essential to fulfilling project objectives comes in the form of contractual agreements. When individual consultants are required, we outline the need for each consultant, provide a work plan for each one, and detail tasks to be accomplished. Also note that the budget preparation guidelines limit the sponsor's portion of compensation paid to a consultant to $500/day for a full day of work.

For each proposed contract we provide an explanatory paragraph that outlines the contractor, key dates, dollar amounts, and specific tasks and deliverables. Following the budget preparation guidelines, the

IV. EQUIPMENT: None.

V. CONSULTANT/CONTRACTUAL AGREEMENTS:

Consultants: None.

Contractual Agreements: A separate contract outlining the contractor, dates, dollars, and specific tasks/deliverables will be made and entered between Children's Health System and the Subcontractor. The Robert Wood Johnson Foundation will not be party to the contract. Children's Health System will maintain fiscal responsibility for its contracts including reporting expenses to the Foundation. We will include accounting and right to audit provisions and record retention and report expectations in the contracts identified in Sections 4 and 5 of the Conditions of Grant. We also will include public reporting expectations in the contracts as identified in Section 7 of the Conditions of the Grant.

The Project Director, John Meurer, MD, MBA, is Assistant Professor of Community Pediatrics and Health Services Research in the Center for the Advancement of Urban Children at the Medical College of Wisconsin and Children's Health System. He is directly responsible for developing the proposed activity, its implementation, and day-to-day direct supervision of the project. He is accountable for planning, organizing, and directing the implementation and operations of this project. Specific responsibilities include directing staff, orientation, training, counseling, evaluation, and discipline in accordance with institutional standards. He directs the implementation and operations, distributes work, directs and personally handles public relations, estimates costs of programs, develops the budget, oversees and negotiates contracts with subcontractors, monitors and assesses project performance and performs other related coalition duties. He develops the agenda for meetings with all Committee Chairs. He contributes to and facilitates as many of the Committee meetings as possible. With the Project Coordinator, he also plans the quarterly conferences. He plans manageable processes based on theoretical models and focused on objectives and outcomes. He builds social relations and communicates to foster linkages, including collaboration with the National Program Office and other Coalitions. He ensures all five Committees remain accountable to one another. The Project Director directly supervises the Project Coordinator. For Dr. Meurer's total 40% effort, the requested budget is $22,000 plus an additional $22,000 will be supported in-kind by the Medical College of Wisconsin.

The Project Coordinator, Phoebe Ross, MPA, is Research Coordinator in the Center for the Advancement of Urban Children at the Medical College of Wisconsin and Children's Health System. She assists the Project Director in all of the above activities. Specific responsibilities include scheduling and recording minutes and communicating information for the Steering, Surveillance and Coalition Evaluation, and Environmental Risk Reduction Committees. She schedules and plans the quarterly conferences. She helps develop the agenda for meetings with all Committee Coordinators. She also serves as the Project Coordinator for the Environmental Risk Reduction Committee and assists the Chair with planning and facilitating meetings and communicating information. She directly supervises optical scanning of primary survey data in the Center for the Advancement of Urban Children. For Ms. Ross's total 40% effort, the requested budget is $9,000 plus an additional $9,000 will be supported in-kind by the Medical College of Wisconsin.

The Surveillance & Coalition Evaluation Committee Chair, Ramesh Sachdeva, MD, PhD, MBA, is Associate Professor of Critical Care Pediatrics and Epidemiology at the Medical College of Wisconsin and Director of the Center for Outcomes Research and Quality Management at Children's Hospital of Wisconsin. He designs observational and experimental studies with the assistance of academic and community-based researchers. He supervises collection of secondary data from data managers at hospitals, health plans, and public health agencies. He controls the quality of primary and secondary data. In his data management, he respects the confidentiality of individuals and organizations. He appropriately designs and directs analysis of primary and secondary data. He clearly reports findings to coalition partners. He also contributes to the Steering Committee and quarterly coalition conferences. He directs and supervises the Evaluation Committee Coordinator. For Dr. Sachdeva's total 10% effort, the requested budget is $9,750 plus an additional $9,750 will be supported in-kind by the Medical College of Wisconsin.

The Steering Committee Chair, Kevin Kelly, MD, is Professor of Pediatrics at the Medical College of Wisconsin and Director of the Asthma and Allergy Center at Children's Hospital of Wisconsin. He provides vision and leadership to the coalition, builds social relationships, recognizes achievements, and communicates to foster linkages. Through his efforts, he develops a sustainable coalition and an integrated strategic plan and targeted interventions. Specifically, he develops Steering Committee meeting agendas with the Project Director. He identifies, recruits, and retains Steering Committee and coalition members through respectful, participatory management approaches. He also contributes to Surveillance and Evaluation Committee Meetings and quarterly coalition conferences. For Dr. Kelly's total 5% effort, the requested budget is $5,125 plus an additional $5,125 will be supported in-kind by the Medical College of Wisconsin.

The Family Advocacy Committee Member and Surveillance & Evaluation Committee Member, Sharon Tilly, MD, MPH, is Associate Professor of Community Pediatrics and Director of the Center for the Advancement of Urban Children at MCW and CHS. She helps design studies, select survey instruments, and collect primary survey data. For Dr. Tilly's total 5% effort, the requested budget is $4,125 plus an additional $4,125 will be supported in-kind by the Medical College of Wisconsin.

Fringe Benefits for Sub-Contracts with the Medical College of Wisconsin: Fringe benefits for sub-contracted partners at the Medical College of Wisconsin may include vacation, holidays, sick leave, short-term and

> Robert Wood Johnson Foundation will not be listed as a party to the contracts. We will maintain fiscal responsibility for our contracts, which includes reporting expenses associated with the contract to the sponsor. We also include right to audit provisions and record retention expectations when negotiating contracts.

long-term disability, Family Medical Leave Act, leave of absence, life insurance, health insurance, dental insurance, retirement plan, dependent care reimbursement plan, education, child care, and professional liability, depending upon the type of individual position or appointment held. The fringe benefit rate is 25% at the Medical College of Wisconsin.

Contractual agreements will be established to compensate individuals serving as co-chairs and members of various committees. The Co-Chair of the Family Advocacy Committee, the Co-Chair of the Provider Quality Improvement Committee, and the Evaluation Committee consultant will receive stipends of $4,000 each. Two members of the Family Advocacy Committee, a Provider Quality Improvement member, and Environment Committee member will each receive stipends of $2,000 for their efforts.

A variety of other organizations in the coalition will not require subcontracts for their contributions to committees, but are providing $120,297 in in-kind support.

In total, Milwaukee Allies Against Asthma requests $150,000 in planning funds from the Robert Wood Johnson Foundation and coalition partners will contribute in-kind an additional $261,265.

* * *

The University of Michigan
School of Public Health
Allies Against Asthma
109 S. Observatory Street
Ann Arbor, Michigan 48109-2029

August 23, 2000

Dr. John Meurer
Fight Asthma Milwaukee Coalition
Children's Health System
9000 W. Wisconsin Avenue
P.O. Box 1997
Milwaukee, WI 53201

Dear Dr. Meurer:

The Allies Against Asthma National Program Office is currently coordinating site visits for those coalitions that have been selected to move forward to the next stage of the proposal review process. This letter contains information which we hope will assist you as we work together to coordinate the visit.

STAGE THREE: SITE VISIT

Preparing for the Site Visit.

Our full proposal to the Robert Wood Johnson Foundation's "Allies Against Asthma" program received a favorable review, and we were selected for a site visit. That is, as part of the evaluation process, the sponsor wanted to see firsthand our operation—its environment and people. Information gathered in a single day by a team of reviewers can decide the fate of an application that has taken us months to prepare. In essence, a site visit represents a "quality control" measure for the sponsor, a way for them to verify our credibility and establish a level of trust with us before awarding project funding. In this case, the sponsor decided to conduct site visits with 13 of the remaining 26 applicants (50 percent); eight sites will be awarded project funding.

We begin to prepare for the site visit by reading through and analyzing three documents provided by the sponsor: the site visit announcement, the site visit sample agenda, and the site visit questions. Then, as requested, we develop written responses to the site visit questions and submit them to the National Program Office five business days in advance of the site visit. Our answers to the "proposal specific" and "general" site visit questions will form the basis of our oral presentation to the site visit team and set the stage for further interview questions.

Site Visit Team

The site visit team will include 3–4 people representing the National Advisory Committee, the Robert Wood Johnson Foundation, and the National Program Office (NPO). We will provide you with a resume of each site visitor prior to the visit. A copy of any handouts or other written information you provide throughout the day should be made for each member of the team.

Logistics

Most site visits will be conducted during one day, between approximately 8:30 am and 3:30 pm. We expect the host coalition to make arrangements for a meeting site, preferably in the office of its host agency or one of its key partners, and to communicate with all local participants.

The NPO will arrange accommodations for the team. Recommendations for hotels and restaurants convenient to the meeting site would be appreciated. Once we have made these arrangements we will contact you to get directions from the hotel to the meeting site.

In the interest of thoroughness, rather than simply providing the site visit team with "a copy of any handouts," we go one step further to provide a "take away" folder that includes

- the agenda,
- the project summary,
- PowerPoint presentation slides,
- written responses to "proposal-specific" and "general" site visit questions,
- a list of other related projects, and
- contact information for all key participants.

These additional items subtly reinforce our three hot buttons. For example, contact information illustrates that our project is a community-based collaborative effort, and a list of related projects underscores our concern for evaluation and sustainability.

Understandably, the site visit team requested directions from their hotel to the meeting site. But to be good hosts—and to help save on overall site visit costs—coalition leaders volunteered to drive the site visit team to and from the airport, their hotels, and the meeting sites. More importantly, this act of goodwill provided coalition leaders with some additional time to get acquainted with site visitors, including an opportunity to drive through the targeted geographic area and an extra chance to discuss key aspects of the project, such as the population to be served.

Agenda

The development of the agenda is a joint process between your coalition and the NPO. We would like you to draft a preliminary schedule based on the information provided in this letter. A member of our staff will be assigned to work with you to be sure the agenda meets our mutual needs. We view the site visit as an opportunity to learn more about your coalition, and are interested in meeting the individuals you identify as important to the coalition's development and its efforts to improve pediatric asthma care in your community. At the same time, there are some specific people we would like to meet and specific issues we would like for you to address during the visit.

Attached is a list of questions that arose during the proposal review process. ***We would like for you to provide a written response to the National Program Office at least five business days prior to the site visit.*** This will give the site visit team time to review your comments before the discussions. Your responses should also be discussed during the site visit, being sure that all questions are addressed by the end of the day.

The visit should be structured so that the individuals most involved in the project's decision-making, planning, implementation, and evaluation are able to participate in all or part of the day. The goal is to include key people, while keeping the number of participants small enough to allow for productive conversation.

Developing the agenda is the most difficult task. The site visit announcement indicates, "Your responses should be discussed during the site visit, being sure that all questions are addressed by the end of the day." With six site-specific and 11 general questions, it would be nearly impossible to discuss all questions in any detail. Consider: The sample site visit agenda allocates a total of two hours with coalition leadership to address these 17 questions—this averages out to seven minutes per question with no time for a break!

Rather than trying to answer each question individually during our presentation, we cluster them into groups according to the three hot buttons we identified and addressed throughout the grant application process. While a detailed agenda gives us an idea of how much time is available to present key information, we remain flexible in case we need to address any unexpected situations or accommodate the wishes of the site visit team.

After listening to our presentation, the site visit team may wish to ask other questions about our project, staff, and organization. This interview process provides us with a vital opportunity to clarify any "fuzzy" aspects of our project, to reinforce our key points, and to establish rapport with the site visitors.

Site visit interviews can range in format from highly structured to unstructured. In structured interviews, the site visit team asks the same questions of all candidates, thus ensuring a level of consistency in their data collection process. This format, however, may not allow enough spontaneity to fully explore candidates' intangible characteristics. In unstructured interviews, candidates have the flexibility to address the issues that are of greatest concern to them. This format effectively prevents the site visit team from biasing the interview with preconceived notions about the proposed project, yet it may also produce a considerable amount of information

In most cases, site visit activities should start at 8:30 am and be completed by 3:30 pm. Given the brief time in which the site visit team will be with you, we have developed a number of recommended site visit components that we feel are important. How you schedule the specific components is up to you. Attached is a sample agenda to give you an idea of how these components might be put together. Be sure to schedule adequate time throughout the day for site visitors to ask questions as they arise.

At some point during the day, the site visit team would like to meet with the following individuals:

➢ Coalition leadership
➢ Key staff of the host agency/fiscal agent
➢ General coalition membership: If at all possible, we would like to attend a general coalition meeting with the full coalition membership. We recognize that this schedule may be difficult for many coalitions, especially those that normally meet outside of business hours. If this is the case, we will work with sites individually to arrange for all or part of the site visit team to arrive early or stay late in order to accommodate this schedule. Other than a brief introduction of the coalition members, we do not require any special agenda for this meeting. As much as possible, we would like to observe the coalition conducting its normal activities and discussions.
➢ Representatives of key partners whose commitment is needed to implement the initiative, including policy makers from the state and local level, hospital and health plan representatives, representatives of the school or public housing systems, and others who may or may not be members of the coalition. When applicable, include representatives of organizations referenced in the attached questions.

All local participants do not need to be present for the entire meeting. The project leader should determine what is feasible and what works best for the project and the day's discussions.

The agenda is designed to allow us to make the most of our time by working through lunch. While we appreciate your arranging the lunch for the site visitors, we are happy to pay for them. It should not be an expense for you to have us visit! Feel free to provide us with a bill for the meal.

A member of our staff will contact you shortly to discuss specific dates for your site visit and your proposed agenda. If you have any questions in the meantime, feel free to contact me (734-647-3179, lindoc@umich.edu) or Hayley Warshaw (734-615-3312, hwarshaw@umich.edu). We look forward to working with and meeting you soon.

Sincerely,
Linda Jo Doctor, MPH
Deputy Director

not directly related to the site visit purpose. Most site visit interviews compromise and follow a moderately structured format.

The tone of the site visit announcement suggested that a semistructured interview format would be used. Semistructured interviews balance the need for consistency and flexibility. Meaning, the site visit team can use a structured list of questions with all candidates to establish a basis for comparing responses and then use varied follow-up questions to probe for additional details. Interview questions may span a continuum of time, from past actions to future intentions. This combination format of fixed and flexible questioning is an effective way for the site visit team to obtain interview results that are valid and reliable.

Successfully managing the site visit is, in large part, a matter of paying attention to many details. Proper preparation will increase the likelihood that the site visit will go smoothly. The "three Rs" to surviving a site visit include:

- *Reviewing*. Bring together all project personnel and collaborators, have everyone reread the proposal, and review in detail the components of the project.
- *Rehearsing*. Ask outside colleagues to come in and conduct a practice site visit. The most common mistake in a site visit is for project personnel to be unfamiliar with proposal details. Rehearsing the site visit will help key participants to learn their roles in the interview process and to stay on schedule during the main event. Presenters should note their own verbal and nonverbal behaviors to ensure that they appear friendly, positive, and engaged.
- *Responding*. Ask sponsors if they have a particular agenda they wish to follow or if they want to see any special background documents. Arrange a private room for them to meet in and conduct interviews. Allow plenty of time

for reviewers' questions. Do not bombard reviewers with a lot of new information that was not in the application. Do not unnecessarily repeat material already presented in the application.

Before the sponsor will award project funding, they need to feel comfortable with us, to trust that our coalition understands their concerns and shares their values. The site visit sample agenda is designed so that the site visit team can observe our coalition in action, as much as possible, in a natural environment. During the visit they will be looking at intangible characteristics among coalition leaders and other members, such as:

- Passion—do we exhibit enthusiasm for this project?
- Energy—do we demonstrate the drive to make this project a success?
- Trust—do we act as a team working together to achieve a common goal?
- Commitment—do we display a sense of dedication toward each other and for completing the project?
- Ownership—do we claim responsibility for our successes and challenges?

Especially for collaborative projects, the site visit team may take a "divide-and-conquer" approach to assessing programmatic features such as project leadership, community involvement, communication, accountability, and sustainability. By meeting with key partners individually, the site visit team can quickly determine whether the project is real or a "phantom" collaboration. Phantom collaborations—relationships that exist only on paper—don't get funded. In real collaborations, project partners' roles are well-defined in themselves and in relation to overall project goals. Collaborators can explain how they plan to cooperate administratively, fiscally, and programmatically to make the project a success.

Allies Against Asthma

Site Visit Sample Agenda

The following is a ***sample*** agenda. We understand the need to revise the agenda based on availability, and will work with each site individually to develop a final schedule.

8:30–10:30	**Participants:** Coalition leadership **Agenda:** The site visit team will provide a short introduction to its members and the purpose of the visit. The coalition leadership should provide a *brief* overview of the proposal and begin to address the questions attached. Time should be included for the site visit team to ask questions based on the discussion.
10:30–11:30	**Participants:** Key staff of the host agency/fiscal agent **Agenda:** Clarify relationships between host agency/fiscal agent and coalition. Discuss any of the attached questions related to this relationship.

11:30–1:00 **Participants:** Coalition leadership and key coalition partners
Agenda: The team should meet individually with "key players" whose commitment is needed to implement the initiative, including state and local policy makers. A working lunch is probably necessary to provide sufficient time for such meetings.

1:00–1:30 **Participants:** Site Visit Team
Agenda: The Site Visit Team should meet privately in order to discuss the morning's activities.

1:30–3:00 **Participants:** Full coalition membership
Agenda: Provide a brief introduction of coalition members and their affiliation. Conduct general coalition business.

3:00–3:30 **Participants:** Coalition leadership
Agenda: Final opportunity to address remaining questions, outstanding issues.

While the site visit team will spend time interviewing the coalition leadership and fiscal agent, the site visit sample agenda also requests that the team should "meet individually with 'key players' whose commitment is needed to implement the initiative, including state and local policy makers." Participation from government officials was a distinctive feature that we identified in the RFP for the letter of intent, and has taken on an increasing level of importance as we advance through the grant application process.

In addition to state and local officials, we include key players from the community, such as parents and members of community-based organizations, and representatives from health care delivery systems and health plans. We select individuals from these groups because, as necessary, they can answer the "proposal specific" (S) and "general" (G) site visit questions about their:

- Roles in coalition leadership: S3, S4, and G1
- Access to data and data collection systems: G6, G7, G8, G9, G10

The site visit team may also ask collaborative partners the following types of questions: "Why is this program important to you?", "How long have you been involved with the program?", "What was your involvement in developing the grant application?", "What are your connections to the community?", "If your program is selected for funding, what do you see as your role?", and "How do your contributions fit into the 'big picture'?"

The sponsor identified 17 questions that needed to be answered in writing prior to the site visit. Of these questions, six were specific to our coalition and 11 were general questions for all coalition sites. In the RFP for the letter of intent and full proposal, the sponsor limited the number of pages they would accept. This time, they did not. That said, even conservative estimates of one half to a full page written answer per question would mean that our responses are 8.5 to 17 pages long. This is approximately the length of another full proposal! Accordingly, we aim to find a balance between length and completeness. Abbreviated answers may cast doubt on our understanding of the planning process. Verbose answers may frustrate reviewers, especially when they have many pages to read in a very short time; written responses are due a mere five business days prior to the site visit. Thus, we must answer questions thoroughly yet concisely.

The three hot buttons identified in our letter of intent and full proposal are once again repeated throughout the "proposal-specific" (S) and "general" (G) site visit questions. They provide a basis around which our responses can be organized. In particular, hot buttons relate to the following questions:

- Community-based collaborative efforts: G1, G2, G3, G4, and S3, S4
- Evaluation and outcomes: G5, G6, G7, G8, G9, G10, and S1, S2, S5
- Matching funds and sustainability: G11 and S6

Allies Against Asthma

Site Visit Questions

Proposal Specific Questions: Fight Asthma Milwaukee Coalition

S1. Please clarify the target population. What is the geographic focus? Is this a city or countywide focus? How many and which children will be targeted?

S2. The proposal states that the project will target children, especially those residing in the inner-city. However, the data provided suggests hospitalization rates for African Americans outside of the city are significantly higher. Why exclude this group?

S3. The leadership role of parents is clear, however the role of grassroots community-based organizations in leadership and decision-making is not clear. Please clarify.

S4. Who is on the steering committee?

S5. The objectives listed on pages 1 and 2 include a combination of both objectives and action steps. Please clarify your key objectives.

S6. What portion of the matching funds is cash vs. in-kind contributions?

General Questions for All Sites

G1. Please provide some examples of how community representatives are involved in the leadership and decision-making process of the coalition. How will you ensure this level of involvement continues during the planning and implementation phases?

G 2. Are there any constituencies who are missing from the coalition membership? If yes, who and how and when will you secure their participation?

G 3. A mission of Allies Against Asthma is to develop "connectivity" among intervention strategies in the home, clinical practice, school, health care delivery system, and other community systems. How will the planning process you propose ensure links across the various domains? Which links will you consider as most critical?

Over half of all the site visit questions relate to the sponsor's concern for systematic evaluation and measurable outcomes. Foremost among these is the first specific question: "S1. Please clarify the target population. What is the geographic focus? Is this a city or countywide focus? How many and which children will be targeted?" That is to say, we need to know exactly *which* and *how many* children we are targeting for services before we can assess whether or not we are achieving our goal of controlling pediatric asthma.

More than one third of the site visit questions focus on determining the extent to which project efforts are community based and collaborative. The third specific question (S3) and the first general question (G1) both call for examples of how community representatives participate in the leadership and decision-making processes of the coalition. This concern for inclusive participation is reinforced through the design of the site visit sample agenda, which allocates an hour and a half for the site visit team to meet with community members individually. During this time, site visitors will assess whether this project is a real or phantom collaboration.

While only two site visit questions (S6 and G11) focus on the hot button of matching funds and sustainability, during the site visit interview, all coalition members should be prepared to answer a potentially loaded question: "What will happen to this project if it is not selected for funding?" That is, without sponsor support, will the project: Continue as planned? Continue on a reduced scale? Cease to exist?

From the site visit sample agenda, we knew that our initial presentation would be based on the structured "proposal-specific" and "general" site visit questions. During the interview, we will pay particular attention to the style of follow-up questions asked by the site visit team. Follow-up questions may be open ended or closed ended and probe for clarification, solicit new information, or refocus responses in more productive directions. Said differently, we can take verbal cues from the site visit team depending on whether they pose follow-up questions in a neutral or leading style.

Consider the following pairs of open-ended questions; one is asked in a neutral style (N), and the other asked in a leading style (L). Neutral questions do not provide any indication of the values of the site visit team. Leading questions provide brief glimpses into the preferences of the site visitors and allow us to shape our answers to match their priorities:

- (N) "What did you mean when you said . . .?" and (L) "When you said . . . did you mean . . .?"
- (N) "What would you do next?" and (L) "As your next step, would you consider doing . . .?"
- (N) "Tell me about the target group of children that you have selected." and (L) "Wouldn't you agree that children from urban, suburban, and rural communities should be included in the target group?"
- (N) "Describe the value of this communication process." and (L) "Why does this communication process work so well?"

G 4. What is the coalition's approach to cultural competency during the planning and implementation phases and evaluation of the project?

G 5. The national evaluation effort is a partnership of the local coalitions and the National Program Office. In addition to the local evaluations, the National Program Office will look across sites to assess the role of coalitions in improving systems of care and pediatric asthma outcomes. For this evaluation each coalition may be asked to identify a number of priority components for their implementation action plan.

Your coalition has done a significant amount of research and planning related to community concerns about asthma care. Thinking to the future and based on your current information, what would you now consider as your top three priority activities?

G 6. What data at the target population level would be available to evaluate the activities listed above?

G 7. What kind of data is accessible from the state/county/local and/or facility based (e.g., hospital, health plan) surveillance systems to track asthma outcomes related to the activities? How will you gain access to these data? Who will manage the data for you?

G 8. Would the coalition be able to identify a population of children who will be exposed to the prioritized activities who could be followed over time in order to evaluate the initiative's impact on health status, health care use, and quality of life?

G 9. Do you have the capacity, e.g., data systems, collaborative arrangements, that would enable you to compare outcomes for a population of children exposed to the coalition activities with outcomes for a population of children not exposed? If so, please describe.

G 10. What data will illustrate that efforts of the coalition were essential to the activities and outcomes? How will your coalition assess and manage these data?

G 11. If new systems of care are shown to be effective, how will they be institutionalized?

* * *

Compare the following pairs of closed-ended questions, where one is asked in a neutral style (N) and one is asked in a leading style (L). Whereas open-ended questions encourage in-depth responses, closed-ended questions typically require brief "yes/no" answers.

- (N) "Are you going to . . .?" and (L) "So, what you're saying is . . ., right?"
- (N) "What types of intervention strategies do you intend to use in your overall implementation plan?" and (L) "One-time interventions have limited effectiveness and pose challenges for measuring outcomes. Do you plan to use them as part of your overall implementation strategy?"
- (N) "How often will nurses communicate with parents of children with asthma?" and (L) "Will nurses communicate with parents of children with asthma at least twice per month?"
- (N) "Would you be willing to participate in the national cross-site evaluation?" and (L) "As part of your participation in the national cross-site evaluation, do you prefer video conferencing or face-to-face meetings?"

In short, the site visit team may—intentionally or unintentionally—provide verbal prompts indicating the shape and direction they believe the project should take. They may ask leading questions. They may express approval or disapproval of an answer. They may summarize and paraphrase answers to hear what they want to hear. They may begin to talk too much and finish an answer for us. By listening closely to their questions, we can better target our answers to match their values.

STAGE THREE: SITE VISIT

Celebrating the Grant Award Notification.

The time between reading the Request for Proposal (RFP) for the "Allies Against Asthma" program and receiving the grant award notification from the Robert Wood Johnson Foundation was more than 14 months. In particular, three months passed from the submission of our letter of intent to the arrival of the invitation to submit a full proposal; three months passed after we submitted our full proposal until we learned that we were selected for a site visit; and an additional two months passed between the site visit and the arrival of the grant award notification. The application process was long (and rigorous) yet rewarding.

The grant award notice is symbolic of our ability to make a "connection" with the sponsor. Through a balanced presentation of logical, emotional, and relational elements we made a compelling case for project support, one that demonstrated to the sponsor the correlation between our project idea and their funding priorities. In essence, we are a means to fulfilling an end that they value. Namely, funding our coalition will help develop a sustainable strategy for asthma management that will improve the health status of vulnerable urban youth.

THE ROBERT WOOD JOHNSON FOUNDATION

December 1, 2000

Dr. John Meurer
Children's Health System
9000 W. Wisconsin Avenue
P.O. Box 1997
Milwaukee, WI 53201

Dear Dr. Meurer:

It is a pleasure to inform you that the Robert Wood Johnson Foundation has approved a grant of $150,000 to Children's Health System, Inc., in 12 month support of its participation in the Foundation's program, Allies Against Asthma.

The funds are to be used in accordance with the proposal to the Foundation and the terms and conditions outlined in the Request for Project Support. They are also to be used in accordance with the final budget and are to be applied over the period January 1, 2001, through December 31, 2001. Our Treasurer's Office will be in touch concerning payment of this grant and reporting requirements.

If your organization wishes to issue a news release on this grant, please feel free to do so. We ask that a copy of the draft text be sent to us for our review and information in advance of dissemination. Please allow three days for this process. Address the copy to the Foundation to the attention of Maureen Cozine in our Communications Department.

All of us at the Robert Wood Johnson Foundation wish you success in carrying out this important undertaking.

Sincerely,

Steven A. Schroeder, M.D.
President and CEO

CHAPTER 5

The Retirement Research Foundation

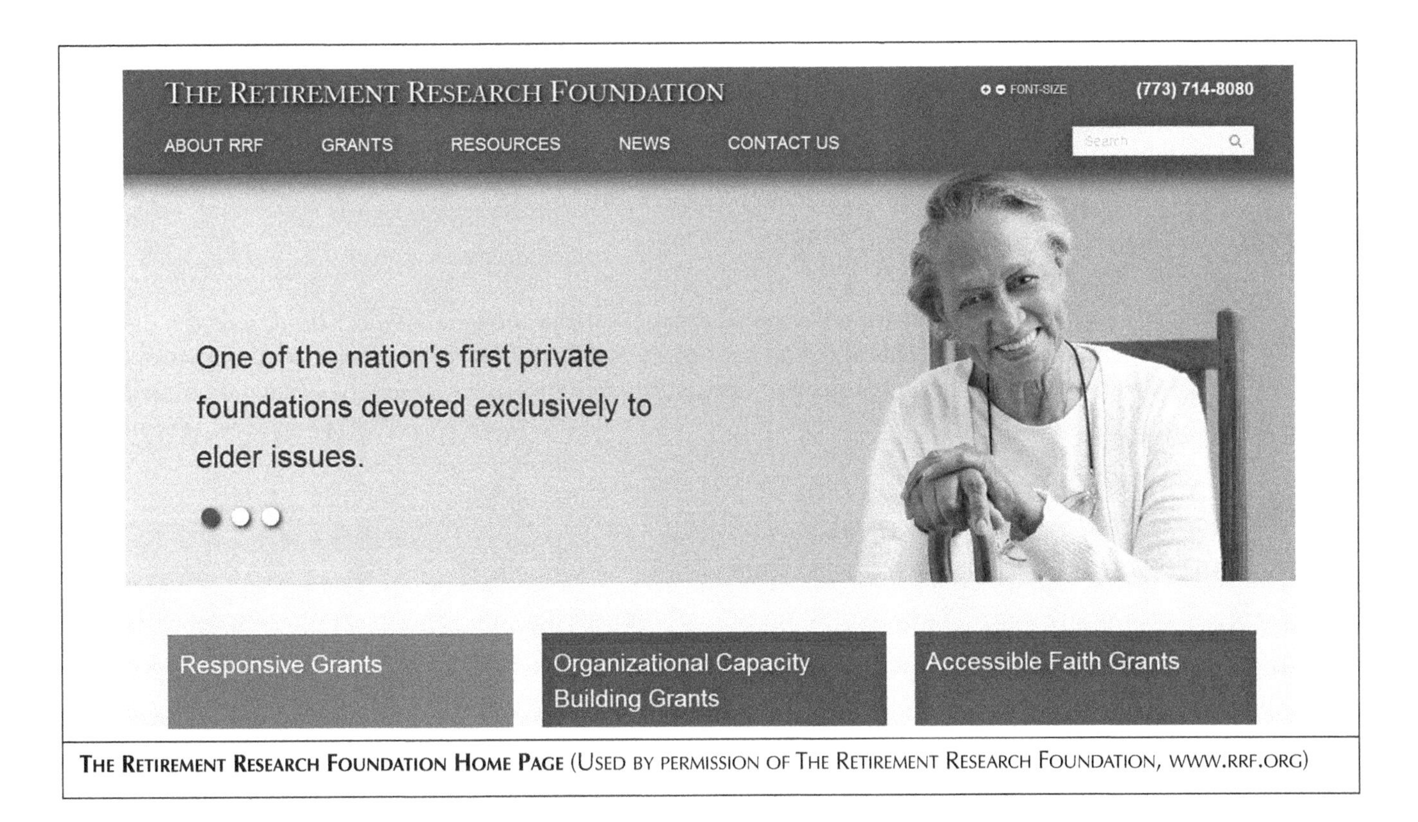

THE RETIREMENT RESEARCH FOUNDATION HOME PAGE (USED BY PERMISSION OF THE RETIREMENT RESEARCH FOUNDATION, WWW.RRF.ORG)

"Improve the quality of life for our nation's elders" is the mission of The Retirement Research Foundation. Three main funding categories—responsive grants, organizational capacity building grants, and accessible faith grants—drive its grantmaking. Endowed by philanthropist John D. MacArthur in 1978, The Retirement Research Foundation currently has assets of $134 million (2013 figure) and awards more than $5 million annually.

The Retirement Research Foundation Web site (www.rrf.org) is rich with information about its history, mission and goals, board of trustees and staff, funding priorities, funding history, grant recipients, grant resources, aging-related resources, and application processes. In contrast to the previous chapter where the sponsor issued a detailed Request for Proposal (RFP), the Retirement Research Foundation publishes application guidelines that are brief and very broad.

In this chapter we examine a successful proposal to the Retirement Research Foundation under their responsive grants category. Within this category, there are four funding priorities: advocacy, direct service, professional education and training, and research. An analysis of giving patterns between 2012 and 2014 suggests that approximately 50 percent of total awards and 40 percent of dollars went to direct service; approximately 20 percent of awards and 30 percent of dollars went to research; approximately 16 percent of awards and dollars went to advocacy; and approximately 11 percent of awards and dollars went to professional education and training. The proposed project falls into the research category, where a typical award averages $100,000 for one year, and the grant request rekindles a long-term relationship with the sponsor.

The Retirement Research Foundation uses a single-stage application process, but offers applicants the option of submitting a brief two-page letter of inquiry prior to submitting a full application. In this instance, a strategic encounter with the program officer in a professional setting served as an acceptable substitute to submitting a letter of inquiry; the program officer encouraged submission of a full proposal. Unlike most other sponsors, the Retirement Research Foundation does not impose page limitations on the proposal narrative; applicants must strike a balance between being thorough and concise.

Stage One: Full Proposal

- The Request for Proposal
- The Executive Summary
- The Proposal Narrative
- The Grant Award Notification

This application is a model of proposal planning and writing; it presents the right balance of logic, emotion, and relationships to connect with the values of the sponsor. Figure 4 overviews the key elements that we brought together to reach the Persuasion Intersection.

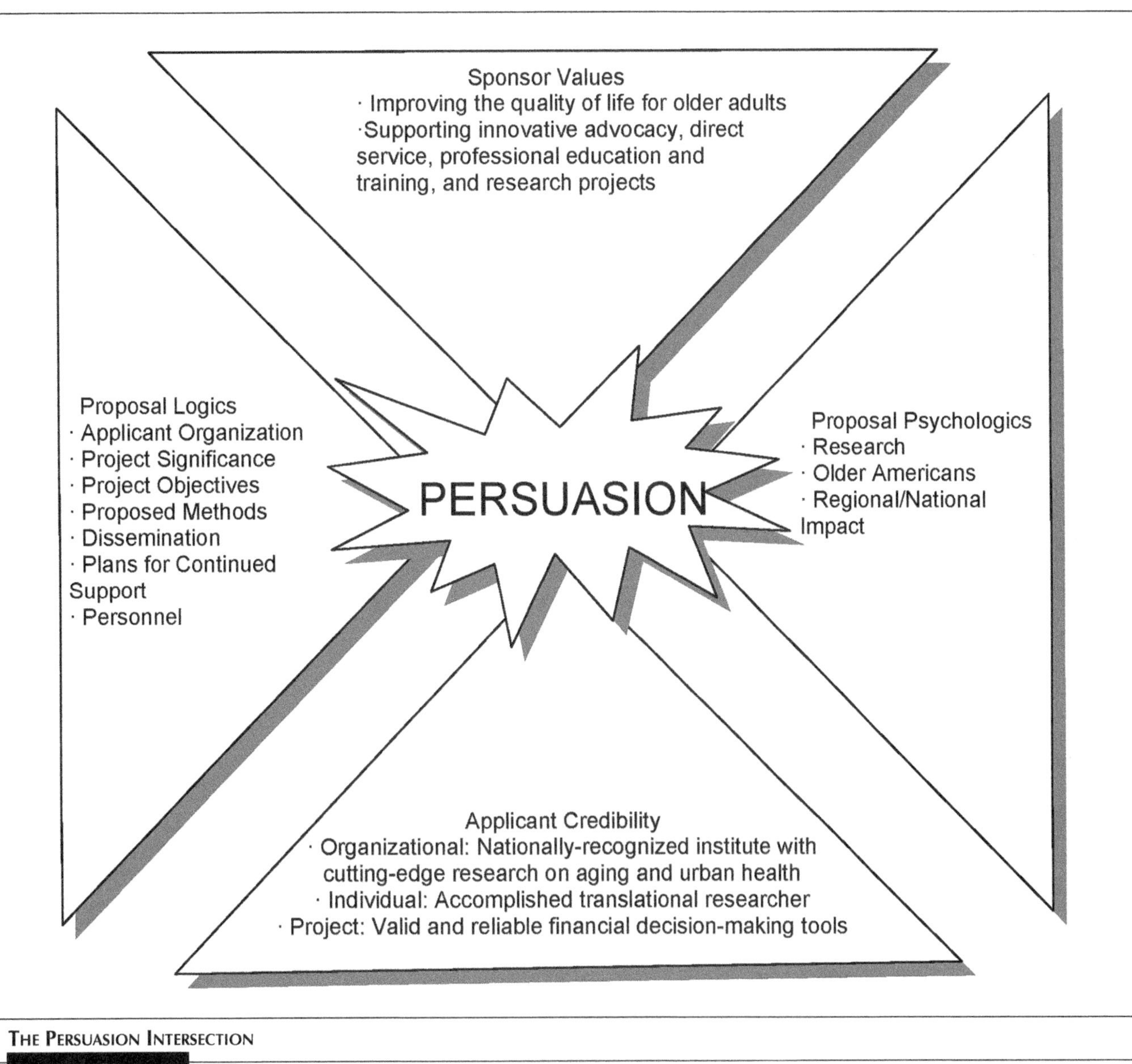

THE PERSUASION INTERSECTION

FIGURE 4

STAGE ONE: FULL PROPOSAL

Analyzing the RFP.
A Request for Proposal (RFP) is an invitation to submit a grant application. Sponsors may issue RFP guidelines that range from broad and flexible to specific and rigid. Analyzing the RFP means asking a series of iterative questions about *relevance, feasibility*, and *probability* to determine whether a proposal can be developed that will persuade sponsors that we can be a change agent to solve a problem important to them.

The following call-out thought bubbles provide insight into the process of planning and writing a successful proposal. Because the RFP Analysis Process is iterative by nature, the three steps may not always appear sequentially.

Step One: Relevance.
The Retirement Research Foundation supports projects that benefit older Americans and makes responsive grants in the areas of advocacy, direct services, professional education and training, and research. There are no stated minimum or maximum requests; however, it is not uncommon for research requests to be for $100,000. There are no page length restrictions for the narrative; proposals may be submitted to any of three annual deadlines (February 1, May 1, or August 1). The proposal review process generally takes four to eight weeks.

The Retirement Research Foundation

The Retirement Research Foundation (RRF) is devoted exclusively to improving the quality of life for our nation's older adults, especially those who are vulnerable due to advanced age, economic disadvantage, or disparity related to race and ethnicity.

Since its endowment by the late John D. MacArthur in 1978, The Retirement Research Foundation has awarded more than $200 million in grants.

RRF fulfills its mission through grantmaking programs which support innovative advocacy, direct service, professional education and training, and research projects that benefit older Americans.

Responsive Grants: Research—Overview

The Retirement Research Foundation funds research projects that have a regional or national impact on older Americans. Of particular interest are projects that:

- Seek causes and solutions to significant problems facing older adults through support of applied and policy research for which federal funding is not available.

Responsive Grants: Research—Eligibility

Research Grants are provided to organizations that are:

- Tax exempt under Section 501(c)(3) of the Internal Revenue Code; OR non-profit organizations that are not required to have a 501(c)(3) designation, such as state-funded universities.
- Nonprofit organizations, including but not limited to institutions of higher education.

RRF does not fund the following:

- Biomedical, theory development, or dissertation research.
- Conferences or fundraising events.
- Governmental agencies, except for state universities, area agencies on aging, and programs of the Veterans Administration.

The Retirement Research Foundation acknowledges the time and effort needed to submit a proposal and invites interested applicants to submit a brief **Letter of Inquiry (LOI).**

This step is optional, but may offer valuable feedback as you prepare a full proposal.

Step Two: Feasibility.
The RFP is very brief at only 1,000 words, yet two hot buttons and one distinctive feature stand out.

Research is a hot button that is in the sponsor's name, is a funding priority, and is repeated in the RFP. The RFP even clarifies the sponsor's preference for applied and policy research over theory development research. Further, the RFP contains broad descriptive words including *nation's older adults, older Americans,* and *advanced age* to call attention to the hot button of older Americans.

A distinctive feature noted in the RFP is regional/national impact. In the absence of this detail, an organization might have tried to argue that improving the quality of life for older Americans is best accomplished at the local community level. Applicants that confirm their projects will have a regional or national impact may be perceived as being more competitive than those who do not.

Step Three: Probability.
Preproposal contact questions might ask "Even though the Retirement Research Foundation does not fund theory development, is it expected that applicants elaborate on the theoretical basis for the proposed applied research?'" and "Are there models of development underpinning applied research that are more favorably received?"

Step Three: Probability.
Strategic thinking questions might include "To what extent is there value in submitting an optional Letter of Inquiry?" and "To what extent would it be more advantageous to have a conversation about the proposed project with the program officer?"

Step Three: Probability.
Preproposal contact questions might ask "Which dimensions of research on financial decision making in older adults are most pressing?" and "What difficulties linger that are still not being addressed?"

Step Three: Probability.
Preproposal contact questions might ask "When the Letter of Inquiry asks about 'potential regional or national impact of the research finding,' is it really asking for the same thing as when the RFP for the full proposal asks about 'anticipated contribution to the field?'" and "To what extent do reviewers expect to see matching funds already committed to the project?"

Step Two: Feasibility.
Evaluation criteria in the RFP indicate that the full proposal should describe the applicant organization, project significance, project objectives, proposed methods, dissemination, plans for continued support, and personnel. There are no page limitations for the proposal narrative. The RFP offers a writing tip for success related to the evaluation criteria, namely, to include the information in the order listed.

Step Two: Feasibility.
The RFP offers a writing tip for success, namely, to use lay terminology in the executive summary. The Retirement Research Foundation board of trustees may review the executive summary prior to making funding decisions, and lay terminology may help keep them focused on the project's significance and regional/national impacts rather than technical specifications of the research.

An LOI may be emailed to info@rrf.org as a Word or PDF attachment. To allow enough time for feedback, please submit LOIs at least six weeks prior to the application deadline (February 1, May 1, or August 1).

Include the following information in your two-page Letter of Inquiry:

- The issue the study will address.
- Why this research is needed at the present time.
- Potential regional or national impact of the research findings.
- Outline of research questions, study design, and study methods.
- Why the applicant (and partner organizations, if any) are qualified to lead the effort.
- Estimated cost of the project, the amount of funding already secured (if applicable), and the amount requested from RRF.

Responsive Grants: Research—Apply

For applicants from universities or hospital organizations, please note that RRF prefers that the applicant is the university or the hospital, rather than a foundation affiliated with the university or hospital. If you have questions about this, please contact RRF directly before you submit your application.

Although the Foundation does not use a standard application form, RRF requests that proposals include the following components as outlined in 1–5, preferably in the order listed below. Please note that, except for the Executive Summary, there is no page or length restriction.

1. The Grant Application Cover Sheet is available electronically as a PDF file and as a Word document. Choose the format that works best for you. Please complete and print the Cover Sheet and include it with your proposal. The Cover Sheet contains a checklist to help ensure that you include all information needed for your proposal.
2. The Executive Summary is a separate two- to three-page summary that concisely describes the project. The Executive Summary offers a succinct overview of your project and allows RRF to better understand what you are trying to accomplish. Include brief information about the project's need, objectives, methods, total project cost, and amount requested from RRF. If the proposed study is technical in nature, please use lay terminology in the Executive Summary.

3. The Proposal Narrative provides an opportunity for you to describe your project thoroughly to RRF by addressing the following:
    - Applicant Organization – Include a brief history of your organization, recent accomplishments, and the organization's qualifications to lead this project.
    - Project Significance
        - Importance and relevance of the proposed project
        - Literature review, describing existing knowledge related to the study's aims and methods
        - How the project complements or extends existing knowledge in the field
        - Anticipated contribution to the field
    - Project Objectives
        - Provide clear, concise, and complete objectives
        - State the study's hypotheses or specific research questions
    - Proposed Methods
        - Research design
        - Study hypotheses, if relevant
        - Sequence of the investigation
        - Sample size and how samples will be identified and/or recruited
        - Eligibility and exclusion criteria
        - Types of data to be obtained

Step Three: Probability.
Strategic thinking questions might include "Should the applicant organization information be more brief than thorough and, thus, move reviewers more quickly to the project significance?" and "Should the literature review be a subheading unto itself or should appropriate literature be cited throughout the proposal narrative?"

Step Three: Probability.
Preproposal contact questions might ask "Why are the study hypotheses requested in both the 'Project Objectives' section and the 'Proposed Methods' section?" and "Is it reasonable to have only two or three objectives given that the project period is only one year in duration?"

Step Two: Feasibility.
Research is a hot button reinforced not only through repetition of the word *research* but also through the extensive bulleted list of research-related considerations: *study hypotheses, sample size, sample recruitment, eligibility and exclusion criteria, data analyses, data interpretations,* and *ethical issues regarding the use of human subjects*. The Proposed Methods have nine bulleted items whereas the next largest section, Project Significance, has only four items, thus creating the expectation for significant detail in research plans.

Step Three: Probability.
Strategic thinking questions might include "Even though there are no page limitations, what level of detail is reasonable to include to persuade reviewers that project methods are well thought out and, at the same time, not to burden them with sub-specifics?" and "Is it expected that the Institutional Review Board will have approved the human subjects research prior to the application being submitted or simply prior to conducting the research, if funded?"

Step Three: Probability.
Strategic thinking questions might include "To what extent are there preferred professional journals to which articles should be submitted for publication?" and "Is there an expectation that products and tools developed under a grant award would become part of the public domain?"

Step Three: Probability.
Preproposal contact questions might ask "Given the Retirement Research Foundation's interest in supporting research 'for which federal funding is not available,' are there strategies for future funding that will be more favorably received?" and "What level of detail do reviewers expect to see about plans for funding future phases of research when the results of the proposed project have not yet been realized?"

    - Data analyses planned
    - Data interpretation planned
    - Ethical issues regarding the use of human subjects (if applicable)
- Dissemination
    - Products, tools, reports, briefs, policy research papers, professional journals, etc., that will be developed (include samples, if applicable)
    - Target audiences that findings will be disseminated to, including groups, meetings, symposiums, etc., where the outcomes will be discussed
- Plans for Continued Support
    - Describe plans to fund any next phases of the research
- Personnel
    - Provide information about project director or principal investigator, co-investigators, and other key personnel and their qualifications to lead this project

4. Budget, Budget Narrative, and Timeline – While RRF does not require a standard form for these documents, samples are provided for illustrative purposes. If possible, please start each of these documents on a new page. You may use more than one page for each.
   - The Line Item Budget includes all expenses and income, including grant funds requested from RRF and funds received and/or requested from other sources for this project, if any. Up to 10 percent of the budget may be requested from RRF for indirect project costs. See RRF's Budget Sample.
   - The Budget Narrative describes how the budget relates to the proposed project activities. Budget narratives generally contain a description for each line item identified in the budget. If the project director and/or principal investigator are engaged in other projects, identify the percentage of time and compensation from these projects. See RRF's Budget Narrative Sample.
   - The Timeline corresponds directly to the activities that are described in the proposal. See RRF's Timeline Sample.
5. Attachments – Please include three copies of the following:
   - Resumes or curricula vitae for the project director and other key personnel
   - Signed copies of commitment (or memoranda of understanding) from partnering organizations (if applicable)

   Include one copy of:
   - IRS 501(c)(3) designation letter
   - Most recent audited financial report
   - Most recent annual report

* * *

Step Two: Feasibility.
Evaluation criteria in the RFP indicate that there are no page limitations or standard forms to be used for completing the budget, budget narrative, and timeline. A writing tip for success is offered: "If possible, please start each of these documents on a new page."

Step Three: Probability.
Strategic thinking questions might include "Will reviewers have a favorable view toward principal investigators who are engaged in other projects, a sign that other sponsors are willing to invest in a related activity, or have a critical view, a red flag concern about time commitments?" and "Is there a certain level of effort that is expected of the principal investigator?"

Step Three: Probability.
Preproposal contact questions might ask "Is it reasonable to use the National Institutes of Health's biosketch format for the project director and other key personnel?" and "Are there expected categories of information to be included beyond education and training, personal statement, positions and honors, significant contributions to science, and ongoing and completed research support?"

Step Three: Probability.
Strategic thinking questions might include "Is the audited financial statement readily available?" and "Is the annual report readily available?"

STAGE ONE: FULL PROPOSAL

Developing the Executive Summary.
Following the RFP guidelines, the executive summary is presented as a three-page, condensed substitute for the proposal narrative. In 710 words, the executive summary identifies key points of the proposal and introduces two sponsor hot buttons—research and older Americans—and a distinctive feature—regional/national impact.

While the executive summary is usually the first read section of the full proposal, it was the last written. Nearly 60 percent of the executive summary is composed of sentences repeated verbatim from the narrative, which helps ensure consistency in content and style.

Boldface headings address each of the elements in the RFP: "Include brief information about the project's need, objectives, methods, total project cost, and amount requested from RRF."

Reading this stand-alone document that uses lay terminology, members of the board of trustees can quickly understand the entire project and its alignment with foundation values.

The opening paragraph leans in to the sponsor hot button of older Americans. The key words *older adults* appear 11 times, nearly once per sentence. The first and last sentences also foreshadow the hot button of research. The key words *relevant literature* and sample citations suggest that, as requested in the RFP, a more comprehensive literature review will be included in the proposal narrative that "describes existing knowledge related to the study's aims and methods."

THE PROPOSAL: ASSESSING FINANCIAL DECISION-MAKING AND FINANCIAL EXPLOITATION

Executive Summary

Overview of Need and Significance

Older adults continue to be financially exploited at disturbing rates (Conrad, Iris, Ridings, Langley, & Wilber, 2010; MetLife, 2009, 2011). Sadly, financial exploitation is committed by trusted professionals, families and friends. The loss of many financial abilities due to cognitive disorders makes older adults especially susceptible to exploitation. Despite the growing prevalence and adverse impact of financial abuse of older adults, cases of financial exploitation are difficult to detect and to prosecute. Criminal justice professionals are appreciably challenged when determining how best to balance protection of older adults with their right to autonomy. Both under and over-protection of older adults can lead to damaging consequences. Under protection for older adults can lead to gross financial exploitation that can impact every aspect of the older adult's life, including the ability to pay for needed services during times of vulnerability. Moreover, the dilemma is that over protection can be equally as costly. Many older adults have very strong needs for autonomy and control and to unnecessarily limit autonomy can lead to increased health problems and shortened longevity. The same difficulties arise in other professional groups serving older adults such as attorneys, financial planners, bankers etc. Thus, assessing the integrity of older adults' financial judgment abilities is often the key to protecting older adult's rights to autonomy and to protection when needed. However, assessment tools of financial judgment are sorely lacking as a review of the relevant literature indicates.

Introducing new investigative tools for professionals, improving measurement of financial decisional abilities, and making these tools widely available, has the potential to transform the field of financial exploitation. The introduction of reliable and valid measures enables professionals to efficiently and effectively complete case detection and intervention. The specific aims for the current proposal include:

Project Objectives
This proposal presents two major, measurable objectives.

Objective # 1: Determine the concurrent and predictive validity of both the newly created diagnostic tool the Lichtenberg Financial Decision Rating Scale (LFDRS) and LFDSS.

Objective # 2: Implement the newly created Lichtenberg Financial Decision-making Screening Scale (LFDSS) across a variety of professional settings and measure its utility as an investigative screening tool.

Project Methods
To reach Objective # 1, we will recruit an additional 100 older adult participants. This group will include at least 30 older African-Americans who are part of the Healthier Black Elders Participant Registry, a database established and managed by Dr. Lichtenberg at the Institute of Gerontology. The remaining members of the control group will come from referrals from front line financial planners, accountants, and attorneys as well as volunteers who learn of the study via our website postings, flyers, and targeted emailing and who wish to participate.

The need overviewed in the first paragraph justifies *why* this research project is necessary, touching on the frequency and severity of the problem—financial exploitation is occurring at disturbing rates—and the inability of the current situation to deal with the problem—cases of financial exploitation are difficult to detect and to prosecute and both under- and overprotection of older adults can lead to damaging consequences. The second paragraph transitions to the proposed solution—provide professionals with valid and reliable tools to help them assess the integrity of older adults' financial judgment abilities. In other words there are two audiences *who will benefit* from the project: professionals serving older adults are the direct beneficiaries and older adults themselves are the ultimate beneficiaries.

Two project objectives are expressed in two succinct sentences, explaining exactly *what* will be accomplished during the granting period. The objectives and methods expand further on the hot button of research. Key words include *concurrent and predictive validity, diagnostic tool, investigative screening tool, control group, scale and item analysis, internal consistency, factor analysis, item response theory, reliability*, and *convergent validity*.

Project methods describe *how* the objectives will be realized and *where* the project will take place. The first paragraph identifies *who* is responsible for leading project efforts and confirms that the principal investigator has direct access to the target population of older adults, which reinforces project feasibility.

The second paragraph of the methods confirms that the principal investigator has buy-in from practitioner professionals in the community to help pilot test the financial decision-making tools. That is to say, the professionals *who will benefit* from the project are also taking an active role in its planning and development, which increases the likelihood of sustained engagement.

The third paragraph of the methods highlights our credibility and capacity to carry out the project. Namely, the principal investigator has assembled a team that includes foremost experts for tool development.

The final paragraph of the methods touches on the distinctive feature of regional/national impact. The key words *dissemination methods* and *widespread distribution* suggest that the financial decision-making tools themselves, not just the results of the research, will be shared extensively.

The last paragraph of the executive summary overviews *how much* the research project will cost, delineating the amount requested from the sponsor and the level of matching funds contributed by the organization. The significant level of matching funds is likely to catch the attention of reviewers. The final sentence suggests that the project will continue beyond the granting period, which brings the impacts back to a humanistic focus.

To reach Objective # 2, we will recruit 100 older adult participants (age 60 years and older). Professionals across a variety of professions have agreed to utilize the LFDSS screening form in their interviewing or investigative work. These include financial planners, elder law attorneys, bankers, prosecutors, police, and sheriff personnel. In addition, these professionals have agreed to fill out an LFDSS usage survey each time they use the scale. All of the interviews will take place in the office of the professionals.

Working with one of the foremost experts in scale and item analyses, a number of sophisticated statistics will be used to test the full diagnostic tool as well as the screening tool. Internal consistency, factor analysis, and item response theory will all examine reliability and internal scale characteristics, while measures of convergent validity will also be examined by comparing the scores on the evaluation tool to neurocognitive abilities and a second measure of financial judgment and procedural abilities. Finally, the screening scale will be evaluated for implementation and also validity.

At the end of this study, the broader launch of the full evaluation and screening tools will be implemented. Our final sections of the grant describe dissemination methods and how we will leverage RRF funding to further the scientific study of and widespread distribution of the scale.

Project Cost

We will achieve these objectives with an RRF investment of $69,075.00 for this one year grant. An additional $39,000 will be funded through an internal Wayne State research pilot grant and a small amount of development monies. Finally, some sustainability mechanisms are identified.

* * *

1.0 Applicant Organization

The Institute of Gerontology (IOG), an interdisciplinary research center at Wayne State is dedicated to conducting edge-cutting research in social and behavioral sciences and cognitive neuroscience regarding to issues of aging and urban health. With absolute consistency, the IOG pursues a four-part mission.

1. **Research:** Improving our community's health through research
2. **Education:** Preparing tomorrow's leaders in aging research
3. **Outreach:** Connecting seniors and their families to current knowledge
4. **Partnerships:** Building programs that will stand the test of time

Since 1999 when Dr. Peter Lichtenberg became the Director of the Institute of Gerontology, the Institute's research funding doubled, and its focus on translating research to both practitioners and older adults increased. Broadly speaking, the IOG focuses on cognitive neuroscience and aging, health disparities, financial gerontology and aging and disability. The IOG also serves as an interdisciplinary research training environment for both pre and post-doctoral trainees. Since 1999, 50 Ph.D. students and 10 post-doctoral fellows completed their training at the IOG. Dr. Lichtenberg also brought community engagement to the IOG, first starting with a few conferences each year for professionals and older adults, and growing the program so that in the past year the IOG had over 100 community programs, training over 5,000 professionals and older adults. The IOG's efforts were noted by Wayne State University which in 2013 granted a 6-year rechartering. Since 2011 IOG faculty have begun to focus more and more on issues related to financial gerontology; from investigating financial vulnerability at the population level to national and local studies of fraud.

STAGE ONE: FULL PROPOSAL

Developing the Proposal Narrative.

Following the RFP guidelines, the proposal narrative begins with "brief" organizational history, list of accomplishments, and summary of organizational qualifications to lead the project. In 256 words, approximately one double-spaced page, the "Applicant Organization" section establishes the credibility of our organization and program. The opening sentences define the purpose and mission of the Institute of Gerontology, tying directly to the sponsor hot buttons of research and older Americans.

The first sentence of the second paragraph identifies *who* is responsible for leading project efforts and, further, establishes individual credibility in terms of the sponsor's preference for supporting applied and policy research over theory development research: "its focus on *translating research* to both practitioners and *older adults* increased."

The third and fourth sentences of the paragraph offer a quantitative example of an organizational accomplishment—50 doctoral and 10 postdoctoral fellows have been trained—that provides an early hint at sustainability. That is to say, the next generations of health professionals are likely to be trained on and use in their future practice the financial decision-making tools being developed with the generosity of sponsor support.

The final sentence of the paragraph touches on the distinctive feature of regional/national impact. Strategic placement of hot buttons and distinctive features at the opening and closing of paragraphs makes memorable for reviewers our sensitivity to the sponsor's logical and psychological concerns.

The "Project Significance" section justifies to the sponsor *why* this research project is needed. In 81 words, this introductory paragraph overviews the details that will unfold over the next nine double-spaced pages. Specifically, the second sentence foreshadows that the force of example—a synopsis of 26 studies published in the 2000s—will demonstrate the inadequacies of current tools to assess financial decision making in older adults. More importantly, the final sentence appeals directly to the values of the sponsor: the project will make a contribution to the scholarly field (i.e., the hot button of research) and have a humanistic impact (i.e., the hot button of older Americans). Developing the proposed diagnostic and screening tools is a means to a greater end, not an end in itself, one that is articulated in the sponsor's mission statement, "improving the quality of life for our nation's elders."

2.0 Project Significance

This proposal section will examine the importance and relevance financial capacity and financial exploitation by reviewing the literature and concepts relative to both research and practice. Specifically, a synopsis of 26 studies will demonstrate that few existing clinical research and assessment tools fail to assess financial decision-making and financial judgment relative to specific transitions being questioned. The validation of the two proposed tools (screening and diagnostic) not only contributes to the stockpile of knowledge, it affords financial protection of the elderly.

The review of literature was so comprehensive that to present it in an organized fashion, it was necessary to cluster existing research into a few smaller themes. Five subheadings are used to group articles into legislative history, elder justice, financial exploitation, financial capacity, and the intersection of financial exploitation and financial capacity.

This first subheading uses roughly two thirds of a double-spaced page to recap a historical perspective. It provides an operational definition of elder mistreatment, from which the entire basis for the project is derived. The bulleted list highlights that though protections have been enacted each decade through federal legislation, exploitation of older Americans continues to be a significant issue nationally.

2.1 Historical Perspective

Elder mistreatment is defined as intentional actions that cause harm or create serious risk of harm to an older adult by someone who stands in a trust relationship to the elder or is a caregiver (Dong & Simon, 2012). Blancato (2012) reviewed the legislative history regarding elder abuse and elder mistreatment highlighting key legislation:

- 1970's Authorization for Adult Protective Services under the Social Security Act.
- 1980's First national center on Elder Abuse at Administration on Aging is formed.
- 1987 OBRA for Long Term Care: Defined elder abuse and mandated state investigations.
- 1992 Amendment to Older Americans Act regarding elder mistreatment which provided a broader definition for what constituted abuse of older adults—but funding remained static for 20 years and counting.
- 1992 & 2006 Title VII of Older Americans Act—authorized elder abuse prevention activities.
- 2011 Elder Justice Act as part of the Affordable Care Act which recognized in federal law older adults' rights to be free from abuse and exploitation.

2.2 Financial Autonomy and Elder Justice

Stiegal (2012) vividly described the fact that financial capacity and financial exploitation are "entwined" (p.73). That is, older adults' vulnerability is twofold: (1) the potential loss of financial skills and financial judgment; and (2) the inability to detect and therefore prevent financial exploitation. Nerenberg (2012) highlighted the term *elder justice*, which holds that older adults have the fundamental right to live free from abuse, neglect, and exploitation. Although it is critical as it is to protect older adults from financial exploitation, it is equally essential to protect older adults' financial autonomy. Both under and over-protection of older adults can lead to damaging consequences. Under protection for older adults can lead to gross financial exploitation that can affect every aspect of the older adult's life. The dilemma is that over protection can be equally costly.

> The second subheading is succinct, approximately one half of a double-spaced page, yet carries a heavy psychological weight: the paragraph balances the need for additional protections to be provided to older adults with the need to safeguard their autonomy. The final three sentences were included verbatim in the executive summary and begin to foreshadow that the proposed new tools will be able to help professionals find an appropriate equilibrium between over- and underprotecting older adults.

2.3 Financial Exploitation

Older adults continue to be financially exploited at disturbing rates (Conrad, Iris, Ridings, Langley, & Wilber, 2010; MetLife, 2009, 2011). Compared to their MetLife 2009 study, Teaster et al. (2012) found 389 unduplicated media articles about financial exploitation across three months. These accounted for $530M losses, including $240M losses tied to other family members and stunningly, 51% of cases involving strangers.

> The third subheading dives into greater detail, nearly three double-spaced pages. The opening sentence of the first paragraph was included verbatim in the executive summary to introduce the frequency and severity of the problem. The second and third sentences of the paragraph quantify the situation: 389 unduplicated media articles about financial exploitation across three months report $530 million in losses. Reviewers might intuitively extrapolate these numbers to reason that in a single year there could be 1,550 articles reporting $2.1 billion in losses—staggering sums of money taken from a population, some of whom may be considered at risk or vulnerable.

Conrad et al. (2010) suggested six pertinent domains of financial exploitation: (a) theft and scams, (b) abuse of trust, (c) financial entitlement, (d) coercion, (e) signs of possible financial exploitation, and (f) money-management difficulties. Specifically, Conrad and colleagues defined financial exploitation as illegal or improper use of an older adult's funds or property for another person's profit or advantage. Conrad and colleagues rank ordered their domains by severity of the problem, with thefts and scams being the most severe form of financial exploitation. Thefts and scams represent the taking of an older adult's monies without permission either by outright stealing or committing fraudulent activities (i.e. scam). Terms such as "abuse of trust" or "financial entitlement" are financial exploitation categories that imply an ongoing relationship between the parties.

> The second paragraph in this subheading takes the next step, categorizing and ranking the types of exploitation that are producing the greatest financial losses for older adults.

Paragraphs three through seven in this subheading further humanize the financial exploitation of older adults. Paragraph three tugs at emotional sympathies: financial exploitation is perpetrated by family members—and because of an ongoing relationship among family members, the violation of trust may occur more than once. Paragraphs four and five offer possible reasons why exploitation continues: some victims are less likely than others to report the mistreatment.

In paragraph six, the principal investigator strategically inserts his own published research into the review of the current knowledge in the field. The second sentence highlights the uniqueness of the research, namely, it is "the first population-based study to gather prospective data to predict financial exploitation of any kind." In contrast to paragraphs three through five, which summarized key research results, this paragraph details the research process as well: sample size, survey instruments, analysis techniques, and statistical significance levels. As a whole, this paragraph helps to establish the credibility of the principal investigator: he has experience conducting the type of research described in the "Project Methods" section, including disseminating the results in professional journals.

Five recent random sample studies of community dwelling older adults have documented the alarming rates of financial exploitation and their correlates, while a fifth provided a new way to classify financial exploitation. For the most part, these studies gathered data on abuse of trust, coercion, and financial entitlement. **First**, Acierno et al. (2010) reported that 5.2% of all respondents have experienced financial exploitation by a family member during the previous year. Sixty percent of the mistreatment consisted of family members' misappropriation of money. The authors also examined a number of demographic, psychological, and physical correlates of reported financial exploitation. Only two variables—deficits in the number of activities of daily living (ADLs) and nonuse of social services—were significantly related to financial exploitation.

Second, Laumann, Leitsch, and Waite (2008) reported that 3.5% of their sample was a victim of financial exploitation during the previous year. Younger older adults, ages 55–65, were the most likely to report financial exploitation. African Americans were more likely than Non-Hispanic Caucasians to report financial exploitation, whereas Latinos were less likely than Non-Hispanic Caucasians to report having been victimized. Finally, participants with a romantic partner were less likely to report financial exploitation.

Third, Beach, Schulz, Castle, and Rosen (2010) found that 3.5% of their sample reported experiencing financial exploitation during the six months prior to their interviews, and almost 10% had at some point since turning 60. The most common experience was signing documents the participant did not fully understand. The authors found that, directly related to theft and scams, 2.7% of their sample believed that someone had tampered with their money within the previous six months. In their sample, African Americans were more likely to report financial exploitation than were Non-Hispanic Caucasians. Depression and ADL deficits were other correlates of financial exploitation.

Fourth, Lichtenberg, Stickney & Paulson (2013) focused on older adults' experience of fraud (defined as someone else inflicting financial losses other than by robbery or theft). This is the first population-based study to gather prospective data to predict financial exploitation of any kind. Forty-four hundred (4,400) older adults participated in a Health and Retirement Survey sub-study, the 2008 Leave-Behind Questionnaire. The prevalence of fraud across the past five years was 4.5%, and among measures collected in 2002, age, education, and depression were significant predictors of future fraud from 2003–2008. Using depression and social need fulfillment to determine the most psychologically vulnerable older adults, Lichtenberg and colleagues found that fraud prevalence in those with the highest depression and the lowest social need fulfillment was three times as high (14%) as compared to the rest of the sample's 4.1% prevalence (χ^2=20.49; p<.001).

Fifth, Jackson and Hafemesiter (2012) compared the experiences of pure financial exploitation with hybrid financial exploitation. Hybrid financial exploitation refers to cases where psychological abuse, physical abuse or neglect was found along with the financial exploitation. In cases of hybrid financial exploitation, the older adults were less healthy and more likely to be abused by those who cohabitated with the older adult. This important research underscored the variability and heterogeneity of financial exploitation of older adults.

The final paragraph in this subheading adds one more humanistic dimension to the financial exploitation of older adults: psychological abuse, physical abuse, or neglect may happen concurrently with financial exploitation and may be perpetuated by the cohabitating adults on whom they are most dependent.

2.4 Financial Capacity and Neurocognitive Abilities

Although financial exploitation research demonstrates the significant need for protection of older adults in the pursuit of elder justice, financial capacity research highlights the importance of protecting autonomy and autonomous choices of capable older adults. Specifically, financial capacity, defined here as the ability to manage "money and financial assets in ways consistent with one's values or self-interest" (Marson 2001; Flint, Sudore & Widera, 2012), is assumed until evidence to the contrary is brought forward. Pinsker et al. (2010) proposed that three abilities underlie financial capacity: (1) *declarative knowledge* (e.g., the ability to describe financial concepts); (2) *procedural knowledge* (e.g., writing checks); and (3) judgment to make *sound financial decisions*. Since dementia is a key part of financial incapacity, Pinsker et al. concluded that a comprehensive cognitive evaluation should be an integral part of the financial capacity assessment of older persons. Mental health conditions, such as depression, anxiety, and psychosis, can also affect capacity.

The fourth subheading is the longest in this section, nearly four double-spaced pages, and calls attention to the limitations of the existing instruments to assess financial decision making in older adults. The opening paragraph establishes an operational definition of financial capacity and identifies its component characteristics. The last two sentences of the paragraph contend that health professionals are in a prime position to help determine the capacity of older adults to make reasonable financial decisions.

The impact of age-related dementia (e.g., Alzheimer's disease) on financial capacity (Marson, 2001) also threatens financial autonomy. Marson and his group have compared financial capacity in cognitively intact older persons, to those suffering from mild Cognitive Impairment to mild and moderate Alzheimer's disease. Marson noted that a disproportionately high number of older adults subject to conservatorship proceedings suffer from dementia. Marson (2001) conceived of financial capacity as relating to three things: (1) specific financial abilities, (2) broad domains of financial activity, and (3) overall financial capacity. In his 2001 study, for example, financial capacity was strongly linked to stage of Alzheimer's disease. In comparing mild vs. moderate stages of Alzheimer's, differences in capability existed relative to basic monetary skills (53% vs. 10%), financial concepts (47% vs. 5%), and financial judgment (13% vs. 0%). When taking into account marginally capable individuals, it is clear that having mild stage Alzheimer's disease does not equate with incapable financial capacity. Fully 50% of older adults with mild stage Alzheimer's disease were judged capable or marginally capable of financial judgment, whereas 70% and 60% of Alzheimer's patients in the mild stage were fully or marginally capable of basic monetary skills and financial concepts. In regression analyses, memory functioning and word finding skills were significant predictors of financial judgment, accounting for 25–49% of the variance.

The second paragraph in this subheading focuses on Alzheimer's disease, the most common cause of dementia among older adults. Stages of Alzheimer's disease can range from mild to moderate to severe; thus, older adults with the brain disorder may have a wide range of financial capacity. This baseline information provides a smooth transition to the following paragraphs, which introduce the tools available to evaluate financial capacity.

The third paragraph in this subheading introduces the first of two leading psychometric instruments for determining financial capacity in older adults. The Financial Capacity Instrument assesses eight domains, ranging from simple tasks such as counting coins to complex tasks such as making financial judgments with respect to an inheritance.

In each subsequent study, Marson and colleagues have utilized the eight-domain Financial Capacity Instrument (FCI) (Martine et al. 2008) or a semi-structured interview to evaluate financial capacity (Marson et al., 2009) including assessments of:

1. Basic monetary skills
2. Financial knowledge
3. Cash transactions
4. Checkbook management
5. Bank statement management
6. Financial judgment
7. Bill payment
8. Knowledge of personal assets and estate arrangements.

Martine et al. (2008) investigated declining financial capacity using the FCI in normal older adults and those with mild Alzheimer's disease across a 12 month time period. At baseline, persons suffering from Alzheimer's disease scored below the healthy elders on the eight domains of the FCI and an overall rating of financial capacity. Over the year long period, Alzheimer's patients showed declines of about 10% in almost every domain. Scores of healthy older adults remained stable. Among the patients, bank statement management, investment decisions, financial judgment, and cash transactions showed the greatest decline over the year period, whereas knowledge of assets and estate arrangements showed the least change. The Mini Mental State Exam (MMSE) was strongly related to the FCI overall score at baseline ($r=.71$; $p<.05$).

The fourth and fifth paragraphs summarize several studies that used the Financial Capacity Instrument with older adults. The results of the studies were somewhat mixed, which leads to the assertion in the final sentence of the fifth paragraph that better tools are needed: "Thus, the great variability of the impact of early cognitive decline and early dementia on financial judgment highlights the need for new and more specific instruments to assess specific financial judgments in older adults suffering from cognitive impairment." In other words, a review of the literature sets the stage for appealing to both of the sponsor's hot buttons—more research is needed to develop psychometric tools that accurately assess financial decision making in older adults.

Sherod et al. (2009) investigated the neurocognitive predictors of FCI domains across 85 healthy normal elders, 113 older adults with MCI, and 43 with mild Alzheimer's disease. Arithmetic was the single best predictor of FCI scores; accounting for 27% of the variance in healthy elders and 46% of the FCI variance in those persons with mild Alzheimer's disease. When it came to self-assessment, Okonkwo et al. (2009) reported that even those older adults in the earlier stages of cognitive decline, with only mild Cognitive Impairment were more likely to over-estimate their cognitive skills compared to normal controls. However, financial judgment remained intact among those with mild Cognitive Impairment, relative to normal controls. Thus, the great variability of the impact of early cognitive decline and early dementia on financial judgment highlights the need for new and more specific instruments to assess specific financial judgments in older adults suffering from cognitive impairment.

Kershaw and Webber (2008) introduced a financial capacity test similar to Marson's, titled the Financial Capacity Assessment Instrument (FCAI). The 38-item measure comprises six subscales. The subscales include everyday financial abilities, financial judgment, estate management, cognitive function related to financial tasks, debt management, and support resources. The FCAI is presented as a scale with broader validation than Marson's FCI, including adult populations suffering from schizophrenia and traumatic brain injury. Its initial reliability and validity data were promising relative to other measures of general financial abilities and to overall cognitive skills. The authors reported that the FCAI domains were significantly related to the MMSE and the Independent Living Scales Money Management subtest. Finally, unlike the FCI, the FCAI is widely available for clinical and research use.

The sixth paragraph in this subheading introduces a second leading psychometric instrument for determining financial capacity in older adults. The Financial Capacity Assessment Instrument has six subscales, ranging from everyday financial abilities such as paying bills to estate management matters such as understanding Power of Attorney. Note that the final sentence raises consideration about the accessibility of the current instruments, subtle foreshadowing of and justification for making the proposed diagnostic and screening tools widely available.

Although several studies have documented good inter-rater reliability and construct validity for the FCI, and some preliminary validity data for the FCAI, financial judgment had one of the lowest percent agreements by raters among those with mild Cognitive Impairment and mild Alzheimer's disease. One significant weakness of the otherwise excellent current financial domain assessment instruments (e.g., Kershaw & Webber, 2008; Marson, 2009) is that they use hypothetical stimuli (e.g., how could you be sure the price of a car is fair?) as opposed to individualized real-life situations. Accordingly, it is critical that valid and reliable tools exist to adequately assess specific financial decision-making abilities relevant to the individual at risk, especially regarding "sentinel financial transactions," defined as transactions that can result in significant losses or harmful consequences.

The final paragraph in this subheading summarizes the strengths and weaknesses of the two dominant instruments for determining financial capacity in older adults. Specifically, while both have reliability and validity characteristics, they use hypothetical stimuli rather than real-life situations. As a consequence, raters have highly variable scores for assessing financial decision-making abilities of older adults, particularly those with mild cognitive impairments and mild Alzheimer's disease.

Human Resource managers might say it this way: "If you ask a hypothetical interview question, then you will get a hypothetical interview answer." Hence, Human Resource managers have moved toward competency-based interview questioning, where candidates provide examples based on their personal experiences. It's the difference between asking, "What would you do to ensure compliance with institutional policy?" (a hypothetical scenario) to "Describe a time when a staff member went against institutional policy and tell me how you handled the situation" (a real-life scenario).

2.5 The Intersection of Financial Exploitation and Financial Capacity

Shulman, Cohen and Hull (2005) examined 25 cases in which there were legal challenges to the testamentary capacity of an older adult. Testamentary capacity is heavily weighted toward financial judgment skills as opposed to actual management of finances or even performing cash transactions. Examples of testamentary capacity include making a donation, signing a real estate contract (e.g., reverse mortgage), or changing a will. In 72% of the challenged cases, radical changes were made to the previous will. Fifty-six percent of the cases had documented issues of undue influence, and 40% of the cases were associated with dementia. Other psychiatric and neurologic conditions were found in 28% of the cases. Flint, Sudore and Widera (2012) also found that impaired financial judgment was not only linked to cognitive impairment, but also to behavioral and psychological symptoms of dementia, including lack of awareness and delusional thinking. Thus, financial incapacity assessment must include assessments related to values, undue influence, and other contextual variables in addition to assessing neurocognitive functioning and diagnostic issues.

In this fifth subheading, approximately two thirds of a double-spaced page is dedicated to exposing the boundaries between financial capacity and financial exploitation. The fourth, fifth, and sixth sentences cite select statistics to document the frequency and severity of the problem: "Fifty-six percent of the cases had documented issues of undue influence, and 40% of the cases were associated with dementia." The final sentence of the paragraph articulates what needs to be done to help bridge the gap: "Thus, financial incapacity assessments must include assessments related to values, undue influence, and other contextual variables in addition to assessing neurocognitive functioning and diagnostic issues." That is, psychometric instruments must examine more dimensions in order to portray a more accurate picture of the financial decision-making abilities of older adults.

2.6 A New Approach to Financial Decision-making Capacity for Specific "Sentinel Financial Decisions or Transactions"

None of the available instruments directly assesses financial judgment and the underlying decisional abilities of the older adult. As described below, we carried out an in-depth process to create a new *diagnostic tool*, The Lichtenberg Financial Decision Rating Scale (LFDRS), and a new *screening tool* The Lichtenberg Financial Decision Making Screening Scale (LFDSS). Both of these instruments are unique in that they provide a standardized, structured approach to assess the decisional abilities surrounding the significant financial decision or transaction in question.

This sixth subheading starts to make the turn from describing the problem situation to proposing a potential solution: "None of the available instruments directly assesses financial judgment and the underlying decisional abilities of the older adult. As described below, we carried out an in-depth process to create a new diagnostic tool . . . and a new screening tool." At the same time, it establishes the credibility of the principal investigator, for whom the tools are named. This three-sentence paragraph, which is roughly one third of a double-spaced page, also effectively addresses both hot buttons—research and older Americans—and the evaluation criteria for "describing existing knowledge related to the study's aims and methods."

2.7 Relationship to Existing Knowledge in the Field

Sections 2.1 through 2.6 summarize in detail the existing knowledge in the field and point out gaps that will be addressed. In sum, no available instrument assessing financial exploitation deals with sentinel, real-world circumstances. Instead, they deal only with theoretical or hypothetical circumstance that may or may not be relevant to existing circumstances.

2.8 Anticipated Contributions to the Field

Upon completion of project objectives, we will contribute two near assessment tools for determining financial decision-making and identifying financial exploitation. These tools will possess the critical psychometric characteristics of reliability and validity and are based on previously unused models of test construction.

3.0 *Project Objectives*

Older adults continue to be financially exploited at disturbing rates (Acierno et al., 2010; Beach et al., 2010; Conrad, Iris, Ridings, Langley, & Wilber, 2010; Lichtenberg et al, 2013 MetLife, 2009, 2011). One-year prevalence rates of financial exploitation in older adults range from 3.5 to 5.2% with thefts and scams being the most serious form of abuse. Although a majority of cases of financial exploitation involve close family or friends, financial exploitation involving strangers is growing, even among professionals in financial or legal services. Despite the growing prevalence and adverse impact of financial abuse of older adults, cases of financial exploitation are difficult to detect and to prosecute. Criminal justice professionals are appreciably challenged when determining how to balance protection of older adults with their right to autonomy. Both under and over-protection of older adults can lead to damaging consequences. *Under protection* for older adults can lead to gross financial exploitation that can impact every aspect of the older adult's life, including the ability to pay for needed services during times of vulnerability. Moreover, *over protection* can be equally as costly. Many older adults have very strong needs for autonomy and control; and to unnecessarily limit their autonomy can lead to increased health problems and shortened longevity. The problem of financial exploitation is also intimately related to the vulnerability of older adults due to dementia and social isolation. The sheer increasing numbers of older adults (i.e. 10,000 baby boomers reaching 65 years of age each day over the next several years) in general, and with dementia, make financial exploitation one of the fastest growing public health problems in America.

Assessing the integrity of older adults' financial judgment abilities falls on the shoulders of "front line professionals" who work with older adults. A scarcity of tools exists for professionals to assess financial exploitation risks when working with older adults when making significant financial decisions or transactions. Specifically such professionals as elder law attorneys, bank tellers, and financial planners, accountants, and securities brokers must collaborate with criminal justice professionals (e.g. police, sheriff, adult protective service, prosecutor professionals) who investigate alleged exploitations.

The final two subheadings in this section, which constitute approximately one half of a double-spaced page, reflect two sides of the same coin: the seventh subheading summarizes the gaps in knowledge in the field and the eighth subheading identifies the specific deliverables—a diagnostic tool and a screening tool—that will extend knowledge in the field.

"Project Objectives" describe exactly *what* we are going to do to solve the identified problem and *who will benefit* from the project.

As a lead-up to the objectives, just over two double-spaced pages are dedicated to summarizing the problem statement. The opening sentences in the first paragraph of this section recap the frequency and severity of elder mistreatment: 3.5–5.2 percent of older adults are victims of financial exploitation, often by close family and friends. The closing sentences suggest that if nothing is done to change the current situation, it's only going to get worse: more than 10,000 baby boomers will reach 65 years of age each day over the next several years. This sentence helps creates a sense of urgency for tackling this problem right now.

The final sentence of the paragraph calls attention to the fact that financial exploitation of older adults is not simply a local problem, it is a national problem. This also serves as an initial hint at the distinctive feature of regional/national impact.

The second paragraph underscores the shortcomings of the present situation. Namely, there is a lack of valid and reliable tools for professionals to use to assess financial decision-making abilities of and risks to older adults.

The third paragraph states the humanistic consequences of professionals not having access to appropriate financial assessment tools: increased vulnerability to exploitation and decreased quality of life for older adults. When sandwiched between several longer paragraphs, this single 42-word sentence stands out—on paper and in reviewers' minds.

As a result of the lack of efficient and effective financial risk assessment tools, this quality of life dimension is grossly neglected, thereby leaving older adults vulnerable to exploitation even, for example, when a complaint has been made to criminal justice professionals.

The fourth paragraph begins to transition from the problem to the solution. The first sentence draws on the research literature to justify the approach used to design two new tools, named after the principal investigator, which can be used by professionals to examine financial decision making in older adults. The final sentence speaks to the heart of the funding request and, simultaneously, hints at both hot buttons (research and older Americans) and the distinctive feature (regional/national impact): though tools have been created, they need to be validated further before they can be implemented on a wide-scale basis.

In a preliminary project we used a well-established approach (Conrad et al, 2010) during 2012–2013 to engage over 30 experts in creating two new tools, the Lichtenberg Financial Decision Making Rating Scale (LFDRS) and the Lichtenberg Financial Decision Making Screening Scale (LFDSS). This work resulted in new multiple choice tools that examine financial decision making and can be used by front line professionals (LFDSS) and consulting health professionals (LFDRS) in cases where the integrity of an older adult's financial decision or transaction is called into question. Further validation and implementation of these tools is needed.

The fifth paragraph states the anticipated project contribution, one that speaks directly to the sponsor's values: new investigative tools that have the potential to transform the field of financial exploitation of older adults.

The use of the phrase "specific aims" in the last sentence was a deliberate effort to mirror the language of the sponsor, which in the "Project Significance" section asks for a literature review that describes existing knowledge related to the study's aims and methods. At the same time, "specific aims" is language common to the largest public funder of medical research in the United States, the National Institutes of Health.

Introducing new investigative tools for professionals, improving measurement of financial decisional abilities, and making these tools widely available, has the potential to transform the field of financial exploitation. The introduction of reliable and valid measures enables professionals to efficiently and effectively complete case detection and intervention. The specific aims for the current proposal include:

3.1 Objective # 1: Determine the concurrent and predictive validity of both the LFDRS and LFDSS.

- ***Hypothesis***: By using the scales with a mixed population of older adults (at-risk and not at risk) validity can be more fully examined.
- ***Methodology***: 200 vulnerable and non-vulnerable older adults will be administered the LFDRS and LFDSS and results will be correlated with neuropsychological and financial capacity tests. We will measure the predictive validity of the assessment for cases under investigation.
- ***Outcomes***: The psychometric properties of the scales will be thoroughly evaluated.

3.2 Objective # 2: Implement the LFDSS across a variety of professional settings and measure its utility as an investigative screening tool.

- ***Hypothesis***: Having criminal justice and other professionals use the LFDSS and provide feedback about its efficiency and usefulness will enable us to better evaluate the tool.
- ***Methodology***: Across a variety of settings (i.e., elder law, financial planning, banks, police, sheriff, adult protective services), professionals will administer and score the LFDSS.
- ***Outcomes***: The LFDSS will provide a structured and efficient way for professionals to assess core financial decisional abilities of the older adult.

4.0 Preliminary Studies

This proposal section describes the creation and inter-rater reliability of the LFDRS and LFDSS. In developing the full scale (LFDRS), a Concept Mapping approach (Conrad et al., 2010) was followed to generate the conceptual model and the stimulus items. The screening scale consists of a subset of items from the larger scale (LFDSS). The larger scale has its roots in the MacArthur studies approach to capacity, which represents its core decisional abilities (Appelbaum and Grisso, 1998).

The fifth and sixth paragraphs introduce two specific, measurable objectives. In response to the sponsor's request in the "Project Objectives" section to "State the study's hypotheses or specific research questions," we applied a hypothesis-methodology-outcomes template. In a mere 180 words, approximately three fourths of a double-spaced page, reviewers understand exactly *what* is going to be done, *what* research questions will be tested, *how* the investigations will be conducted, and *what* results are likely to occur. This template also serves as a transitional device to the section on "Proposed Methods."

The "Preliminary Studies" section is *not* a specific heading included in the RFP. Nearly 10 double-spaced pages are dedicated to explaining the work that has been accomplished so far to create the screening tool and the diagnostic tool. In essence, the purpose of this section is twofold: (1) report on past actions to establish the credibility of the principal investigator and the project, and (2) generate enthusiasm for completing the research study and bringing it to the implementation phase. This contextualization helps reviewers to understand that the proposed scope of work described in the "Proposed Methods" section is realistic and feasible within the constraints of a one-year grant period.

Of note, it was possible to include this "Preliminary Studies" section only because the sponsor does not have page or length restrictions. If the sponsor did have page limits, it's likely that this section would have been condensed to a few sentences and integrated into the "Proposed Methods" section as part of the justification for the research design and sequence of the investigation. In essence, the Retirement Research Foundation's RFP allowed a flexibility that is atypical to many sponsors.

This subheading, approximately two double-spaced pages in length, establishes credibility for the project and for key personnel.

The opening paragraph describes how the research study is grounded in an established approach for securing input from multiple participants and reaching consensus in theory development. An inclusive process secured feedback from two groups with expertise in financial capacity assessment: a national panel of researchers and a local panel of practitioner professionals. Since dissemination is an evaluation criterion, note the credibility-building statement in the sixth sentence for the national panel of researchers: "Three of the six panelists have published extensively in the area of capacity assessment of older adults and one in the Traumatic Brain Injury literature." Similarly, the seventh and eighth sentences identify the criterion used to select members of the local panel of practitioner professionals: active participation in Institute of Gerontology conferences. In other words, the principal investigator is drawing on established networks to enlist feedback from individuals who are deeply knowledgeable and passionate about serving older adults. Grassroots engagement increases the likelihood that panelists will utilize the newly validated tools and advocate for others to use them as well.

4.1 Conceptual model. We developed an initial conceptual model by drawing on studies of decisional abilities in general and as specifically related to financial exploitation. This model included the intellectual factors, values and issues of undue influence. Using the Concept Mapping Model, we then assembled two groups of experts: six of them were engaged in financial-capacity work across the nation (i.e. psychologists and psychiatrists who do research and/or clinical work in the area of capacity assessment of older adults) and 14 were local and worked daily with older adults who are making sentinel financial decisions and transactions (e.g., law enforcement, bank personnel, adult protective services, financial planners, elder law attorneys). The national panel consisted of five psychologists and a psychiatrist. All of the panelists had been qualified as an expert in financial capacity assessment cases with older adults. Three of the six panelists have published extensively in the area of capacity assessment of older adults, and one in the Traumatic Brain Injury literature. The Institute of Gerontology has co-sponsored conferences on legal, financial and psychosocial matters related to older adults. From contacts through these conferences, the second, local group was formed. Separate conference calls were held with each group to present the conceptual model for review. Based on their extensive feedback, the final conceptual model was refined and, in separate meetings with each group, finalized. Specifically, the groups broadened the conceptual model to include a variety of important contextual factors (detailed below).

A new model was created and included contextual factors, intellectual factors and values. The contextual factors were chosen from studies of financial exploitation. Conrad et al. (2010) identified themes of financial coercion and financial entitlement as part of financial exploitation. These are included in contextual factors of past financial exploitation and undue influence. Different studies highlighted different aspects of the importance of financial situational awareness and psychological vulnerability; from Beach and Schultz (2010) predictors of financial exploitation to the Lichtenberg et al. (2013) work on scams. Intellectual factors were drawn from the 25-year tradition of decisional abilities work (Appelbaum and Grisso, 1988) and echoed by more recent work (ABA-APA, 2008; Sherod et al., 2009). The ABA-APA Handbook for Psychologists *Assessing Diminished Capacity in Older Adults* also highlighted the importance of an older adult's values.

As can be seen in Figure 1, contextual factors include Financial Situational Awareness (FSA); Psychological Vulnerability (PV), which includes loneliness and depression; Undue Influence (I); and Financial Exploitation (FE). Contextual factors, as illustrated by the model, directly influence the intellectual factors associated with decisional abilities for a sentinel financial transaction or decision.

Intellectual factors refer to the functional abilities required for financial decision-making capacity and include an older adult's ability to (1) express a choice (C), (2) communicate the rationale (R) for the choice, (3) demonstrate understanding (U) of the choice, (4) demonstrate appreciation (A) of the relevant factors involved in the choice, and (5) make a choice that is consistent with past values (V). Intellectual factors—unless they are overwhelmed by the impact of contextual factors—are the most proximal and central to determining the integrity of financial decisional abilities.

Figure 1. Key Components of the Financial Decisional Abilities Model

Whereas the first paragraph in this subheading establishes the integrity of the process, the second paragraph establishes the credibility of model creation. The literature cited throughout the paragraph demonstrates an awareness of "existing knowledge related to the study's aims and methods," as requested in the evaluation criterion for "Project Significance." A strategic citation published by the principal investigator helps to establish individual credibility and appeals to both sponsor hot buttons; the principal investigator has the most recently published research on financial exploitation of older Americans. An equally significant though more subtle credibility statement occurs in the final sentence: The American Bar Association and American Psychological Association's "Assessment of Older Adults with Diminished Capacity" handbook for psychologists is a widely respected publication in the field and the principal investigator was an instrumental member of the project work group that created it.

Paragraphs three and four describe and the subsequent figure illustrates the relationship between contextual and intellectual factors that influence the financial decision-making ability of older adults. The figure helps to break up long blocks of text as well as display connections in the new model that may otherwise have gone unnoticed in the narrative alone. As described in paragraph four and depicted in the figure, intellectual factors "are the most proximal and central to determining the integrity of financial decisional abilities." The figure intentionally follows the final paragraph in this subheading—rather than being inserted immediately after paragraph three when it was introduced—to act as a visual summary of the previous two pages.

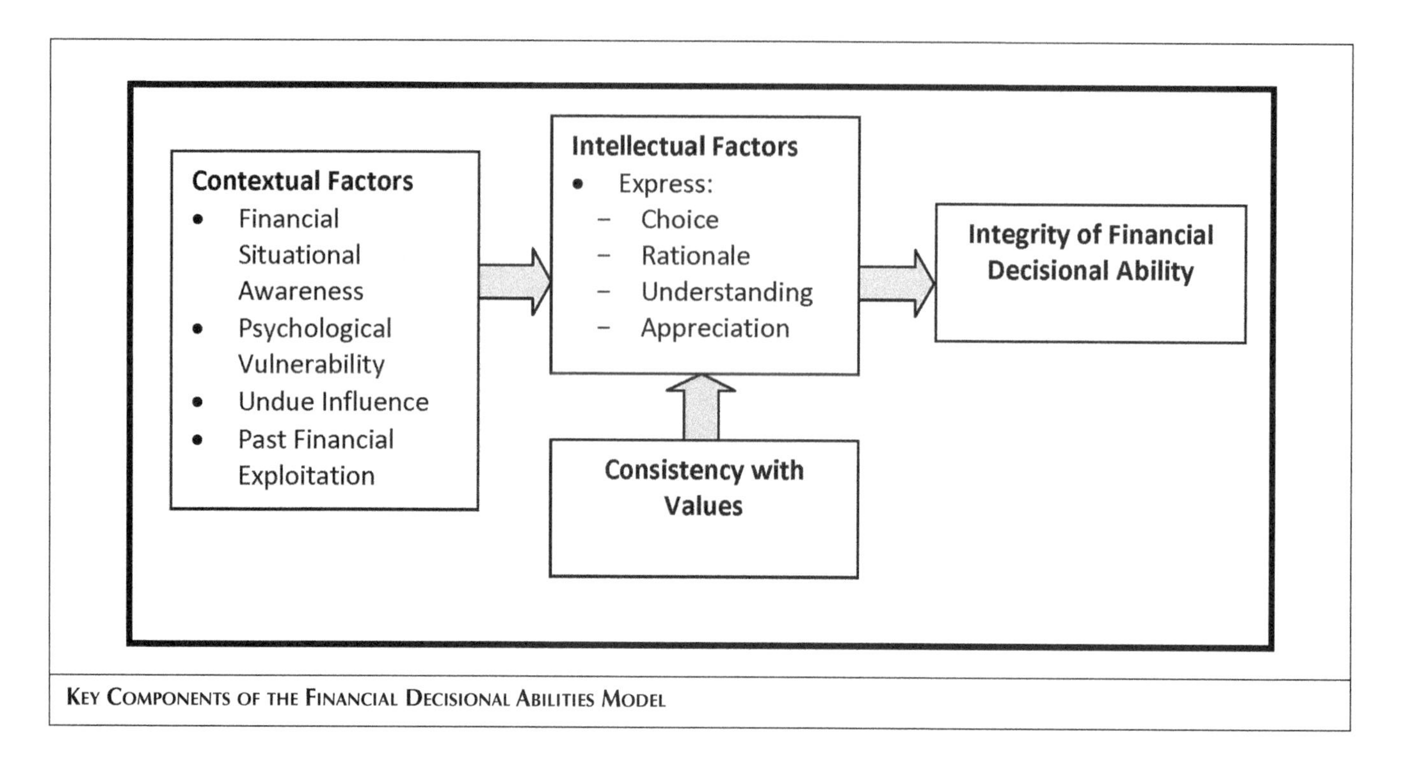

KEY COMPONENTS OF THE FINANCIAL DECISIONAL ABILITIES MODEL

The second subheading in this section is the second longest in the entire proposal narrative, roughly five double-spaced pages. A detailed description is provided for the process used to create the diagnostic tool. Whereas in the "Project Significance" section the force of examples was used to call attention to the inadequacies of current tools to assess financial decision making in older adults, here the force of examples is used to demonstrate that the new tool has exactly the detail and sensitivity needed.

In this opening paragraph, the second sentence highlights the number of questions initially identified for the tool; the third sentence indicates that the list of questions was expanded; the fourth sentence reveals that the question format was changed based on panel feedback; and the fifth sentence specifies the amount of time that passed before a second iteration of the tool was shared. These steps prepared the diagnostic tool for testing.

4.2 Lichtenberg Financial Decision Making Rating Scale (LFDRS) Construction In parallel with the development of the conceptual model, we also worked with the expert groups to identify and choose items for the Lichtenberg Financial Decision Making Rating Scale (LFDRS). Originally 28 open-ended stems were proposed as potential questions. Based on expert group feedback, a broader set of questions than we had originally proposed was created. It was further agreed that a multiple-choice format would be used for questions. Three months after the first set of conference calls, the revised LFDRS was distributed and additional feedback elicited during a second set of conference calls. This resulted in only minor revisions, and the final version of the LFDRS was ready for testing soon after. Instructions for administration and scoring were also finalized at this time. *The full scale is to be used by health or mental health professionals who have a background in assessing financial capacity or financial judgment, and who are trained in clinical interviewing.*

The final scale consists of 61 multiple-choice questions that were asked of all five participants. Depending on the answers to certain items, it is possible to be asked up to 17 additional questions. The questions are presented in separate sections that measure Financial Situational Awareness (18 questions; including some undue influence and financial exploitation), Psychological Vulnerability (12 questions), Current Financial Transaction (20 questions; including intellectual factors) and a final section on undue influence and financial exploitation (11 items). Sample stems of the items from the LFDRS are shown in Table 1. Examiners can score single items according to awareness and accuracy or examiner rated risk. Single items are tallied, and each of the decisional abilities is rated which then leads to the examiner using all of the information from the scale to determine a final overall rating of the integrity of financial decisional abilities. This approach is entirely consistent with the MacArthur scales such as the MacCat-T, which was "designed to be consistent with a basic maxim in the legal definition of competence. No particular level of ability is always associated with competence or incompetence. (Grisso and Appelbaum, 1998, p. 2).

Table 1. Sample Items from the Lichtenberg Financial Decision Making Rating Scale

Financial Situational Awareness
• What are your current sources of income?
• How worried are you about having enough money to pay for things?
• Who manages your money day to day?
• Do you regret or worry about financial decisions you have made recently?
• Are you helping anyone financially on a regular basis?
• Have you gifted or lent money to someone in the past couple of years?
Psychological Vulnerability
• How often do you wish you had someone to talk to about financial decisions or plans?
• Have you recently lost someone who was a confidante?
• How often do you feel downhearted or blue about your financial situation or decisions?
• Is your memory, thinking skills, or ability to reason with regard to finances worse than a year ago?
• When it comes to making financial decisions, how often are you treated with less courtesy and respect than other people?
Sentinel Financial Decision/Transaction
• What current major financial decisions or transactions are you intending to make?
• What are your personal (financial) goals with this transaction?
• Now and over time, how will this decision and/or transaction impact you financially?
• How much risk is there that this transaction could result in a loss of funds?
• Who will be adversely affected by the current decision/ transaction? How will they react?

The second paragraph elaborates on the process of assessment administration. The first four sentences consider the perspective of the older adult completing the assessment: 61 multiple choice questions with 17 possible follow up questions that measure 5 dimensions of financial decision making. The last four sentences consider the perspective of the professional scoring the assessment: items can be evaluated individually or collectively to reach a final rating, yet as the final sentence points out, a certain flexibility exists with respect to interpreting the rating to mean competence or incompetence.

The table following the second paragraph provides 28 sample items from the diagnostic tool. The breadth and depth of questions reveals the tool's ability to discern internal and external motivations, past actions and future intentions, and baseline understanding and consequences of choices.

• To what extent did you consult with anyone before making the financial decision?
• Who did you discuss this with?
• Would someone who knows you well say this decision was unusual for you?
Financial Exploitation
• Have you ever had checks missing from or out of sequence in your checkbook?
• Do you have a credit or debit card that you allow someone else to use?
• Has anyone ever signed your name to a check?
• How often in the past few months has someone asked you for money?
Undue Influence
• Have you had any conflicts with anyone about the way you spend money or to whom you give money?
• Has anyone asked you to change your will?
• Has anyone recently told you to stop getting financial advice from someone?
• Was this transaction your idea or did someone else suggest it?
• Did this person drive or accompany you to carry out this financial transaction?

In our first work with the LFDRS, we studied inter-rater reliability of expert judges. Adults aged 60 and older were eligible to participate in a videotaped interview using the LFDRS if they had completed a major (relative to their circumstances) financial transaction or decision within the previous two months or if they were contemplating making a major financial transaction or decision in the next two months. All participants were referred by an elder-law attorney. Approval for the videotaped interviews was obtained from the Wayne State University IRB, and all participants signed release forms approved by the university's Office of the General Counsel. One of the authors (PL) performed all of the interviews. Interviews varied in length from 15 to 40 minutes; with the majority running 23–28 minutes. The instructions to the participants were as follows: "I am going to be asking you a number of questions related to your financial situation and financial decision making. For each question there will be multiple-choice answers. If any of the questions are confusing or unclear, please tell me."

The third paragraph details the considerations that went into ensuring that interview questions are scored consistently across professionals administering the tool with older adults. The first sentence identifies participant eligibility criteria; the second sentence describes a standardized referral process; the third sentence substantiates that research protocols for the protection of human subjects were followed; and the fourth and fifth sentences confirm a uniform interviewer and format were used. More broadly, this transparency of process helps to establish the credibility of the principal investigator and of the work that has led up to the proposed project.

Participants. Five participants, who are briefly described here, completed the LFDRS on videotape:

Participant # 1: Deanna is a 65-year-old single, retired mother of one adult child. She has a master's degree and had retired within the previous six months. The decision being weighed is whether to set up a trust and change her will so that her son—who lives with her and attends graduate school—would be her Durable Power of Attorney for Finances (DPOA). Specifically, she is considering a "springing" DPOA, which does not require that two physicians designate her as incapacitated. Deanna currently reports no significant current health problems.

Participant # 2: Kathy is a 70-year-old single, retired woman with no children. She has an associate's degree, and worked as a secretary during her career. Kathy suffers from bipolar disorder, for which she had experienced an acute episode and been hospitalized six years prior to the LFDRS interview. The decision being weighed is whether to change her will so that one of her nieces will no longer be included in her estate.

Participant # 3: Shirley is a 60-year-old married woman who had been seen by a neurologist two weeks prior to her LFDRS interview and received a diagnosis of probable Alzheimer's disease, mild stage. She and her husband have one adult son. Shirley completed high school and has been a homemaker since her marriage. Three weeks prior to her LFDRS interview, she purchased an annuity.

Participant # 4: Tim is a 61-year-old married factory worker with one child. He has a high school education and is married to Shirley (Participant #3). On the advice of his financial advisor and separate from Shirley, he had recently purchased an annuity with a nursing-home rider. Afterward, Tim learned from his attorney that the annuity could be a threat to his financial assets.

Participant # 5: Jan is a 76-year-old widow with two adult children. She has a high school education and worked as a bookkeeper until her retirement 10 years earlier. Jan recently established a special-needs trust for one of her adult sons, who is emotionally disturbed.

4.3 Reliability Ratings The five videotaped interviews were rated by five experts from each of the two expert groups for a total of 10 raters. Five experts were psychologists trained in geropsychology and experienced in older adult capacity assessments, and the remainder also worked extensively with older adults and included two attorneys, one Adult Protective Service worker, and two financial planners. The videotaped interviews were sent to the raters and independently rated in their own offices. The raters were given the LFDRS written instructions and were given three weeks to rate the interviews. Raters were instructed to view each interview and rate the integrity of a participant's financial decisional abilities as fully capable, marginally capable, or not capable. Following Marson's (2009) methods, excellent judgment agreement was defined as 100% agreement ("exact"), and very good judgment was defined as 80% or greater agreement.

The final paragraphs in this subheading profile the five individuals who would become part of the case studies for professionals to test the diagnostic tool. Collectively, these paragraphs also bring in a humanistic element: reviewers can see in their minds eye the older adults who will ultimately benefit from this research project.

The third subheading in this section uses just over two double-spaced pages to elaborate on inter-rater reliability, looking at levels of agreement among raters when they observe the same event. In the opening paragraph, the first two sentences share that five experts from the national panel of researchers and five experts from the local panel of practitioner professionals served as raters. The third, fourth, and fifth sentences describe the conditions under which the ratings occurred. The sixth sentence establishes the yardstick against which the ratings are measured: 100 percent agreement is exact and 80 percent agreement or better is very good.

Establishing the reliability of the diagnostic tool is a fundamental precursor to determining its validity, the focus of Objective #1. Whereas *reliability* refers to consistency of scoring, *validity* refers to accuracy of assessment, the extent to which the tool measures what it claims to measure. The paragraphs in this subheading confirm reliability and, thus, help justify the next phase of research to determine validity.

The second paragraph relates the instructions given to raters for scoring. Overall decisions are rated on a three-point scale, where 0 = lacks decisional abilities, 1 = has marginal decisional abilities, and 2 = has full decisional abilities.

The third paragraph indicates that while exact agreement existed among raters on three cases, differences emerged in two cases. Raters do not always agree, nor should they be expected to; they bring different experiences and perspective to the process. Though raters met the threshold of very good judgment established in the literature, the less-than-perfect agreement convinced the principal investigator to develop a training video that would provide additional context for future users of the diagnostic tool.

In Table 2 are the details for the inter-rater judgment agreement for the gerontology experts using the LFDRS. Raters were told ahead of time about the specific financial decision in question but were not given any medical or personal background information on the older adults that were interviewed. The raters' judgments were based solely on their observations of the LFDRS interview. Instructions for scoring the integrity of the financial decisional abilities were as follows: "Overall decisional abilities are a clinical judgment based on both the contextual and intellectual factors. In a case with few concerns raised by contextual factors, scores on the intellectual factors would determine the overall decisional ability judgment. An interviewer may determine, however, that contextual factors, such as undue influence and/or psychological vulnerability, overwhelm the individual's intellectual factors and, as a result, use contextual factors and intellectual factors in making an overall decision. Overall decisional abilities are rated on a 3-point scale:"

0 = Lacks decisional abilities
1 = Has marginal decisional abilities to make this decision/transaction
2 = Has full decisional abilities to make this decision/transaction

Significant challenges existed in the cases where the raters lacked agreement. In cases one, two and three, there was perfect agreement, with cases one and two being deemed fully capable and case three being judged as not capable. In case four there was 80% agreement. In this case eight of the raters judged Tim fully capable and two of the ten judged Tim marginally capable. These latter two experts believed that Tim did not fully understand the decision he made. Finally in case 5 there was 90% agreement, with nine raters judging Jan fully capable and one judging her marginally capable.

In the course of this study it was decided to create a YouTube training video to describe the LFDRS, its construction, usage and scoring (see

Table 2. Inter-Rater Judgment Agreement for the 10 Experts using the LFDRS.

	Observed	% Agreement
Case 1	10/10 Fully Capable	100%
Case 2	10/10 Fully Capable	100%
Case 3	10/10 Not Capable	100%
Case 4	8/10 (8 Fully Capable; 2 Marginally Capable)	80%
Case 5	9/10 (9 Fully Capable; 1 Marginally Capable)	90%

Appendix for listing of the YouTube interviews of all 5 older adults and the introduction). It also became apparent that 10 items taken from the Current Financial Transaction section represented an excellent screening tool. *The screening tool was created to be used by front line professionals who work with older adults making significant financial decisions or transactions from both the civil (e.g. elder law attorney, CPA, Certified Financial Planner, banker) and criminal justice sectors (e.g. Adult Protective Services; Police, Sheriff, Prosecutors).*

The final paragraph in this subheading calls attention to the genesis of the screening tool. Namely, while the diagnostic tool was being developed for health and mental health professionals who are trained in clinical interviewing and have a background in assessing financial decision-making judgment, the principal investigator realized that a subset of questions could be used to create a screening tool for use by professionals in financial and criminal justice fields who work with older adults.

The hot buttons of research and older Americans are woven throughout the "Preliminary Studies" section. What's more, the final sentence in this paragraph clearly indicates the applied nature of the research activity, which the sponsor prefers over theory development.

5.0 *Proposed Methods*

5.1 Research Design This project uses a descriptive as opposed to an experimental design. Specifically, it samples several populations with screening and diagnostic forms of a financial decision-making tool in order to determine if the resulting reliability and validity characteristics, assessed through rigorous statistical analyses, warrant adoption by financial and criminal justice professionals serving the elderly.

The "Proposed Methods" section describes *how* the research will be carried out. It contains more than 19 double-spaced pages of detail, roughly double the length of the "Preliminary Studies" section. In hindsight, several subheadings would have benefitted from greater consistency and clarity and in doing so would have made reading easier for reviewers. For instance, in this section we broke our own pattern of presentation: each of the previous four sections began with an overview paragraph before introducing a subheading. In this case, there is no narrative accompanying the section heading; it jumps right into the first subheading prescribed in the evaluation criteria. The research design is a systematic extension of the approach described in the preliminary studies: multiple populations will be sampled and now statistical analyses will help determine validity characteristics, the focus of Objective #1.

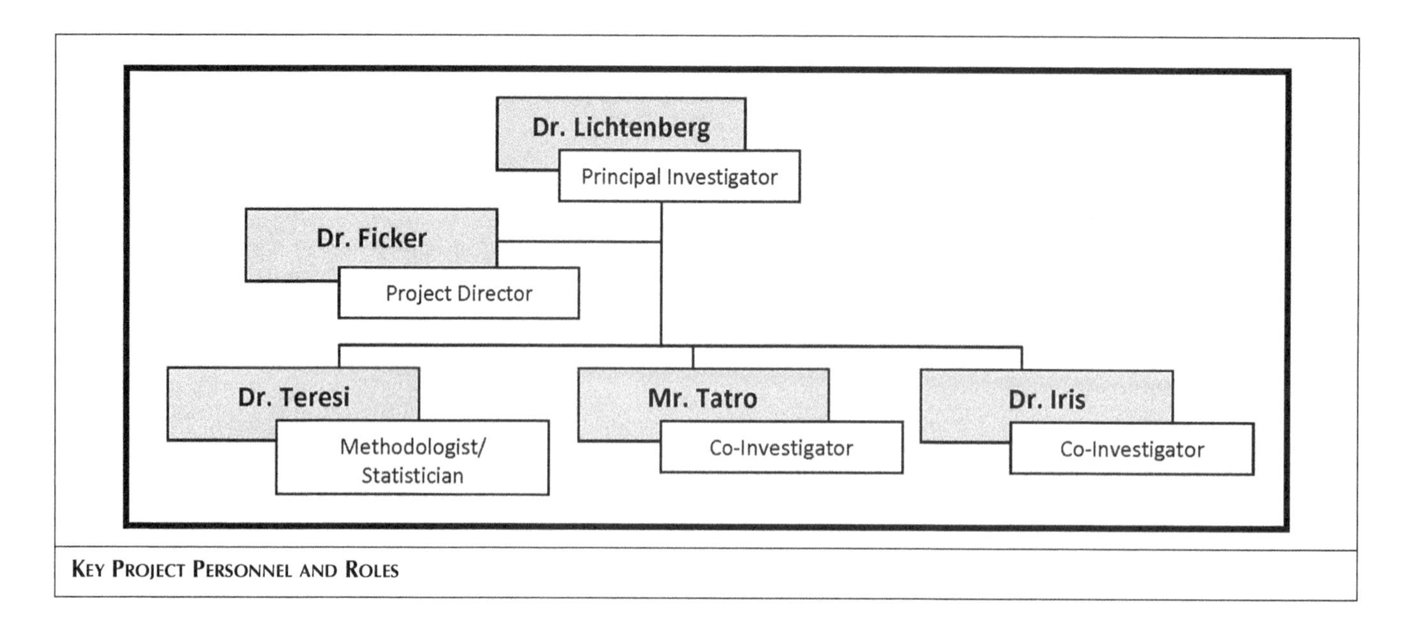

KEY PROJECT PERSONNEL AND ROLES

The second subheading breaks from the sequence presented in the evaluation criteria. Key project personnel are introduced over three and a half double-spaced pages here rather than at the end of the proposal narrative in the "Personnel" section. In hindsight, maintaining parallel structure might have facilitated reading fluency. The figure provides a visual overview of the relationships between five key project personnel.

The format for introducing each of the five key project personnel is the same: a boldface heading with role, name, and academic degree; a paragraph that highlights relevant experience and expertise with research and/or older Americans (sponsor hot buttons); and a concluding sentence specifying responsibilities in the project.

The first paragraph of this subheading describes the qualifications of the principal investigator to lead this research initiative. The opening sentence identifies individual credentials and institutional affiliations. The second sentence speaks to both sponsor hot buttons, "A *researcher*

5.2 Key Project Personnel Figure 2 shows the key project personnel and their interrelationships.

Principal Investigator: Peter Lichtenberg, Ph.D., ABPP is the Director of the Institute of Gerontology at Wayne State University and Professor of Psychology, and Physical Medicine and Rehabilitation. A researcher immersed in both the clinical and normative aging processes, Dr. Lichtenberg's research trajectory focuses on financial exploitation and capacity in older adults. His work in neuropsychology, mental health, medical rehabilitation and financial exploitation and capacity has resulted in over 150 peer reviewed publications and six books. He has served on several national panels to create practice guidelines in geropsychology and on the assessment of decision making of older adults with diminished capacity. Recently, Dr. Lichtenberg has published research on thefts and scams in older adults and the role that social factors play in contributing to susceptibility and influence. Dr. Lichtenberg has also published on the importance of accurate diagnosis in potential financial exploitation and capacity cases, and over the past five years has been involved in 35 forensic capacity assessment cases as an independent evaluator, appearing in county probate court to give testimony seven times. **Project Role**: Dr. Lichtenberg will be responsible for managing the entire project and he will conduct all of the interviews and assessments.

Co-Principal Investigator: Ron Tatro, BA is responsible for leadership and collaborative networking for enhancing safety and the quality of life of older victims and survivors of elder abuse, domestic violence, neglect and financial exploitation. A former police chief for nearly a decade, Mr. Tatro turned his attention to issues of older adult health and the prevention of elder abuse. He is a national certified trainer in elder abuse and expert on elder abuse issues. He has trained criminal justice and human services professional throughout Michigan. These programs work with professionals to help identify, investigate, and utilize community resources to respond to cases of abuse and exploitation of vulnerable adults. He is engaged with other prevention colleagues in creating a statewide elder abuse response protocol for first responders. He has extensive experience and expertise with a background in law enforcement, social services, non-profit management, and Department of Justice grants administration. He is a frequent presenter and facilitator on issues related to elder abuse prevention and intervention. He is participating with the Department of Justice's Elder Justice Roadmap Project, which is developing a national "roadmap" intended to improve how the nation conceptualizes and addresses elder abuse, neglect and exploitation. **Project Role**: Mr. Tatro will serve as a liaison to the criminal justice partners in the project and will facilitate the interviews with the older adults and assist in the dissemination of the project at later stages.

immersed in both the clinical and normative *aging* processes, Dr. Lichtenberg's *research* trajectory focuses on financial exploitation and capacity in *older adults*." The third and fourth sentences recognize the sponsor's interest in widespread dissemination—the principal investigator has over 150 peer reviewed publications, six books, and several best practice guidelines—which relates to the distinctive feature of regional/national impact. The fifth sentence harks back to the published literature cited in the "Project Objectives" and "Preliminary Studies" sections. The sixth sentence underscores that the principal investigator is well established among both researchers and practitioner professionals. The final sentence confirms overall managerial responsibilities.

The second paragraph describes the qualifications of one of two co-principal investigators. The first sentence identifies current responsibilities and the last sentence identifies proposed project roles—note the significant overlap between the two. The second sentence showcases the unique credibility that the co-principal investigator brings to the project: a decade's worth of experience as a police chief provides a vast network of relationship connections with practitioner professionals. The fourth, sixth, and ninth sentences hint at the distinctive feature of regional/national impact because of experience conducting trainings throughout the state and participation in other national initiatives that aim to address elder abuse, neglect, and exploitation.

Chief Methodologist and Statistician: Jeanne Teresi, Ph.D. Dr. Teresi is the Administrator and Director of the Research Division at the Hebrew Home at Riverdale. Dr. Teresi is the Director of the Research Core for the Center for Stroke Disparities Solutions (CSDS). She has doctorates in both Gerontology and Measurement and Statistics, and 30 years of experience in health disparities research, measurement and applied biostatistics, and extensive experience in the oversight of analyses from multi-site studies. Dr. Teresi has served as an associate editor of Biometrics, and is currently a deputy editor of Medical Care. She also serves on the editorial boards of the Gerontologist and Psychological Test and Assessment Modeling. She is a consultant to the national Resource Centers for Minority Aging Research (RCMAR) projects. For decades, she has worked in the area of item response theory (IRT), differential item functioning (DIF). She is a consultant to national measurement projects such as the NIH-funded roadmap project, Patient-Reported Outcomes Measurement Information Systems (PROMIS) and Toolbox. **Project Role**: Dr. Teresi will be responsible for conducting the data analyses for the project, including data collection, statistical analyses, and data interpretation.

The third paragraph describes the qualifications of the chief methodologist and statistician. The third sentence lists her credentials: dual doctoral degrees in the project's topic (gerontology) and the project's approach (measurement and statistics) as well as three decades' worth of research experience. The ninth sentence makes a strategic reference to her consultant work with the National Institutes of Health, the largest public funder of medical research in the United States. The final sentence clarifies her specific responsibilities on the project: collecting, analyzing, and interpreting data.

Project Director: Lisa Ficker, Ph.D. Dr. Ficker worked with Dr. Lichtenberg on the creation of the scales, and has experience using the LFDRS and administering and scoring neuropsychological tests. **Project Role**: Dr. Ficker will assist Dr. Lichtenberg in all aspects of the project, including coordinating the interview schedules, taking notes during liaison and prosecutor calls, assisting with Human Investigation Committee (IRB) reporting, and troubleshooting unforeseen difficulties.

The fourth paragraph describes the experience the project director has had with developing the diagnostic tool and summarizes the administrative role she will have with its validation.

Co-Investigator: Madelyn Iris, Ph.D. Dr. Iris is the Director of Research at the Leonard Schanfield Research Institute, CJE SeniorLife in Chicago, and an Adjunct Associate Professor at Northwestern University. Dr. Iris has been a leader in research on elder abuse for over 25 years. In 2012, she was awarded the Rosalie Wolf Memorial Award from the National Protective Services Administration for her research contributions to our understanding of elder abuse. Along with colleague Dr. Conrad, Dr. Iris developed a conceptual model and measures for both self-neglect and financial exploitation. For the past year she has served as a consultant to the Financial Decision making Rating Scale which will be a key instrument used in this project. Dr. Iris' past work has been supported by grants from the National Institute of Justice, and the Retirement Research Foundation, and she is currently a co-investigator (Dr. Conrad PI) on an NIJ project on a computerized decision support system to determine cases of elder abuse. Dr. Iris was a consultant during the creation of the LFDRS and LFDSS. **Project Role**: She will assist with the interpretation of data and national dissemination.

The fifth paragraph describes the qualifications of the second co-investigator. While on one hand it might have made sense to present the two co-investigators back-to-back, a strategic decision was made to end the subheading with a strong anchor: in addition to being a leading researcher (second sentence), award winner (third sentence), and consultant on the development of the diagnostic tool (fifth sentence), she is a seasoned grantseeker who has been supported by grants from the National Institute of Justice and the Retirement Research Foundation (sixth sentence). That is to say, there is psychological weight in listing two key project personnel who have been successfully funded by the sponsor in the past—the principal investigator and the co-investigator—in the opening and closing paragraphs of the subheading. The final sentence articulates her specific role with data interpretation and dissemination, hinting at the distinctive feature of regional/national impact.

5.3 Study Hypotheses Our overarching hypothesis is that both the screening and diagnostic form will yield valid and reliable information enabling professionals to efficient and effectively identify and intervene is cases of potential financial exploitation. More precisely, for Objective # 1, we hypothesis that the validity of the screening and diagnostic forms is increased when using the scales with both at-risk and not-at-risk elderly adults. With Objective # 2, we hypothesize that feedback from criminal justice and other professionals regarding their experiences with the screening and diagnostic forms will strengthen the clinical utility and investigative effectiveness of both tools.

5.4 Sequence of Investigation In graphic form (Table 2), the project sequence or chronology is specified. Roles will be carried out as defined in the key project personal discussion, Section 5.2.

Table 2. Project Timeline: Month by Month

	Months											
	1	2	3	4	5	6	7	8	9	10	11	12
Staff Working on Project	X	X	X	X	X	X	X	X	X	X	X	X
Recruit LFDSS Participants	X	X	X	X	X	X	X	X	X	X	X	X
Recruit LFDRS Participants	X	X	X	X	X	X	X	X	X	X	X	X
Add New Sites for Study	X	X	X	X	X	X	X	X	X			
Data Entry and Analysis						X	X	X	X	X	X	X
Dissemination Efforts						X	X	X	X	X	X	X
Manuscript Preparation											X	X

This third subheading returns to the sequence prescribed in the evaluation criteria and, in less than 100 words, draws attention to the research hypothesis associated with each of the two project objectives. The hypotheses are meant to be succinct, one sentence each.

In hindsight, it's conceivable that reviewers could interpret the third sentence—the hypothesis for Objective #2—to be less of a hypothesis and more of a study rationale. The proposal narrative could have been strengthened by sharpening the questions that would be answered, such as, how much time did it take professionals to complete the screening and diagnostic tools, were the tools perceived to be useful, which professionals were more likely to integrate the tools into their practice, and what barriers would prevent tool adoption?

Of note, there is a mildly embarrassing typo in the second sentence—"we hypothesis" rather than "we hypothesize." While it is always important to pay attention to the mechanics of grammar, spelling, and punctuation, a single mistake does not automatically mean a proposal will be rejected. Proposals do not need to be perfect to be funded; rather, they must be persuasive.

The fourth subheading relies on a visual device to highlight *what* activities will be occurring and *when.* Rather than name specific calendar months, the table identifies project months. This allows a certain flexibility for the starting and ending dates in case an extended time passes between proposal submission and a grant award notification. Logically, the entries for dissemination and manuscript preparation come near the end of the project period. Psychologically, they hint at the distinctive feature of regional/national impact and are well positioned to be the last things in reviewers' minds as they finish reading this subheading.

The fifth subheading is slightly more than one double-spaced page in length and, in two paragraphs, describes plans for sample size and recruitment for Objective #1 and Objective #2. The two paragraphs identify *where* the project will take place and *who will benefit* from targeted activities. The paragraphs follow a parallel structure, identifying the number of older adult participants who will be recruited, confirming pathways to access the target populations, summarizing a history of successfully working with the populations on other research initiatives, and specifying the location where interviews will occur. The seventh sentence in this paragraph even underscores the quota sampling process that will be used to ensure that an appropriate gender ratio of participants is secured. Together, these details help establish the credibility of the project, saying in essence, "We have an established history of working with the target populations on research projects that benefit older adults. We can do it again."

In hindsight, the second paragraph would have benefitted from greater specificity. While reviewers may appreciate the comprehensive engagement with financial planners, elder law attorneys, bankers, prosecutors, police and sheriff personnel, they may wonder whether the sample selection will be stratified to ensure equal numbers among these subgroups. Additional detail could have been added about collecting demographic data on the professionals to consider whether trends in tool usage correlate with variables such as age, gender, years of experience, training, and percent of population served who are older adults. These types of details would provide additional justification for taking a mixed sample approach.

5.5 Sample Size and Recruitment

Objective # 1:

Determine the concurrent and predictive validity of both the LFDRS and LFDSS. For this objective, we will recruit 100 older adult participants. This group will include at least 30 older African-Americans who are part of the Healthier Black Elders Participant Registry, a database established and managed by Dr. Lichtenberg at the Institute of Gerontology. The remaining members of the control group will come from referrals from front line financial planners, accountants, and attorneys as well as volunteers who learn of the study via our website postings, flyers and targeted emailing and who wish to participate. The IOG maintains an annually updated email list comprised of nearly 2000 older adults who regularly volunteer to participate in gerontology-related research projects. Over the past three years nearly 1000 of older adults connected to the IOG have participated in research. We will use quota sampling to get a ratio of women to men that match the population (i.e. depending on ages of participants this can range from 55 to 65% being women). Interviews will take place at a mutually convenient place such as Wayne State University, the older adult's home, or the offices of a referring professional.

Objective # 2:

Implement the LFDSS across a variety of professional settings and measure its utility as an investigative screening tool. For this objective, we will recruit 100 older adult participants, age 60 years and older from the offices of professionals who are partnering with us. Professionals across a variety of professions have agreed to utilize the LFDSS in their interviewing or investigative work. These include financial planners, elder law attorneys, bankers, prosecutors, police, and sheriff personnel. In addition, these professionals have agreed to fill out an LFDSS usage survey each time they use the scale. All of the interviews will take place in the office of the professionals.

5.6 Subject Eligibility and Exclusion Criteria In total, 200 subjects will be recruited for this project. All must be age 60 or older. At least 30 subjects will be of African-American descent. Approximately one-half of the subjects will be females. All subjects must sign a consent form affirming their willingness to participate in the study.

The sixth subheading is the shortest in the entire proposal narrative, five sentences that comprise less than a quarter of a double-spaced page, and in hindsight presented the biggest source of confusion for reviewers. The opening sentence indicates "In total, 200 subjects will be recruited for this project," which seems consistent with the previous subheading where 100 subjects will be recruited for Objective #1 and 100 subjects will be recruited for Objective #2 but is inconsistent with the "Project Objectives" section that indicates 200 subjects will be engaged for Objective #1 and an unspecified number will be engaged for Objective #2. This discrepancy was not enough for reviewers to reject the project idea outright. It did, however, provoke a call for a clarification and an explanation of power analysis, a statistical technique for estimating the population size required to detect a meaningful change.

5.7 Types of Data Obtained Two types of data will be collected, namely, financial decision-making (two assessment tools) and neuropsychological and financial capacity (six assessment tools) data. Each type is discussion in this proposal section.

Financial Decision Making Data.

Lichtenberg Financial Decision Making Rating Scale (LFDRS): The PI developed an initial conceptual model and set of questions to generate the FDRS. Guided by financial exploitation and assessment tool experts Ken Conrad and Madelyn Iris, we pulled together two groups of experts: those expert in financial capacity work, and those who work directly with older adults making sentinel financial decisions and transactions on a daily basis (e.g. law enforcement, bank personnel, adult protective services, financial planners, elder law attorneys). We held separate conference calls with the group of experts, presenting the model and questions. Based on their extensive feedback, the final conceptual model was refined as was a broader set of questions and a multiple choice format. Three months after the first set of conference calls were held; we distributed new versions of the FDRS and set up new conference calls to receive a second round of feedback. The feedback given during the second round of calls indicated a need for only minor revisions, and the FDRS was thus completed soon afterwards.

The seventh subheading uses nearly three and a half double-spaced pages to describe eight tools that will be used to collect financial decision-making and neuropsychological and financial capacity data. Given this breadth and depth of information, to prevent reviewers from getting lost in the narrative flow, two new levels of organization were introduced, for a total of four levels of headings and subheadings:

- Level one headings are boldface font, italicized, and on a line by themselves.
- Level two headings are boldface font and on a line by themselves.
- Level three headings are indented, boldface font, punctuated with a period and further text follows.
- Level four headings are indented, italicized, punctuated with a colon and further text follows.

Headings are concise and informative. Effective use of vertical and horizontal white space sets off headings and enhances readability.

Two paragraphs describe the creation of the diagnostic tool and the process used to establish its reliability. In essence, these paragraphs recap in truncated form the details introduced in the "Preliminary Studies" section.

The final scale consisted of 65 multiple choice questions with separate sections measuring Financial Situational Awareness, Psychological Vulnerability, Undue Influence, Past Financial Exploitation, and Intellectual Factors. Final instructions for administration and scoring of the FDRS were also completed at this time. Videotaped FDRS interviews were recently conducted with five older adults and inter-rater reliability is currently being established by having multiple raters view the videotapes and score the FDRS. The resulting data consists of a global score and subtest scores on the five indices. Administration time averages 27 minutes.

One paragraph restates from the "Preliminary Studies" section the creation of the screening tool. A new detail is added in the final sentence, "The average administration time is 7 minutes." In other words, by spending approximately 45 seconds on each of 10 screening items, front-line professionals can have a preliminary indication of the financial decision-making abilities of older adults; reviewers understand that professionals are more likely to adopt into practice tools that are simple and quick to use and provide valid responses.

Lichtenberg Financial Decision Screening Scale (LFDSS): Subsequent to interviewing five older adults and performing the first inter-rater reliability testing on the LFDRS 10 items were chosen as the screening items. These items come mostly from the Intellectual Factors subtest and a couple of the Undue Influence questions. The resulting data consists of core aspects of decisional abilities. The average administration time is 7 minutes.

Whereas the previous level three subheading introduced two financial decision-making measures, this level three subheading introduces six neuropsychological measures. These overview sentences provide justification for their selection, namely, they assess a wide range of cognitive functioning and they are well-established, validated tools.

More broadly, by validating the diagnostic and screening tools for financial decision making and using them in concert with existing valid tools for testing memory, concentration, problem solving, and communication, professionals will be able to better serve older adults and improve their quality of life.

Neuropsychological Measures. The six neuropsychological measures described below were chosen for two reasons; (1) they cover the broad areas of cognitive functioning, and (2) they have been widely used and well validated in older adult populations, including among African Americans.

Wide Range Achievement Test IV-Reading and Arithmetic: The WRAT IV reading subtest has been found to be an excellent measure of quality (versus only quantity) of a person's educational experience (Schneider & Lichtenberg, 2011). The test consists of 16 letters and 64 words that are read aloud.

Boston Naming Test: The purpose of the test is to assess the ability to name pictured objects. This 60 item test is particularly sensitive to word finding difficulties. The resulting data provides insights into a common and debilitating feature found among the elderly, namely, the ability to name objects.

The Rey Auditory Verbal Learning Test: This 15 item word recall test (over 5 trials) measures immediate memory span, a learning curve and reveals learning strategies. The resulting data represents a measure of immediate recall, thereby providing insights into short-term memory capacity.

Animal Naming Test: This category naming measure of verbal fluency is highly sensitive to cognitive change in older adults and measures verbal executive functioning and semantic fluency. The resulting data helps differentiate among different types of dementia.

Trailmaking Test: The Trailmaking Test consists of A and B parts. In part A, older adults are timed as they connect circles in order by number. This part is a test of basic visuo-motor attention. A mental flexibility component is added in part B in which the older adult connects the circles in order but this time alternating between number and letter. The resulting data provides insights on visual attention and task switching abilities.

Independent Living Skills—Financial subtest: This is a test of more basic domains of financial capacity including recognition of money, ability to make change, to write a check and balance a checkbook. The resulting data indicate one's to competency to manage personal financial affairs.

These neuropsychological tests were chosen for the following reasons: (1) Word finding plays a key role in the older adult articulating his or her choice. (2) Memory is related to rationale for the choice, understanding of the choice and expressing a consistent choice, and executive functioning is related to the ability to appreciate the consequences of a choice. (3) Arithmetic and reading skills give an indication of quality of an individual's education and that may be related to financial decision making also. (4) Basic financial skills are related to the ability to make financial judgments.

Collectively, this neuropsychological test battery **covers** the broad areas of cognitive functioning. Further, these instruments have been widely used and well validated in older adult populations, including among African Americans. The average administration time for the entire neuropsychological test battery is roughly 1.5 hours

Each of the next six paragraphs are two to five sentences long and identify key characteristics of the six tests. In each paragraph, the first sentence answers the question "What?"—what is the tool designed to measure—and the final sentence answers the question "So what?"—why is the information important: data collected from the tests will provide insights on specific dimensions of older adults' cognitive functioning.

In practical terms, the same amount of text—approximately 330 words—was used to describe the two financial decision-making tools as was dedicated to depicting the six neuropsychological measures. This strategy keeps an overall balance between the level three subheadings and yet maintains a focus on the proposed aims to validate and implement the diagnostic and screening tools. Notice the first paragraph includes a strategic literature citation that lends further credibility to the principal investigator being ensconced in the field.

The final two paragraphs justify the neurological tests at local and global levels. Locally, the tests identify potential gaps in word recall, memory, math and reading skills, and basic financial skills, which may be indicators of diminished cognitive functioning. Globally, the collective battery of tests provide a comprehensive assessment of the cognitive functioning of older adults. As highlighted in the final sentence, while an individual screening tool might take a few minutes to administer, the wide-ranging battery of tests will take an hour and a half to complete.

The eighth subheading takes a bit of an artistic liberty with the evaluation criteria and combines two items—"Data analyses planned" and "Data interpretation planned"—into one: "Data Analyses and Interpretation." As a result, this is the longest portion of the entire proposal narrative, nearly seven double-spaced pages. The text is heavy on the hot button of research, describing theoretical approaches, conceptual models, and statistical analyses. To help guide reviewers through the sometimes dense text, there are eight level three subheadings and expanded definitions that explain methodological jargon.

5.8 Data Analyses and Interpretation Our dual approach to data analysis focuses both on psychometric approaches and statistical computations.

Four paragraphs describe the theoretical approach to how the diagnostic and screening tools will be validated, namely, using item response theory. Since some reviewers may not be thoroughly familiar with item response theory, the second and third paragraphs include a broad explanation of the approach and contrast it with other more familiar approaches. The fourth paragraph justifies the selection of this particular approach, highlighting its uniqueness (i.e., no other studies have used item response theory to develop measures of financial decision making) and value (i.e., greater precision than classical approaches).

Psychometric Analyses. An aim of this study was to examine the psychometric properties of the *Lichtenberg Financial Decision Making Rating Scale* and the *Lichtenberg Financial Decision Screening Scale* using item response theory (IRT) among an ethnically diverse sample that includes African Americans.

In broad terms, item response theory (IRT) is a paradigm for the design, analysis, and scoring of tests, questionnaires, and similar instruments measuring abilities, attitudes, or other variables. Unlike simpler alternatives for creating scales evaluating questionnaire responses, it does not assume that each item is equally difficult. This distinguishes IRT from, for instance, the assumption in Likert scaling that all items are assumed to be replications of each other or in other words items are considered to be parallel instruments. By contrast, item response theory treats the difficulty of each item as information to be incorporated in scaling items. It is based on the application of related mathematical models to testing data. Because it is generally regarded as superior to classical test theory, it is the preferred method for developing scales, especially when optimal decisions are demanded, as is the case with financial decision-making capacity.

IRT is based on the idea that the probability of a correct/keyed response to an item is a mathematical function of person and item parameters. The person parameter is construed as (usually) a single latent trait or dimension. Examples include general intelligence, the strength of an attitude, or decision-making capacity. Parameters on which items are characterized include their difficulty (known as "location" for their location on the difficulty range), discrimination (slope or correlation) representing how steeply the rate of success of individuals varies with their ability, and a pseudo guessing parameter, characterizing the (lower) asymptote at which even the least able persons will score due to guessing (for instance, 25% for pure chance on a 4-item multiple choice item).

Little work has been conducted among ethnically diverse samples and to our knowledge no studies have used item response theory (IRT) to develop measures of financial decision making. IRT (Lord & Novick, 1968) incorporates latent variable models that confer many advantages over traditional methods of item analyses, and is the methodology used in item banking projects sponsored by the National Institutes of Health (Reeve, et al., 2007). Unlike those derived from classical test theory (the method most often used to examine measures), IRT parameter estimates are theoretically invariant and can be compared across groups. Classical test theory (CTT) parameters and statistics such as proportion positive, corrected item-total correlations and coefficient alpha are affected (confounded) by sample characteristics, and thus cannot be compared. Moreover, CTT internal consistency estimates are omnibus statistics in the sense that they are summary measures of reliability, whereas IRT precision or reliability estimates can be examined at varying points along the attribute continuum. It is more realistic to expect that precision is greater at varying points along the continuum than to assume that one value summarizes measure performance for all levels of the state or trait. Finally, information functions derived from the models and analyses provide a means for selection of the best item subsets when short forms are developed

Conceptual Model for the Psychometric Analyses. According to the literature, we can hypothesize that the diagnostic measure is essentially unidimensional with one single underlying attribute, but additional variance may be explained due to additional factors or subscales. The items were posited to be effect indicators in that the underlying latent variable—financial decisional abilities—gives rise to the indicators and accounts for the variance in the item set. The rationale for positing essential independence for the screening measure is that the 10 items for the LFDRS are from the Intellectual Factors subtest with two items from the Undue Influence questions. On the other hand, the actual LFDSS, the diagnostic version, consists of 65 multiple choice questions with separate sections measuring Financial Situational Awareness, Psychological Vulnerability, Undue Influence, Past Financial Exploitation, and Intellectual Factors. Thus several underlying dimensions are hypothesized.

Statistical Approach. Prior to statistical analyses, item distributions will be examined. Exploratory factor analyses with principal components estimation and tests of scree will be performed, followed by a confirmatory bi-factor analysis. The bifactor model assumes that a single general trait explains most of the common variance, but that group traits explain additional common variance for item subsets (see Reise, Moore, & Haviland, 2010). For the screening test, factor analyses will be first performed to examine essential unidimensionality. The diagnostic tool (FDRS) will be examined using confirmatory factor analyses and specifying the factor loadings, based on the theoretical specifications shown in the appended measure.

Briefly, traditional factor analysis (merged exploratory factor analysis [EFA] and confirmatory factor analysis [CFA]) fitting a unidimensional model with polychoric correlations will be conducted. A robust parameter estimation procedure, based on a mean and variance adjusted weighted least squares procedure (WLSMV) contained in *Mplus* will be used (Muthén & Muthén, 2007). Second, following

One paragraph is used to acknowledge the underlying assumptions that drive the approach to the analysis of variance. In hindsight, it's about here in the "Data Analysis and Interpretation" section where the force of example approach begins to obfuscate rather than clarify the project methods. An effort to show a depth of consideration for data analyses perhaps pushed too far into "research-ese" and clouded the details upon which we were trying to shine extra light.

Two paragraphs identify the statistical approaches that will be used on the diagnostic tool and screening tool to assess variance.

In the first paragraph, considerable detail is provided in the second sentence identifying the sequence of exploratory factor analyses, tests of scree, and confirmatory bi-factor analyses that will occur; the third sentence cites pertinent literature to acknowledge assumptions of the analyses that explain common variance.

In the second paragraph, there is a step-by-step portrayal of the traditional factor analysis (first sentence), parameter estimation procedure (second sentence), and Schmid-Leiman transformation (third sentence) that will be performed.

In hindsight, the presentation of analyses might have been better organized around reliability (i.e., internal consistency and item response theory) and validity (i.e., confirmatory factor analysis, correlations, and multiple regression). That is to say, potential for confusion exists because the "Data Analyses and Interpretation" subheading contains discussion of validity and reliability tests and characteristics and the subsequent "Validity Testing" subheading also contains an account of validity tests and characteristics.

One paragraph is used to summarize tests of dimensionality, a consideration of whether tool questions measure a single construct or separate facets of a construct. The third sentence refers to the literature to validate the calculation of common variance and the fourth sentence acknowledges how a worst-case scenario will be treated: the amount of distortion can be calculated for instances where data is applied to the wrong model. These sentences point to a depth of methodological detail—the principal investigator understands how data should be analyzed and can account for adjustments in the off-chance it is analyzed incorrectly.

One paragraph is used to give details on tests of internal consistency reliability. The first sentence cites the literature to justify the preferred statistical approach; the third sentence explains the basis of calculations; and the fifth sentence describes how results will be interpreted.

One paragraph is used to give details on a second way internal consistency reliability will be assessed. The second sentence cites literature to justify this approach, namely, item response theory has been used to model other data sets on older adults. The third, fourth, and fifth sentences answer the question of "What?"—what calculations will be performed and what functions will be graphed. The sixth, seventh, and eighth questions answer the question of "So what?"—why is the information important: it reveals the extent to which the tool item measures financial decision making capacity in older adults. The final sentence identifies the software that will be used to perform the calculations and justifies its use by citing appropriate literature.

recent guidelines (Revelle & Zinbarg, 2009), a Schmid-Leiman (S-L) (Schmid & Leiman, 1957) transformation using the "psych" R package (Rizopoulus, 2006) will be performed in order to find an alternative set of group factors for a bi-factor model (Gibbons, et al., 2007). All items will be specified to load on the general factor, and the loadings on the group factors will be specified following the S-L solution. Factor loadings will be presented along with communalities (h^2) and general factor variance. Both eigenvalues and fit statistics will be examined, including root mean square error of approximation (RMSEA) and comparative fit index (CFI).

Tests of Dimensionality. The explained common variance (ECV) provides information about whether the observed variance/covariance matrix is close to unidimensionality. The ECV can be estimated as the percent of observed variance explained. It is calculated as the eigenvalue for the general factor divided by the sum of the eigenvalues for the general and group factors from a bi-factor model (see Reise et al., 2010): $ECV = \sum \lambda^2_{Gen} / \sum \lambda^2_{Gen} + \sum \lambda^2_{G1} + \sum \lambda^2_{G2} \ldots \sum \lambda^2_{GK}$. The difference in the loadings between the unidimensional model and the general factor loadings (λ_1) in the bi-factor model will also be examined as an indication of the degree of distortion that would occur by fitting a unidimensional model to data that are multidimensional.

Tests of Internal Test Reliability. The methods for assessing reliability that have emerged from the psychometric literature as the preferred statistics include McDonald's (McDonald, 1970) omega total and hierarchical (ω_t and ω_h). Omega total is based on the proportion of total common variance explained. Omega Hierarchical (ω_h) is calculated as the sum of the squared loadings on the general factor, divided by the total scale score variance (V_x). Classical test theory-derived internal consistency coefficients (e.g. Cronbach, 1951) will also be computed. This information will be interpreted in terms of the number of items, the reliability of individual items, and item prevalences. Mean inter-item correlations will also be examined.

Item Response Theory (IRT). Additionally, IRT (Lord & Novick, 1968) will be used to evaluate scales. IRT has been used to model gerontological data sets (see Teresi, Cross, & Golden, 1989; Teresi, Kleinman, Ocepek-Welikson, 2000). The estimates for the discrimination and severity parameters (*a* and *b*, respectively) will be evaluated, the item and test information functions graphed and the reliability estimates calculated at points along the underlying attribute dimension (θ). Because items are binary (correct or incorrect), a two parameter logistic IRT model will be used. The estimates for the discrimination and severity (location) parameters (*a* and *b*, respectively) will be evaluated, the item and test information functions will be graphed and the reliability estimates calculated for points along the dimension of the underlying construct, denoted as θ (theta). The discrimination parameter informs about the strength of the relationship between an item and the trait measured, e.g., satisfaction. The severity (location) parameter indicates at what point along the satisfaction continuum the item maximally discriminates (separates or differentiates among examinees at different satisfaction levels or groups). These parameters are useful in determining which items are most informative in terms of the measurement of the underlying construct, financial decision making capacity. IRTPRO (Cai, Thissen, & du Toit, 2011) will be used for IRT parameter estimation and tests of model fit.

Model Fit. Although model fit statistics represent an area of controversy, and each has pros and cons, ur approach will be to evaluate the root mean square error of approximation for values <0.10, although it is acknowledged that lower values, e.g., 0.06 to 0.07, are often recommended (Cicchetti & Feinstein, 1990; Hu & Bentler, 1999). The comparative fit index (CFI) will be examined using a cutoff value of 0.90. This value is high; however, model complexity (more variables, for example) can impact this statistic. In general, there have been recommendations to move away from fit tests alone because these statistics are affected by many factors.

Power for Factor Analyses and IRT. Several factors affect power in the context of the measurement model (Edelen-Orlando, Thissen, Teresi, Kleinman, & Ocepek-Welikson, 2006); skewed, sparse data in some response categories (leading to large standard errors and spuriously high parameter estimates); model fit (larger samples are required with poor fit); sampling distributions of respondents and the distribution of the latent attribute, where items located at the extreme points along the latent continuum will have higher standard errors because few subjects are located there, and precision will be less at the extremes of the latent continuum. Also, fewer indicators per latent variable and lower reliability of indicators may result in reduced power. The effect of unreliability on power is well known; however, the necessity for high reliability of measures in the context of power for latent change models has recently been affirmed by simulation studies (Prindle & McArdle, 2012). Thus we have focused on the selection of highly reliable indicators and propose to examine these carefully.

Power can be considered both in terms of hypothesis testing and precision of parameter estimation. The literature dealing with sample size in relation to structural equation modeling has focused on Monte Carlo trials and goodness-of-fit tests for covariance structures rather than power in relation to estimation of structural parameters (Gerbing & Andersen, 1993). The effects of sample size on goodness of fit tests are well-known (Bollen, 1986). Early evidence from Monte Carlo studies of samples sizes required for robust maximum likelihood estimation in structural equation modeling (SEM) indicates that n's should be at least 100.

One paragraph is used to describe the approach to model fit statistics. The first, second, and third sentences identify the specific cutoff values that will be applied and the fourth sentence provides the rationale for examining the results from multiple statistical analyses.

Two paragraphs are used to explain considerations that went into determining an appropriate sample size.

In the first paragraph, the first three sentences recognize specific situations in sampling that can have a negative impact on reliability. More significantly, the fourth sentence identifies the particular actions that will be taken to overcome these potential problems, namely, examining carefully a targeted selection of dependable indicators.

In the second paragraph, the second and third sentences draw upon the literature to document the effects of sample size in relation to statistical tests and, as a result, the final sentence confirms that at least 100 participants will be sampled. Reviewers should not be surprised by this sample size calculation—it's the logical extension of and justification for the number of older adults to be engaged in Objective #1 and Objective #2.

In the ninth subheading, we break once again from the sequence presented in the evaluation criteria to provide an expanded description of validity testing. Over two double-spaced pages, details are presented about the specific tests that will be used with older adults, the process for collecting data, and the approach for establishing tool validity. The two sentences in this opening paragraph aim to situate the diagnostic tool and screening tool among the best tools—the gold standards—currently available, which is pretty good company to keep.

One paragraph is used to describe the approach for establishing the validity of the diagnostic tool. The vast majority of the paragraph is repeated verbatim from the "Types of Data Obtained" subheading and is essential for setting up the information that will be introduced in the next paragraph for establishing the validity of the screening tool.

5.9 Validity Testing. One purpose of the analyses is to examine the convergent and divergent construct validity as well as the concurrent criterion validity of the screening measure against a gold standard global rating. In this case, the gold standard is represented by neuropsychological test scores and financial ability scores.

Convergent and Discriminant Validity. The convergence of the measure of financial decision making capacity and neuropsychological tests will be examined. It is expected that the FDRS will be correlated with cognitive measures. For example, the *Wide Range Achievement Test IV-Reading* (WRAT IV) reading subtest measures quality of educational experience. The *Boston Naming Test* assesses the ability to name pictured objects and is sensitive to word finding difficulties. *The Rey Auditory Verbal Learning Test:* is a measure of word recall and examines immediate memory span. The *Animal Naming Test is a* category naming measure of verbal fluency which is sensitive to cognitive change in older adults and measures verbal executive functioning and semantic fluency. The *Trailmaking Test* consists of A and B parts. In part A, older adults are timed as they connect circles in order by number. This part is a test of basic visuo-motor attention. A mental flexibility component is added in part B in which the older adult connects the circles in order but this time alternating between number and letter. The *Independent Living Skills—Financial subtest* is a test of more basic domains of financial capacity including recognition of money, ability to make change, to write a check and balance a checkbook. Word finding plays a key role in the older adult articulating his or her choice. Memory is related to rationale for the choice, understanding of the choice and expressing a consistent choice, and executive functioning is related to the ability to appreciate the consequences of a choice. Arithmetic and reading skills give an indication of quality of an individual's education and that may be related to financial decision making also. Finally, basic financial skills are related to the ability to make financial judgments.

Concurrent Criterion Validity. Because we have a gold standard measure, we can examine the relationship of the screening measure and the FDRS with the gold standard ratings of financial decision making competency. We will create an expectancy table so that at each possible cut score of the screening measure we will examine positive predictive power, negative predictive power, sensitivity and specificity. Additionally, the Receiver Operating Characteristic Curve will be examined, plotting sensitivity against 1-specificity in order to examine the performance of the measure.

One paragraph is used to describe the approach for establishing the validity of the screening tool. The second sentence addresses key statistical concepts including *sensitivity*, the ability to correctly identify older adults who have financial decision making abilities; *specificity*, the ability to correctly identify older adults who do not have financial decision-making abilities; and *cut score*, the determination point for considering an older adult as qualified for financial decision making. The challenge is to find a cut score that produces an optimal balance between sensitivity and specificity, maximizing positive predictive value (i.e., the proportion of older adults who test positive who actually are qualified to make financial decisions) and negative predictive value (i.e., the proportion of older adults who test negative who actually are qualified to make financial decisions). The final sentence identifies the specific analysis that will be conducted to illustrate true positive rates and false positive rates.

Implementation Data. These analyses, will enable us to assess the usage and utility of the screening scale according to a number of different professionals. Each time the professionals use the screening scale, they will completed the LFDSS usage survey that asks questions about efficiency and utility. We will also compare the screening results to actual decisions made by the professionals using the scale.

One paragraph is used to describe the process for collecting data on screening tool usage and comparing screening tool results against final determinations made by professionals who used the diagnostic tool.

More broadly, whereas the previous two paragraphs focus on determining validity of the diagnostic tool and screening tool, the aim of Objective # 1, this paragraph focuses on determining the utility of the screening tool, the aim of Objective # 2.

The 10th subheading returns to the sequence prescribed in the evaluation criteria and, in 55 words, acknowledges that standard human subjects research protocols will be followed. The second sentence harks back to the pilot phase when it was determined that professionals would benefit from training prior to administering the screening tool and/or diagnostic tool and serves as evidence of a "lesson learned." In hindsight, additional details could have been included to clarify, for instance, protections enacted for subjects who may lack the capacity to consent to the research study.

5.10 Ethical Issues The ethical issues in this project all focus around the protection of human subjects. IRB approval has already been secured. Professionals administering both instruments will be first trained and special emphasis will be placed on subject confidentiality. Identifiers will be used instead of names and only the PI will retain names in a secured location.

The final subheading in the "Proposed Methods" section employs an artistic liberty: the RFP calls for a project timeline to *follow* the proposal narrative yet we decided to include it here as a one-page visual summary of the preceding section. It is modeled on the template provided on the sponsor's Web site and reviewers can quickly understand *what* activities will be occurring and *when*. Though the timeline was first introduced in the "Sequence of Investigation" subheading, 14 double-spaced pages have passed since then, so it seemed reasonable to reproduce it again. Select repetition can be a proposal strength.

5.11 Project Timeline Below is the timeline for the project. Because of some initial pilot funding by Wayne State University, the project staff is ready to begin the project on the first day of RRF funding. We will begin with no fewer than 8 different partner sites. Throughout the project, additional partner sites for the study will be brought on board.

Project Timeline

	Months											
	1	2	3	4	5	6	7	8	9	10	11	12
Staff Working on Project	X	X	X	X	X	X	X	X	X	X	X	X
Recruit LFDSS Participants	X	X	X	X	X	X	X	X	X	X	X	X
Recruit LFDRS Participants	X	X	X	X	X	X	X	X	X	X	X	X
Add New Sites for Study	X	X	X	X	X	X	X	X	X			
Dissemination Efforts						X	X	X	X	X	X	X
Data Entry and Analysis						X	X	X	X	X	X	X
Manuscript Preparation											X	X

6.0 *Dissemination*

6.1 Recent Prior Experience with RRF. The Principal Investigator has a successful track record in developing educational and training materials and ensuring their widespread usage. In his previous RRF grant (Integrating Mental Health into Occupational Therapy Practice with Older Adults), Dr. Lichtenberg used a Community-based participatory research (CBPR) partnership approach that equitably involved community members, organizational representatives, and researchers in all aspects of the research process and in which all partners contribute expertise and share decision making. This CBPR method built a strong team to develop and test a 6-DVD set for training. The steps taken for success in widespread usage of the DVD series included:

1. Excellence in the product created.
2. Empirical work and peer reviewed publications on the product
3. Reaching out to partner nationally and regionally with providers of similar type of products (ex. American Occupational Therapy Association CE division, Chex Corridor Home Health CE).
4. Presenting nationally and regionally on the product
5. Creating attractive web-based materials to advertise and draw attention to the product.

This dissemination strategy was very successful as evidenced by the fact that users of the training have come from over 30 of the states in the U.S. Ninety-three percent (93%) of those who purchase the product for continuing education (CE) have completed the CE questions and submitted the material for CEUs. Our conservative estimates are that over 2000 users in the past four years have viewed some or all of the DVD training series.

6.2 Dissemination Strategies for Proposed Project. In creating the diagnostic tool (LFDRS) and the screening tool (LFDSS), we intend to attract the broadest possible set of users. The LFDRS is a longer,

The "Dissemination" section describes *how* the research results will be shared with key constituents. It contains nearly five double-spaced pages of detail, citing past successes as well as future plans for having a regional/national impact, a distinctive feature.

The first subheading uses approximately one double-spaced page to fortify the credibility of the principal investigator. The opening sentence asserts, "The principal investigator has a successful track record in developing educational and training materials and ensuring their widespread usage," and the remainder of the paragraph documents this claim in terms of a project funded previously by the sponsor. The fourth sentence and numbered list outline the procedural steps taken as part of the dissemination strategy, and the fifth, sixth, and seventh sentences quantify meaningful outcomes: users represent 30 states, 93 percent complete the questions for continuing education units, and 2,000 users have viewed DVD training materials. The not-so-subtle message is "We've done it before; we can do it again."

The second subheading uses approximately two and one third double-spaced pages to elaborate on specific dissemination strategies. Whereas the executive summary included a single sentence that acknowledged thought has been given to dissemination, this subheading presents seven paragraphs and a table's worth of detail. The first paragraph targets the intended audiences: the researchers and practitioner professionals who will be interested in the diagnostic tool (second sentence) and the practitioner professionals who will be interested in the screening tool (third sentence). The fourth sentence lends further credibility to the dissemination approach, confirming that not only is a plan in place but it is already being acted on. The final seven words of the last sentence—"will be furthered by funding from RRF"—appeal directly to the sponsor, saying, in effect, "Though we are taking proactive steps to share our work broadly, with your support we can do even more."

Two succinct sentences introduce a synopsis of major dissemination strategies. The strategies identified represent a mix of active approaches (i.e., audiences are actively engaged in processing information, such as participating in a training session) and passive approaches (i.e., audiences respond passively to information, such as reading a journal article). The table uses a three-column format to call attention to the what-who-how of the dissemination approach. Not only does the table touch on the hot button of research, but it also appeals to the sponsor's preference for applied research. In the "Specific Information" column, for instance, researchers will want to know about the reliability and validity characteristics of the diagnostic and screening tools and practitioner professions will want to know about the availability of training on how to use the tools properly.

Of note, there are three almost consecutive mistakes around the table due to hurried editing. The sentence above the table begins "Table x," where "x" was a placeholder until the exact table number could be inserted—oops #1. The boldface table heading indicates that this is "Table 1" when, in fact, it is Table 3—oops #2. The first sentence after the table refers to "Expanding on the Table 4 information" when, in reality there is no Table 4 and, again, it should be Table 3—oops #3. While editorial mistakes can be distracting to reviewers and should be eliminated to the extent possible, in this instance they did not take away from the ability of the proposal overall to connect with the values and priorities of the sponsor.

more thorough and complicated diagnostic tool; it is intended for health and mental health professionals who are well versed in aging issues. The LFDSS, in contrast, is a screening tool designed for use by a very broadly by professionals who work with older adults and their financial decisions/transactions, including those from multiple professions outside of an in the criminal justice system. The plans for ensuring widespread usage of the LFDRS and LFDSS have already begun and will be furthered by funding from RRF.

Briefly, our project uses a strategic mix of active and passive dissemination strategies to communicate project results to various stakeholders. Table x summarizes our primary dissemination strategies.

Table 1. Synopsis of Major Dissemination Strategies

Specific Information	Target Audience	Dissemination Strategy
• Reliability of Screening Tool • Reliability of Diagnostic Tool • Validity of Screening Tool • Reliability of Diagnostic Tool • Availability of Training Approaches	• Elder law attorneys • Bank tellers • Financial planners • Accountants • Securities brokers • Estate planners • Police • Sheriff • Adult protective service • Friend of court • Prosecutorial professional	• Poster Sessions at professional society meeting • Presentations as professional society meetings • Journal articles to various professional and trade journals • WSU IOG Web site • Webinars • Training Manual • Videos

Expanding on the Table 4 information, we are confident the target audience will be attracted to the quality of the LFDRS and LFDSS. The strong conceptual approach, use of experts and initial reliability give us confidence that our tools address a neglected area; these are tools that assess the specific financial decision/transaction in question. Support from RRF will allow us to collect important validity and implementation data. With these data in hand we can approach commercial distributors.

The second paragraph in this subheading justifies why the target audience will be attracted to the diagnostic and screening tools; namely, as highlighted in the second sentence, researchers will appreciate the sound methodological approach and practitioner professionals will appreciate easy-to-use tools that help address a pressing problem. Further, the third and fourth sentences work together to justify why the sponsor should be attracted to the tools. The third sentence restates the purpose of the project—to research (a hot button) the validity of the diagnostic and screening tools—and the fourth sentence calls attention to the implications of the resulting work—commercializing the tools to have a regional/national impact (a distinctive feature). In other words, the third sentence conveys "what" the sponsor's investment will afford and the fourth sentence answers "So what?"

The third paragraph in this subheading speaks again to project credibility. Not only is there a plan for dissemination, but concrete steps have already been taken through the creation of overview, demonstration, and training videos. The final sentence reaffirms that network relationships are already in place to facilitate dissemination to additional audiences of researchers and practitioner professionals.

We have already taken the first few steps towards dissemination. For instance, we have already created videos of (a) an overview of the LFDRS and how to use it; and (b) video clips of both the LFDRS and LFDSS to be seen as adjuncts to training in the instruments. We will expand these demonstration and training videos, and use our consultants to help us identify opportunities across many professions.

Since both the screening and diagnostic tools represent important pieces of intellectual property, we are working with the intellectual properties office at Wayne State University. They have chosen our instruments to be high priority for developing a complete web-based approach to training and implementation. In addition, we would consider working with publishers such as Professional Resources Inc. who publish and market tools in this area of work.

The fourth paragraph dives deeper into the approach for making training materials available to practitioner professionals. Namely, the first two sentences call attention to the institutional interest in developing Web-based training, and the third sentence identifies a specific publisher with a history of producing professional development tools and training.

If time had allowed for initial contacts to occur with potential publishers, the third sentence might have been written to include a bit more punch: "In addition, preliminary conversations with senior editors at select publishers, such as Professional Resources Inc. who publish and market tools in this area of work, have generated great enthusiasm for commercial distribution of the diagnostic and screening tools."

We have a chapter in the APA Handbook of Clinical Geropsychology which will describe the scale's conceptual framework and its creation, and we will be submitting an article to the Clinical Gerontologist on the scale creation, reliability and case application by April 2014. We will also submit an abstract to the GSA by March 2015 on the LFDRS.

We are developing materials for continuing education (CE) presentations to be used locally, state-wide and nationally. Since not all target audiences will be able to attend CE presentations, we will also develop webinars to introduce the LFDSS and LFDRS to a variety of professionals working with older adults.

The fifth paragraph addresses the two most common forms of dissemination used in academia: publications and presentations. Note the level of detail: the first sentence identifies the topic and names the book in which a chapter will be published and identifies the topic and names the journal and submission date by when an article will be submitted; the second sentence specifies the topic, professional society, and date by when a conference abstract will be submitted. These details are more persuasive to reviewers than a generic statement of "an article will be submitted for publication and a presentation will be given at a professional society meeting."

The sixth paragraph stresses, again, current action and future plans. The first sentence indicates that materials are currently being developed for presentations locally, state-wide, and nationally, a distinctive feature. The second sentence expresses that webinars will be developed for those who cannot attend the presentations.

The final paragraph in this subheading casts a slightly wider dissemination net, acknowledging that while the primary audience includes researchers and practitioner professionals, a secondary audience of individuals in the general public may be interested in the project as well. As a result, institutional resources will be engaged to distribute a press release nationally.

While our primary target audience consists of professionals, we recognize that the general public also has interest in our work as evidence by inquiries from both the print and electronic media. Accordingly, we will develop a press release based on the completed project and distribute it nationally with the assistance of the Wayne State Public Relations office.

The "Sustainability" section aligns with the RFP guidelines call to address "Plans for Continued Support." One and a half double-spaced pages are used to describe for the sponsor *what comes next*.

Just like a good literature review, the proposed work is situated within the context of what has come before and what is likely to come after. Notice how the first sentence foreshadows the ability of sponsor funding to be leveraged to secure additional extramural support. The second sentence states the purpose of the proposed project and the third sentence leads into two examples of previously funded projects and two examples of future planned funding requests.

7.0 Sustainability

This proposal builds upon other previously funded work; RRF funding can help leverage future federal funding. Funding from RRF will allow us to collect data on validity and implementation of both the LFDRS and LFDSS. Below are the previous funded projects and planned submissions for funding.

1. A philanthropic gift of $25,000 in fall 2012 to support Dr. Lichtenberg's work enabled him to hire consultants, bring expert panelists together, create the LFDRS and perform the first reliability study.
2. An internal Wayne State University BOOST grant of $35,000 in December 2013 was granted to support the development of new relationships with professionals serving older adults and the collection of a small amount of pilot data (25 cases) and prepare applications to the RRF to complete an initial validity and implementation study and a re-submission to the National Institute of Justice for a larger and more definitive study of validity and implementation. This grant was awarded based on the strength of the peer reviews obtained from the first National Institute of Justice submission (May 2013). The BOOST grant is enabling Dr. Lichtenberg to hire staff, hire a nationally renowned statistician and methodologist, and establish a working relationship with professionals with aging clients and professionals who work with older adults in the criminal justice field.
3. A resubmission to the NIJ is planned for summer 2014. Being able to document support from RRF will significantly strengthen the resubmission.
4. Ongoing work with the Wayne State University intellectual property office will enable us to develop easier access and distribution of the scales to professionals across the country.

Numbered list items 1 and 2 help to establish credibility for the principal investigator and for the project. Namely, a philanthropic gift from an individual provided support to conduct the first reliability study, and an internal grant from the institution provided support to gather project pilot data. These gifts and grants demonstrate that other funders trust the principal investigator and believe in the significance of the research being conducted and the potential benefits for older adults. The further implication is that since a proof of concept has been established, the time is now right for the Retirement Research Foundation to invest in the next phase of research to validate the diagnostic and screening tools.

Numbered list items 3 and 4 also help to establish the credibility of the principal investigator and of the project, but in a different way. They speak to a vision for and commitment to the future. The principal investigator knows exactly what needs to be done next—to whom an application needs to be submitted by when and for what—to continue translating the research on financial decision making in older adults into practical tools that can be used by health, financial, and criminal justice professionals.

Notice how the second sentence in Item 3 speaks to the weight the sponsor carries with other grantmakers: "Being able to document support from RRF will significantly strengthen the [NIJ] resubmission." The sponsor's willingness to invest in the principal investigator and project will inspire others to do so as well. Said differently, funds and reputation both can be leveraged to realize far-reaching gains benefiting older adults.

The proposal ends on a humanistic note. Viewed narrowly, project sustainability is about finances, identifying the sources of internal and external funding that could be used to continue project activities. A broader view of sustainability means considering other ways the project will "live on" beyond the grant. In this case, the first sentence highlights structural sustainability, that a seasoned project team is in place and committed to this line of research, and the second sentence underscores social sustainability, that the benefits will continue to accrue for older adults because of the practitioner professionals who serve them. Not so coincidentally, the final sentence systematically touches both sponsor hot buttons.

Beyond these mechanisms for *financial sustainability*, the project *structural stability* remains in place; that is, we have the same infrastructure, systems, and procedures to continue on with our prior work, thereby, helping to root this research trajectory in permanence. Further, we enjoy *social sustainability* that will sustain this project initiative. Specifically, we have the same research team continuing on and also enjoy support for the financial professionals and volunteer subject participants. These enduring advantages benefit both our direct and indirect audiences. In essence multiple types of sustainability mechanisms will not only leverage RRF support but underpin further scholarly research in the field of financial decision-making and financial exploitation.

* * *

The Retirement Research Foundation
8765 West Higgins Road, Suite 430, Chicago, Illinois 60631-4170
773/714-8080 773/714-8089 fax www.rrf.org

August 15, 2014

Neva Solana
Assistant Vice President for Sponsored Program Administration
Wayne State University, Office of Research and Sponsored Programs
Sponsored Programs Administration
5057 Woodward Avenue, Suite 13001
Detroit, Michigan 48202

RE: RRF Grant #2014-024

Dear Neva Solana:

The Retirement Research Foundation is pleased to inform you that a grant award in the amount of $69,075 to the Wayne State University, Office of Research and Sponsored Programs has been approved. This award is being made in support of the project entitled: Assessing Financial Decision-Making and Financial Exploitation.

Grant funds will be available for one year beginning October 1, 2014. Payment will be made after receipt by the Foundation of this countersigned letter. To facilitate your receipt of the payment check, please include the name of the official to whom the check is to be sent. This award is not to be construed as a commitment for any future awards to your organization.

The grant is made subject to the following conditions:

1. Under United States Law, grant funds may be expended only for charitable, religious, scientific, literary, or educational purposes. The grant is to be used only for the purposes specified in the proposal submitted to the Foundation, and it is understood that these grant funds will be used substantially in accordance with the attached approved budget. It is also understood that no substantial variances will be made from the budget or timeline without the Foundation's prior approval in writing. Any grant funds not expended or committed for the purpose of the grant, or within the period stated above will be returned to the Foundation.
2. Full and complete reports are to be submitted according to the attached schedule. These reports should contain a financial statement and a narrative account of what was accomplished by the expenditure of funds. A reporting schedule is enclosed. The financial statement should reflect expenditure of the grant funds, according to the categories of the attached approved budget.
3. Records of receipts and expenditures will be maintained and made available to the Foundation at reasonable times.
4. The Foundation is to be notified promptly if the organization's 501(c)(3) classification or IRS determination that it is not a private foundation is revoked or modified.
5. The Foundation may monitor and conduct an evaluation of operations under this grant which may include a visit from

STAGE ONE: FULL PROPOSAL

Celebrating the Grant Award Notification.

The motivation to submit a proposal to the Retirement Research Foundation stemmed from a strategic encounter with the program officer in a professional setting. The entire process took about a year: four months went by as the proposal moved from conception to submission, three months passed while the proposal was under review, two months were needed to prepare responses to reviewer follow-up questions, and two more months passed before the Retirement Research Foundation's board of trustees made a final determination of grant awards.

The grant award notice is strong evidence that our proposal was able to convey to the sponsor that funding us will help them achieve their mission. We were able to balance successfully the relationship between sponsor values and organizational capabilities and between proposal logics and proposal psychologics. The proposal is persuasive because it presents a seamless argument that stands the test of reason, addresses psychological concerns, and connects project ideas to the values of the sponsor.

Foundation personnel to observe your program, discuss the program with your personnel and review financial and other records connected with the activities financed by this grant. The Foundation may include information on this grant in its periodic public reports.

6. Any reports, materials, books, articles, presentations which result from this grant are to indicate the Foundation's support of the program.
7. Any press releases or public announcements of this grant are to be approved by the Foundation in advance of release.

Your acceptance of these agreements should be indicated below by the signature of the officer who is authorized to execute contracts on behalf of the organization.

We wish you success with your project and look forward to learning of your progress.

Sincerely,

Irene Frye
Executive Director

Materials from the Retirement Research Foundation are used by permission.

CHAPTER 6

The Wisconsin Partnership Program, Community-Academic Partnership Fund

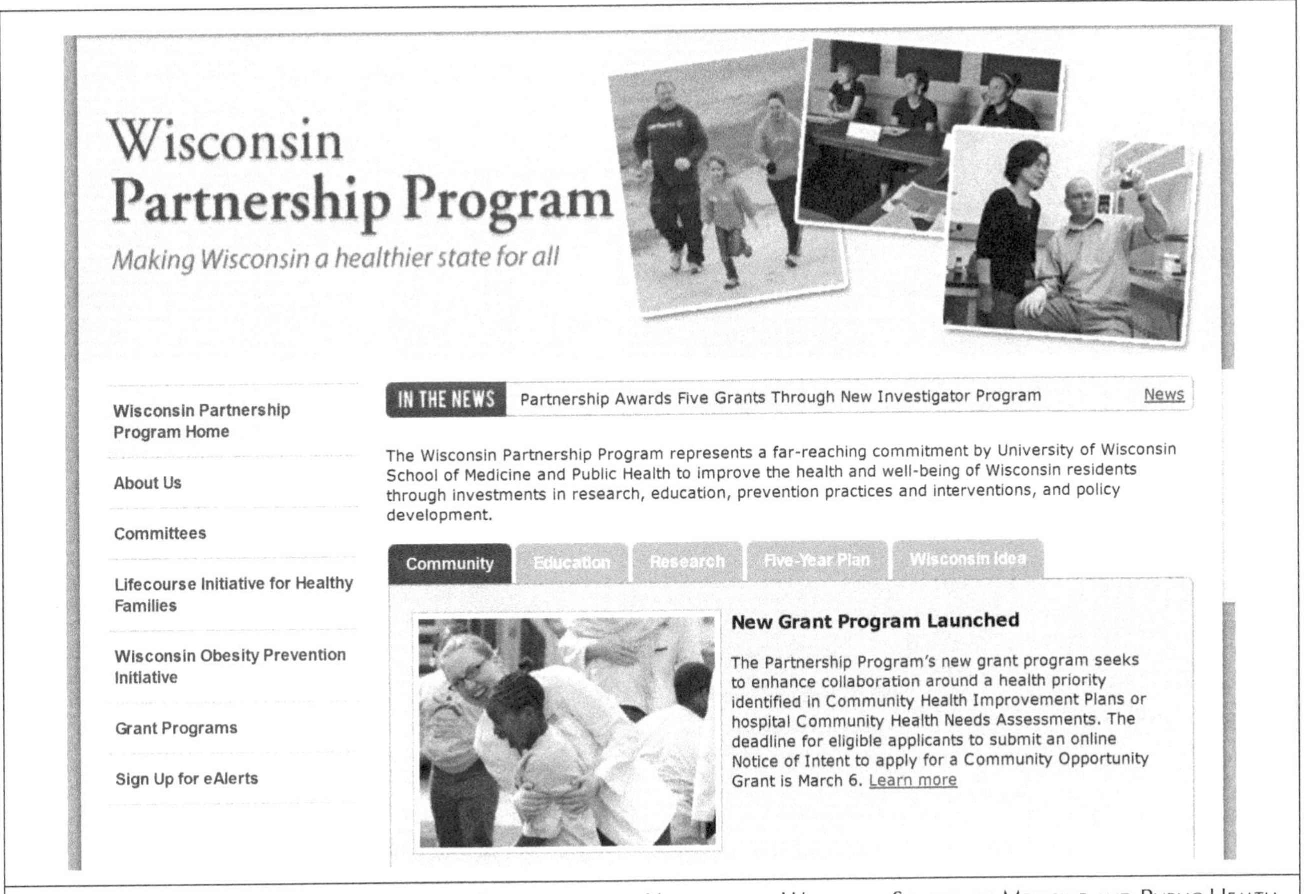

WISCONSIN PARTNERSHIP PROGRAM HOME PAGE (COURTESY OF THE UNIVERSITY OF WISCONSIN SCHOOL OF MEDICINE AND PUBLIC HEALTH, WWW.MED.WISC.EDU/WISCONSIN-PARTNERSHIP-PROGRAM/MAIN/499. USED BY PERMISSION.)

The Wisconsin Partnership Program was created in 2004 with funds from the conversion of Blue Cross/Blue Shield United of Wisconsin from a nonprofit insurer to a for-profit corporation. Their mission is "to serve the public health needs of Wisconsin, and to reduce health disparities through research, education and community partnerships." With an endowment of $338 million (2013 figure), the Wisconsin Partnership Program administers multiple grant programs, including the Community-Academic Partnership Fund. The fund supports the development of partnerships between community organizations and academic institutions, and the implementation of small- and large-scale projects that aim to improve the health of Wisconsin communities and residents. A wealth of information about grantmaking priorities, application processes, and funding history is available online at http://www.med.wisc.edu/wisconsin-partnership-program/main/499.

In this chapter we take an in-depth look at a successful application to the Wisconsin Partnership Program, Community-Academic Partnership Fund. With its priorities to eliminate health disparities; address rural and urban areas in Wisconsin; promote healthy weight, physical activity, and good nutrition; and reduce the incidence and severity of overweight and obesity, this program was identified as a potential source of support for a special project to expand a coalition and its efforts to increase access to healthy foods for low-income and food-insecure families.

The Wisconsin Partnership Program, Community-Academic Partnership Fund uses a two-stage application process. In the first stage, applicants submit a two-page letter of interest that responds to the Request for Partnerships. In the second stage, the sponsor invites select applicants to submit a six-page full application. Accordingly, this chapter is divided into two sections, one for each stage of the application process. The elements of each stage are as follows.

Stage One: Letter of Interest

- The Request for Proposal
- The Letter of Interest

Stage Two: Full Application

- The Executive Summary
- The Narrative
- The Work Plan
- The Logic Model
- The Roles and Responsibilities
- The Budget and Budget Narrative
- The External Reviewer Comments
- The Grant Award Notification

This application is a model of proposal planning and writing; it presents the right balance of logic, emotion, and relationships to connect with the values of the sponsor. Figure 5 overviews the key elements that we brought together to reach the Persuasion Intersection.

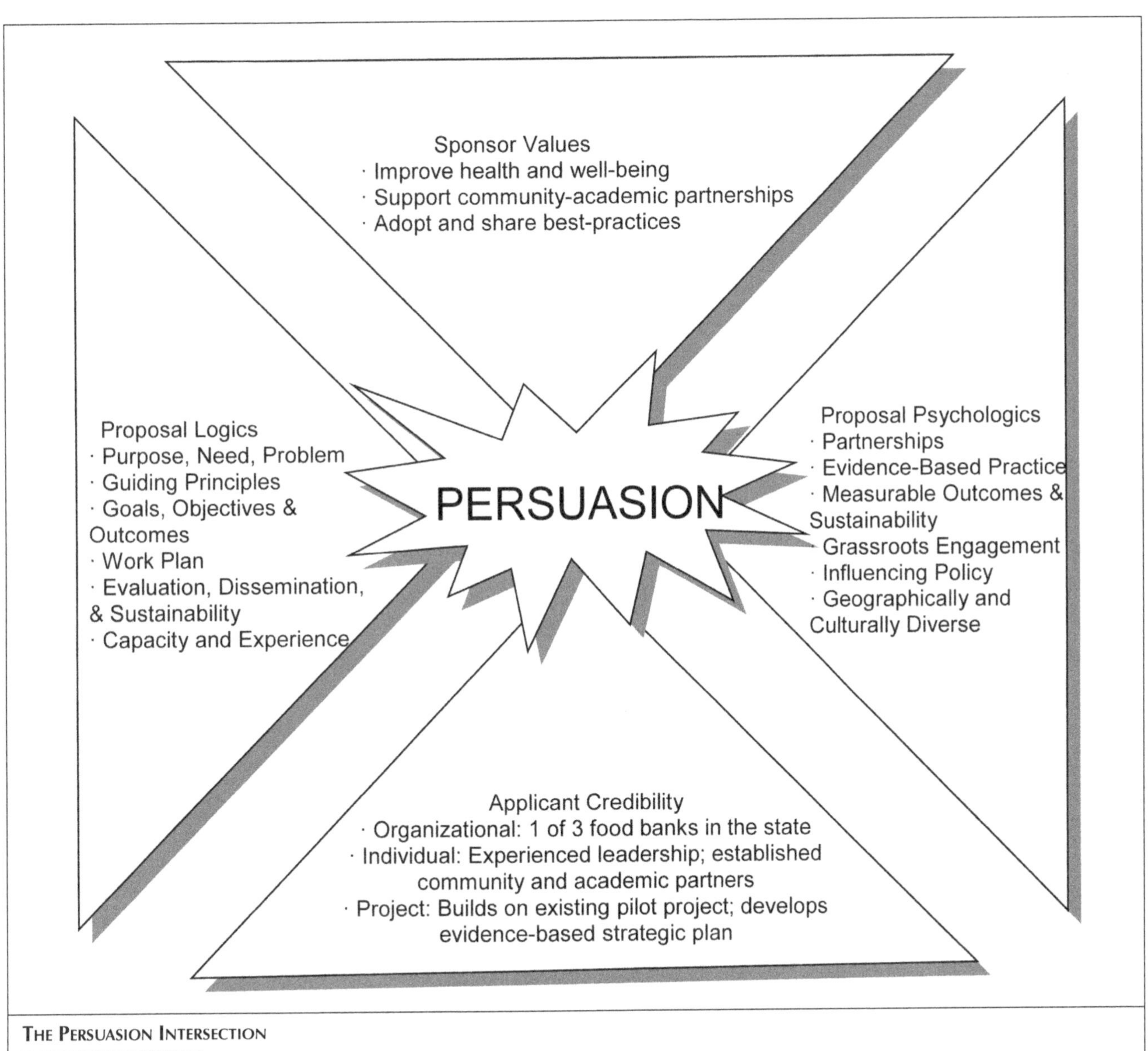

THE PERSUASION INTERSECTION

FIGURE 5

STAGE ONE: LETTER OF INTEREST

Analyzing the RFP.
Analyzing Request for Proposal (RFP) guidelines is a three-step process whereby we ask questions about the *relevance* of our project idea to the sponsor's guidelines, the *feasibility* of developing a proposal, and the *probability* of achieving funding success. The RFP Analysis Process moves us along the Roads to the Persuasion Intersection.

The following call-out thought bubbles provide insight into the process of planning and writing a successful proposal. Because the RFP Analysis process is iterative by nature, the three steps may not always appear sequentially.

Step One: Relevance.
According to the RFP guidelines, the Wisconsin Partnership Program offers development grants of up to $50,000 for one to two years to improve public health and well-being of state residents in rural and urban underserved areas. Prevention activities must align with the state's health plan, *Healthiest Wisconsin 2020*. A two-page letter of interest is due June 6 and, if invited, a six-page full proposal is due September 12.

Step Two: Feasibility.
Hot button phrases for evidence-based practice are repeated more than two dozen times in the RFP: *evidence, effectiveness, best practice, promising practice, models,* and *social determinants of health*. The RFP aggressively advocates for using the What Works database, including dedicating an entire section to "Finding Evidence." Further, this hot button relates directly to the sponsor's guiding principle of effectiveness.

Wisconsin Partnership Program Community-Academic Partnership Fund Request for Partnerships

PROGRAM OVERVIEW

KEY DATES

June 6, 2013	Notice of Intent/Letter of Interest due
September 12, 2013	Full application due
December 30, 2013	Notification of awards
April 1, 2014	Expected project start date

PURPOSE AND GRANT DESCRIPTION

The Wisconsin Partnership Program was created with funds from the conversion of Blue Cross & Blue Shield United of Wisconsin. The Program is dedicated to improving the health and well-being of the public through investments in research, education and evidence-based practices leading to environmental, institutional or policy change. The 2009–2014 Five-Year Plan, available at med.wisc.edu/wpp, guides the work of the Wisconsin Partnership Program.

Priority Areas:

- Programs aimed at eliminating health disparities.
- Programs that address the health needs of rural and urban underserved areas in Wisconsin.
- Programs targeted to promoting healthy weight, physical activity and good nutrition, and reducing the incidence and severity of overweight and obesity.

REVIEW CRITERIA

- Aligns with Wisconsin Partnership Program grant priorities.
- Aligns with Wisconsin Partnership Program mission, vision and guiding principles.
- Enhances existing or promising community and academic partnerships.
- Uses promising practices or evidence-based strategies.
- Aligns with the Wisconsin State Health Plan.

ELIGIBILTY

- Must be a Wisconsin-based organization.
- Must be a state, tribal or local governmental agency or a charitable organization that is tax-exempt under
- Section 501(c)(3) of the Internal Revenue Code.
- Must work with a UW System academic partner.

FUNDING CATEGORIES AND DURATION

Development Grant (6-page limit)

- Partnership development awards are up to $50,000 for 1 to 2 years.
- Pilot/feasibility awards are up to $50,000 for 1 to 2 years.

TECHNICAL ASSISTANCE/CONTACT INFORMATION

Wisconsin Partnership Program
wpp@hslc.wisc.edu
608-265-8215, or Toll Free - 866-563-9810

INTRODUCTION

The University of Wisconsin School of Medicine and Public Health Oversight and Advisory Committee (OAC) is pleased to announce the availability of the 2013 Community-Academic Partnership Fund grants through the Wisconsin Partnership Program.

The Wisconsin Partnership Program provides funding to Wisconsin community-based organizations in partnership with faculty from the UW School of Medicine and Public Health or from other UW System campuses to improve the health of Wisconsin residents. Through a competitive Request for Partnerships (RfP), the OAC will fund prevention activities promoting the goals of Wisconsin's health plan, *Healthiest Wisconsin 2020: Everyone Living Better, Longer* (dhfs.wisconsin.gov) and aligning with Wisconsin Partnership Program's mission, vision and guiding principles.

BACKGROUND

Created with funds from the conversion of Blue Cross & Blue Shield United of Wisconsin, the Wisconsin Partnership Program is dedicated to improving the health and well-being of the public through investments in research, education and evidence-based practices leading to environmental, institutional or policy change. The 2009–2014 Five-Year Plan, available at med.wisc.edu/wpp, guides the work of the Program.

PURPOSE

These grants allow community applicants to: (1) have an impact on the health of Wisconsin residents, (2) work in partnership with faculty and staff from the University of Wisconsin System and (3) adopt evidence-based programs or best-practices that can be shared or taken to scale, or develop innovative programs to serve as models of best practice.

FUNDING PRIORITIES

- Programs aimed at eliminating health disparities.
- Programs that address the health needs of rural and urban underserved areas in Wisconsin.
- Programs targeted to promoting healthy weight, physical activity and good nutrition, and reducing the incidence and severity of overweight and obesity.

COMMUNITY PARTNER

Eligible community partners are Wisconsin-based, nonprofit, IRS tax-exempt 501(c)(3) and tribal or governmental organizations. Fiscal sponsors are permitted, but must be approved by the Wisconsin Partnership Program. Contact the program officer to discuss fiscal sponsorship.

Step Two: Feasibility.
Partnership is a hot button that appears more than one hundred times in the RFP. Not only is "partnership" in the name of the program, the sponsor redefined RFP to mean Request for Partnerships and requires collaboration between a community agency and an academic institution as part of the eligibility criteria. This hot button is also one of the sponsor's guiding principles.

Step Three: Probability.
Strategic thinking questions might include "To what extent is it possible to integrate elements of the Five-Year Plan into the narrative?" and "Is there additional information on the sponsor's Web site—annual reports, grantee profiles, recognition garnered by staff and board members—that will provide insight into their expectations?"

Step Three: Probability.
Preproposal contact questions might include "What are some of the biggest dissatisfactions with the current approaches to promoting healthy weight and good nutrition?" and "Which dimensions of the problem need to be addressed next?"

Step Three: Probability.
Strategic thinking questions might include "To what extent is it possible to design a project that addresses multiple funding priorities?" and "Are the odds of getting funded good enough to merit submitting a proposal?"

Step Three: Probability.
Preproposal contact questions might include "Does Institutional Review Board (IRB) approval need to be secured prior to submission or prior to an award?" and "What is the relationship between the academic partner IRB and the UW-Madison IRB?"

Step Three: Probability.
Preproposal contact questions might ask "What percentage of development grantees have subsequently secured funding for implementation grants?" and "Are there any specific characteristics that development projects shared which positioned them for success as implementation projects?"

Step Three: Probability.
Preproposal contact questions might ask "To what extent are the same reviewers used in subsequent review cycles?" and "What percentage of applications represent first-time submissions compared to resubmissions?"

ACADEMIC PARTNER (*Must have Principal Investigator status with an institutional IRB of record.*)

- UW School of Medicine and Public Health tenure, Clinical/Health Sciences (CHS) and clinician-teacher track faculty.
- UW School of Medicine and Public Health academic staff and emeritus professors with approval of a UWSMPH department chair or center director.
- UW School of Medicine and Public Health volunteer staff and other UW System faculty, including UW Extension, with Principal Investigator (PI) status with an institutional IRB of record.

CONTINUATION/EXPANSION APPLICATIONS

Applicants can apply for a continuation or expansion of a Wisconsin Partnership Program funded project. All continuation/expansion applicants must submit a final report or an evaluation demonstrating successful completion of project objectives and a successful partnership with an academic partner.

RESUBMISSION

Applicants may resubmit an unfunded proposal from a previous grant cycle. Resubmissions are considered new applications and, as a result, will be part of the same competitive process as all other grant applications.

DEVELOPMENT GRANTS **(limit of 6 pages, single-spaced)**

- **Partnership Development Up to $50,000 1 to 2 years**
  Community partners and UW faculty/staff seeking to form sustainable relationships to identify ways they can work together to address public health issues at the local, regional or state level. *Examples of outcomes can include a formal strategic plan, a community action plan or community assessment results.*
- **Pilot/Feasibility Up to $50,000 1 to 2 years**
  Community partners and UW faculty/staff working together to pilot test the effectiveness or feasibility of implementing an intervention and to determine if a particular intervention is appropriate, adoptable or adaptable in a community, a geographic region or with a targeted population. *For example, testing an evidence-based program or promising practice used in an urban area, with a rural population.*

APPLICATION TIMELINE

Request for Partnerships (RfP) and electronic Notice of Intent (NOI) released	May 3, 2013
Technical assistance available (Wisconsin Partnership Program website)	Ongoing
Notice of Intent due	**June 6, 2013 – 4 p.m.**
Invitation to submit full application	July 31, 2013
Technical Assistance Days	August – dates to be determined
Full application due	**September 12, 2013 – 4 p.m.**
Notification of awards	**By December 30, 2013**
New grantee orientation	February 2014
Earliest project start date	April 1, 2014

Step Three: Probability.
Strategic thinking questions might ask "If selected to submit a full proposal, can this be accomplished during the sponsor's scheduled timeframe?" and "Is the sponsor's projected timetable consistent with our strategic plan for partnership and program development?"

NOTICE OF INTENT/LETTER OF INTEREST

Submission of the Notice of Intent is the responsibility of the community agency. It is advisable to work in conjunction with your academic partner (if you have already identified an academic partner) to submit this Notice of Intent and Letter of Interest. Projects will be considered for further development based on alignment with Wisconsin Partnership Program goals and priorities. Submitting a Notice of Intent *does not automatically qualify* the applicant organization for the full submission process. Selected applicants will be notified by July 31, 2013.

The Letter of Interest is the narrative portion of the Notice of Intent and is part of the web-based application. The Letter of Interest must be in PDF format only, not to exceed **two (2) single-spaced pages.** Use a minimum of 11- point font and address the following:

- Describe what the project is proposing to do, including the need for the project and the expected impact.
- Define the target audience, including geographic area, rural/urban, etc.
- Explain how the project team will work with the academic partner to address the public health issue.
- Describe the applicant organization and its ability to successfully complete the project.
- Identify the evidence for project activities or intervention (use the What Works Database or other public health evidence-based sources (whatworksforhealth.wisc.edu).
- Describe how the project will measure success.
- Indicate how the project aligns with the Wisconsin Partnership Program's guiding principles, mission and vision, and the State Health Plan (dhfs.wisconsin.gov).

Step Two: Feasibility.
Evaluation criteria in the RFP indicate that the two-page letter of interest should describe the project purpose, target audience, partnerships, applicant organization, evidence-based sources, measures of success, and alignment with grant program.

Two evaluation criteria—partnerships and evidence-based practice—are also sponsor hot buttons. A third sponsor hot button, measurable outcomes and sustainability, is repeated throughout the RFP but is *not* stated directly as evaluation criteria. Addressing evaluation criteria represents a minimum performance standard: Proposals are more persuasive when the sponsor's logical and psychological concerns are met, which in this case means appealing to all three hot buttons in the narrative.

TIPS FOR WRITING THE NOTICE OF INTENT/LETTER OF INTEREST

1. Learn about the Wisconsin Partnership Program (med.wisc.edu/wpp).
   - ✓ Review the RfP in detail before starting.
   - ✓ Review the Wisconsin Partnership Program's strategic Five-Year Plan and annual reports.
   - ✓ Review the Wisconsin Partnership Program website, including grants awarded in the past.
2. Keep the scope of the project manageable.
   - ✓ Start with a logic model and be sure outcomes are measurable (www.uwex.edu).
   - ✓ Write the Letter of Interest with precision and clarity of purpose.
3. Ask others to review the Letter of Interest before submitting it.

Contact the program officer for more information:
wpp@hslc.wisc.edu

FULL PROPOSAL GUIDELINES

A limited number of applicants will be invited to submit full proposals. Submission of the full application is the responsibility of the community agency. The link to the web-based full application will be provided to applicants. Submit online by 4:00 p.m. CDT September 12, 2013. **Five hard copies, double-sided and fastened, must be postmarked on or before September 12, 2013.**

GENERAL GUIDELINES

- All documents must be uploaded onto the online application as PDF with minimum 11-point font, and one-inch margins (single-spaced lines are acceptable)
- Narrative page limits:
  - ➢ Development proposals – 6 pages
- References are not included in the page limit.
- The logic model, work plan, appendices and optional materials are not part of the narrative page limit.

EXECUTIVE SUMMARY

The executive summary must summarize the following elements and will be used as a "stand alone" description of the project (Tip: Write this section last). Limit 1 page.

Step Two: Feasibility.
Proposal writing hints and resource Web sites related to evaluation criteria are given repeatedly to applicants: starting first with the logic model to plan inputs, outputs, and short-, medium-, and long-term outcomes will ensure that descriptions of key activities and evaluation strategies align across the entire narrative.

Step Three: Probability.
Preproposal contact questions might ask "Historically, what percentage of applicants are invited to submit full proposals?" and "What are the most common mistakes that you see in applications that are not invited to submit full proposals?"

Step Two: Feasibility.
The RFP is filled with tips for success related to the evaluation criteria, such as this one that encourages writing the executive summary last. This tip comes from a lesson of experience: when the executive summary is written first, it is likely to contain points that are not explained in the narrative because project ideas were still being formed. Writing the executive summary after the narrative is completed ensures alignment between the two.

✓	Required Elements (Scoring: 0 points)
	Brief background on the significance of the health issue or health topic
	Goal of the project
	Brief description of the project
	Intended measurable outcomes
	Funding request and timeframe
	Indication of next steps following project completion
	Brief statement about the impact of this project for residents of Wisconsin Description of how the project addresses the State Health Plan, *Healthiest Wisconsin 2020* (dhfs.wisconsin.gov), and Wisconsin Partnership Program mission, vision and guiding principles

Step Two: Feasibility.
Even though the executive summary does not receive a point score on the reviewer's evaluation form, it has a significant impact: because the executive summary is often the first thing that reviewers read, it establishes the mindset for understanding the entire proposal.

NARRATIVE

The narrative (not including footnotes, references, logic model, work plan and appendices) must be submitted as a PDF. Use these six (6) section headings and instructions to write the narrative.

Step Two: Feasibility.
Evaluation criteria in the RFP indicate that the six-page full proposal should describe the project purpose, need and statement of problem; outcomes related to the guiding principles; goals, objectives and outcomes; work plan; evaluation, dissemination and sustainability plans; and capacity and experience of partners and key staff.

✓	1. Project Purpose, Need and Statement of the Problem (Scoring: 15 points)
	Describe the purpose and need for the project and the significance of the issue being addressed.
	Identify and describe the target population; include demographic information.
	Use community, county, regional or state-level data to provide evidence of project need; refer to County Health Rankings, the Wisconsin Report Card and trend data for Wisconsin.
	Describe how the project will advance one or more of the health and/or infrastructure focus areas of the State Health Plan and specifically address the objectives associated with the focus area. (dhfs.wisconsin.gov).
	*This section should incorporate current local, regional or statewide data to support the need and purpose.

Step Two: Feasibility.
The asterisk calls extra attention to a tip for success related to the evaluation criteria: do not rely exclusively on national data to justify a local need. Data should be as specific as possible to the target population and community being served.

Step Two: Feasibility.
The RFP offers asterisked tips for success related to the evaluation criteria for each section of the narrative except for "2. Outcomes Related to the Guiding Principles." It is unclear why this is the only section that does not offer friendly advice. Applicants might value knowing, for instance, whether reviewers give greater credence to narratives that address all versus some of the guiding principles.

Step Two: Feasibility.
The asterisked tips for success in sections 3, 4, and 5 all relate to ensuring consistency across documents. In practical terms, this may mean that there will be select redundancy between the narrative, work plan, and logic model.

Step Two: Feasibility.
Grassroots engagement with the target population is a distinctive feature that carries weight with reviewers. Whereas the Letter of Intent simply asks applicants to "define the target audience," the Full Application additionally asks for a description of "plans to include the target population in the planning and design of activities and interventions" and "experience in working with the target population."

✓	**2. Outcomes Related to the Guiding Principles (Scoring: 15 points)**
	Describe how the project incorporates the Wisconsin Partnership Program's guiding principles; provide examples and address at least one guiding principle: *Prevention*: Promote health and prevent disease, injury and disability *Partnership*: Seek out, encourage and support community-University partnerships *Enhancement*: Advance and replicate innovative and transformational population health programs *Responsiveness*: Accelerate existing and stimulate new initiatives with the greatest potential to improve population health *Effectiveness*: Support the translation and application of evidence-based practices and policies *Sustainability*: Enhance and leverage other resources to help programs evolve and become self-sustaining
✓	**3. Goals, Objectives and Outcomes (Scoring: 15 points)**
	Discuss the project's goals, objectives and outcomes, along with potential activities or interventions *This section should be consistent with the work plan and logic model.
	Summarize the evidence-base, existing knowledge or research that supports the project or program design, approach or strategy; for more information, refer to *What Works for Health* database at whatworksforhealth.wisc.edu.
	Describe how the community-academic partnership contributes to the goals, objectives and outcomes of the proposed project.
	Describe plans to include the target population in the planning and design of activities and interventions.
✓	**4. Work plan (Scoring: 15 points)**
	Use the template provided in the web-based application. Submit a PDF project work plan and corresponding timeframe of activities. * The work plan should be consistent with the logic model and evaluation efforts described in the evaluation section.

✓	5. Evaluation, Dissemination and Sustainability Plans (Scoring: 20 points)
	Logic Model. Using the template provided in the web-based application, submit a logic model. The logic model should be a snapshot of all project activities and expected outcomes. *Outcomes listed on the logic model should match the overall evaluation plan. Outcomes must be measurable. The logic model should be consistent with the work plan. See www.uwex.edu for more information on building a logic model.
	Describe details of the evaluation plan (including plans to measure success, who will measure, what tools will be used, what will be measured and why).
	Dissemination. Describe a plan for communicating project results to the public health community, other organizations and to policy-makers.
	Sustainability. Explain how the project will continue beyond the funded period, including how the project can impact environmental, institutional and policy change.
✓	**6. Capacity and Experience of Partners and Key Staff (Scoring: 20 points)**
	Describe the capacity of the applicant organization to carry out the project (include the agency's mission, key staff, clientele, and experience in working with the target population).
	List staff responsibilities.
	Describe the role of collaborating organizations, if applicable. *If this is a continuation/expansion of a funded development or implementation grant, describe the progress made to date.

Step Two: Feasibility.
The RFP highlights the expectation that outcomes be measurable and sustainable. Indeed, sustainability is one of the sponsor's guiding principles. Hot button phrases are used nearly 40 times: *outcomes, measurable, sustainable, long-term,* and *logic model.*

Step Two: Feasibility.
The parenthetical comment calls added attention to the level of detail necessary to persuade reviewers to assign full points to this evaluation criterion. The evaluation plan should describe who will be using what tools to collect which data and with what frequency.

Step Two: Feasibility.
Influencing policy is a distinctive feature. While grant funds cannot be used for lobbying purposes, projects that are able to affect policy change may be well received by reviewers; changes to policy can contribute to sustainability, a sponsor hot button.

Step Two: Feasibility.
Though the budget does not receive a point score per se on the reviewer's evaluation form, alignment still needs to exist between the narrative and the budget. Financial concerns might manifest in the scoring of the final section on capacity. Points might be deducted, for instance, because of an uncertainty as to whether sufficient funds were budgeted to support the scope of activity to be carried out by key personnel and collaborators.

Step Three: Probability.
Preproposal contact questions might clarify "Are there preferred levels of cash and in-kind matches?" and "What level of cost sharing is expected of grantees?"

Step Three: Probability.
Strategic thinking questions might include "Are all of the proposed expenses allowable under the terms and conditions of the program?" and "Are there expenses beyond those supported by grant funds that must be borne by the community and academic partners?"

Step Two: Feasibility.
The RFP offers a tip for success related to the evaluation criteria: a budget justification must explain project costs in relation to the goals, objectives, and activities proposed, not just narrate the basis of calculations.

BUDGET

The project budget should clearly indicate how the grant funds will be spent. Expenditures must:

- Be fully justified, reasonable and clearly related to project goal(s);
- Reflect the activities/tasks listed in the proposal; and
- Explain the sources and amounts of any cost sharing funds, either in-kind or cash match.

Requests should be made by expense type (salary, fringe benefits, travel, supplies, etc.). Provide sufficient detail for individuals unfamiliar with the project so they can accurately review the proposal.

- **Use of Funds:** Complete guidelines for allowable/unallowable expenses are available for review on the Wisconsin Partnership Program website along with the 2013 Request for Partnership application materials.

Funds may be used for project-related costs such as:

- Personnel expenses, such as salaries and benefits
- Salary support for academic partners
- Consultant and contract services
- Travel

Funds may **not** be used for:

- Clinical services related to treatment or follow-up for specific health conditions; however, clinical services that involve screening and education, or mobilizing resources to promote health care access may be funded.
- General overhead expenses
- Lobbying
- Capital expenditures costing $5,000 or more with a useful life of two (2) years or more; exceptions may be made for capital expenditures if such equipment is crucial to the primary objectives of the project; Wisconsin Partnership Program approval is required.
- Projects outside the state of Wisconsin
- Supplanting (see below)

- **Budget Justification:** A budget justification narrative is required for purposes of describing in detail the major budget line items: salary, fringe, travel, equipment, supplies, consultants/contracts and other costs. The narrative should provide the specifics of why an expense is necessary to achieve the goal(s) and objective(s) of the project.

ONE-PAGE RESUMES OR BIOGRAPHICAL SKETCHES

Submit in PDF, resumes or biographical sketches for the project manager and lead staff person (if different people), and the academic partner involved. Limit resumes or biographical sketches to **one page** each.

LETTERS OF COMMITMENT (mandatory for each academic partner)

The letter(s) must provide evidence of collaboration, with specific details on how the collaborating organization(s) and academic partner(s) will be involved or support the project. Explain roles and responsibilities of both the community and the academic partner. Applicants will be asked to submit the letter(s) in the narrative section of the online application. Letters of Commitment can be addressed to the Wisconsin Partnership Program, Oversight and Advisory Committee.

NON-SUPPLANTING

Supplanting means to replace, take the place of, or to supersede. The Wisconsin Partnership Program prohibits any funds from being awarded that will supplant funds or resources otherwise available to applicants from other sources for the proposed project.

All applicants must answer the nonsupplanting questionnaire as part of the application process. As an ongoing check against supplanting, grant recipients will be asked annually to recertify that other funds for the proposed project have not become available or been declined. No grant can be awarded if a determination of supplanting is made.

FINANCIAL STATEMENTS

Submit in PDF, a copy of the community organization's and/or fiscal sponsor's (if applicable) prior year financial statements or current annual revenue and expense budget.

IRS DETERMINATION LETTER

Submit in PDF, a copy of the community organization's (applicant agency) and fiscal sponsor's (if applicable) IRS determination letter of tax exempt status, if appropriate.

COMPLIANCE

Answer the compliance questions in the online application. A UW-Madison Institutional Review Board (IRB) evaluates all projects involving human subjects research conducted under the auspices of the university.

TRADE SECRET AND PROPRIETARY INFORMATION

Applicants must identify and request confidentiality of any trade secrets and/or proprietary information in their applications.

Step Three: Probability.
Strategic thinking questions might include "Would there be a psychological advantage to having the résumés of lead partners use the same template?" and "Would it make sense to adopt the National Institutes of Health's biosketch format as the preferred model?"

Step Three: Probability.
Strategic thinking questions might consider "Would it be reasonable to have the letter of commitment cite evidence of successful collaborative projects in the past that form the basis of this proposed initiative?" and "Should a sample letter of commitment with pertinent details be drafted for the collaborative partner to put on their letterhead?"

Step Three: Probability.
Strategic thinking questions might include "Does this ongoing check against supplanting suggest that it would be unwise to even apply for funding for complementary project activities?" and "Does this ongoing check against supplanting suggest that, in the event other funds do become available, it is not permissible to renegotiate with both sponsors to reach a mutually agreeable arrangement?"

Step Three: Probability.
Strategic thinking questions might include "Are prior year financial statements and current budget documents readily available?" and "Is the IRS determination letter of tax exempt status readily available?"

Step Three: Probability.
Strategic thinking questions might consider "Given that the full proposal is only six pages long, what is a reasonable amount of optional material to include?" and "Assuming that less is more when it comes to attachments, which ones will have the greatest impact on reviewers?"

Step Three: Probability.
Preproposal contact questions might inquire "Of the six guiding principles, are there any that are considered to be foremost among equals?" and "To what extent are partnerships expected to adopt these guiding principles verbatim versus establish collaborative principles of their own that reflect the spirit of prevention, partnership, enhancement, responsiveness, effectiveness, and sustainability?"

Step Two: Feasibility.
While partnerships is a hot button, geographically and culturally diverse community partnerships is a distinctive feature. Projects that serve rural areas of the state and are inclusive to diversity populations may be perceived as being more competitive than those who do not.

OPTIONAL MATERIAL

Submit letters of support or relevant and appropriate materials (PDF only) such as survey forms, training materials, evaluation instruments or draft tools to help describe the work plan and activities proposed.

WISCONSIN PARTNERSHIP PROGRAM MISSION, VISION AND GUIDING PRINCIPLES

The Wisconsin Partnership Program is dedicated to improving the health of the public through investments in research, education, prevention practices and interventions and policy development. The goal is to show progress in improving the health of individuals, families and communities in Wisconsin.

The following mission, vision and guiding principles are the framework for forming partnerships and collaborations to make Wisconsin a healthier state for all:

Mission: The Wisconsin Partnership Program will serve the public health needs of Wisconsin and reduce health disparities through initiatives in research, education and community partnerships.

Vision: Making Wisconsin a healthier state for all.

Guiding Principles:

- *Prevention*: Promote health and prevent disease, injury and disability
- *Partnership*: Seek out, encourage and support community-University partnerships
- *Enhancement*: Advance and replicate innovative and transformational population health programs
- *Responsiveness*: Accelerate existing and stimulate new initiatives with the greatest potential to improve population health
- *Effectiveness*: Support the translation and application of evidence-based practices and policies
- *Sustainability*: Enhance and leverage other resources to help programs evolve and become self-sustaining

Health improvement is defined in two ways: improving health indicators and health related quality of life, and reducing health disparities. Progress will be determined through effective health policies, interventions and practices over the short-term, and through improvements in health care, health behaviors, social determinants of health and the physical environment over the long-term.

To accomplish the mission and vision, the Wisconsin Partnership Program will invest in a balanced portfolio of geographically and culturally diverse community partnerships, education and research initiatives and community engagement strategies, and support the transformation to an integrated school of medicine and public health.

The Wisconsin Partnership Program is an integral part of the UW School of Medicine and Public Health with partners and resources statewide. Through collaboration and partnerships, the people of Wisconsin will benefit from the shared knowledge, experience and resources of the School and communities.

Step Three: Probability.
Preproposal contact questions might probe further the importance of geographically and culturally diverse community partnerships: "Will awards be made on the basis of any special criteria, such as geography, size of target population, or ethnic diversity of the partners?" and "Could a higher scoring proposal get bumped out in favor of a lower scoring proposal that meets other special criteria?"

Step Two: Feasibility.
Evidence-based practice is a hot button, but also note how references to the What Works database gain force through repetition in the RFP: the first mention is a soft parenthetical "(use the What Works Database or other public health evidence-based sources)"; the second mention is a casual statement, "refer to What Works for Health Database"; and this third mention is more directive, "Applicants are strongly encouraged to use What Works for Health."

FINDING EVIDENCE
Applicants are strongly encouraged to use "What Works for Health: Policies and Programs to Improve Wisconsin's Health." This database is based on a wide scan of analyses assessing evidence of effectiveness and provides information on what works and does not work for many different health issues.

Step Three: Probability.
Preproposal contact questions might ask "What would be the key features of an ideal solution?" and "Would this approach be useful for cost reasons or something else?"

COMMUNITY-ACADEMIC PARTNERSHIPS
The Community-Academic Partnership Fund is guided by the belief that collaborations between community organizations and academic partners can yield beneficial results in improving the health of Wisconsin. Partnerships begin with a community-identified need and an academic interest. Community leaders bring an understanding of the public health needs of specific populations, access to local resources and a commitment from dedicated staff and volunteers. The University of Wisconsin brings education and research expertise and a service commitment to the state exemplified by the Wisconsin Idea.

Step Three: Probability.
Strategic thinking questions that need to be addressed internally to assess organizational competitiveness include "What health-related needs have been identified as being the most pressing for the community?" and "Which additional resources would provide the greatest benefit to the community?"

> **Step Three: Probability.**
> Preproposal contact questions might ask "Are there preferred roles for the academic partner to ensure appropriate levels of active engagement?" and "Should evaluations be conducted by the academic partner, externally by a consultant, or both?"

- **Community and Academic Partner Roles:** The community partner is responsible for submission of the application. The OAC expects academic partners to be actively engaged in the project from serving in an advisory or consulting role to advising on evaluation methods and design, to conducting community engaged research. A document outlining roles and responsibilities of both community and academic partners is required and submitted as part of the online application process. The applicant must include a letter of commitment from the academic partner outlining intended roles and responsibilities.
- **Finding an Academic Partner:** It is important to work with an academic partner who has experience and interest in the project idea. Resources are available to help applicants find a partner, think through project ideas or partnership plans and prepare applications. Contact the program officer if assistance is needed.

> **Step Three: Probability.**
> Preproposal contact questions might ask "Is there an a priori number or percent of Letters of Interest that will move forward to development of Full Applications?" and "Will a point system be used for scoring Letters of Interest akin to the one used for scoring Full Applications?"

REVIEW PROCESS

Notice of Intent/Letter of Interest

- **Initial Technical and Content Review by Wisconsin Partnership Program Staff**
  Staff will review each Notice of Intent (NOI) and Letter of Interest (LOI) to ensure requirements, including eligibility, have been met. Any NOI that does not comply with the submission requirements will not be considered for final review. *Passing this initial technical and content review does not guarantee submission of a full proposal.*
- **Final Content Review**
  OAC members, along with staff, will review the content of the Notice of Intent/Letter of Interest to determine if further development as a full application is warranted. Evaluation of these preliminary "notices" will be based on a combination of alignment with the Wisconsin Partnership Program goals and priorities, the applicants' presentation of clear goals, measurable outcomes, use of evidence and alignment with the State Health Plan 2020.

> **Step Three: Probability.**
> Preproposal contact questions might ask "Should proposals be written for reviewers with nontechnical backgrounds?" and "Do reviewers fill certain roles on the panel as specialists or generalists?"

Full Application

- Technical Review by Wisconsin Partnership Program Staff
  Staff will review each full application to ensure that minimum application requirements, including a nonsupplanting review, have been met. Any application that does not comply with the submission requirements will not advance for further review.
- **Expert Review Panel**
  Each application will be reviewed and scored individually by external review members. Following the review, they will provide a ranked list along with a critique of each ranked proposal to the OAC. The review panel is comprised of health care professionals, community and public health advocates and practitioners and UW faculty and academic staff. The review panel is advisory to the OAC.
- **OAC Review**
  The OAC will make the final determination of awards in December 2013 based on rank, program objectives and alignment with the Wisconsin Partnership Program mission, vision and guiding principles. The OAC's decisions are final and cannot be appealed. The OAC may also request that applicants respond to concerns prior to making a decision on the award.

> **Step Three: Probability.**
> Preproposal contact questions might investigate "Does the Oversight and Advisory Committee (OAC) tend to accept the recommendations of the expert review panel without revision?" and "What types of concerns have been raised by the OAC in the past prior to making award determinations?"

AWARD INFORMATION

The OAC and program staff will negotiate the terms of each grant with applicants and enter into contractual agreements with successful applicants prior to the distribution of any funds. Successful applicants will participate in project orientation, project and fiscal monitoring activities as defined and delineated in the contract terms and conditions.

The OAC reserves the right to establish award amounts and to authorize budget items, program goals and other terms of the proposal prior to entering into an agreement with award recipients. Award recipients may make justifiable modifications in the approved grant budget or project plan only through prior consultation with and written approval of Wisconsin Partnership Program staff.

By applying to the Community-Academic Partnership Fund, applicants agree and consent, without reservation, substitution or limitation, to each of the following:

- Application submission requirements and rules, and the procurement process, procedures and specifications identified in this application, including all appendices and any application forms.
- The evaluation methods, evaluation process, evaluation criteria, scoring and project budget described in this Request for Partnerships.
- The OAC's sole, unrestricted right to reject any or all applications submitted in response to this Request for Partnerships.
- Supplanting prohibition as dictated by the Insurance Commissioner's Order and as identified on the nonsupplanting questionnaire.

Step Three: Probability.
Preproposal contact questions might ask "How does the project orientation that successful applicants are required to complete fit into the work plan timeframes?" and "Who exactly is expected to participate in the project orientation and what is the anticipated time commitment?"

Step Three: Probability.
Strategic thinking questions might consider "If a grant is awarded, are these terms and conditions acceptable?" and "If a grant is awarded, will there be additional terms and conditions that are not listed here?"

FISCAL SPONSOR ROLE

Use of a fiscal sponsor must be approved by the Wisconsin Partnership Program. A fiscal sponsor is a governmental or tax-exempt, 501(c)(3) organization that can distribute funds to organizations or groups that have not received IRS recognition of 501(c)(3) status. Fiscal sponsors must ensure adequate financial control and discretion for specific projects in furtherance of the sponsor's own exempt purposes. A fiscal sponsor, specifically its board of directors, accepts significant financial and legal liability when it sponsors a project under its 501(c)(3) designation. The fiscal sponsor acknowledges authority over and responsibility for the project including at minimum the following:

- Receipt and disbursement of Wisconsin Partnership Program grant funds.
- Maintaining proper financial record keeping and reporting for the project based on generally accepted accounting practices consistent with the organization's policies and procedures.
- Preparing all Wisconsin Partnership Program financial reporting requirements.
- Submitting a signed fiscal sponsor agreement with the project applicant identifying the roles and responsibilities of each partner toward the financial compliance of the project.

Step Three: Probability.
Strategic thinking questions might include, "Are systems and procedures in place to maintain and report on financial records?" and "Is it reasonable to complete the final performance and financial status reports within 90 days after the end date of the award period?"

The fiscal sponsor may assume additional roles and responsibilities as directed and negotiated by the applicant organization. This may include coordination, organizing or staffing roles. The Wisconsin

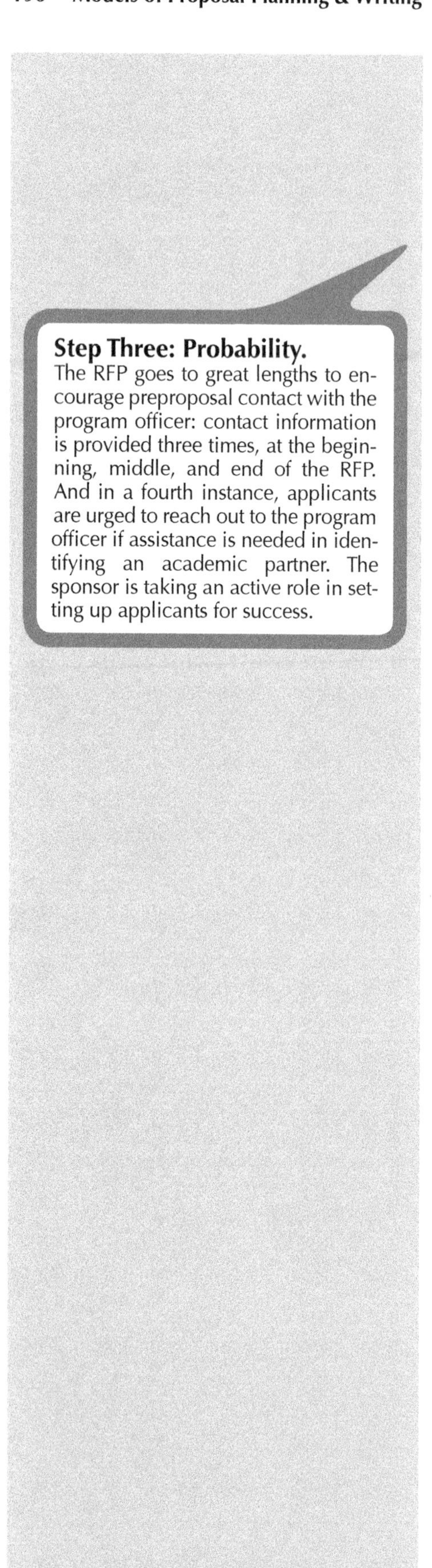

Partnership Program expects that fiscal sponsors will take an active role in the implementation and sustainability of project activities.

- **Fiscal sponsor criteria:**

– Wisconsin-based organization
– State, tribal or local governmental agency or charitable organization that is tax-exempt under Section 501(c)(3) of the Internal Revenue Code

Contact the WPP at wpp@hslc.wisc.edu.

* * *

Title: Changing Views of Hunger: One Community at a Time

Project Description: In 2012, according to the Feeding America, Map the Meal Gap report, almost one out of five Eau Claire County (ECC) children were food insecure.[1] During the same period, ECC WIC respondents reported their family experienced low food insecurity (54%) or very low food insecurity (21%).[2] These numbers are disturbing as increasing evidence links food insecurity to a variety of negative outcomes for children, including lower test scores, poorer school achievement, and higher frequency of behavioral problems.[3] Currently, two rural school districts have higher free and reduced lunch participation than the urban school district. To be effective in improving community health and wellness, communities need to be cognizant of the impact of food insecurity and worsening health disparities. Recent research has observed an association between adults in food insecure households and a higher risk of hypertension and diabetes than those living in food secure households.[4] Anecdotal evidence indicates that community awareness about these relationships, especial among health professionals, is low.

The purpose of the proposed project is to expand community awareness of the impact of hunger, and its increased risk for chronic disease, as well as the impact of the built environment. The project team plans to engage the Eau Claire City-County Health Department Health Communities Program and other health agencies in Western WI including Mayo Health System, the largest health care provider. Community partners will identify specific strategies for how qualitative data collected from a completed ECC family food insecurity study can be utilized to educate health professionals and the broader community about how social determinants of health impact hungry families. As insights are gained about these issues, specific mechanisms for addressing the problems can be identified and a strategic plan for implementation can be developed.

STAGE ONE: LETTER OF INTEREST

Developing the Letter of Interest.
The boldface heading at the top of the Letter of Interest identifies the public health issue—hunger—that will be the focus of the proposed project and foreshadows the approach that will be used— grassroots engagement.

In two paragraphs the "Project Description" justifies to the sponsor *why* this project is needed and states *what* the project will do.

Of note, the final two sentences of the opening paragraph touch on the hot button of evidence-based practice. Together these sentences show a familiarity with the published literature and with the specific needs of the community.

The second paragraph hits all three hot buttons: partnerships, evidence-based practices, and measurable outcomes and sustainability. Collaborative efforts extend beyond the minimum of having a community partner and academic partner to including health departments and health agencies in the community. "Social determinants of health" represents an established framework for considering conditions that affect health status. A major output of this development grant is a strategic plan to guide partners as they implement activities designed to reduce hunger in the community.

The "Target Audience" describes *who will benefit* from project efforts and *where* the project will take place.

Two distinctive features are addressed in this paragraph: grassroots engagement with the target population and geographically and culturally diverse community partnerships. In particular, citing previous focus group work with food-insecure families demonstrates a history of success working with the target population, and reinforcing the rural nature of the community appeals to a funding priority area of the sponsor.

Target Audience: The project team plans to educate the broader community with a targeted emphasis involving two particular groups in ECC: Community agencies that serve food insecure families yet are unaware of the interrelationship between hunger and chronic disease; and health professionals working with families. Participants in the food insecurity focus group study identified these two groups as potential advocates. ECC's 99,000 residents include the city of Eau Claire, with 65,000 residents, and small rural communities, dispersed across 638 square miles. The urban-rural mix increases the challenge for educating communities and health professionals and identifying strategies to reduce food insecurity. For example, although urban and rural families experience difficulties related to transportation and access to healthy and nutritious food, there are distinct differences in how to address these barriers depending on where a family lives. A diverse stakeholder coalition is therefore essential.

In one lengthy paragraph, "Partnerships" tells the sponsor *who* is participating in the project.

This entire paragraph is a hot button for partnerships. It names the community partner, academic partner, project managing partner, and current public and private health partners. They have experience working together on a non-grant-funded activity and are ready to take their relationship to the next level, building a coalition of like-minded organizations and individuals to tackle the problem of food insecurity in the community.

What's more, this paragraph hints at the hot button of measurable outcomes and sustainability; namely, the first sentence acknowledges the nearly 20-year history of the Hunger Prevention Coalition for Eau Claire County, which suggests that collaborative endeavors will continue to exist beyond the conclusion of the grant period.

In back-to-back sentences, appeals are made to two distinctive features: naming the Hmong Mutual Assistance Association recognizes geographically and culturally diverse community partnerships and citing results from focus groups with Hmong families confirms grassroots engagement with the target population.

Partnerships: The Hunger Prevention Coalition for Eau Claire County (HPC), established in 1995, has long recognized the problem of food insecurity and has been involved in efforts to reduce hunger. Recently, HPC partnered with UW-Eau Claire nursing faculty (2011–13) to conduct a focus group study to hear the voices of food insecure parents and agency staff who serve them. This team, led by HPC members from Feed My People Food Bank and ECC UW Extension Nutrition Education Program and academic partner, UW-Eau Claire Department of Nursing, will continue to collaborate on the proposed project with the goal of connecting the existing team with other community groups concerned about hunger and community wellness. EC City recently completed a Health Chapter in their comprehensive five year plan. EC City County Health Department also completed its community assessment and identified chronic disease as one of the key areas to address during the next 5 years. The project team will collaborate with the Chronic Disease Prevention Action Team (includes representatives from hospitals, health department and community) to formulate next steps for increasing awareness of hunger among community residents with a particular focus on health professionals. Feed My People team member Emily Moore was recently elected to the Mayo Clinic Health Systems board of directors. The team also has strong relationships with the Hmong community, through the Hmong Mutual Assistance Association (HMAA). UW Extension team member Nancy Coffey serves on the HMAA board of directors. Anecdotal and focus group data indicate many Hmong families are low-income and experience food insecurity. Hmong focus group study participant voiced unique needs that are not currently being met through standard food assistance services. This minority group is disproportionately affected by hunger and requires targeted attention. A partner from HMAA will be a key stakeholder for the proposed project.

Applicant Organization: Feed My People's mission is to eliminate hunger in west central Wisconsin. It works in collaboration with national, regional, and local partners to accomplish this. The organization has been a key voice for hunger relief in Eau Claire for 30 years. Feed My People manages gross receipts valued at over $10 million annually, including small grant management. Emily Moore has served as the executive director for 9 years. She is an active member of the Hunger Prevention Coalition and will serve as the lead collaborator in this project.

"Applicant Organization" identifies *who* is responsible for project activities.

This paragraph is a testimonial to credibility. It establishes organizational credibility, including an established mission to eliminate hunger in the region, a 30-year history of working collaboratively to serve community needs, and experience managing multimillion-dollar budgets. It also establishes individual credibility, citing a lengthy tenure with the organization and active participation in related coalition activities. In other words, this partnership development grant represents a systematic continuation of prior efforts to support the community.

Evidence: The project team is well positioned to move forward utilizing RWJF's Roadmap to Health Action Model, the WI What Works database, and the socio-ecological model for improving health. Key components of the RWJF model that will be followed include: Working Together, Assessing Needs and Resources, and Communication. For example, stakeholders with connections to clinical care will lead efforts to identify evidence-based strategies for educating health professionals, while stakeholders with knowledge of the built environment will lead efforts to improve transportation, a key barrier to health identified by focus group participants. Needs and resources to educate a broader community about hunger will be assessed. For example, while food insecure participants identified the internet as a source of information and potential resource, evidence from the What Works database indicates that social media and technology are effective communication tools. Therefore, connecting the needs with the resources related to social media and technology will be essential. What Works evidence also indicates that farmers' markets increase availability of fresh fruits and vegetables yet many focus group participant were not aware that the EC farmers' market accepts Food Share. This is another area that supports the importance of media representatives as partners in this communication effort.

The "Evidence" section tells the sponsor *how* project objectives and activities will be accomplished.

This entire paragraph is a hot button for evidence-based practice. In addition to acknowledging that the What Works database will be used, as applicants were "strongly encouraged" to do, this paragraph calls attention to the use of another nationally recognized model, the Robert Wood Johnson Foundation's Roadmap to Health Action Model. RWJF is perhaps the best known special-purpose foundation in the United States and specializes in funding health and health care issues; reviewers will recognize the credibility of RWJF immediately, even if they are unfamiliar with the specific Roadmap to Health Action Model.

This paragraph touches on the distinctive feature of grassroots engagement with the target population. Citing the results of previous focus group work with food-insecure families suggests that it will be easy to connect with them again.

"Measurement of Success" summarizes *how* effectiveness will be determined.

This paragraph appeals to the hot button of measurable outcomes and sustainability; namely, the partners will develop a strategic plan during the granting period that will guide implementation activities for several years beyond the granting period.

Measurement of Success: Project success will be measured based on development of a community action plan that includes: 1. Specific strategies for how urban and rural communities can begin to address the needs of food insecure families; 2. An outreach plan including identification of specific educational materials designed to assist urban and rural health professionals to establish best practices to message/frame social determinants of health with families who are food insecure; and 3. A communication plan which identifies strategies for educating individual families and agency staff about resources while informing the broader community about the impact of hunger on health and chronic disease. The project team's successful completion of the food insecurity focus group study demonstrates ability to collaborate and meet these project goals. Existing partnerships will be broadened to engage the ECC community, including the EC City Planner, EC City-County Health Department Health Communities Program, regional media outlets, and local health care systems.

For the third time in this 1,369-word narrative, there is a brief touch on the distinctive feature of geographically and culturally diverse community partnerships. Reviewers are reminded that the project will address rural and urban underserved areas in the state.

This closing paragraph speaks directly to the sponsor's review criteria, confirming alignment with the Wisconsin Partnership Program mission to improve public health and reduce health disparities; the WPP grant priorities to promote healthy weight and good nutrition in a rural area of the state; and the state health plan goals to improve health across the life span and eliminate health disparities and achieve health equity. Building on a foundation of existing community and academic partnerships, new collaborators will be recruited and evidence-based practices will inform a plan to implement new initiatives that aim to change views of hunger.

Alignment with WPP: The proposed project is in alignment with the mission of the WPP and State Health Plan. The goal is to develop a community action plan with specific educational and media strategies that will promote healthy weight, good nutrition and thereby reduce the incidence of chronic disease of ECC residents who are disproportionately affected by poverty and hunger. Partnerships between stakeholders from health, education, transportation, social services, and the HMAA will collaboratively develop a plan that promotes the health of children and families, educates community and health professionals, and ultimately reduces health disparities among low-income families. Goals will be accomplished through strengthening existing community-academic partnerships while stimulating new initiatives through broader coalitions including the EC City-County Health Department and local health care systems. By becoming cognizant of the relationship between food insecurity and health disparities, the ECC community will be more effective in improving community health, wellness, and quality of life. Ultimately, these efforts align with Healthiest WI 2020 by contributing to improvements in health across the lifespan for children and families and reducing health disparities among those who are food insecure.

1. Feeding America (2010). Map the Meal Gap. Retrieved from: http://feedingamerica.org/hunger-in-america/hunger-studies/map-the-meal-gap.
2. WIC, Division of Public Health, WI Dept. of Health Services (2012). Retrieved from: www.dhs.wisconsin.gov/wic/WICPRO/data/foodsecurity.
3. Center on Hunger and Poverty, 2002. The Consequences of Hunger and Food Insecurity for Children: Evidence from recent Scientific Studies. Waltham, MA: The Heller School for Social Policy and Management, Brandeis, www.hungernwnc.org/about-hunger.
4. Seligman, Laria & Kushel. Food Insecurity is Associated with Chronic Disease among Low-Income NHANES Participant, Amer Soc of Nutrition, 2010.

* * *

The final two sentences wrap up the narrative on a positive, humanistic note: they reinforce the long-term aims to improve health and quality of life for children and families. That is to say, the development grant—securing funding to bring together a variety of community and academic partners and develop an evidence-based strategic plan—is a means to an end rather than an end in itself.

The RFP is silent about the extent to which references should be included in the letter of intent; preproposal contact suggested that it would be reasonable to include a few strategic end notes to show familiarity with the literature and document the frequency and severity of the food insecurity problem in the community.

STAGE TWO: FULL APPLICATION

Developing the Executive Summary.
The boldface heading at the top of the page identifies this as the executive summary and *not* the first page of the narrative. Boldface subheadings follow the prescribed sequence of the eight elements, reflecting past actions as well as future intentions. The executive summary also adheres to the length requirement and the RFP's expectation that it be a "stand alone description of the project."

Following the tip provided in the RFP, the executive summary was written *after* the narrative was completed. Indeed, approximately half of the executive summary is composed of sentences lifted verbatim from the narrative; this select repetition ensures an overall consistency in presentation style and tone.

EXECUTIVE SUMMARY: Changing Views of Hunger: One Community at a Time

Background: Located in Western WI, Eau Claire County (ECC) is home to 99,000 residents, including the city of EC with 65,000 residents, and small rural communities, dispersed across 638 square miles. The rural nature of the region and the large agricultural industry mask the reality that food insecurity exits. Although ECC's health is ranked 17th overall in the state, 8% of residents report limited access to healthy food, compared to 5% in WI, and significantly above the national benchmark of 1%. Food insecurity and the lack of access to affordable healthy foods contribute to increased risk of chronic disease. These risks are further compounded in ECC, because of its urban-rural mix and large geographic size, which pose additional challenges to identify strategies to increase access to healthy food for all low income residents. Challenging public health problems such as these require multiple approaches and an effective collaborative framework for planning public health interventions. To be effective in improving residents' health and wellness, communities need to move systems and public policy interventions forward to increase access to adequate and appropriate healthy food for all.

Project goal: The goals for this development project is to convene a broad-based Coalition to create and evidence-based strategic plan to increase access to healthy foods for low-income ECC residents.

Project description: To achieve this goal, the project team will build upon an existing community-academic partnership and recently completed community assessments. The project team will convene a Coalition, representing 8–10 community organizations from diverse private, public, non-profit, geographic and ethnic interests. A strategic plan will be developed that is grounded in evidence from the literature, local food security data, and recent focus group research, and aligned with health assessment plans from EC City, City-County Health Department, and Mayo Clinic Health System. Individuals who are food insecure will be engaged throughout the process to provide feedback on the plan as it progresses. As part of the Coalition's effort, an outreach-media plan will be developed to assist coalition members and their organizations to mobilize the community to implement the strategic plan.

The executive summary introduces three hot buttons that will be reiterated throughout the narrative. Key words referring to partnerships appear 20 times and include *coalition, partnership, collaborative,* and *team.* Phrases denoting evidence-based practices are incorporated six times and include *evidence-based, evidence, focus group research,* and *determinants of health.* Key phrases that address measurable outcomes and sustainability are presented six times and include *strategic plan, measurable outcomes,* and *continue the Coalition's work.*

Measurable outcomes:

1. Coalition members will create a community-driven, evidence-based strategic plan to increase access to healthy foods and reduce stigma associated with food insecurity.
2. Coalition members will demonstrate increased knowledge of broad determinant of health—social, economic, and physical environment—and their effect on access to healthy foods.
3. Coalition members will demonstrate readiness—knowledge, skills, and confidence—to mobilize the ECC community to implement the strategic plan.

The executive summary also foreshadows three distinctive features that will be integrated systematically into the narrative. Notice that grassroots engagement with the target population is touched upon in one sentence, "individuals who are food insecure will be engaged throughout the process . . . ." There is a singular reference to influencing policy in the narrative, "communities need to move systems and public policy interventions forward . . . ." And geographically and culturally diverse community partnerships are addressed twice: "the rural nature of the region" and "convene a Coalition, representing 8–10 community organizations from diverse private, public, non-profit, geographic and ethnic interests."

Funding request and time frame: 24-month, $50,000

Next steps: The Coalition's developed strategic plan will align city, county, and health system plans to streamline efforts dedicated to improving access to healthy food for low-income residents. This alignment provides direction for collaborative effort across multiple systems. To support implementation of the strategic plan, a search of relevant funding mechanisms will be conducted to continue the Coalition's work.

The RFP requires the executive summary to include a "brief statement about the impact of this project for residents of Wisconsin," which is slightly unusual because a directly comparable section is not required in the narrative. Rather, the RFP requires the narrative to define how project success will be measured and describe how the project aligns with the sponsor's mission and guiding principles, which are related to the impact of the project but not necessarily for "residents of Wisconsin." So in this instance, long-term impacts—increased access to adequate and appropriate healthy food—are operationally defined for the target population of Wisconsin residents in Eau Claire County.

The final paragraph speaks directly to the sponsor's review criteria, confirming alignment with the sponsor's mission and funding priorities as well as with the state health plan goals and focus areas.

Impact on WI residents: Through increased public awareness, education, and understanding, the Coalition will mobilize the ECC community to implement the evidence-based strategic plan. Ultimately, ECC residents will have increased access to adequate and appropriate healthy food. The ECC community will align resources to reduce health disparities and improve health outcomes through reduced chronic disease rates associated with inadequate healthy food intake.

Link to 2020 and WPP mission: The project aligns with the State Health Plan's "Nutrition and Healthy Foods" health focus by improving access to *adequate, appropriate and safe food and nutrition* for our state's neediest citizens. It meets the "Collaborative Partnerships" infrastructure focus by building an effective Coalition among organizations and identifying supportive resources. By increasing access to safe and healthy food the project advances the WPP's mission and meets the funding priorities to: "eliminate health disparities," "address the health needs of rural and urban populations," and "promote a healthy weight & good nutrition and reduce overweight & obesity." The project follow three of the Partnership's GuidingPrinciples:"Prevention,""Partnership,"and"Responsiveness."

* * *

NARRATIVE: Title: Changing Views of Hunger: One Community at a Time

1. Project Purpose, Need and Statement of the Problem

Purpose and Need for Project, Significance of Issue, and Evidence of Project Need: Located in Western WI, Eau Claire County (ECC) is home to 99,000 residents, including the city of EC with 65,000 residents, and small rural communities (2 villages and 13 townships), dispersed across 638 square miles.[1] The rural nature of the region and the large agricultural industry mask the reality that food insecurity exists. Food insecurity is defined as limited or uncertain availability of nutritionally adequate and safe foods or limited or uncertain ability to acquire foods in socially acceptable ways.[2] Although ECC's health is ranked 17th overall in the state, 8% of residents report limited access to healthy food, compared to 5% in WI and significantly above the national benchmark of 1%.[3] Limited access to healthy food is often linked to geographic and economic issues. Research indicates that people who live in a neighborhood with access to a grocery store are more likely to eat healthy.[4] Unfortunately, many low-income communities lack a grocery store and have a saturation of fast food and convenience stores. In ECC 54% of restaurants are designated as fast food, compared to 41% in the state, and again, significantly above the national average of 27%.[3] Food insecurity is often coupled with poverty as in ECC where the poverty rate is 15.1%, above the state average of 12% and the national average of 14.3%.[3] These numbers are disturbing, particularly in light of the growing body of evidence linking poverty and food insecurity to negative health outcomes.

STAGE TWO: FULL APPLICATION

Developing the Narrative. Because the Full Application recaps and expands the Letter of Interest, some overlap will exist in the information presented. Select redundancy is a proposal strength, particularly in this case because some reviewers will see only the Full Application.

In this paragraph, the opening sentence is repeated almost verbatim from the Letter of Interest. Though Eau Claire is the eighth largest city in the state, reviewers, many of whom typically are from Madison and Milwaukee, may not be familiar with the area. Thus, additional context is provided, describing its small, rural nature, which helps establish the mindset for understanding the magnitude and significance of the food insecurity problem.

Given that Wisconsin ranks in the upper one third of states in the nation in obesity, "food insecurity" may not be a top-of-mind concept for some reviewers. Accordingly, the term is defined in the third sentence of this paragraph. Subsequent sentences contextualize the problem, citing local, state, and national data to document its frequency, severity, and long-term implications.

The "Purpose and Need for Project, Significance of Issue, and Evidence of Project Need" is the longest section of the narrative, just over one third of the total length, and explains *why* the project is necessary, *where* the project is taking place, *who* is participating in the project, and *who will benefit* from targeted activities.

The Full Application builds on the foundation laid in the Letter of Interest. The association between adults in food-insecure households and increased risk of hypertension and diabetes was established in the Letter of Interest. The link to increased risk for obesity was a strategic addition in the Full Application, a direct appeal to sponsor priority areas.

Equally significant, the problem statement is framed as an endemic public health issue, aligning precisely with the sponsor's mission, vision, and guiding principles—its raison d'etre.

Eating nutritious foods is one of the major modifiable determinants of chronic diseases[5] yet residents need supportive environmental and policy interventions to optimize access to affordable healthy food choices. Poverty puts households at a much higher risk of food insecurity.[6] Due to the additional risk factors associated with poverty and food insecurity, low-income people are especially vulnerable to chronic diseases.[7–8] For the purpose of this project, low-income is defined as living below 185% of poverty. With this definition in mind, nearly one out of three ECC residents—30%—live below 185% of poverty[9] compared to 24% in WI.[10] Recent research reported an association between adults in food insecure households and a higher risk of hypertension and diabetes compared to those living in food secure households[8] and with other research linking food insecurity and increased risk for obesity.[7] These chronic health conditions further exacerbate low-income residents' ability to live healthy lives. To be effective in improving residents' health and wellness, communities need to become cognizant of the relationships between food insecurity, poverty and chronic diseases, and their long-term impacts on health disparities.

The lack of access to affordable healthy foods contribute to increased risk of chronic disease.[7–8] These risks are further compounded in ECC, because of its urban-rural mix and large geographic size, which pose additional challenges to identify strategies to increase access to healthy food for all low-income residents. Challenging public health problems such as these require multiple approaches and an effective collaborative framework for planning public health interventions. Coordinating the activities of multiple programs or agencies is therefore essential. The Healthiest WI 2020 Partnership Model will be utilized to address these complex issues through a collaborative leadership approach that is designed to effectively align systems for better health.[11]

This one-sentence paragraph serves as a transitional device, shifting emphasis in this section from anguishing over the problem to advocating for a solution. Equally significant, it effectively hits all three sponsor hot buttons: "the purpose of the proposed project is to convene a *Coalition* . . . to align resources and develop an *evidence-based* strategic *plan*."

In an effort to reduce health disparities and chronic disease rates, the purpose of the proposed project is to convene a Coalition of private, public, and non-profit community organizations to align resources and develop an evidence-based strategic plan for increasing access to healthy foods, in particular fresh fruits and vegetables, for low-income ECC residents.

The Coalition is needed to align and build upon recently completed community health assessments and plans and an existing community-academic partnership. The newly presented Health Chapter of the city's 5-year comprehensive plan includes policy 2.2 on improving access to healthy foods (see letter of support). The EC City-County Health Department's community health assessment, completed in February 2013, identified chronic disease as one of three core health priorities and noted the need for adequate, appropriate and safe food and nutrition as an element in that selection. Additionally, as part of the Mayo Clinic Health Systems community health needs assessment process, the NW WI Regional Board of Directors adopted a strategic plan in July that identified "prevention and management of chronic disease" and "adequate, appropriate and safe nutrition" as two of its three priorities. Combining resources to develop a unified strategic plan that addresses access to healthy food will align and unify community efforts, producing more effective results.

The RFP allowed optional letters of support to be included and a deliberate effort was made to be judicious in their use—too many letters can be distracting for reviewers. Note the strategic cross-reference in the narrative to "see letter of support," where additional details can be found about the City's interest in improving the built environment and willingness to participate in coalition activities as a technical resource aid. That is to say, this letter goes beyond project endorsement to detailing specific partner contributions. Reviewers will find this level of commitment much more compelling.

The project team, composed of members from Feed My People Food Bank, UW-Extension (UWEX) and UW-Eau Claire (UWEC) nursing department, has worked together as a community-academic partnership for two years and is therefore well positioned to lead this effort. Since completing a two-year focus group research study on food insecurity in ECC in 2013, they have pilot date and an increased understanding of food insecurity experiences among local residents. Key themes as to why people in ECC are hungry fell into two main areas: economic (assistance gaps and employment issues) and physical environment (especially issues related to transportation).

This paragraph appeals simultaneously to the hot button of partnerships and the review criteria of enhancing existing community and academic partnerships. The partnering institutions are identified by name for the first time in the narrative and their history of working together successfully on a related research project is summarized. The significance of this existing relationship cannot be overstated: it takes time to build a coalition. Through regular meetings, phone calls, and countless e-mails, partners crystalized their shared commitment to changing views of hunger and forged bonds of trust. Reviewers will recognize that this partnership development project is not a knee-jerk response to a funding opportunity; rather, it is a systematic extension of prior collaborative efforts to produce change in the community.

This paragraph is a testament to credibility. It documents that the academic and community partners have experience working together and achieving results. Their grassroots approach is driven by the needs of the community and the educational campaign relates directly to the proposed project. That is to say, the elements for success are already in place. Partners are poised to take the next logical step in their relationship and engage other like-minded organizations and individuals.

The impetus for the initial community-academic food insecurity study was a community round-table with media representatives. The round table was convened to identify what information was necessary to gather to increase community understanding of the extent and impact of food insecurity and to reduce judgment about individuals experiencing it. After the project team shared the focus group study results with these same media representatives, they have invested time and energy in developing and promoting an educational campaign for September 2013 Hunger Action month, entitled, "Turning the Tables on Food Hardship: A Community Partnership to Improve Access to Adequate, Healthy Food in the Chippewa Valley." This educational effort is limited in scope, with input primarily from the project team. It would therefore be greatly enhanced through the creation of a broader coalition that would utilize evidence-based practices to develop a strategic plan that moves beyond awareness to action.

This paragraph addresses the distinctive feature of grassroots engagement with the target population. In particular, the academic and community partner have direct experience securing feedback via focus groups from food insecure Hmong families. This detail was first introduced in the Letter of Interest. More significantly, in the Full Application, focus group feedback is used to predict future impacts, namely, "after two years of implementation of the strategic plan, 20% (6,000) of low-income residents will have increased access to healthy food." Said differently, this extrapolation from past to future behavior leverages the distinctive feature of grassroots engagement with the target population into a hot button for measurable outcomes and sustainability.

Target Population: The primary target population is low-income ECC residents (30,000) experiencing food insecurity.[9] This target population includes families with children under 18 years of age, elders, veterans, and those with disabilities. Another targeted group will be Hmong residents, who comprise the largest ethnic minority group in ECC.[1] Demographic and focus group data indicate that many Hmong families are low-income and experience food insecurity. Hmong focus group participants voiced unique needs that are not currently being met through standard food assistance services. We anticipate that after the first two years of implementation of the strategic plan, 20% (6,000) of low-income residents will have increased access to healthy food. This figure is based on the successful implementation of a recent effort that made it possible to use Food Share (food stamp) dollars at the farmers market. The Project's ultimate beneficiaries are low-income, food insecure Wisconsinites who are, by definition, at risk of hunger and inadequate nutrition due to limited access to obtain sufficient food for an active, healthy life. The Project also seeks to reduce residents' risk for chronic nutrition-related diseases by improving access to healthy foods, especially fresh fruits and vegetables.

Alignment with State Health Plan: The Project will advance the "Infrastructure" focus of the State Health Plan by developing an effective "Collaborative Partnership" between the project team, city/county health work groups, city planners, businesses, health care providers, individuals and groups that work with or represent low-income residents, and media outlets to improve community health. The Project Manager (UWEX) and the Community Partner (Feed My People) have extensive networks within the community that will assist in identifying Coalition members. UWEC will provide research-based healthcare expertise and best practices, as well as connections to healthcare providers and university resources. UWEX will expand on existing relationships with city and county workgroups ensuring involvement of low-income geographic and varied ethnic voices. Feed My People Food Bank's connections with non-profit food assistance agencies and healthcare providers will be utilized to increase Coalition membership. The project will advance the "Health" focus of the State Health Plan by addressing the "Nutrition and Healthy Foods" focus area. The project's main objectives will directly address the health objective of *access to adequate, appropriate and safe food and nutrition for all.* This objective will be met through the project team's effort to build a diverse Coalition, in conjunction with city and county health work-groups focused on improving food access through built environmental and policy interventions, and the creation of an evidence-based strategic plan. The project also aligns with Healthiest WI 2020 by contributing to improvements in health across the lifespan for children and families and reducing health disparities among those who are low-income.

Whereas the Letter of Interest, when appealing to the review criteria, contained only sweeping generalizations about the project being aligned with the state health plan, the Full Application provided concrete details to pinpoint the alignment. Specifically, the project advances the "Infrastructure" focus by developing an effective collaborative partnership and advances the "Health" focus by increasing access to "Nutrition and Healthy Foods."

2. Outcomes Related to the Guiding Principles

Guiding Principles: The proposed project is in alignment with the mission of the WPP. Through the creation of a diverse community Coalition and a community-driven, evidence-based strategic plan, the project will address the following WPP guiding principles:

1. *Prevention:* The strategic plan will identify specific evidence-based practices (EBP) to increase access to healthy food which will prevent the incidence of chronic disease among low-income ECC residents who are disproportionally affected by food insecurity. The strategic plan will also address factors associated with the built environment that create barriers to accessing healthy food for food insecure residents. Identifying structural factors within the environment and identifying specific strategies to address these such as initiating grocery stores in low-income neighborhoods or Supplemental Nutrition Assistance Program (SNAP) Health Bucks incentives at farmers markets will also prevent chronic conditions through increased access to healthy food.

In 707 words (18 percent of the total), this section speaks directly to the review criteria, confirming alignment with sponsor's guiding principles. The initial reaction to the RFP's guidance to "address at least one guiding principle" was that if commenting on one was "good," then more would be "better," even though it would limit narrative space available to dedicate to other sections. However, the pre-proposal contact confirmed that it was *not* necessary to relate to all six guiding principles; reviewers assign points based on how well the guiding principle(s) are addressed, not how many are addressed. Some past grant winners noted only one or two guiding principles.

2. *Partnerships*: The newly formed Coalition will build on existing partnerships between project team agencies to include stakeholders from local governments, health, business, social services, and organizations representing diverse racial/ethnic groups such as the Hmong Mutual Assistance Association (HMAA). Goals will be accomplished through strengthening existing community-academic partnerships while stimulating new initiatives through broader coalitions including the EC City-County Health Department and local health care

This first sentence is repeated verbatim from the Letter of Interest and helps to establish credibility of the partners in addressing this cause. A 20-year history of service to individuals and families in the community speaks to the hot buttons of measurable outcomes and sustainability as well the distinctive feature of grassroots engagement with the target population.

This paragraph introduces and makes cross-references to a second and third optional letter of support. These letters, just like the first one, summarize briefly a history of collaboration—a hot button—and commit to future contributions. For instance, the health department promises to make connections with various health councils and county boards, touching the distinctive feature of policy implications, and the Hmong Mutual Assistance Association pledges to "recruit individuals for the project Coalition as well as food insecure individuals to represent the Hmong families' views and perspectives in the area of food insecurity," touching on the distinctive feature of grassroots engagement with the target population.

systems. The expanded partnerships will collaboratively develop a plan that promotes the health of low-income families, educates the community, and ultimately reduces health disparities among low-income residents. Through increased public awareness, education, and understanding, the Coalition will mobilize ECC residents to implement the evidence-based strategic plan.

Partnerships: The Hunger Prevention Coalition for Eau Claire County (HPC), established in 1995, has long recognized the problem of food insecurity and has been involved in efforts to reduce hunger. Since HPC focuses primarily on serving individuals and families and providing direct access to food, their efforts toward changing the built environment or addressing broad determinants of health have been very limited. Recently however, a sub-committee of HPC partnered with UW-Eau Claire nursing faculty (2011–2013) to conduct a focus group study to hear the voices of food insecure parents and agency staff who serve them. This team, led by HPC members from Feed My People Food Bank and ECC UW-Extension Nutrition Education Program and academic partner, UW-Eau Claire Department of Nursing, will continue to collaborate on the proposed project with the goal of connecting the existing team with other community groups concerned about hunger and community wellness.

EC City recently completed a Health Chapter as part of their comprehensive five year plan and specifically identified access to fresh food as a component of the built environment (see letter of support). EC City-County Health Department (ECCCHD) also completed its community assessment and identified chronic disease as one of three key areas to address during the next 5 years (see letter of support). The Chronic Disease Prevention Action Team, which includes representative from hospitals, the ECCCHD, and community representatives, will lead the effort in addressing this key health concern. Representatives from these government, non-profit, and community entities will be invited to be part of the Coalition; they will provide depth of understanding and assistance in identifying ways to align these existing plans to create an effective system for increasing access to healthy food for low-income residents. Feed My People team member, Emily Moore, is a Mayo Clinic Health Systems Board Member. Her relationships create a foundation for the development of further partnerships between Mayo Clinic and the Coalition. The team also has strong relationships with the Hmong community, in particular through HMAA. UWEX team member, Nancy Coffey, serves on the HMAA Board of Directors and has collaborated with the HMAA on numerous educational efforts. A partner from HMAA will be a key stakeholder for the proposed project (see letter of support). These existing relationships and those newly formed through the coalition development process will strengthen ECC overall and provide a foundation for taking action to reduce community stigma, increase ECC's awareness of community food insecurity, and the need for increased access to healthy food for all residents.

3. *Responsiveness*: By building a strong Coalition of a broad spectrum of community organizations already invested in addressing access to

healthy foods and prevention of chronic disease, this project will accelerate existing initiatives with the greatest potential to improve population health.

3. Goals, Objectives and Outcomes

Goals: The goal for this development project is to convene a broad-based Coalition to create an evidence-based strategic plan to increase access to healthy foods for low-income ECC residents.

Objectives:

1. Complete literature review of relevant evidence-based practices (EBPs)
2. Increase size (from 3 to 10) and organization representation (from 3 to 8) of Coalition membership
3. Evaluate Coalition cohesion & motivation to act (readiness measures).
4. Complete strategic and outreach-media plans with next steps identified.
5. Evaluate Coalition members regarding the collaborative process (satisfaction measures)
6. Collect and integrate feedback from food insecure community members regarding strategic plan
7. Disseminate plan to key stakeholders
8. Complete search for possible funding mechanisms to support implementation of strategic plan

The "Goals, Objectives and Outcomes" uses 553 words (14 percent of the total) to describe *what* the project is going to do and *how* objectives will be accomplished.

The goal statement evolved slightly from the Letter of Interest to the Full Application, narrowing its focus and becoming more succinct—contracting from 41 words to 28 words. Nevertheless, it still touched on all three hot buttons: "The goal for this development project is to convene a broad-based *Coalition* to create an *evidence-based* strategic *plan* to increase access to healthy foods for low-income ECC residents."

The objectives are expressed in specific and measurable terms, detailing exactly what will occur during the course of the project. Not surprisingly, the objectives touch on all three hot buttons. Objective 1 relates to evidence-based practice, Objectives 2–3 and 5–7 relate to partners, and Objectives 4 and 8 relate to measurable outcomes and sustainability.

Of note, while it might be unusual to include an objective to "complete literature review" in an implementation grant—reviewers would expect that to have been completed already—it is appropriate for a development grant that aims to "form sustainable relationships to identify ways they can work together to address public health issues."

As a writing tip in the RFP suggested, this section of the narrative is consistent with the work plan and logic model. In fact, the goals and objectives are repeated verbatim in the work plan and the outcomes are repeated verbatim in the logic model. Reviewers expect to see uniformity across documents in the complete grant application.

The first sentence of this paragraph is identical to a sentence in the Letter of Interest and confirms the evidence-based practices—a hot button—that will be used. More significantly, the second sentence, which is unique to the Full Application, justifies the selection of these specific practices; it clarifies for reviewers why these approaches were chosen and not some other alternatives. The third sentence goes a step further to indicate exactly which elements of a national model will be most valuable to this project.

More broadly, nearly half of the sentences in this paragraph are very similar or identical to ones in the Letter of Interest. This select repetition reflects a consistency in development of goals, objectives, and outcomes and, at the same time, an added depth on how they will be attained.

Outcomes:

1. Coalition members will create a community-driven, evidence-based strategic plan to increase access to healthy foods and reduce stigma associated with food insecurity.
2. Coalition members will demonstrate increased knowledge of broad determinants of health—social, economic, and physical environment—and their effect on access to healthy foods.
3. Coalition members will demonstrate readiness—knowledge, skills, and confidence—to mobilize the ECC community to implement the strategic plan.

The project team is well positioned to move forward utilizing RWJF's Roadmap to Health Action Model[3], the WI What Works database, and the socio-ecological model for improving health.[12] These frameworks were selected for their evidence-based approaches, relevancy to Wisconsin, and attention to the broad determinants of health, in particular social, environmental, and economic factors. The key components of the RWJF model that are relevant to the proposed project include: Working Together, Assessing Needs and Resources, and Communication. The existing community-academic partnership provides a solid foundation from which to recruit key stakeholders into a broader coalition. For example, the director of Feed My People is a member of the board from the largest health system in the region. Her connections will assist with recruitment of stakeholders affiliated with the medical community. The UWEC and UWEX partners have university and community-wide connections that will lead efforts to identify evidence-based strategies for educating and mobilizing the newly formed Coalition and the broader community. Because of the completed focus group study with ECC food insecure participants, the project team already has connections with and data from the target population. For example, since focus group participants' identified transportation and food deserts as key barriers to accessing healthy food, stakeholders with knowledge of the built environment will be recruited to lead efforts to address these infrastructure issues. Needs and resources to educate the broader community about hunger will also be assessed. Food insecure participants identified the internet as a source of information and potential resource; parallel evidence from the What Works database indicates that social media and technology are effective communication tools. Therefore connecting the needs with the resources related to social media and technology will be essential. What Works evidence also indicates that farmers markets increase availability of fresh fruits and vegetables yet many focus group participants were unaware that the EC Downtown Farmers Market accepts Food Share. This is another area that supports the importance of media representatives as partners in this communication effort. The project team will continue to integrate focus group data into planning and development and will also recruit low-income residents experiencing food insecurity to participate directly in the Coalition and/or provide feedback on the strategic plan.

4. Work Plan (see separate document)

We will add a community organizer to the project team to assist the project manager, including recruitment of coalition members and residents experiencing food insecurity, facilitation of coalition meetings, and day-to-day operations of the project. The community organizer will have existing relationships within the ECC community and with the target population.

The "Work Plan" identifies *when* specific activities will occur and *who* will be responsible for their completion.

In a strategic use of limited narrative space, the description of the work plan is deliberately short, one paragraph with 51 words in two sentences, which represents 1 percent of the total length. The details of the work plan are in a separate document that is not part of the narrative page limitations. Similarly, the community organizer is introduced here as a new hire and key roles and responsibilities are outlined in a separate required document that does not count against narrative page limitations.

5. Evaluation, Dissemination and Sustainability Plans (For Logic Model see separate document)

Evaluation: Project success will be measured based on achievement of the previously described outcomes. Formative and summative evaluation data will be collected primarily by the academic partner to ensure outcomes are achieved. The existing partnership, representing three (3) organizations, will be expanded to create a broader community Coalition, composed of 10–12 additional representatives from relevant organizations.

The academic partner will develop, administer, and analyze pre and post-test surveys to evaluate charges in Coalition members knowledge regarding broad determinants of health, food insecurity, and associated stigma as well as their readiness to mobilize the ECC community (see work plan for survey timeline) Surveys will be designed based on existing instruments and revised to meet local needs. Since active engagement is the process is essential for long-term sustainability, Coalition members' satisfaction with the process itself will also be evaluated through meeting check-ins and minutes of a group discussion at the conclusion of the project. Meeting minutes will also document attendance, which is another means to monitor engagement in the process. The project team's successful completion of the food insecurity focus group study demonstrates our ability to collaborate and meet these project goals.

In 554 words (14 percent of the total), the "Evaluation, Dissemination and Sustainability Plans" section answers *how* project effectiveness will be assessed.

Most of the second paragraph is dedicated to explaining who will be responsible for developing survey tools, administering data collection procedures, and analyzing results to determine Coalition member satisfaction and community readiness to act on proposed changes. The final sentence, however, is a testimony to partner credibility. In essence it says, "We've done work successfully like this before, and we can do it again."

Dissemination: The evidence-based literature review, Coalition strategic plan, and funding priorities will be disseminated to Coalition members who will in turn share the developed documents with their respective organizations. In conjunction with the Coalition, the project team will create a dissemination plan that can be implemented across various member organizations. The continuing involvement of the media in the Coalition will provide a mechanism for communicating with the broader community on a regular basis. The existing partnership between the project team and local media representatives will be expanded through the Coalition with resulting wider community exposure of the Coalition's efforts and increased readiness to act. The project team also has experience presenting regionally and state wide including the 2013 Wisconsin Public Health Association Annual Meeting and the 2013 Wisconsin Prevention Conference. A manuscript has been prepared for submission to Journal of Extension, reporting results of the ECC food insecurity study. Through these venues, the team has gained much experience and is well prepared to continue dissemination activities in relation to the proposed project.

Given the nature of the community-academic partnership, dissemination strategies reflect the best of both worlds. Community partners have established networks to communicate via print and electronic media. Academic partners have experience presenting at statewide conferences and publishing in peer-reviewed journals. This combination of dissemination strategies will ensure project results have a broad reach.

The final sentence of this paragraph appeals to the distinctive feature of policy implications. It is a natural segue to the next section on sustainability. That is to say, when information is widely disseminated, it can lead to changes in policy, which would extend the project impact long after the granting period.

This entire paragraph is a hot button for measurable outcomes and sustainability. In this instance, project continuation is rooted in structural sustainability. The first two sentences describe how the new Coalition will expand existing coalitions and partnerships. The final two sentences describe how the strategic plan will coordinate and align current health plans. In short, building on present infrastructure and processes increases the likelihood for continued action and impacts beyond the granting period.

"Capacity and Experience of Partners and Key Staff" uses 640 words (16 percent of the total) to articulate *who* is participating in the project and *who* is responsible for project activities.

The first two paragraphs in this section establish organizational credibility. The opening sentences establish the uniqueness of the applicant organization to lead the proposed project: it is one of three food banks in Wisconsin and is the only one outside of the state's two largest cities, Milwaukee and Madison. Even reviewers who are unfamiliar with Eau Claire will take note of the applicant organization's 30-year history, 14-county service area, six million pounds of food annual distribution, and extensive local, regional, and national networks.

UWEX state specialists will be consulted to provide support with food security policy development, guiding the translation of proposal products into effective policies that align with ECC systems and culminate in the achievement of better health for all county residents.

Sustainability: The intent of the development grant is to create a Coalition that is community-driven, invested, and mobilized to increase access to health food for ECC low-income residents. The existence of a Coalition dedicated to this particular area of health will provide an avenue for aligning existing systems and health plans and concentrating partnership efforts towards making healthy foods available for all with the ultimate goals of reducing health outcome disparities. Building on existing health plans and coordinating with established, long-term entities such as Healthy Communities Council (health department committee) and EC City Planning, fosters sustainability and increases the likelihood for continued action and long term success. The establishment of an outreach-media plan will support the implementation of the strategic plan by reducing community associated with food insecurity and increasing community commitment to improving the entrenched public health problems of food insecurity and access to healthy food for all ECC low-income residents.

6. Capacity and Experience of Partners and Key Staff

Applicant Organization: Feed My People (FMP) is one of three Feeding America food banks located in Wisconsin. The other two are Second Harvest Food Bank in Southern Wisconsin in Madison and Feeding America Eastern Wisconsin, in Milwaukee. FMP's mission is to eliminate hunger in west central Wisconsin. It does this by improving accessibility to food for low-income individuals and empowering the more than 100 food assistance programs it works with to build their capacity. In ECC, FMP serves 23 food pantries, shelters, and other nonprofit agencies offering food assistance. It also runs a weekend backpack meal program, providing over 1,500 elementary and Head Start children with food for the weekend. FMP distributes over 6 million pounds of food annually within a 14 county area. It has 11 paid staff members. Thousands of individuals volunteer each year, providing more hours than 5 full-time staff members.

FMP has been a key voice for hunger relief in Eau Claire for 30 years. The organization has a strong relationship with the media and appears about once per month in TV, radio and/or newspaper stories. FMP communicates through its quarterly newsletter (circulation 5,400), monthly e-Newsletter, and daily Facebook page. It receives over 6000 unduplicated visits (approx. 200,000 hits) on its website each month. FMP works in collaboration with national, regional and local partners to accomplish its mission. In addition to the three food banks in WI, there are three food banks in MN (Duluth, St. Paul, and Rochester) that serve programs in nine WI border counties. Together these six food banks form the Wisconsin Association of Feeding America Food Banks. FMP is also part of the MN/ND/Western WI Cluster of food banks. EMP's director, Emily Moore, serves as an officer of the WI Association and is an active member of the Cluster. These associations strengthen FMP's capacity, resources, connections and opportunities for collaborative innovation.

FMP manages gross receipts valued at over $10 million annually, including small grant management. Emily has served as the executive director for 9 years. During her tenure, FMP has increased its distribution by more than 10 times and its staff size has quadrupled. Additionally, she managed a successful capital campaign raising sufficient funds to purchase a facility three times the capacity of the previous rented one, debt-free. Emily is an active member of the ECC Hunger Prevention Coalition and will serve as a lead collaborator on this project.

The third paragraph in this section establishes the individual credibility of the project director. With nine years' experience as executive director, including managing $10 million in gross receipts annually and increasing distribution 10-fold in less than a decade, the project director is well suited to lead this initiative.

Collaborating Organizations: The Academic Partner is the University of Wisconsin-Eau Claire, represented by Dr. Mary Canales, Professor, Department of Nursing. Dr. Canales has been a member of the project team since 2011 and continues to collaborate on disseminating results from the food insecurity study and establishing the local media educational campaign, "Turning the Table on Food Hardship." As a co-investigator and evaluator on federally-funded research projects with under-represented groups since 2000, she has gained expertise in qualitative research, EBP literature reviews, and evaluation. The skills and experiences gained through numerous community-based projects will be employed throughout the proposed project.

As part of the eligibility criteria in the RFP, the applicant organization is required to work with an academic partner. This paragraph identifies the partnering institution and cites the credentials of the collaborator. In addition to a history of working with the project director on a food insecurity study, the academic partner has expertise in research, evaluation, and evidence-based practice literature reviews—a hot button. This conforms to the expectation stated in the RFP that academic partners are "to be actively engaged in the project from serving in an advisory or consulting role to advising on evaluation methods and design, to conducting community engaged research."

The Project Manager will be Nancy Coffey, UWEX Nutrition Education Program Coordinator, Eau Claire County. Nancy's work focuses on coordination of the Wisconsin Nutrition Education Program, assisting food stamp and food stamp-eligible county resides improve their food security, food safety and dietary quality. Nancy also is chair of the Hunger Prevention Coalition. The HPC is a community collaboration that works to reduce hunger and improve nutrition and enhance quality of life for residents. Nancy collaborates with over 30 community agencies in her work and has been involved in many community projects as a member or facilitator; she has experience managing programs and budgets. Nancy was one of the key proponents for the initial focus group study on food insecurity in ECC and will continue to be a member of the project team through the project manager role. (See roles and responsibilities for more detail.)

This final paragraph identifies an additional collaborative partner who will be responsible for managing the project. The partner has direct experience working with the target population and has vast networks with organizations that address hunger in the community. Note the final sentence in the paragraph contains a cross-reference to a separate required document that outlines roles and responsibilities of both community and academic partners. This parenthetical comment was a strategic device to overcome limits in narrative space.

References

1. United States Census Bureau (2013). *State and County Quick Facts-Wisconsin*. Washington, D.C.: Department of Commerce. Accessed online at: http://quickfacts.census.gov/qfd/states/55000.html
2. Life Science Research Office (1990). Core indicators of nutritional state for difficult-to-sample populations. *Journal of Nutrition*, 120 (supplement 11), 1559–1600.
3. Robert Wood Johnson Foundation (2013). *County Health Rankings and Roadmaps-Wisconsin*. Accessed online at: http://www.countyhealthrankings.org/app/wisconsin/2013/rankings/outcomes/overall/by-rank
4. Morland, K., Wing, S., Diez Roux, A. (2012). The contextual effect of the local food environment on residents' diets: The atherosclerosis risk in communities study. *American Journal of Public Health*, Nov. 2002, p. 92.

The RFP is clear that "references are not included in the page limit," so the list of citations is much more comprehensive than was included in the Letter of Interest. The literature cited is very current, which lends credibility to the community and academic partners being familiar with the most up-to-date evidence-based practices. The references include entries for the state health plan, which is a review criterion, and for the What Works database, which applicants are "strongly encouraged to use." There are also entries for a dominant national model on making community health change, the Robert Wood Johnson Foundation County Health Rankings and Roadmaps, and for policy and environmental approaches to improving health, which speak to a distinctive feature.

5. Story, M., Kaphingst, K., Robinson-O'Brien, R. & Glanz, K. (2008). Creating healthy food and eating environments: Policy and environmental approaches. *Annual Review of Public Health*, 29, 253–72.
6. Curtis, K. & Bartfield, J. (2011). Poverty and Food Insecurity in Wisconsin and Eau Claire County, Board of Regents of the University of Wisconsin System. Accessed online at: http://apl.wisc.edu/pfs_profiles/Eau_Claire_Poverty_and_Food_Insecurity.pdf
7. Food Research and Action Center (FRAC) (2010). *Why low income and food insecure people are vulnerable to overweight and obesity*. Washington, D.C.: Author. Accessed online at: http://frac.org/initiatives/hunger-and-obesity/why-are-low-income-and-food-insecure-people-vulnerable-to-obesity
8. Seligman, H. et al. (2010). Food insecurity is associated with chronic disease among low-income NHANES participants. *Journal of Nutrition*. 140, 304–310.
9. US Census Bureau. (2011). *American fact finder: American Community Survey one year estimates*. Washington, D.C.: Department of Commerce. Accessed online at: http://factfinder2.census.gov/faces/tableservices/jsf/pages/productview.xhtml?src=bkmk
10. Row, K. (2008). *Hunger close to home*. Cooperative Extension Publishing: Madison, WI. Accessed online at: http://www.uwex.edu/ces/flp/demographics/hunger/pdfs/brown.pdf
11. Department of Health Services (2010). *Healthiest Wisconsin 2020: Everyone living better, longer*. Accessed online at: http://www.dhs.wisconsin.gov/hw2020/
12. University of Wisconsin Population Health Institute and the School of Medicine and Public Health (2010). *What works for health: Policies and programs to improve Wisconsin's health*. Madison, WI: The Board of Regents of the University of Wisconsin System. Accessed online at: http://whatworksforhealth.wisc.edu/

* * *

Changing Views of Hunger: One Community at a Time

Project Goal Statement: Convene a broad-based Coalition to create an evidence-based strategic plan to increase access to healthy foods for low-income Eau Claire County (ECC) residents

Objectives: By May 2016:

1. Complete literature review of relevant evidence-based practices (EBPs)
2. Increase size (from 3 to 10) and representation (from 3 to 8) of Coalition membership
3. Evaluation Coalition cohesion & motivation to act (readiness measures)
4. Complete strategic and outreach-media plans with next steps identified
5. Evaluation Coalition members regarding the collaborative processes (satisfaction measures)
6. Collect and integrate feedback from food insecure community members regarding strategic plan
7. Disseminate plan to key stakeholders
8. Complete search for possible funding mechanisms to support implementation of strategic plan

Outcome measures:

1. Coalition members will create a community-driven, evidence-based strategic plan to increase access to healthy foods and reduce stigma associated with food insecurity
2. Coalition members will demonstrate increased knowledge of broad determinants of health—social, economic and physical environment—and their effect on access to healthy foods
3. Coalition members will demonstrate readiness—knowledge, skills and confidence—to mobilize the ECC community to implement the strategic plan

STAGE TWO: FULL APPLICATION

Developing the Work Plan. The work plan is presented as a stand-alone document; whether quickly skimming or critically reading the work plan, reviewers can understand what the entire project is all about. The project goal, eight objectives, and three outcome measures are repeated verbatim from the Full Application.

The real value of the work plan rests in the table that delineates activities, timeframes, responsible personnel, and anticipated outcomes. Phrases for key activities begin with action verbs and touch on all three hot buttons: "recruit coalition members" addresses partnerships; "conduct literature review of EBP" addresses evidence-based practices; and "conduct search for funding sources" addresses measurable outcomes and sustainability. Further, a simple document design feature, explicitly noting in italics *"Evaluation activity:"* calls extra attention to hot button activities related to measuring outcomes.

Timeframes are expressed in months rather than calendar dates, which allows a certain flexibility in case the project start date changes. Using small units of time—one, two, or three months—is more meaningful to reviewers than saying activities are "ongoing" for the whole grant period.

ACTIVITY	TIMEFRAME	RESPONSIBLE PERSON	ANTICIPATED OUTCOME
Initial Project team meeting to review goals, objectives and plan	Month 1	Project team (Project manager, Academic Partner, Community Partner and Community Organizer)	Ensure goals & objectives of grant are clear to all parties and develop next steps for moving forward; review budget & timeline
Monthly project team meetings during grant period	Grant cycle	Project manager/ Project team	Review objectives to ensure on track. Provide forum for ongoing review of evaluation tools.
Conduct literature review of EBP related to grant objectives	Months 1–3	Academic Partner	Completed review of evidence based community practices relevant to grant activities
Project team discussions to incorporate best practices for preparing and mobilizing coalitions	Month 4–6	Project manager/ Project team	Ensures all Project team members are up to date regarding the most current evidence; provides time to review completed literature review and determine plan for educating and mobilizing the Coalition membership
Evaluation activity: Develop pre-survey form to assess Coalition members' knowledge about broad determinants of health, their relationship to food insecurity, local food insecurity data & stigma: Surveys completed prior to Coalition meeting 1 and 4	Month 4	Academic partner	Process for collecting formative evaluation data identified & tool developed
Evaluation activity: Identify process that will be used for measuring Coalition ongoing satisfaction	Month 5	Academic partner	Project team will agree on a method that will address each Coalition member's satisfaction and sense of being heard. Tool will be used at end of each meeting so that adjustments can be made prior to the next meeting.
Recruit Coalition members from variety of organizations	Months 2–6	Project team	Creation of Coalition that represents inclusive community interests (racial/ethnic, rural/urban)
Recruit 2–4 residents who are food insecure to participate in Coalition and/or provide insight throughout the process	Months 2–6	Project team	Ensure perspectives of targeted group are involved in the Coalition; recognizes that depending on life circumstances, ability to be involved will vary.

Convene Coalition for initial meeting	Month 6	Community Organizer	Introductions, review of grant activities and outcomes, and begin process to develop action plan.
Monthly Coalition meetings	Months 7–9	Community Organizer	During each meeting, specific steps taken towards developing action plan including review literature report, existing EC city & county data, & completed local research studies. Each meeting will also include targeted education to increase coalition member's knowledge of relationship between broad determinants of health and their local impact.
Evaluation activity: Compile survey data from Coalition meetings; identify areas where further education is needed.	Months 9–10	Community Organizer	Formative evaluation data collected to identify areas for further education.
Complete initial draft of action plan	Month 10	Community Organizer	First draft of action plan.
Recruit & engage 6–10 individuals who are food insecure to review initial draft & provide feedback.	Months 9–11	Project team	Gain input from those directly affected by food insecurity. Based on previous research study recognizes the need for additional recruitment time to gain trust and encourage participation.
Evaluation activity: Compile notes and feedback from food insecurity group	Month 12	Academic partner	Summary of feedback to share w/ Coalition members.
Share summary of food insecurity feedback w/ Coalition members, revise action plan accordingly.	Month 13–15	Project Manager/ Coalition sub-committee	Revised action plan that incorporates views of those directly affected by food insecurity.
Develop community outreach-media pal incorporated existing educational campaign; form outreach-media sub-committee to facilitate activities	Month 13–15	Project Manager/ Coalition sub-committee	Formation of sub-committee to develop community outreach-media plan; will include local media representative
Evaluation activity: Facilitate group dialogue among Coalition members to evaluate cohesion, knowledge gained, & confidence to prepare community for action plan	Month 15	Academic partner	Summative evaluation to assess Coalition process & knowledge gained. Addresses satisfaction & knowledge measures. Explore strategies to improve community readiness around food security issues.

Conduct search for funding sources to support implementation of action plan & compile results	Month 15–18	Academic partner	Identification of potential sources of funding to move action plan forward
Evaluation activity: Develop post-survey to measure Coalition members' changes in knowledge, attitudes & beliefs (KAB) regarding broad determinants of health, food insecurity, & stigma	Month 18	Academic partner	Provides tool for formative evaluation of KAB
Celebrate final action and outreach-media plans w/ Coalition members.	Month 19	Community Organizer	Recognizes Coalition members' efforts with completed final products.
Discuss dissemination plan including key stakeholders & funding sources, & distribute post-survey to members	Month 19	Community Organizer	Dissemination plan for reaching key stakeholders identified & funding sources prioritized
Evaluation activity: Post-survey results tabulated, summarizes, & compared to formative data previously collected	Month 19–20	Academic partner	Formative and Summative evaluation data compiled.
Initiate community outreach-media plan	Month 20–22	Coalition outreach sub-committee/ Community Organizer	Based on Coalition direction, outreach-media subcommittee takes initial action.
Finalize dissemination plan based on input	Month 20–22	Coalition outreach sub-committee/ Community Organizer	Project team has dissemination plan to follow
Disseminate action plan throughout community based on Coalition recommendations	Month 20–22	Project team	Disseminate outcome of work to key stakeholders in the broader community & begin to foster community readiness for change.
Disseminate project results including action plan to broader community including regional and state audiences	Month 22–24	Project team	Disseminate outcome of work to regional and statewide audiences to share results especially best practices learned
Compile final report for grantor	Month 22–24	Community partner/ Project team	Summative report of all grant activities completed.

* * *

Program: Changing Views of Hunger: One Community at a Time Logic Model

Situation: Limited access to adequate and nutritious food for low income residents in Eau Claire County

Inputs	Outputs		Outcomes — Impact		
	Activities	*Participation*	*Short*	*Medium*	*Long*
Existing members of Hunger Prevention Coalition of Eau Claire County (ECC)	Conduct literature review of relevant food security evidence based practices (EBP)	Representatives from EC City & County government including planning and health departments	Coalition members will demonstrate increased knowledge of broad determinants of health—social, economic & physical environment—and their effect on access to healthy foods	Coalition members and their organizations will mobilize community and implement the strategic plan	Community members will demonstrate reduced stigma towards food insecure residents
			↓	↓	↓
Feed My People staff time and networking capabilities	Recruit 10–12 Coalition representatives from 8–10 sectors of community	Representatives from businesses that employ large numbers of low-income individuals	Coalition members will create a community-driven evidence-based strategic plan to increase access to healthy foods & reduce stigma associated with food insecurity	Through the Coalition's community awareness campaign, ECC residents and community leaders will demonstrate increased understanding of the need to increase access to healthy food for low income residents	Local government, businesses, medical community, media, non-profits & community members will move system & public policy interventions forward to increase access to adequate and appropriate healthy food for all.
UW-Extension staff time facilitating & networking capabilities	Convene Coalition - provide education & resources related to food insecurity & community readiness	Representatives from local media including radio, TV & print			

STAGE TWO: FULL APPLICATION

Developing the Logic Model. The logic model is presented as a stand-alone document and follows the template provided in the RFP. All three hot buttons are addressed in the description of output activities and short-term outcomes. For instance:

"Conduct literature review of relevant food security evidence based practices" and "Coalition members will demonstrate increased knowledge of broad determinants of health" relate to the hot button of evidence-based practice.

"Recruit 10–12 Coalition representatives" and "Coalition members will demonstrate readiness . . . to mobilize ECC community" relate to the hot button of partnerships.

"Seek funds to support strategic plan, implementation & long term sustainability" and "Coalition members will create a community-driven evidenced-bases strategic plan" relate to the hot button of measurable outcomes and sustainability.

UW-Eau Claire academic partner qualitative research & evaluation skills Community Partner, Extension & university space for meetings & research Existing relationships with media representatives Existing relationships with individuals who are food insecure Funding for strategic plan coordination and implementation	Coalition develops EBP strategic action plan including existing data: • local food security statistics • local focus group research • health assessment & plans from: -EC City-Co Health Dept -EC City Planning -Mayo Clinic Health System Survey coalition members throughout project to evaluate process effectiveness Identify & engage diverse pool of food insecure individuals to provide feedback on proposed action plan Disseminate plan progress to key stakeholders Seek funds to support strategic plan implementation & long term sustainability	Representatives from local medical community including Mayo Clinic Health System, Marshfield Clinic or Sacred Heart Hospital Representatives from the Hmong Mutual Assistance Association, & area veteran groups 6–10 individuals who are food insecure & are of diverse identities (racial, ethnic, age, urban, & rural)	↓ Coalition members will demonstrate readiness—knowledge, skills & confidence—to mobilize ECC community to implement the strategic plan	Communication methods could include outreach & education through: • TV, radio and print media • Public speaking in the community • Community awareness events • Social media	**Long Term Social & Economic Impact** County food insecure residents will have: Increased access to adequate and appropriate healthy food for all ECC Community will: Align resources to reduce health disparities Improve health outcomes through reduced chronic disease rates associated with inadequate nutritious food intake. Everybody living better and longer.

Assumptions	External Factors
Through continuing partnership, media will be a thread for reporting coalition progress to better engage the entire community	Limited time for collaborative work
Coalitions composed of broad community representation are essential for improving long-term public health problems such as food insecurity	Negative societal and political attitudes towards people in need
Poverty, food security and health are intricately related	Recent recession that has increased need for food while further stressing agencies that provide it
Health outcomes for individuals are heavily influenced by broad determinates including social, economic, & physical environment	

* * *

All three distinctive features are addressed as well. Under outputs-participation, "6–10 individuals who are food insecure" addresses the distinctive feature of grassroots engagement with the target population and "Representatives from the Hmong Mutual Assistance Association" addresses the distinctive feature of geographically and culturally diverse community partnerships. Under outcomes-long, "Local government, businesses, medical community, media, non-profits & community members will move system & public policy interventions forward" addresses the distinctive feature of policy implications.

Also note that the last entry under long-term outcomes gives a nod to a sponsor review criterion: the project aligns directly with the state health plan "Healthiest Wisconsin 2020: Everyone Living Better, Longer" in the health focus area of "Adequate, appropriate, and safe food and nutrition."

STAGE TWO: FULL APPLICATION

Developing Roles and Responsibilities.
"Roles and Responsibilities" describes exactly *who* will be participating in the project and *who* will be responsible for project activities.

The first three paragraphs highlight the responsibilities for existing key project staff. The fourth paragraph describes the duties of a new hire, the community organizer. Though the RFP requested these details in the narrative, space limitations necessitated that they be summarized in the narrative and presented in full in a required appendix document. Bulleted items address all three hot buttons.

Roles and Responsibilities

Community Partner, Emily Moore, Feed My People Food Bank

- Serve as fiscal manager
- Provide leadership through participation on Project Team
- Utilize networks to identify and recruit Coalition members and low-income participant advisors
- Engage in Coalition meetings and process
- Disseminate Coalition progress through website, Facebook, e-Newsletter, newsletter
- Utilize existing positive relationship with media

Academic Partner, Mary Canales, University of Wisconsin-Eau Claire

- Complete evidence-based practice literature review related to food insecurity and broad determinants of health, community readiness and mobilization, and best practices for reducing stigma associated with food insecurity
- Assist with recruitment of Coalition members
- Attend Coalition meetings, compile minutes, and review as part of ongoing evaluation process
- Prepare surveys to evaluate changes in knowledge among Coalition members related to food insecurity, stigma, and broad determinants of health and readiness to engage the community to implement the strategic plan
- Complete all evaluation activities associated with the project
- Assist with development of strategic plan to increase presentations, manuscript development
- Complete search of funding sources to share with Coalition and project team
- Work with team to identify specific funding avenues to move forward with EB strategic plan

Program Manager, Nancy Coffey, Eau Claire County UW-Extension Wisconsin Nutrition Education Program

- Overall project management to assure that goals, objectives and outcomes are met
- Utilize networks to identify and recruit Coalition members and food insecure residents involved directly in the Coalition and as well as those providing feedback on the Coalition plan
- Oversight of community organizer to meet work plan activities and outcomes
- Engage in Coalition meetings and process
- Disseminate Coalition progress through website and Facebook
- Utilize existing positive relationship with media to disseminate project outcomes
- Work with team to disseminate project action plan to stakeholders
- Work with team to write final project report for grantor

Community Organizer, TBD

- Carry out day to day management of the project under direction of project manager
- Assist with recruitment of and building relationships with Coalition members
- Prepare agenda, food, and any other needs associated with Coalition meetings
- Submit all bills and make sure within budget under direction of Community partner
- Facilitate Coalition meetings to create strategic action plan
- Assist with recruitment of and building relationships with low-income, food insecure residents; facilitate discussions with this target population and obtain feedback on draft plans
- Develop tracking system to monitor Coalition membership and engagement in the process
- Assist with evaluation through regular updates of tracking systems
- Document Coalition meetings and strategic plan progress, Coalition satisfaction evaluations and feedback of proposed strategic plan from low-income, food insecure residents
- Coordinate community outreach-media plan with Coalition outreach sub-committee
- Work with team to write final report for grantor

* * *

Budget

Year	Expense Category	Salary	Fringe Benefits	Travel	Equipment	Supplies	Consultants & Contracts	Other Costs	Total Budget
1 (12 mo)	Paid through UW	$7,168	$2,939	$0	$0	$0	$0	$0	$10,106
	Paid through Org	$0	$0	$473	$0	$600	$12,765	$0	$13,838
2 (12 mo)	Paid through UW	$7,454	$3,056	$0	$0	$0	$0	$0	$10,510
	Paid through Org	$0	$0	$1,871	$0	$650	$13,020	$0	$15,541
TOTAL	Paid through UW	$14,622	$5,995	$0	$0	$0	$0	$0	$20,671
	Paid through Org	$0	$0	$2,344	$0	$1,250	$25,785	$0	$29,379
PROJECT TOTAL		$14,622	$5,995	$2,344	$0	$1,250	$25,785	$0	$49,996

STAGE TWO: FULL APPLICATION

Developing the Budget and Budget Narrative.

A budget and budget narrative describe *how much* the project will cost. Yet they are more than a simple statement of proposed expenditures. They are an alternate way to express the project's value. The budget and budget narrative demonstrate to the sponsor that sufficient funds have been requested to achieve project goals and objectives in a cost-effective manner.

The budget form divides expenses into seven categories, and for this multiyear initiative, across two 12-month project periods. At a glance, reviewers can determine exactly how much funding is being requested for (a) salary, (b) fringe benefits, (c) travel, (d) equipment, (e) supplies, (f) consultants and contracts, and (g) other costs. Broadly, the budget request is split 60 percent for the community partner and 40 percent for the academic partner.

Budget Narrative

Salary & Fringe

The project team is made up of the academic partner, project manager, community partner and community organizer. These four individuals will meet together monthly in addition to participating in meetings with the Coalition and doing assigned tasks as determined by the team (see roles and responsibilities). The costs basis for the academic partner and project manager is 10% of their full-time compensation. The costs basis for the community partner is 5% of her full-time compensation. Funds are requested from WPP for the academic partner. The project manager and community partner will participate through in-kind support from their respective organizations. The community organizer will be contracted for this project (see consultant/contracts section).

Year 2 is a continuation of year 1. The academic partner's figures are based on a 4% increase (includes expected increases in health benefits). The other two positions are based on an increase of 2%.

Travel

The funds requested from WPP for outreach mileage are for the community organizer to do outreach including one-on-one meetings with a wide variety of people representing various sectors of the community and meeting with low-income, food-insecure residents in rural Eau Claire County. Budget is based on 20 miles per week for 43 weeks of the year and includes visits in rural Eau Claire County (roughly 40 miles RT per visit).

The other requested funds will be used in year 2 to present project results at conferences. Coalition members will be encouraged to participate in these activities. The mileage expense is based on one round trip from Eau Claire to Madison, but the expectation is that there will be multiple opportunities to present at varying distances with one requiring lodging, meals and registration. Per person costs include: motel at $300 for 2 nights, meals at $100 for 3 days, registration at $200. In-kind funds are generally available to support academic partner presentations at conferences. The in-kind portion is not itemized but will be used to increase the total number of Coalition members that will be able to participate in dissemination activities.

Supplies

$25 food and $10 gas cards will be given to 10 low-income residents each year that participate in meetings or spend 2 hours or more providing advice and feedback—and are not doing so during paid work time. Our assumption is that other participants will be compensated (financially or socially) through their work or volunteer positions.

Healthy food will be provided at Coalition meetings to encourage additional networking and coalition relationship building. The food

The budget narrative provides an explanation for every line item, describing in detail the specific item (*what* is needed), its relevance to the project (*why* it is needed), and the basis of cost calculation (*how much* it will cost) for each year.

Nearly 93 percent of the budget reflects personnel costs—salary, fringe benefits, and consultants—which is reasonable for a development grant where the primary activities center on recruiting individuals to develop a strategic plan. Pilot projects and implementation projects, on the other hand, may have lower percentages for personnel costs because more funds would be allocated to travel, equipment, materials, supplies, and other costs related to key activities.

Of the funding requested for nonpersonnel items, one category that might initially jump out at reviewers on the budget table is travel because of the nearly fourfold increase from year one to year two. The budget narrative clarifies that year one costs focus on outreach activities and year two costs include dissemination activities. Specifying the breakdown of conference registration, lodging, and meals helps to justify the sizable increase in the year two travel budget.

budget is slightly larger in the second year because more meetings are envisioned in year 2 than year 1. Additionally, we will hold a celebration gathering when the final products are complete in order to engage and inform a larger number of individuals connected with participating organizations. Over the two years, the food budget is based on an average of $30 per meeting.

Educational materials will be needed to educate coalition members on the broad determinants of health—social, economic and physical—and their effect on access to nutritious foods. Funds will be used primarily for printing and binders ($8–$15/person per year).

Consultants/Contracts

Funds requested from WPP will be used to pay a consultant to serve as a locally-based community organizer (see roles and responsibilities for a list of duties). This person will have strong connections across multiple organizations and strengths in building collaborative partnerships. We have identified three people with strong credentials and passion for this work. The project manager, academic partner and community partner will have in-depth conversations with one or more of these individuals before making a selection. The budgeted expense is based on about 345 hours of work per year (20% time for 10 months). The rate is based on the rate for similar job descriptions, duties, and experience. $37/hr × 345 hr = $12,765. Year 2 is based on a 2% increase.

Other Sources of Funds

University of Wisconsin-Eau Claire additional in-kind support

- Private office with computer, printer, and locked filing cabinets
- Clerical support for printing, copying, and miscellaneous administrative requests
- Office of Research and Sponsored Programs (ORSP) provides support for grant management, budget, and assistance in conducting grant searches
- Learning Technology Services (LTS) provides technical support staff for problem-solving
- Center for Excellence in Teaching and Learning (CETL) provides assistance with designing innovative educational strategies including use of social media
- McIntyre Library provides access to research librarians and multiple databases for conducting literature searches
- Faculty in psychology available for consultation with designing evaluation tools

Note that the budget narrative identifies types of in-kind contributions made to the project but, consistent with a standard practice at a federal agency, does not include any quantifiable financial information. This presentation allows reviewers to understand the human resources, physical space, and technological tools that will support the project without getting hung up in the details of the value for each specific asset.

Eau Claire County UW-Extension Wisconsin Nutrition Education Program additional in-kind support

- Private office with computer, printer, and locked filing cabinets
- Clerical support for printing, copying, and miscellaneous administrative requests

- UW-Extension Cooperative Extension specialist support will provide assistance to develop: plans with coalitions, coalition effectiveness evaluation, build community awareness on local issues and community policy interventions

Feed My People Food Bank additional in-kind support

- Private office with computer, printer, and locked filing cabinets
- Meeting space
- Utilization of FMP website, Facebook page, e-Newsletter and newsletter to disseminate coalition progress

* * *

Wisconsin Partnership Program

Community Academic Partnership Fund

External Reviewer Comments

Type: Development

Applicant: Feed My People

Project: "Changing Views of Hunger: One Community at a Time"

AVERAGE SCORE: 92

REVIEWER 1

I.I: PROJECT PURPOSE, NEED, AND STATEMENT OF THE PROBLEM
SCORE: 15

STRENGTHS OF SECTION:
The statement of problem/need is strong in providing local/county, state and national statistics to very clearly lay out the problem of disproportionately high levels of poverty and concomitant risks pertaining to health and chronic illnesses in Eau Claire County (ECC)—including (lack of) access to sufficient and nutritious food. This project is well grounded in data.

The plan of developing infrastructure to better serve the needs of specific high-risk populations in ECC for better and more food and the potential for increasing health and wellbeing is very well in line with the priorities set for in the State health plan and the goals of WPP more specifically. Given that the Health Dept in Eau Claire has outlined the need for appropriate nutrition as critical for their state priority of addressing chronic diseases—there seems to be great local buy-in.

STAGE TWO: FULL APPLICATION

Analyzing External Reviewer Comments.
The sponsor had three grant reviewers critique the proposal independently via a mail review. Overall, the proposal earned high marks, ranging from 88 to 95 points out of 100, with an average score of 92. The sponsor considers proposals with scores of 90–100 to be "outstanding"; 80–89 to be "excellent"; 70–79 to be "very good"; 60–69 to be "good"; and below 59 to be "fair/poor."

Reviewer 1 awarded full points—15 out of 15—to the "Project Purpose, Need, and Statement of the Problem" and found the use of local, state, and national statistics particularly compelling.

Reviewer 1 awarded 15 out of 15 points to "Outcomes Related to the Guiding Principles." The description of strengths touch on all three hot buttons: "key project collaborators seem to be well connected" refers to partnerships; "identify and try to apply best practices" addresses evidence-based practices; and "very good potential for sustainability" represents measurable outcomes and sustainability. Further, the phrase "project will integrate even more local representation (inclusiveness)" alludes to the distinctive feature of geographically and culturally diverse community partnerships.

Reviewer 1 awarded 14 out of 15 points for the "Goals, Objectives, and Outcomes." Two strengths noted—"inclusion of target community members in all planning processes; the availability of focus group data on food insecurity from the local communities"—explicitly address the distinctive feature of grassroots engagement with the target population. Though two weaknesses were identified, they were minor enough that the section lost only one point.

AREAS FOR IMPROVEMENT: None.

I.II: OUTCOMES RELATED TO THE GUIDING PRINCIPLES
SCORE: 15

STRENGTHS OF SECTION:
This project has very good potential for sustainability as it expands upon collaborative relationships already in place and which have been productive heretofore. The key project collaborators seem to be well connected and positioned to mobilize various stakeholders—and the project will integrate even more local representation (inclusiveness).

The project is prevention oriented and essentially an embodiment of most of the principles set forth in WPP—it seems to address a demonstrable local need by leveraging local resources in a more efficient way (responsiveness).

And it promises to identify and try to apply best practices in approaching the challenge of increasing community access to good food—such that it may be become a model for other areas of the state.

AREAS FOR IMPROVEMENT:
None.

I.III: GOALS, OBJECTIVES, AND OUTCOMES
SCORE: 14

STRENGTHS OF SECTION:
As this is a development grant, it is understandable that the goal and objectives s are not well defined but rather process oriented. As such, the objectives and outcomes are suitable relative to the aims.

Particular strengths of this project's goals include the inclusion of target community members in all planning processes; the availability of focus group data on food insecurity from the local communities to inform the goal and interventions; attention to coalition building processes (satisfaction, readiness) in order to ensure that the essence of collaboration is as receptive and responsive to stakeholder needs as possible; and the attention to media outlets as important partners in educating the community and disseminating information about access.

AREAS FOR IMPROVEMENT:
The proposal includes a projection of how many individuals will have better access to food after the implementation of the strategic plan—which was a bit confusing as I assume that implementation outcomes will depend on the processes that have yet to be developed. (Putting the cart before the horse?)

While there is an explicit plan to evaluate growth in knowledge on the part of coalition members over the planning phase, it was not clear whether the project plans on including research to evaluate reductions in stigma and increase in awareness/understanding on the part of the community members.

I.IV: WORK PLAN
SCORE: 13

STRENGTHS OF SECTION:
The work plan is detailed, well aligned with the project narrative and logic model.

AREAS FOR IMPROVEMENT:
In surveying the project work plan, it was not clearly evident how the collaborative plans on educating itself about best practices—will the academic partner share results of literature review in meetings? Will there be a systematic search for models for addressing food insecurity around the country? Site visits or invitations for speakers?

From the project work plan it was not clear how food insecure members from different communities and representing diverse interests will be identified.

Reviewer 1 assigned 13 out of 15 points for the "Work Plan." A perceived weakness was the lack of clarity on "how the collaborative plans on educating itself about best practices." Apparently the work plan's fourth entry, which included the activity "Project team discussion to incorporate best practices for preparing and mobilizing coalitions" and outcome "Ensures all Project team members are up to date regarding the most current evidence," was insufficient by itself. Perhaps adding a phrase to the third entry in the work plan, "Conduct literature review of EBP related to grant objectives *and share with project team during monthly meetings*" would have better detailed the approach for keeping Coalition members informed.

I.V: EVALUATION, DISSEMINATION AND SUSTAINABILITY PLANS
SCORE: 18

STRENGTHS OF SECTION:
The logic model is detailed and well aligned with the project narrative and work plan. The dissemination plan is well thought out and diversified—academic publication outlets, regional and Statewide conferences, and coalition members educating staff in their respective agencies.

As noted above, a particular strengths of this study is the plan for working with media (though the plan for media outlets could be more specifically laid out in the proposal).

As several project members are well connected with local administrators in ECC, and the project is well aligned with ECC local priorities, and as ongoing collaboration would not be 'expensive' necessarily, it seems that there is good potential for new policies and inter-agency partnerships to continue well beyond the development stage.

AREAS FOR IMPROVEMENT:
It is not clear if anyone on the project team has experience with federal grant proposals. If not, it may be helpful to obtain consultation.

Reviewer 1 awarded 18 out of 20 points for "Evaluation, Dissemination and Sustainability Plans." The description of strengths touches on the distinctive feature of policy implications, namely, "there is good potential for new *policies* and inter-agency partnerships to continue well beyond the development stage." Though media was not identified as a hot button or distinctive feature, engaging media as a project partner was recognized repeatedly as a project strength.

Of all the weaknesses cited by Reviewer 1, this one is the most intriguing: "It is not clear if anyone on the project team has experience with federal grant proposals. If not, it may be helpful to obtain consultation" for these reasons: (1) the RFP does not require or give preference to project teams with federal grant experience; (2) the narrative does not state that federal grants will be sought as part of sustainability efforts; and (3) the project team does have federal grant experience, which is highlighted in the next section on "Capacity and Experience of Partners and Key Staff." In short, the two point deduction seemed, in this instance, to be based on a new subjective criterion imposed by the reviewer more so than an application of the objective criteria presented in the RFP.

I.VI: CAPACITY AND EXPERIENCE OF PARTNERS AND KEY STAFF
SCORE: 20

STRENGTHS OF SECTION:
It seems evident that the applicants are each well-connected and passionate individuals who have been working on food insecurity issues for some time and have had success in completing previous data collection projects.

As the applicant/lead organization has been serving the ECC community for 30 years (!) and seems to be well known in the community—it has good credibility.

The roles and responsibilities are detailed and seem reasonable.

AREAS FOR IMPROVEMENT:
None

II: OVERALL REVIEWER COMMENTS

SUGGESTIONS FOR STRENGTHENING THE PROPOSAL?
None.

Reviewer 1 offers high praise for the proposal, recognizing that it is well thought-out and well-written.

GENERAL/OVERALL COMMENTS ON THE PROPOSAL:
I think this is a strong (detailed, well thought-out, and well-written) proposal. Other than the few very minor details noted along the way, I do not have any major suggestions for improvement.

REVIEWER 2

I.I: PROJECT PURPOSE, NEED, AND STATEMENT OF THE PROBLEM
SCORE: 15

Reviewer 2 awarded full points—15 out of 15—to the "Project Purpose, Need, and Statement of the Problem." Reviewer 2, just like Reviewer 1, complimented as a strength the effective use of local, county, state, and national data to document the need for the project.

STRENGTHS OF SECTION:
The applicant clearly and effectively uses local, county, state and national data sources and statistics to define the focus population and as evidence to demonstrate the importance of the food insecurity and the need to improve access to healthy food.

The applicant has developed a project based on local focus group input from the focus population, recent experience with similar projects, and the recent identification of this issue in the City Comprehensive Plan and County Health Department community health assessment.

The narrative effectively demonstrates how the project will advance the infrastructure focus of Collaborative Partnership and the health focus of Nutrition and Healthy Foods.

AREAS FOR IMPROVEMENT:
I found only strengths in this section.

I.II: OUTCOMES RELATED TO THE GUIDING PRINCIPLES
SCORE: 15

STRENGTHS OF SECTION:
The narrative demonstrates that the project is well-aligned with key WPP guiding principles of Prevention and Partnerships.

The applicant notes the attention to evidence-based practices to increase access to healthy food, the use of an evidence-based strategic planning process to develop a plan for action, and bases the project on the City and County health plans which are consistent and aligned.

The narrative addresses the partnership development principle effectively by including examples which indicate an effort to build on existing coalition, diversify the coalition, grow the coalition with appropriate partners, and expand to local health care systems.

AREAS FOR IMPROVEMENT:
The narrative could be improved with further detail about the project alignment with the responsiveness principle which is mentioned briefly.

Reviewer 2 assigned a score of 15 out of 15 points to "Outcomes Related to the Guiding Principles." The description of strengths touches on all three hot buttons: "The applicant notes the attention to *evidence-based practices* . . . to develop a *plan* for action" and "The narrative addresses the *partnership* development principle effectively." Though an identified weakness was the limited description of the project's alignment with the guiding principle of responsiveness, full points were still awarded to this section. The RFP instructed applicants to "provide examples and address *at least one* guiding principle" and since this criterion had been met, perhaps Reviewer 2 did not feel it necessary to subtract points for understating an additional guiding principle.

I.III: GOALS, OBJECTIVES, AND OUTCOMES
SCORE: 13

STRENGTHS OF SECTION:
This section describes goals, objectives and outcomes which are largely consistent with the work plan and logic model. In addition, the focus on use of the existing media relationship to improve access is a key asset of this project.

The applicant demonstrates understanding of the evidence based databases and models that are relevant to improving public health - RWJF, CDC, What Works.

Through effective use of consumer focus group input and plans to continue to include the consumer perspective, the applicant shows an understanding of the importance of focus population role in planning.

Reviewer 2 awarded 13 out of 15 points to "Goals, Objectives, and Outcomes." The description of strengths touches on the distinctive feature of grassroots engagement with the target population, namely, "the applicant shows an understanding of the importance of the *focus population* role in planning." Reviewer 2, just like Reviewer 1, recognized engaging media as a project strength, even though media was not used intentionally as a hot button or distinctive feature.

Though crediting, "The applicant demonstrates understanding of the evidence based databases and models that are relevant to improving public health," Reviewer 2 tempers this strength with "The narrative could be improved with expanded description about existing evidence based practices that are relevant." Reviewer 2 seems to desire greater clarity on the implementation processes to be used, which is exactly the opposite of Reviewer 1, who cited as an area for improvement: "I assume that implementation outcomes will depend on the processes that have yet to be developed. (Putting the cart before the horse?)"

Reviewers do not always agree, nor should they be expected to; they bring different experiences and perspective to the review process. Proposals do not have to be perfect to be funded; rather, they must be persuasive.

Reviewer 2 awards 13 out of 15 points to the "Work Plan." An identified weakness relates to the hot button of measurable outcomes and sustainability, namely, "the search for potential *funding sources* in months 15–18 could be lengthened, made slightly earlier." Reviewer 2 makes an astute observation: it may take sponsors 6–9 months to make a decision about project funding, so an application would need to be submitted by months 15–18 for there to be even a chance of receiving funding for implementation activities by month 24.

Reviewer 2 awards 17 out of 20 points to "Evaluation, Dissemination and Sustainability Plans." Note that many of the comments center on the logic model and its content and presentation. The content is a strength: "the goals and outcomes of this project are doable and critical to addressing a well-defined issue." The presentation is an area for improvement: "The logic model could be improved by separating the activities into the key work components . . . by aligning each category/column with its key work area." Reviewer 2 is correct that readability of the logic model is an important consideration.

Other comments address sustainability, which reflects the hot button of measurable outcomes and sustainability. Viewed narrowly, project sustainability is about finances, identifying the sources of funding

AREAS FOR IMPROVEMENT:
The narrative could be improved with expanded description about existing evidence based practices that are relevant.

Description of the evidence based approach under consideration for strategic planning would strengthen the narrative.

The link between the narrative, work plan and logic model could be strengthened by more consistent use of language - strategic plan/action plan, outreach-media plan/dissemination plan.

I.IV: WORK PLAN
SCORE: 13

STRENGTHS OF SECTION:
The work plan is clear, concise, and effectively reflects the narrative.

The activities and scope of work outlined the work plan are feasible and realistic to accomplish the intended project goals.

The work plan and evaluation plan are consistent.

AREAS FOR IMPROVEMENT:
The work plan could be improved with an activity addressing the hiring/orienting of the community organizing consultant and adjusting timeframes that allow more time to complete some of the activities, i.e., the search for potential funding sources in months 15–18 could be lengthened, made slightly earlier, and be followed up with activities to write proposals and secure funds.

The proposal could be improved by using the logic model format provided by WPP for the short, medium and long term outcomes.

I.V: EVALUATION, DISSEMINATION AND SUSTAINABILITY PLANS
SCORE: 17

STRENGTHS OF SECTION:
Although the Logic Model requires some re-structuring, it is clear that the goals and outcomes of this project are doable and critical to addressing a well-defined issue.

The dissemination section effectively addresses getting the findings out to several levels of the social ecology—coalition, key constituents, broader community.

The sustainability section points to the timing which makes this project appropriate with the alignment of the food insecurity study, focus group feedback, City and County plans and effective plans for outreach to engage the broader community.

AREAS FOR IMPROVEMENT:
The logic model could be improved by separating the activities into the key work components for instance: Partnership/Coalition Building, Strategic Plan Development, Dissemination Plan Development, Sustainability Plan Development.

The logic model could be strengthened by aligning each category/column with its key work area so that reading across would result in a logical progression of activity/output to outcome all related to one another.

The sustainability section could be strengthened with some emphasis on potential funding sources and financial partners to supplement the necessary and noted community and partner buy-in.

I.VI: CAPACITY AND EXPERIENCE OF PARTNERS AND KEY STAFF
SCORE: 20

STRENGTHS OF SECTION:
All organizations, staff and partners are well qualified and have extensive experience needed to accomplish the project goals. The importance of community organizing and incorporating the consumer perspective comes through as a priority to the lead applicant and its collaborating partners.

Feed My People has an organizational mission and experience that is perfectly aligned and critical to the proposed project and clearly demonstrates its reach through a strong relationship with the media and its member organizations to be successful as the project community partner.

The collaborating partners are well suited to the project and specifically the academic partner has extensive experience, knowledge and specialization in the field of food insecurity which is spot on for this project.

AREAS FOR IMPROVEMENT:
The capacity section could be improved with a description of the qualifications that will be sought in the consultant.

II: OVERALL REVIEWER COMMENTS

SUGGESTIONS FOR STRENGTHENING THE PROPOSAL?
Re-structuring the logic model as noted is key to improving this proposal.

The narrative would be improved with a more detailed description of the proposed components of the dissemination and sustainability plans.

GENERAL/OVERALL COMMENTS ON THE PROPOSAL:
This proposed project is a strong fit with focus areas of HW2020 and the WPP priorities of improving the health of underserved people in Wisconsin, reducing disparities and specifically addressing nutrition through developing a plan to improve access to healthy food.

Overall this is a well-developed proposal submitted by a very qualified applicant with a partnership plan that can realistically accomplish the goals and outcomes proposed.

that can be used to implement activities. The coalition and strategic plan, however, are grounded in a different type of sustainability—structural sustainability. That is, building on existing infrastructure and processes increases the likelihood for continued action and impacts, even if no further grant funding is received. Perhaps this point could have been made more clearly.

Reviewer 2 assigned full points—20 out of 20—to "Capacity and Experience of Partners and Key Staff." In addition to confirming that individuals and organizations are "well qualified and have extensive experience needed to accomplish the project goals," a strength identified touches on the distinctive feature of grassroots engagement with the target population, namely, "incorporating the *consumer perspective* comes through as a priority." Once again, Reviewer 2 calls out relationships with the media as a key partnership that will contribute to project success.

Reviewer 2 is correct that "the capacity section could be improved with a description of the qualifications that will be sought in the consultant," but does not subtract any points for this weakness.

Reviewer 2 gives a sound endorsement of a "well-developed proposal submitted by a very qualified applicant."

REVIEWER 3

I.I: PROJECT PURPOSE, NEED, AND STATEMENT OF THE PROBLEM
SCORE: 14

STRENGTHS OF SECTION:
Identifying the purpose of this project and the need, were well defined and linked solidly together with evidence based research. There was a nice link between the statistical data and the programs defined needs that made this section very strong. Also identified were existing studies/assessments and coalitions already established to lead this initiative. There was a nice link and connection to the HW2020 State Health Plan and the mission of the WPP.

AREAS FOR IMPROVEMENT:

None at this time.

Reviewer 3 awarded 14 out of 15 points to the "Project Purpose, Need, and Statement of the Problem." It is unclear why one point was deducted since no weaknesses were identified. It could be that philosophical differences existed among reviewers for scoring: Top Down—proposals start with perfect scores of 100 (an "A+") and lose points as weaknesses are identified; Bottom Up—proposals start out with scores of 0 (an "F−") and gain points as strengths are identified; In the Middle—proposals start out with scores of 70 (a "C") and gain points for strengths and lose points for weaknesses. It's conceivable that Reviewer 1 and Reviewer 2 used a Top Down while Reviewer 3 used an In the Middle philosophy.

I.II: OUTCOMES RELATED TO THE GUIDING PRINCIPLES
SCORE: 13

STRENGTHS OF SECTION:
There was a strong focus on prevention and established partnerships. Especially diverse partnership with many community based organizations. The strongest aspect of this section was how these partners were going to build on existing programs to achieve their overall goal. This was brought out in many examples. Involving the Hmong population (the largest minority group in the county) is of high value for the overall success of this project.

AREAS FOR IMPROVEMENT:
While this area describes a lot of different organizations, it is very general in describing how these organizations will work together. The common theme is highlighted, but the specifics are lacking in clarity on how they will be formed and continue long-term.

Reviewer 3 assigned 13 out of 15 points to "Outcomes Related to the Guiding Principles." All three reviewers acknowledged as a strength the commitment to including geographically and culturally diverse community partners, a distinctive feature. Reviewer 3, however, would have preferred to have greater detail about how new partners will be identified, recruited, and retained in the coalition. Perhaps additional information about the partnership development process could have been added to complement the emphasis on the tangible outcome of a formal evidence-based strategic plan.

I.III: GOALS, OBJECTIVES, AND OUTCOMES
SCORE: 14

STRENGTHS OF SECTION:
This area was well defined and concise in its content. There was a direct link to what the objectives were, what outcomes were expected and how the goals would be accomplished. Another area of strength was how social media would be encompassed into meeting the goals and objectives. There was a comprehensive explanation on how the existing professional partners would assist in the recruitment of the key stakeholders.

AREAS FOR IMPROVEMENT:
This section mentioned the frameworks of RWJF's Roadmap to Health Action Model, WI What Works database and the socio-ecological

Reviewer 3 awarded 14 out of 15 points to the "Goals, Objectives, and Outcomes." The distinctive feature of grassroots engagement with the target populations was universally recognized by reviewers as a strength. As an area of improvement, Reviewer 3, similar to Reviewer 2, desired a greater explanation of and justification for the evidence-based models and practices that will drive the project.

model for improving health, but more clarification and detail could have been added to why they would be relevant for this initiative.

I.IV: WORK PLAN
SCORE: 13

STRENGTHS OF SECTION:
The workplan was easy to understand and overall had excellent detail. The "evaluation activity" note was helpful in assisting the reader in understanding the overall activity as it pertained to the previous activities. Very unique.

AREAS FOR IMPROVEMENT:
The anticipated outcomes column could have had more details in their explanations. It had to be cross-referenced with the logic plan to get a richer understanding on what was trying to be communicated.

Reviewer 3 assigned 13 out of 15 points to the "Work Plan." A simple document design feature, explicitly noting "evaluation activity" in the work plan, was acknowledged as a strength. The RFP indicated that "the work plan should be consistent with the logic model and evaluation efforts," and Reviewer 3 would have preferred even greater repetition between the documents in order to minimize the need for flipping back and forth to find key details. Because the work plan and logic model are not part of the narrative page limit, it would have been reasonable to sprinkle in a few more descriptive details.

I.V: EVALUATION, DISSEMINATION AND SUSTAINABILITY PLANS
SCORE: 16

STRENGTHS OF SECTION:
The Logic Model was well designed and coincided with the overall evaluation plan. Another strength of this section was how the project would be sustained over time with the existing coalitions and the organizations that have already been identified as key partners.

AREAS FOR IMPROVEMENT:
This section mentioned the establishment of an outreach-media plan. But no other details or structural definition was mentioned.

Reviewer 3 assigned 16 out of 20 points to "Evaluation, Dissemination and Sustainability Plans," which was the single lowest score in any section by any of the three reviewers. Whereas "strategic plan" is addressed 18 times in the narrative, "outreach-media plan" is mentioned only twice. This imbalance may have contributed to general confusion about the purpose, audience, and rationale for each type of plan.

This section may also be illustrative of scoring philosophy differences. Reviewer 1 and Reviewer 2 seem to use a Top Down approach and the weaknesses cited justify the subtraction of points. For Reviewer 3, however, this approach doesn't quite fit: the weakness cited does not seem commensurate with points subtracted. More likely is that Reviewer 3 used an In the Middle approach and the strengths moved the score up above average while the weakness prevented it from being a top score.

I.VI: CAPACITY AND EXPERIENCE OF PARTNERS AND KEY STAFF
SCORE: 18

STRENGTHS OF SECTION:
The key individuals in this initiative have a strong educational background regarding this topic. They also have experience and are associated with other agencies throughout the midwest that are vital to the success of this project. There appears to be a strong leadership component for this initiative to succeed.

AREAS FOR IMPROVEMENT:
None at this time.

Reviewer 3 assigned 18 out of 20 points to "Capacity and Experience of Partners and Key Staff." Whereas Reviewer 2 identified a weakness and awarded full points, Reviewer 3 didn't identify a weakness and didn't award full points. This section may, again, highlight differences in reviewers' scoring philosophies.

II: OVERALL REVIEWER COMMENTS

SUGGESTIONS FOR STRENGTHENING THE PROPOSAL?
The area of how this initiative will be marketed or communicated to the public was not clearly communicated. A more diverse marketing/media plan would have made for an even stronger proposal.

Reviewer 3 gives a strong endorsement of the proposal even though a number of big-picture and small-picture areas of improvement were cited. Using the sponsor's definitions, Reviewer 1 and Reviewer 2 consider the proposal to be "outstanding" while Reviewer 3 considers it to be "excellent"—high enough marks to merit an overall recommendation for funding.

GENERAL/OVERALL COMMENTS ON THE PROPOSAL:
This is a very strong proposal related to a very important community health problem. The number of partners and support for this initiative is very impressive. Not only is there "buy-in" from a number of agencies and coalitions, but those agencies are also local and diverse and committed to making a difference.

* * *

FORMAL AWARD NOTICE

Congratulations! On behalf of the Wisconsin Partnership Program's Oversight and Advisory Committee (OAC) at the UW School of Medicine and Public Health, I am pleased to inform you that your organization, Feed My People, Inc, has been awarded a 2013 grant from the Community-Academic Partnership Fund for "Changing Views of Hunger: One Community at a Time."

You are listed as the primary contact and community partner for your grant. As the primary contact, you are responsible for informing your grant team, including your academic partner, about this award. You will be asked to convene your grant team (including the academic partner) for an hour-long orientation sometime in February. More information will be emailed to you soon.

We will announce your award by issuing a news release highlighting successful applicants and posting a comprehensive list of grantees on the Wisconsin Partnership Program website. If you send a news release to your local media, please include the following statement: "Funding for this project was provided by the Wisconsin Partnership Program at the UW School of Medicine and Public Health."

We look forward to working with you as you begin to implement your project. If you have questions, it is best to contact us via our Wisconsin Partnership Program email, wpp@hslc.wisc.edu.

Again, please accept our congratulations on your successful application.

Sincerely,
Abigail Grace, MD, MPH
Chair, Oversight and Advisory Committee

The "2013 Community-Academic Partnership Fund" Request for Partnerships is used by permission of the Wisconsin Partnership Program.

STAGE TWO: FULL APPLICATION

Celebrating the Grant Award Notification. The RFP highlights that the recommendations of grant reviewers are considered by the Oversight and Advisory Committee that makes the final determination awards. This grant award notification arrived via e-mail in mid-December, nearly two weeks ahead of the anticipated notification of awards, and was a welcome holiday-season treat.

More broadly, the time between reading the RFP for the Wisconsin Partnership Program development grants and receiving the grant award notification was approximately eight months. Two months passed from submission of the Letter of Interest to the arrival of the invitation to submit a Full Application, and three and a half months passed from submission of the Full Application and the arrival of the grant award notification. For a two-stage application process, this overall timeframe is particularly speedy.

CHAPTER 7

The National Endowment for the Humanities

NATIONAL ENDOWMENT FOR THE HUMANITIES HOME PAGE (COURTESY OF THE NATIONAL ENDOWMENT FOR THE HUMANITIES, WWW.NEH.GOV)

The Preservation Assistance Grants for Smaller Institutions program was created by the National Endowment for the Humanities in 2000. Since that time, more than 1,700 awards have been made to small and mid-sized institutions throughout the United States. According to their Web site (2014), "In the last five competitions the Preservation Assistance Grants program received an average of 313 applications per year. The program made an average of 106 awards per year, for a funding ratio of 34 percent."

The grant program makes $6,000 awards to help institutions improve their ability to preserve and care for their humanities collections. As stated in the RFP guidelines, applicants must draw on the knowledge of consultants whose preservation skills and experience are related to the types of collections and the nature of the activities that are the focus of their projects. Full program details are available online at http://www.neh.gov.

In this chapter, we explore a successful application that demonstrates how timing can play an important role in determining relevance, feasibility, and probability. Several key elements were in place as the organization explored whether to submit for this competition: previous assessments had been conducted, an underused but potentially valuable humanities collection was about to move into a more accessible location, and a new library was being built, which would allow for the opportunity to "start over" regarding conservation efforts.

The Preservation Assistance Grants for Smaller Institutions uses a single-stage application process, which invites online submission of a five-page, single-spaced project narrative via the Grants.gov portal. The elements of this chapter include the following.

Stage One: Full Application

- The Request for Proposal
- The Project Narrative
- The Budget
- The External Reviewer Comments
- The Grant Award Notification

This application is a model of proposal planning and writing; it presents the right balance of logic, emotion, and relationships to connect with the values of the sponsor. Figure 6 overviews the key elements that we brought together to reach the Persuasion Intersection.

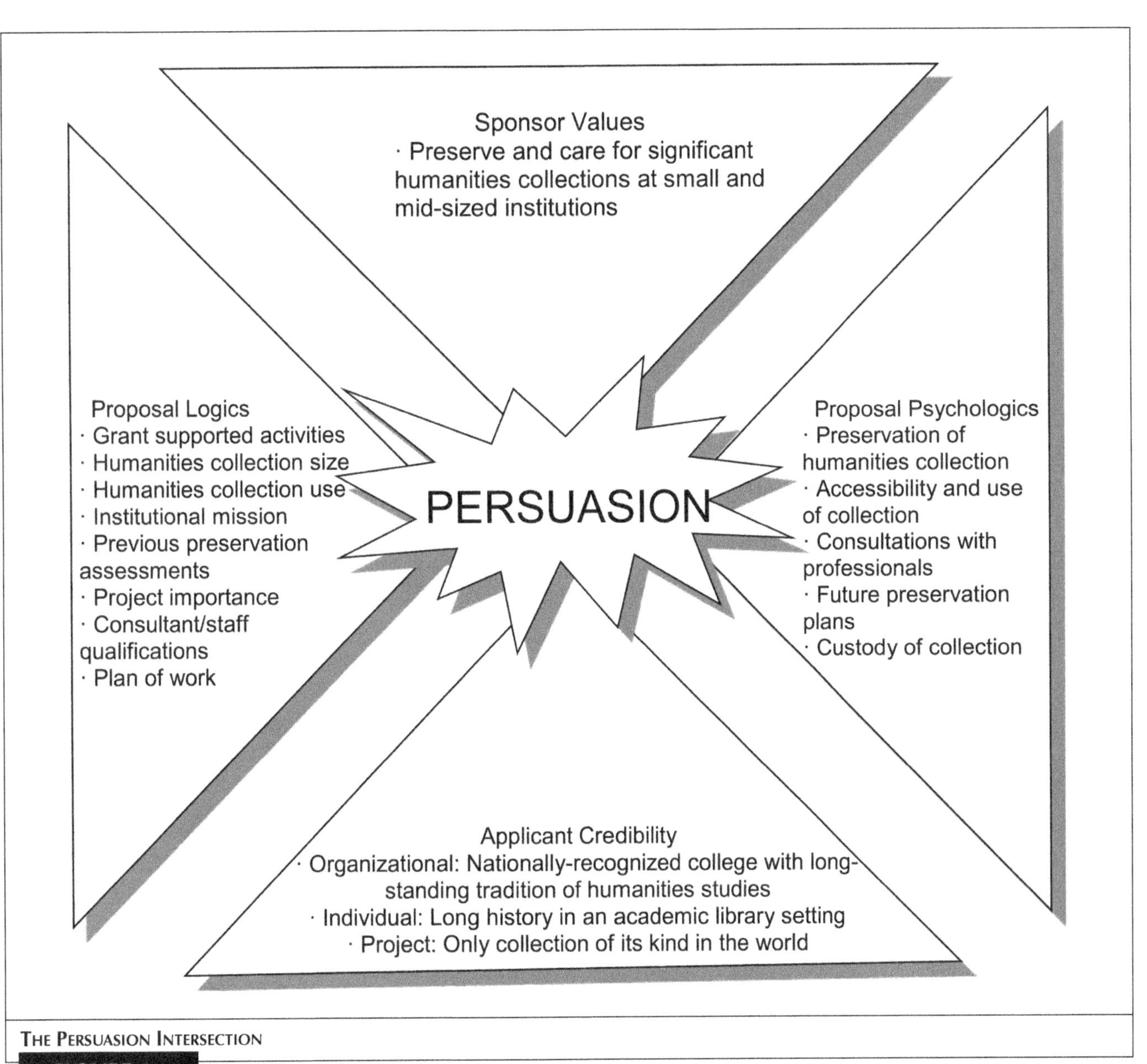

THE PERSUASION INTERSECTION

FIGURE 6

National Endowment for the Humanities

PRESERVATION ASSISTANCE GRANTS FOR SMALLER INSTITUTIONS

Receipt Deadline: May 15, 2008 (for projects beginning January 2009)

Date posted: March 7, 2008
Catalog of Federal Domestic Assistance (CFDA) Number: 45.149

Questions?
Contact the staff of NEH's Division of Preservation and Access at 202-606-8570 and preservation@neh.gov. Hearing-impaired applicants can contact NEH via TDD at 1-866-372-2930.

I. Program Description
Preservation Assistance Grants help small and mid-sized institutions, such as libraries, museums, historical societies, archival repositories, cultural organizations, town and county records offices, and colleges and universities, improve their ability to preserve and care for their significant humanities collections. These may include special collections of books and journals, archives and manuscripts, prints and photographs, moving images, sound recordings, architectural and cartographic records, decorative and fine art objects, textiles, archaeological and ethnographic artifacts, furniture, and historical objects.

STAGE ONE: FULL APPLICATION

Analyzing the RFP.
To determine whether there is interest in applying to a grant program, whether the capacity exists to develop the grant application, and whether the project will be competitive, we systematically analyze the RFP (Request for Proposal) guidelines. By reading, rereading, and reading again the RFP with an increasingly critical eye, we examine *relevance*, *feasibility*, and *probability* with attention toward increasing odds for funding success.

The following call-out thought bubbles provide insight into the process of planning and writing a successful proposal. Because the RFP Analysis Process is iterative by nature, the three steps may not always appear sequentially.

Step One: Relevance.
According to the RFP guidelines, the National Endowment for the Humanities offers Preservation Assistance Grants to help small and mid-sized institutions preserve and care for their "significant" humanities collections. The expertise of "appropriate" and "specifically knowledgeable" consultants will be needed. Grant awards are $6,000, and the project period is for 18 months. Budget items can include costs of consultants, attending workshops, travel, and purchasing and shipping supplies and equipment. A five-page, single-spaced proposal must be submitted online via Grants.gov by May 15. Projects may begin as early as January 1.

Applicants must draw on the knowledge of consultants whose preservation skills and experience are related to the types of collections and the nature of the activities that are the focus of their projects. Within the conservation field, for example, conservators usually specialize in the care of specific types of collections, such as objects, paper, or paintings. Applicants should therefore choose a conservator whose specialty is appropriate for the nature of their collections. Similarly, when assessing the preservation needs of archival holdings, applicants must seek a consultant specifically knowledgeable about archives and preservation. Because the organization and the preservation of archival collections must be approached in tandem, an archival consultant should also provide advice about the management and processing needs of such holdings as part of a preservation assessment that includes long-term plans for the arrangement and description of archival collections.

Small and mid-sized institutions that have never received an NEH grant are especially encouraged to apply.

Step Two: Feasibility.
Hot button words and phrases for preservation of humanities collections are repeated more than 100 times: the exact phrase appears only twice in the RFP but *preservation* appears 50 times, *humanities* appears 22 times, and *collection* appears 45 times. This hot button is not unexpected: it relates directly to the title of the funding program, "Preservation Assistance Grants."

Step Two: Feasibility.
Future preservation plans is a distinctive feature that carries weight with reviewers. Proposals that set the context, situating the current project in relation to long-term plans for collection maintenance and care, will be perceived as being more competitive than those who do not articulate their vision for the future.

Preservation Assistance Grants may be used for:

- **General preservation assessments**

Applicants may engage a conservator, preservation librarian, archivist, digital preservation specialist, or other appropriate consultant to conduct a general preservation assessment and to help draft a long-range plan for the care of collections. The consultant visits the institution to assess policies, practices, and conditions affecting the care and preservation of humanities collections and prepares a report that summarizes the findings and contains prioritized recommendations for future preservation action.

- **Consultations with professionals to address a specific preservation issue, need, or problem**

Applicants may hire a consultant to help address challenges in the stewardship of humanities collections. For example, consultants can provide advice about:

Step Three: Probability.
Preproposal contact questions might include "Do reviewers have a preference for a specific category of grants—general preservation assessments, consultations with professionals, preservation supplies, monitoring equipment, or education and training?" and "Are there a targeted number of grant awards in each category?"

Step Two: Feasibility.
Consultations with professionals is a hot button that is repeated 30 times in the RFP. Consultant fees are specifically included as an allowable expense, but more significantly, the sponsor seems to suggest that consultants are essential to project success: four of the five categories of grants explicitly encourage using funds to engage the services of a consultant.

- developing disaster preparedness and response plans;
- establishing environmental monitoring programs, instituting integrated pest management programs, and developing plans for improving environmental conditions, security, or fire protection for collections;
- studying light levels in exhibition and storage spaces and recommending appropriate methods for controlling light and reducing damage to collections;
- developing plans for arranging, describing, and addressing the preservation needs of archival and manuscript holdings;
- developing detailed plans for improving storage or rehousing a collection; and
- assessing the conservation treatment needs of selected items in a collection.

From preliminary discussions about the proposed assessment, a consultant may be able to anticipate an institution's need for basic preservation supplies. In such cases, the applicant may request funds to purchase the recommended supplies and the consultant should provide a general description of the supplies and justification for their use in the letter of commitment. After the on-site visit, the consultant can refine the list of supplies to be purchased.

Step Three: Probability.
Preproposal contact questions might include "To what extent is there flexibility to purchase different preservation supplies than originally proposed in the narrative and budget?" and "To what extent is there flexibility to change consultants from who was originally proposed in the narrative to who is available at the time of project implementation?"

- **Purchase of storage furniture and preservation supplies**

Applicants who have completed a preservation assessment or consulted with an appropriate professional may request funds to purchase permanent and durable furniture and supplies (e.g., cabinets and shelving units, storage containers, boxes, folders, and sleeves). If an institution's staff and volunteers have limited experience in rehousing collections, the institution should enlist the help of a consultant to provide guidance and training at the beginning of the project. Applicants requesting supplies to rehouse archival collections should discuss how the rehousing activities relate to plans for arranging and describing the materials.

Step Three: Probability.
Strategic thinking questions might include "Will institutions that already have completed an assessment be more competitive?" and "Will the collection need to be rehoused?"

Step Three: Probability.
Preproposal contact questions might include "How much experience is sufficient to justify that expertise exists in-house to rehouse collections?" and "Is it reasonable for the preservation assessment to be completed by staff rather than an external consultant?"

- **Purchase of environmental monitoring equipment for humanities collections**

Applicants may purchase environmental monitoring equipment (e.g., dataloggers, hygrothermographs, and light meters). If the institution's staff does not have experience using the equipment, the application should include a request for training in the use and installation of the equipment and the interpretation of the monitoring data.

- **Education and Training**

Applicants may request support to send staff members who work with humanities collections to workshops and training courses that focus on the care of collections.

Applicants may also hire a consultant to conduct on-site training for staff and volunteers. On-site workshops may be tailored to meet specific needs and holdings of the institution. Staff and volunteers from neighboring organizations may also be invited to participate in on-site workshops.

Education and training requests may address both preservation and access topics. For example, workshops could focus on topics such as the following:

- preservation and care of humanities collections (often offered by collection type, e.g., textiles, paintings, photographs, archives),
- methods and materials for the storage of collections,
- developing environmental monitoring programs,
- disaster preparedness and response,
- best practices for cataloging rare books, art, and material culture collections,
- proper methods for the arrangement and description of archival collections,
- best practices for creating sustainable digital collections,
- digital preservation management, and
- care and handling of collections during digitization.

Applicants may combine two or more elements of the project types listed above in a single application. For example, an applicant may request funds for a consultant to conduct a preservation assessment and an on-site preservation workshop for the institution's staff. In such cases, the consultant's letter of commitment should fully describe both the assessment and on-site workshop.

NEH grants may support consultant fees, workshop registration fees, travel and per diem expenses, and the costs of purchasing and shipping preservation supplies and equipment.

Step Three: Probability.
Strategic thinking questions might include "Is there a disadvantage to spending the vast majority of grant funds on a single piece of equipment and thus having only limited dollars available for a consultant?" and "Is it reasonable to have the vendor provide training on the equipment rather than budgeting separately for a consultant?"

Step Three: Probability.
Preproposal contact questions might ask "If individual environmental monitoring units cost less than $5,000, should they be presented on the budget as 'equipment' or 'supplies'?" and "If a suite of environmental monitoring units cost in excess of $5,000, can they be presented as 'equipment'?"

Step Three: Probability.
Strategic thinking questions might include "Are there representatives from neighboring organizations that would find value in participating in an onsite workshop on environmental monitoring?" and "Will applications that have outreach to neighboring organizations receive preferential consideration?"

Step Three: Probability.
Preproposal contact questions might include "Rather than hiring an external consultant, is it permissible to pay an overload to a current staff member for the additional duty of conducting a preservation assessment?" and "Are there particular education and training topics that are more in favor with reviewers right now?"

Step Three: Probability.
Strategic thinking questions might include "Is the nature of the preservation project such that it can be phased, thus allowing the potential to submit sequential funding requests?" and "Is there an amount of time that must pass between requests in order to be considered for subsequent funding?"

Step Two: Feasibility.
Hot button words and phrases for accessibility and use of collection are repeated more than two dozen times in the RFP: *access, accessibility, open and available, collections are used, collections have been used, for research, for exhibitions, for educational purposes, for public programming, for public education,* and *by students, scholars, or genealogists.* Collectively, these terms describe who will use the collection and how the collection will be used. It's not surprising that the NEH cares deeply about accessibility: the Preservation Assistance Grants program is administered through its Division of Preservation and Access.

Step Three: Probability.
Strategic thinking questions might include "How does this $6,000 project fit into our larger collection preservation strategy?" and "What other resources are available to move this project and strategy forward?"

Previously Funded Projects

An institution that has received a Preservation Assistance Grant may apply for another grant to support the next phase of its preservation efforts. For example, after completing a preservation assessment, an institution might apply to purchase storage supplies and cabinets to rehouse a collection identified as a high priority for improved storage. These proposals receive no special consideration and will be judged by the same criteria as others in the grant competition.

Preservation Assistance Grants may not be used for:

- projects that preserve, organize, or describe materials that are the responsibility of an agency of the federal government;
- projects that preserve, organize, or describe materials that are not regularly accessible for research, education, or public programming;
- projects that focus on collections that fall outside the humanities;
- projects that seek to catalog, index, or arrange and describe the collections;
- projects that focus on preserving or restoring buildings or other structures;
- capital improvements to buildings and building systems, including the purchase of equipment such as air conditioners, dehumidifiers, and security and fire protection systems;
- salaries and fringe benefits for the staff of an institution,
- computers;
- reformatting of collections (e.g., digitizing, photocopying, microfilming, or copying to another medium) or the purchase of equipment for reformatting (e.g., computers, scanners, digital cameras, cassette decks, and CD-ROM drives);
- library binding;
- graduate-level conservation training or training related to advanced conservation treatment;
- conservation of restoration treatments (including deacidification and encapsulation) or the purchase of conservation or restoration treatment supplies and equipment (e.g., mending tape, erasers, and cleaning supplies);
- attendance at regular meetings of museum, library, archives, or preservation organizations; or
- the recovery of indirect costs.

III. Award Information

Grants of up to $6,000 will be awarded.

All grants are awarded for a period of eighteen months, although a grantee may complete a project in a shorter period of time.

Cost sharing

Cost sharing is not required. If eligible expenses are more than $6,000, an applicant may cover the difference and show this as cost sharing in the project's budget.

IV. Eligibility

Any U.S. nonprofit organizations is eligible, as are state and local governmental agencies and Indian tribal governments. Grants are not awarded to individuals. NEH will give priority to smaller institutions and to institutions that have not previously received an NEH grant.

Only one application for a Preservation Assistance Grant may be submitted annually by an institution, although distinct collecting entities of a larger organization may apply in the same year, such as the library and museum of a university or two historic sites within a historical society.

Applicants must also:

- care for and have custody of the humanities collections that are the focus of the application;
- have at least one staff member or the full-time equivalent, whether paid or unpaid; and
- be open and available to provide services or programs at least 120 days per year.

NEH generally does not award grants to other federal entities or to applicants whose projects are so closely intertwined with a federal entity that the project takes on characteristics of the federal entity's own authorized activities. This does not preclude applicants from using grant funds from, or sites and materials controlled by, other federal entities in their projects.

Ineligible applications will not be reviewed.

V. Application and Submission Information Application advice:

Prior to preparing and submitting a proposal, applicants are encouraged to look at the list of sample projects, review sample narratives, and to review the frequently asked questions.

Step Three: Probability.
Preproposal contact questions might include "What is the strategic advantage to offering cost sharing when it is not required?" and "Though not required, is there a level of cost sharing that reviewers believe applicants should contribute?"

Step Three: Probability.
Preproposal contact questions might include "How small does an institution need to be to receive preferential consideration?" and "What consideration is given to institutions that have not *recently* received an NEH grant?"

Step Two: Feasibility.
Custody of collection is a distinctive feature. It stands out as a quirky eligibility criteria, one that might have emerged from the lessons of experience, e.g., the sponsor once unwittingly awarded a grant to an organization to preserve a collection over which it had no ownership, authority, or responsibility. Applicants who reassure the sponsor that they have custody of the collection may be received more favorably than those who remain silent on this point.

Step Two: Feasibility.
The RFP offers a proposal writing tip related to the evaluation criteria: reviewing examples of successful proposals may provide insights on how other applicants included persuasive levels of detail in the narrative and budget and how sponsor hot buttons and distinctive features were addressed.

Step Two: Feasibility.
The National Endowment for the Humanities will use the following stated evaluation criteria in their selection process: a five-page full proposal should describe the grant-supported activities, content and size of the humanities collection, use of the collection, nature and mission of the institution, prior preservation assessments, project importance, qualifications of consultants and staff, and plan of work.

Step Three: Probability.
Preproposal contact questions might include "Do reviewers favor applications that focus on a single or a suite of activities?" and "What outcomes are expected of grantees?"

Step Two: Feasibility.
The RFP offers a writing tip for success related to the evaluation criteria: questions B "content and size of humanities collection" and C "use of the collection" should each be one full page in length. Clearly, reviewers are expecting a certain level of detail in these sections. In practical terms, at least 40 percent of the project narrative (two pages) is dedicated to these two questions and 60 percent (three pages) remains to answer the other six questions.

Step Three: Probability.
Strategic thinking questions might include "What is the significance of the collection to the humanities?" and "Will a larger collection be perceived as more valuable than a smaller collection with other distinguishing features?"

HOW TO PREPARE YOUR APPLICATION

You will prepare your application for submission via Grants.gov just as you would a paper application. Your application should consist of the following parts:

1. Project Narrative

Answer the following questions in order. State each question as the heading for the answer to that question. Project narratives are limited to five single-spaced pages. The font size should be no smaller than eleven point and all pages should have one-inch margins. Applicants should keep the application review criteria (see below) in mind when writing their narratives.

A. **What activity (or activities) would the grant support?**
State the specific activity or activities that the grant would support and the goals of the proposed project.

B. **What are the content and size of the humanities collections that are the focus of the project?**
Describe the collections that are the focus of the project, emphasizing their significance to the humanities. Identify the categories of materials and indicate, where pertinent, the date ranges, quantities, and intellectual content. Highlight specific examples of important items in the collections. The description of your collection should be about one full page in length.

A description of an archival collection, for example, might begin by stating that the collection comprises two hundred letters written by a school teacher between 1870 and 1885; twenty-four linear feet of records pertaining to a local business active from 1940 through 1970; fifty-two maps documenting the history and development of the locality; twelve volumes of birth and death records for local residents from 1860 to 1950; and nine hundred photographs depicting community life during the 1930s and 1940s. The description should then proceed to discuss in detail the content of these materials and their significance to the humanities.

If only a portion of an institution's collection is the focus of the project, briefly describe the overall collections and then provide a detailed account of the portion that is the focus of the project.

C. **How are these humanities collections used?**
Explain how the collections are used. If collections are used for exhibitions or educational programs, describe the nature of these programs. For example, explain how the collections have been used in an exhibition that explores a community's history or how they have been used in school programs and classroom instructional materials. If the collections are used for research, describe the range of subjects that have been (or could be) explored and show how these materials could contribute to new interpretations of national or regional history. Provide examples of research projects conducted by students, scholars, or genealogists. By discussing the use of collections, an applicant will help evaluators understand their importance to the humanities and to the institution's mission. This section of the application should be about one full page in length.

D. **What is the nature and mission of your institution?**
Describe the mission of the institution and discuss specific budget or staffing considerations that characterize it as a small or mid-sized institution, including:

- type of institution: museum, archives, arts or cultural organization, historical organization, public library, historic site or house, college, university, or research library (if other, explain)*;
- amount of operating budget in the most recently completed fiscal year*;
- number of full-time paid staff members*:
- number of part-time paid staff members*;
- number of volunteer staff*; and
- number of days or hours per year on which the institution is open.*

*-Libraries, archives, or museums, etc., that are part of a larger organization, such as a college or university, should provide this information for their institutional unit and explain the specific budget or staffing considerations that characterize the unit as a smaller or mid-sized institution.

Step Three: Probability.
Preproposal contact questions might include "Do reviewers demonstrate a preference for a narrow focus on selectively unique items in a collection or a broad focus on a vast collection of disparate items with value to the humanities?" and "What's the desired impact on an institution's collection, balancing project breadth, depth, and financial resources available?"

Step Three: Probability.
Strategic thinking questions might include "Which local, regional, national, and international researchers would find value in this collection?" and "How might the work of scholars internal and external to the organization contribute to new knowledge and understandings?"

Step Three: Probability.
Preproposal contact questions might include "Are there specific thresholds for budget and staffing that must be met to be considered small or mid-sized?" and "Do reviewers demonstrate a preference for institutions whose missions are more research than public service oriented?"

E. **Has your institution ever had a preservation or conservation assessment or consultation?**

If yes, provide the date of the assessment, the name(s) of the assessor(s).

Has your institution ever engaged a preservation consultant for purposes other than a general preservation or conservation assessment? If yes, briefly elaborate.

F. **What is the importance of this project to your institution?**

Discuss how this project fits into the institution's overall preservation needs or plans. Describe the current condition of collections. Explain how the proposed activities build on previous preservation efforts and how the project fits into future preservation plans.

Applicants proposing to attend workshops or training courses should describe their content and explain how the knowledge gained would be used to improve preservation practices at the institution. Workshops must be attended during the period of the grant. If a regularly offered workshop has not been scheduled at the time of application, contact the workshop's provider to confirm that it will be offered. In an appendix, provide information about the workshop (e.g., a description, announcement, or program) obtained from the provider.

G. **What are the names and qualifications of the consultant(s) and staff involved in the project?**

Using short paragraphs, provide the name(s) and qualifications of the consultant(s) selected for the project, as well as the names and relevant experiences of the participating staff. Applicants requesting training in the care and preservation of humanities collections must seek a consultant specifically knowledgeable about the collection type or types that are the focus of the project. For preservation training projects, identify the staff member(s) who will attend the training and state their positions and responsibilities.

Step Three: Probability.
Strategic thinking questions might include "Is there a disadvantage to having completed an assessment many years ago but not being able to fully implement all of the recommendations?" and "Is listing the name of the consultant from a previous assessment really more important than attaching a copy of the executive summary of the report?"

Step Three: Probability.
Strategic thinking questions might include "Is there a regularly offered workshop that will produce the desired benefits?" and "Will a customized training produce a better return-on-investment than sending multiple staff to a regularly offered workshop?"

Step Three: Probability.
Preproposal contact questions might include "What degree of 'future preservation plans' will reviewers expect to see—one year, five years, 10 years?" and "What value do reviewers assign to the condition of a collection—is an existing collection that is at-risk perceived as having greater need than a newly acquired collection for which a preventive maintenance approach is being pursued?"

Step Two: Feasibility.
The RFP offers another writing tip for success in relation to the evaluation criteria: responses to question G "qualifications of consultants and staff" should be short paragraphs. While "short" is not quantified in the RFP, it might be inferred to be between half and three quarters of a page, given that the writing tip for questions B and C were targeted to be "about one full page in length."

H. **What is the plan of work for the project?**
Outline the steps of the project, the sequence in which they will occur, the amount of time they will take, and indicate who is responsible for which activities.

2. Budget
Provide an itemized budget showing the project's expenses rounded to the nearest dollar. A sample budget is provided here to illustrate the format you should follow:

Step Three: Probability.
Preproposal contact questions might include "What level of detail will reviewers be expecting in the plan of work if preservation supplies and equipment have already been identified?" and "What level of detail is expected in the timetable since purchasing and installation are one-time, short-term events?"

Sample Preservation Assistance Grant Budget					
Applicant Organization: The Town Museum and Library					
Consultant Fees. Provide the following information for each consultant.					
Name of Consultant:	**First Name Last Name**				
No. of days on project:	**Daily rate of compensation:**				**Total:**
4	$550				**$2,200**
Travel: For each trip, indicate the number of persons traveling, the total days they will be in travel status, and the total subsistence and transportation costs for that trip. The lowest available commercial fares for coach or equivalent accommodations must be used.					
From/To:	**No. of persons**	**Total travel days**	**Subsistence costs**	**Transportation costs**	**Total**
Minneapolis, MN, to Boise, ID	1	3	$200/per day = $600	$400	$1,000
Supplies, materials, equipment, and workshop registration fees.					
Item: 2 dataloggers from "Company Name" catalog at $275 each					$550
Item: 1 light meter from "X company" catalog at $216 + shipping					$250
Item: 1 storage cabinet from "Y company" vendor quote incl. shipping					$3,500
Item: 50 sheets 8 ply Museum Board catalog price					$800
Item: 30 archival boxes from "Vendor" catalog price $10 each					$300
Item: workshop registration					$250
Total of Request: Total requested from NEH (up to $6,000)					**$6,000**
Cost sharing by applicant (optional)					$2,850

Cost sharing is not required for Preservation Assistance Grants. However, if eligible expenses are greater than $6,000, the applicant will need to cover the difference and should enter the amount in excess of $6,000 on the cost-sharing line of the Supplementary Cover Sheet and in the budget. For example, if a project costs $8,850, the applicant may request $6,000 from NEH and provide cost sharing in the amount of $2,850.

Step Three: Probability.
Preproposal contact questions might include "Do reviewers give preferential consideration to applications that include cost sharing?" and "If cost sharing is included, is there a preference for organizational funding being used to support consultant fees or preservation supplies?"

3. Appendices

- **Supporting Documentation**

For projects based on a previous preservation assessment, attach a copy of the executive summary of the assessment.

For projects that involve purchasing supplies and equipment, provide a list that identifies each item, quantity, unit cost, and the name of the vendor.

For projects that involve purchasing storage furniture, provide a description of the furniture, the materials from which it is made, unit cost, and the name of the vendor.

For projects that involve the hiring of a consultant, attach a résumé for and letter of commitment from the consultant.

Step Three: Probability.
Preproposal contact questions might include "Are there page limits associated with supporting documentation? vendor quotes for multiple items could more than triple the length of the application." and "To what degree are reviewers concerned with exactly which vendors and products are used—that is to say, do they recommend different vendors and products as a means, for example, to reduce budget costs or increase item quality?"

- **Brief résumés (no longer than two pages) for project director and other key staff**
- **Résumés and letters of commitment for project consultant(s)**

Any project that uses a consultant must provide a résumé and a letter of commitment from the consultant.

Step Three: Probability.
Strategic thinking questions might include "Would there be a psychological advantage to have the résumés of the project director and key staff all use the same format?" and "Are there any expected categories of information to be included on résumés beyond the standard: education, positions held, publications and presentations, professional activities, association memberships, and honors and awards?"

Step Three: Probability.
Strategic thinking questions might include "How much lead time is necessary to secure the required letter of commitment and résumé from the

HOW TO SUBMIT YOUR APPLICATION VIA GRANTS.GOV

Register or Verify Registration with Grants.gov

Applications for this program must be submitted via Grants.gov. Before using Grants.gov for the first time, an organization must register with the website to create an institutional profile. Once registered, your organization can then apply for any government grant on the Grants.gov website.

If your organization has already registered and you have verified that your registration is still valid, you may skip this step. If not, please see our handy checklist to guide you through the registration process. **We strongly recommend that you complete or verify your registration at least two weeks before the application deadline, as it takes time for your registration to be processed.** If you have problems registering with Grants.gov, call the Grants.gov help desk at 1-800-518-4726.

DEADLINE

Applications must be received by Grants.gov by May 15, 2008. Grants.gov will date and time stamp your application after it is fully uploaded. Applications submitted after that date will not be accepted. Supplementary materials must also arrive by May 15, 2008, to be considered as part of the application.

VI. Application Review

NEH asks panelists knowledgeable about the preservation and use of humanities collections to assess applications according to the following criteria:

The collections and their use in humanities programming, education, or research.

- How adequately has the applicant described the content of the collections that are the focus of the project? Is there a detailed description of the type of materials, their quantity, date ranges, and intellectual and historical content?
- How persuasively has the applicant made its case that the collections are important for humanities purposes, such as exhibitions and public programming, public education, or research?

The proposed activities and the justification of their importance to the institution.

- Are the proposed activities clearly described and are they feasible?
- How will this project contribute to the institution's capacity to preserve its collections?

consultant?" and "Should a sample letter of commitment with pertinent details be drafted for the consultant to review and put on letterhead?"

Step Three: Probability.
Strategic thinking questions might include "Has the Grants.gov registration process been completed and confirmed to be valid?" and "Are there any additional steps that need to be taking internally to ensure 'buy-in' for a proposal submission?"

Step Two: Feasibility.
The RFP outlines three broad criteria to which reviewers need to respond when evaluating grant applications. The criteria relate to the questions posed in the "How to prepare your application" section, though some differences exist in sequencing. For example, criteria #1 "collections and their use" relates to questions B "content and size of the humanities collection" and C "use of the collection"; criteria #2 "proposed activities and importance to the institution" relates to questions A "grant-supported activities," D "nature and mission of the institution," E "prior preservation assessments," and F "project importance"; and criteria #3 "plan of work" relates to questions F "project importance," G "qualifications of consultants and staff," and H "plan of work."

Step Three: Probability.
Preproposal contact questions might include "What are the biggest hurdles grantees face in reaching their project goals and objectives?" and "To what extent is it expected that a formal evaluation of the project will be conducted?"

Step Two: Feasibility.
The National Endowment for the Humanities typically assigns a panel of three to six reviewers to score proposals. For any given application, reviewers are more likely to be educated generalists than disciplinary specialists. Reviewers assign scores individually to proposals on a five-point scale: excellent, very good, good, some merit, and not competitive. Reviewers may raise or lower their initial scores after the panel discussion, but they do not need to reach consensus. The program officer synthesizes panel results and assembles a slate of funding recommendations for consideration by the National Council on Humanities. The NEH chair makes final funding decisions.

Step Three: Probability.
Preproposal contact questions might ask "What percentage of awards represent first-time submissions compared to resubmissions?" and "What are the most common mistakes in proposals that lead to their rejection?"

The adequacy of the plan of work.

- Has the applicant provided a feasible and clearly described plan of work, timetable, and budget?
- Have supplies and equipment been adequately described and do they meet preservation standards?
- Have workshop topics been described and are the topics appropriate for the applicant's needs?
- Are the roles of the consultants and staff explained?
- Do the consultants and staff have experience and qualifications appropriate to the project's goals?

Late applications will not be reviewed.

Review and Selection Process

Knowledgeable persons outside NEH will read each application and advise the agency about its merits. The Endowment's staff comments on matters of fact or on significant issues that otherwise would be missing from these reviews, then makes recommendations to the National Council on the Humanities. The National Council meets at various times during the year to advise the NEH chairman on grants. The chairman takes into account the advice provided by the review process and, by law, makes all funding decisions.

VII. Award Administration Information

Award notices

Applicants will be notified by mail in January 2009. Institutional grants administrators and project directors of successful applications will receive at that time award documents by mail. Applicants may obtain the reasons for funding decisions on their application by sending a letter or e-mail to NEH, Division of Preservation and Access, Washington, D.C. 20506 or preservation@neh.gov.

Administrative requirements

Before submitting an application, applicants should review their responsibilities as an award recipient.

Award Conditions

The requirements for awards are contained in the General Terms and Conditions for Awards to Organizations, any specific terms and conditions contained in the award document, and the applicable OMB circulars governing federal grants management.

Reporting Requirements

A schedule of report due dates will be included with the award document.

A final performance report will be due within 90 days after the award period ending date or may be submitted earlier if project activities have been completed. Further details can be found in *Performance Reporting Requirements*.

A final Financial Status Report (2-page PDF) will be due within 90 days after the completion date of the award period. Further details can be found in Financial Reporting Requirements.

VIII. Points of Contact

If you have questions about the program, contact:
Division of Preservation and Access
Room 411
National Endowment for the Humanities
1100 Pennsylvania Avenue, N.W.
Washington, DC 20506
202-606-8570

If you need help using Grants.gov, refer to
Grants.gov: www.Grants.gov
Grants.gov help desk: support@grants.gov
Grants.gov support line: 1-800-518-GRANTS (4726)

IX. Other Information

Privacy Policy

Information in these guidelines is solicited under the authority of the National Foundation on the Arts and Humanities Act of 1965, as amended, 20 U.S.C. 956. The principal purpose for which the information will be used is to process the grant application. The information may also be used for statistical research, analysis of trends, and Congressional oversight. Failure to provide the information may result in the delay or rejection of the application.

Application Completion Time

The Office of Management and Budget requires federal agencies to supply information on the time needed to complete forms and also to invite comments on the paperwork burden. NEH estimates that the average time to complete this application is fifteen hours per response. This estimate includes time for reviewing instructions, researching, gathering, and maintaining the information needed, and completing and reviewing the application.

Please send any comments regarding the estimated completion time or any other aspect of this application, including suggestions for

Step Three: Probability.
Strategic thinking questions might consider "If a grant is awarded, are these general terms and conditions acceptable?" and "If a grant is awarded, will there be additional terms and conditions that are not listed here?"

Step Three: Probability.
Strategic thinking questions might ask "Are systems and procedures in place internally to meet these financial reporting expectations?" and "Is it reasonable to complete the final performance report within the specified timeframe?"

Step Three: Probability.
Preproposal contact questions might ask "Would you review a draft proposal if it was shared four to six weeks in advance of the submission deadline?" and "Do you plan to offer a workshop, teleconference, or webinar that offers guidance on how to prepare an application?"

Step Three: Probability.
Strategic thinking questions might ask "Given the NEH estimate of needing an average of 15 hours per response to complete the application, is sufficient time available to assemble a competitive proposal?" and "What additional resources can be brought to bear to distribute the proposal planning workload and streamline the proposal writing process?"

STAGE ONE: FULL APPLICATION

Developing the Project Narrative.
The RFP guidelines instruct, "State each question as the heading for the answer to that question," so to help springboard development of the project narrative, we outlined headings A–H from Section V "Application and Submission Information." In addition, the three broad criteria to which the reviewers need to respond were incorporated into the outline to provide a checklist of information that must be provided.

The response to question A "What activity would the grant support?" provides an overview of the narrative, explaining in 425 words, about two thirds of one page, *what* the project is going to do, *why* the project is needed, and *where* the project is taking place.

The special collection was rarely used, which was a less than ideal scenario for this grant competition. However, it was about to move from an off-campus to on-campus location and become more accessible, thus creating the opportunity to address one of the hot buttons raised in the RFP: accessibility and use of collection. Detail about the move to the new location also builds the case for the distinctive feature of custody of collection.

Mentioning that the organization was not currently doing a good job with preservation was a calculated risk. However, it creates urgency and

reducing the completion time, to the Office of Publications, National Endowment for the Humanities, Washington, DC 20506; and the Office of Management and Budget, Paperwork Reduction Project (3136-0134), Washington, DC 20503. According to the Paperwork Reduction Act of 1995, no persons are required to respond to a collection of information unless it displays a valid OMB number.

* * *

Preserving the Center for Norbertine Studies Special Collections: Where Nine Centuries of History Intersect with a Liberal Arts College in Northeastern Wisconsin

A. What activity (or activities) would the grant support?

St. Norbert College has rare books and periodicals that are not available or accessible elsewhere in North America; however, these materials—which have great potential for researchers worldwide and embody the heritage of the College—might be damaged or lost if immediate action is not taken. This special collection is currently rarely used by only the Norbertines at St. Norbert Abbey and by a small group of scholars. However, once the collection is made accessible to the campus community of St. Norbert College through the Center for Norbertine Studies and properly preserved, catalogued, displayed and digitized, it can be further utilized by faculty and students of the College, by local historians and researchers, and by the wider national and international community of scholars.

A poor storage environment is recognized as the greatest cause of collection decay. As a result, one of the most pressing collection needs is to preserve St. Norbert College's special and archival collections. The College has never had a building that was designed exclusively to be a library throughout its 110-year history. Our current library, the Todd Wehr Library, was established through the remodeling of an existing campus dormitory in 1977. Because the building was not originally planned as a library, numerous concerns exist about quality climate control and space; the HVAC system is old and has never been retrofitted for a library. The Todd Wehr Library historically has been "reactive" to preservation needs instead of being proactive.

Ensuring that the College remains on the leading edge of learning opportunities, we are currently constructing the approximately 80,000 square foot Miriam B. and James J. Mulva Library, which will include a special collections suite and reading room, showcasing our collections and providing improved organizational and environmental conditions. We formally broke ground for our new library on April 25, 2008, and our construction manager indicates that the building process will take 14 months; thus, the library will be open prior to the 2009 academic year.

It is essential to have the required environmental monitors and training prior to the move, so we do not take current shortcomings with us to the new library. Drawing on the knowledge of two consultants who recently assessed the College Archives and the Archives at nearby St. Norbert Abbey respectively, the goal of this project is to improve the environmental climate surrounding the College's rare materials through training and the purchase and installation of environmental monitoring equipment, including a climate control monitor with software and peripherals to measure the temperature and relative humidity, light meters, water alarm and sensors.

lays the foundation for the importance of this project. The explanation that the preservation thus far has been reactive rather than proactive addresses the hot button of preservation of the humanities collection as well as explains *why* the project is needed.

Consultations with professionals is a hot button repeated more than 30 times in the RFP. While it might seem like an off-hand phrase, "drawing on the knowledge of two consultants who recently assessed" the archives foreshadows that the organization has experience working with consultants and that the archives have already been through a general preservation assessment by experts.

B. What are the content and size of the humanities collections that are the focus of the project?

The Humanities and Fine Arts Division is one of St. Norbert College's three academic divisions and is well represented in our current library. Of the library's total collection, 38% of the titles are in the humanities. The library also subscribes to approximately 50% of the titles covered in H. W. Wilson's *Humanities Index*. Equally significant, the College has been able to substantially grow its humanities collection thanks to a recent gift bequest of $150,000 that doubled the size of an endowed fund for library acquisitions in the humanities, which was established in 1983 with an NEH Challenge Grant. The collection that best represents who we are as an institution and what we can offer scholars around the world is a humanities collection: our special collections for the Center for Norbertine Studies. St. Norbert College was established upon the foundation of the Norbertine tradition, which continues to be reflected in the educational mission of the College today. Founded by St. Norbert in 1120, the Order ultimately became a distinguished community of priest-scholars and teachers who established a long-standing tradition of excellence in education. Today, the Order consists of a number of abbeys throughout the world including one in De Pere, Wisconsin. As the only Norbertine College in the world, St. Norbert College has the privilege and responsibility to gather and share rare documents concerning the life of St. Norbert and the Norbertine Order.

The response to question B "content and size of humanities collection" is 641 words, about one page in length, as recommend in the RFP. It describes the collection's contents and fit within the organization's larger holdings, mission, and history.

This paragraph was created both to contextualize the collection within a larger Humanities collection as well as to enhance the credibility of the organization. The institution has already received NEH funding, which can enhance credibility. However, the organization does not have a long history of NEH funding and that, coupled with its size, addresses the sponsor values.

By stressing in the last paragraph that the organization is the only college of its kind in the world, the uniqueness of the institution and the collection is stated. Notice, however, that the following paragraph appeals to the hot button of accessibility and use of collection by tying the collection to the local community, which helps to widen the audience for whom the collection might be valuable and keeps the collection from seeming too unique to be useful. It also outlines the connection between the college and the abbey in order to address the distinctive feature of custody of collection.

Since its founding in 1898, St. Norbert College has been the site of a collaborative partnership between the College and the Norbertines of St. Norbert Abbey, located a short distance from campus. This long history has been recorded through photographs, correspondence, books, journals and institutional records. This rich source of 19th and 20th century Catholic missionary activity with the native and immigrant peoples of Wisconsin and the development and institutionalization of these relationships has only recently been fully assessed. The College and the Abbey plan to create a unified information system that preserves the existing collections, fosters their growth, and provides access to the various parts of the collections in a consistent and transparent manner.

The phrase "public presentation" in the last sentence in this paragraph is a subtle way to address the hot button of accessibility and use of collection.

Thus, the Center for Norbertine Studies was established in 2006 to provide scholars and the wider world access to materials on the Norbertine Order and to promote the study of the Order's history. The Center, now located within the Todd Wehr Library, will be located within the new Miriam B. and James J. Mulva Library as part of a suite of special collections that will house the rare collections from the Abbey and the College, as well as the archival collections for the College. The result will not simply be a division of book materials from archival materials. Instead, it will be the public presentation of key collections of the Abbey Archive, the Center for Norbertine Studies, and the College library as a unified whole that offers the best resources with a superior, precise, and accurate means of access to the collections.

This paragraph addresses the first broad criterion to which reviewers need to respond: "Is there a detailed description of the type of materials, their quantity, date ranges, and intellectual and historical content?"

The dates and examples of rare items come from a previously conducted assessment by a consultant familiar with these specific materials. Citing the previous assessment is a way to foreshadow what is coming up in the response to question E "Has your institution ever had a preservation or conservation assessment or consultation?" and "borrows" the credibility of an expert. In other words, here a third-party, objective expert is saying that the collection is unique. It also addresses the hot button of consultations with professionals by demonstrating that the organization has a history of consulting with experts.

According to an assessment conducted in late 2007 by Dr. Matthew Heintzelman, Curator of the Center for Austrian and German Medieval Studies at the Hill Museum and Manuscript Library, and the Rare Books Cataloger at the Alcuin Library at St. John's University, Collegeville, the collection includes titles that are not available or accessible elsewhere in North America, including issues of the *Communicator* (for "The English Speaking Circary of the Order of Premontre), several liturgical books, and Norbertine periodicals, such as *Bibliotheque Norbertine* and *Revue de l'Ordre de Premontre.* There is also a relatively large collection of early (pre-1700) imprints, including one 15th century book, 23 16th century books, and 123 17th century books. Nearly the entire collection consists of materials classed in the 200–299 range in the Dewey Decimal system. While the books are in good shape overall, environmental monitoring is immediately required to preserve the collection for current and future patrons.

C. How are these humanities collections used?

The Center's special collections are an integral component of the College. The mission of the Center for Norbertine Studies is to collaborate in enlivening and strengthening an authentic Catholic culture in the Norbertine tradition at St. Norbert College and in the international community by creating opportunities for undergraduate and graduate scholarship, collaboration among Norbertine houses throughout the world, cross-cultural interaction, and international student and faculty exchange. The purpose of the Center is to sustain and strengthen the knowledge, exploration, and critical engagement with the Catholic intellectual tradition within the Norbertine context and to explore the meaning and significance of the College as the only Norbertine college in the world.

The Center serves as an important resource for students, faculty and staff who want information on St. Norbert and the history and spirituality of the Norbertines. Faculty are encouraged to develop projects that make use of the Center's materials and collections, and students can become involved as research assistants or interns. The Center is also a focal point for international research on the Norbertines and has plans to host scholars from all over the world to do research on the Order. The Center for Norbertine Studies also is exploring the possibility of initiating, in cooperation with the Norbertine Order and outside publishers, a series of publications in the area of Norbertine history and spirituality.

The Center is not only a location with research materials; it also organizes and promotes lectures and events related to Norbertine life and tradition, as well as related topics such as the Rule of Augustine and the place of canonical life within the broader Christian monastic tradition. For example, in February 2008, the editors and translators of *Norbert and Early Norbertine Spirituality*, Fr. Theodore Antry, O. Praem., of Daylesford Abbey, and Professor Carol Neel of Colorado College, presented an informal discussion of this groundbreaking volume, which makes available for the first time in English translation several important early sources for Norbertine spirituality.

Once the collection is properly preserved, catalogued, displayed and digitized, it can be utilized with greater depth and frequency by faculty and students of the College, by local historians and researchers, and by the wider national and international community of historians and scholars. More specifically, the materials in the Norbertine archival collection will be used by researchers in the fields of Immigrant history, Wisconsin history, European history, Christian monasticism, American Catholicism, American frontier history and Native American/Christian encounters. Some examples of projects that could be conducted include studies of the Norbertines' work with Hispanic Catholics in Green Bay; translation projects of important documents pertaining to the early history of the Norbertines; and scholarship using the multi-volume diary of Fr. Gaertner, an Austrian Norbertine who recorded detailed information and his impressions of Native American and European immigrant communities in mid-19th century Wisconsin.

At one page in length, as recommended by the RFP guidelines, the response to question C "How are these humanities collections used?" is one of the longest sections of the narrative at 761 words. This section explains *who will benefit* from the project activities.

As part of the Proposal Logics, applicants must tie the project to the larger organizational mission. Here the connection between the collection and the institution's mission and heritage is explained in more detail to help the reviewers understand the importance of the collection to the Humanities and address the hot button of accessibility and use of collection.

This entire paragraph is a hot button for accessibility and use of collection. Placing the collection within a larger center will increase its accessibility and use by students, faculty, and researchers.

To highlight the "use" dimension of the sponsor hot button for accessibility and use of collection, a specific example of a lecture event related to the special collection is provided.

This collection had not been widely used up to this point so some speculation was needed regarding what fields of humanities and what research projects could make use of these materials. However, specific details were needed here because the RFP noted that the response to question C, "use of the collection," should be one page—one of the longest sections of the proposal. It also addressed both use and proposed activities, two broad criteria that reviewers will be focusing on.

Quantifying the numbers of visitors each year further highlights the accessibility and use of collection in which the archives will be housed, a sponsor hot button. The reference to the digital library collection hints at the future preservation plan's distinctive feature and is a way to expand future access.

Our current library consistently has had over 225,000 visitors each year, and the new library will continue to welcome patrons from Northeastern Wisconsin. As part of the plan for the inauguration of the new Mulva Library, we will highlight items from special collections, including items from the Abbey which were never seen by the public. We will also participate in the Modern Wisconsin Records Collecting Needs project survey, which will enable us to have more archival records available to the public. We also have plans, pending funding, to participate in the WAICU (Wisconsin Association of Independent Colleges and Universities) digital Library Collection.

At 389 words, the response to question D "What is the nature and mission of your institution?" provides organizational level information about *where* the project will take place and *who* is responsible for the project.

D. What is the nature and mission of your institution?

Located in De Pere, Wisconsin, St. Norbert College has an enrollment of 2,086 undergraduate students in 30 academic majors and 83 graduate students in two master's programs. According to the most recent statistics available from the Education Trust, the College's 4, 5, and 6 year graduate rates are among the highest in the state. In addition, more than 98% of our students are employed or attending graduate school when surveyed nine months after graduation.

The organization's mission is explicitly stated in the first sentence of this paragraph as is a brief summary of some of the institution's regional and national achievements.

St. Norbert College is a small liberal arts college committed to providing an educational environment that is personally, intellectually and spiritually challenging. In recognition of St. Norbert College's efforts to encourage students to explore all a liberal arts education offers, the John Templeton Foundation lists St. Norbert among institutions with exemplary Student Leadership programs and names it as one of the 100 institutions on its "Honor Roll for Character-Building Colleges." St. Norbert College also earned national recognition as one of five colleges and universities to receive the inaugural Senator Paul A. Simon Award for Campus Internationalization. The *Princeton Review* continues to designate St. Norbert College as one of the "Best in the Midwest."

The RFP guidelines state that libraries that are part of a larger organization, such as a college, should provide budget and staffing information for just their unit. The second sentence in this paragraph highlights this but also intentionally uses the phrase "smaller institution" to reinforce the sponsor values of collections at small and mid-sized institutions.

The current Todd Wehr Library is and the future Miriam B. and James J. Mulva Library will be the exclusive college library at St. Norbert College. The budget and staffing considerations characterize the Library as a smaller institution:

Amount of operating budget in the most recently completed fiscal year: $832,478 (includes salaries, library materials, office supplies, binding)
Number of full-time paid staff members: 9
Number of part-time paid staff members: 6
Number of volunteers: 0
Number of days or hours per year the institution is open: 4091.5 hours

E. Has your institution ever had a preservation or conservation assessment?

A general preservation assessment survey, awarded as part of the Subsidized Survey Program of the Midwest Art Conservation Center (MACC) and generously funded by a grant from the National Endowment for the Humanities and the St. Paul Travelers Foundation, was conducted at the College's Todd Wehr Library Archives Collection on July 17 and 18, 2006. Elisa L. Redman, Assistant Director of Preservation Services, and Amanda Sorenson, undergraduate intern, at the MACC, conducted the survey.

The survey consisted of evaluating the archival and special collections and their environments in the library and artifact displays in four other building on campus, as well as taking into account the Archive's close connection to the related archival collection and displays at St. Norbert Abbey. The purpose of this survey was to assess the Library's policies, practices, and conditions that influence preservation of the archives and special collections and to aid in the development of a plan of action that addresses the overall care and preservation of these collections. As a result of this general preservation needs assessment survey, it was recommended that the Todd Wehr Library make several immediate changes, including acquiring a visible and UV light meter to regularly monitor and record light levels throughout the Archive storage and exhibition areas and starting a system of monitoring environmental conditions by the purchase and use of data loggers and associated software.

As part of a separate assessment, Dr. Matthew Heintzelman, Curator of the Center for Austrian and German Medieval Studies at the Hill Museum and Manuscript Library, and the Rare Books Cataloger at the Alcuin Library at St. John's University, Collegeville, MN, conducted an examination of the rare books at St. Norbert Abbey and provided his final report to St. Norbert College in October 2007. In addition to other recommendations, Dr. Heintzelman recommended that before extensive cataloging of the book collection can begin, environmental improvement in shelving, monitoring of humidity, temperature, and microenvironments must be addressed.

Section E addresses the hot button of consultations with professionals and explains previous partnerships as well as the results of previous assessments. Having a previous assessment was a key factor in the decision that the timing was right to apply for the competition. Because the Midwest Art Conservation Center is funded by the NEH, this bolsters the organization's credibility by showing that this project is leveraging previous funds.

"Immediate changes," in the last sentence, helps to create a sense of urgency and need. It reinforces to the sponsor *why* the project is necessary. The current archive storage and exhibition areas are not up to par, which is a threat to the preservation of the collection, a sponsor hot button. If something is not done, it might not be wise to move the valuable Norbertine collections into the current space. This addresses the importance of the project and hints at the upcoming plan of work.

Environmental improvements and storage methods are allowable in this funding opportunity; however, cataloging is not. In the last sentence, it is stressed that the improvements that are allowable must occur before the cataloging, which will take place at a later date via a different project. This addresses the future preservation plans and emphasizes to the reviewers that the organization understands what is allowable and what is not.

Section F recaps *why* the project is needed by including more detail about the prior assessments. Reviewers will be examining "proposed activities and importance to the institution" throughout Sections D, E, and F, so some threads from prior sections can be carried through and reinforced.

This paragraph combines two hot buttons: consultations with professionals and preservation of humanities collections by explaining that the previous assessments stated that the collections are in good condition, but the light and humidity are not ideal for the collection's continued preservation.

These bullets explain *when* the activities will take place and stress that there is a window of opportunity for staff to be trained so as to make sure that bad habits are not continued.

We broke the project into "phases" in order to sequentially order tasks and demonstrate that the project is already underway (phase one is complete) and that there is a plan for what will come after the grant period is concluded. In other words, the phases provide a larger context for the grant project.

Section G addresses *who* is responsible for the project. Because consultant résumés are required attachments, only the most relevant and unique qualifications were chosen to appear in the narrative, saving space at 337 words.

F. What is the importance of this project to the institution?

As the only Norbertine College in the world, the College continues to embrace its rich Catholic, Norbertine and liberal arts traditions as it moves through the 21st century. The Center for Norbertine Studies strives to explore, in collaboration with Norbertines throughout the world, how this precious heritage, so rich in its cultural expression and influence, can inform and help shape spiritual, intellectual and cultural life on our campus. Without access to these materials and without proper preservation, historians cannot make use of this collection. A priceless piece of American history has been hidden, virtually unused and unknown. It is our desire to remedy this situation by improving and monitoring the environmental conditions in which materials are stored and make them more accessible to historians and scholars at St. Norbert College and throughout the world.

Preserving the special collections that contain the history and records of the College's mission and heritage is a top priority. Because the current Todd Wehr building was not originally planned as a library, numerous concerns exist about quality climate control, security, and space. As part of his assessment, Dr. Matthew Heintzelman concluded that the rare book collection is in good condition overall. However, Elisa Redman's assessment states that visible light levels are higher than ideal in the Rare Book Room, and the relative humidity readings in the Abbey are higher than desirable. Therefore, it is essential to have the required environmental monitors and training now and take proper care of our special collections prior to the move, so we do not take our current shortcomings with us to the new library.

- The first phase of this project was to assess the Todd Wehr Library Archives Collection (completed July 2006) and the St. Norbert Abbey Archives (completed October 2007).
- The second phase is to address the immediate need of stabilizing the environment surrounding our rare artifacts by purchasing environmental equipment for a special collections room that will bring together and house the rare collections from the St. Norbert Abbey and the College and provide training on this equipment.
- The third phase is to purchase storage furniture to rehouse and stabilize the collections in the new Miriam B. and James J. Mulva Library.
- The fourth phase is to create a long-range preservation plan and disaster plan.
- The fifth phase is to complete other protocol steps, including detailed object-by-object surveys for specific collections and prioritized conservation treatments for individual artworks.
- The sixth phase is to digitize materials to preserve materials and to provide easier access to researchers worldwide.

G. What are the names and qualifications of the consultant(s) and staff involved in the project?

Felice Maciejewski is the Interim Associate Vice President for Information Services and Director of the Library. She has worked in academic libraries for over 24 years and has been a librarian for over 17 years. She is also active member of the American Library Association and the Wisconsin Library Association and was chosen to participate in the 2008 Frye Leadership Institute at Emory University in Atlanta, GA.

Andrea Rolich, Senior Academic Librarian and Director of the Collection Preservation and Assessment Department of the Memorial Library at UW-Madison, is a well respected expert on preservation and will be conducting preservation training along with her staff member, Wayne Gathright. As project leaders for the IPI WebERA (Web Environmental Risk Analysis) project at UW-Madison, they both have experience with the PEM2 climate control monitor. They have been monitoring with PEMs since 2001 and are also experienced in monitoring both UV and visible light levels in various campus libraries. Their experience will help St. Norbert College staff use the recommended equipment and establish best practices.

As project director, Ms. Maciejewski has already secured commitments from the consultants to provide up to 4 days of specialized training to Library staff, including Olivia Dart (Library Operations Assistant), David Bosco (Circulation Supervisor), Sally Hansen (Assistant Library Director), and Kim Boldt (Systems Librarian).

The specific qualifications of the consultants are connected to the project activities. For example, both consultants have experience with the specific climate control monitor requested in the budget. This addresses the question in section VI "Application Review" of the RFP, "Do they [the consultants] have experience and qualifications appropriate to the project's goals?" and addresses the hot button of consultations with professionals.

H. What is the plan of work for the project?

At 339 words, Section H explains *how* the project will be accomplished, *who* is responsible for the project, and *when* the activities will occur.

The organization has a long way to go in improving their archive storage and display. The eventual goal would be to digitize the collection to make it even more accessible. However, all long-term projects must start somewhere, and this provides the rationale for why the project is beginning with the environmental issues.

According to the Image Permanence Institute, a university-based, non-profit research laboratory founded in 1985, the storage environment is recognized as the greatest cause of collection decay, as well as the most effective means of preventing it. There is strong scientific evidence that heat and moisture are the primary rate-controlling factors in almost every mode of decay. Therefore, temperature and relative humidity are the most fundamental factors to consider in environmental management. They are always present, have the broadest effect on the largest number of items in the collection, and they act as enablers (or inhibitors) of damage by other factors such as light or pollutants. Control of these factors in the storage environment is of fundamental importance in preservation and is more broadly effective and much cheaper to implement than other, more limited, preservation actions.

This paragraph provides the strongest connection between the project and the hot button of preservation of humanities collection so far by explaining that correcting environmental factors can prevent decay, have the broadest impact, and be cost effective.

St. Norbert College requires several items for monitoring the environment in our special collections area at the Todd Wehr Library, including a climate control monitor with software and peripherals to measure the temperature and relative humidity, light meters, and water alarm and sensors. Ms. Maciejewski will be responsible for

This section outlines the steps of the project, *when* they will occur, and *who* will be responsible. A detailed plan of action helps the organization's credibility because it shows that thought has been put into the plan and gives the funder confidence that the applicant will be ready to go once awarded rather than spinning its wheels for a while first.

purchasing the equipment, and the St. Norbert College Library staff will install the equipment. With proper training from specialists, the Library staff will learn to monitor the environmental climate surrounding our rare materials. Prior to the 2009–10 academic year, this special collection and library staff will be transferred to the new Miriam B. and James J. Mulva Library.

* * *

STAGE ONE: FULL PROPOSAL

Developing the Budget.

The budget is modeled after the sample illustration presented in the RFP guidelines and includes itemized project expenses rounded to the nearest dollar. This level of detail highlights not only *how much* the project costs but also depicts the distribution of funds, namely, 43 percent of the budget relates to the consultant visits and 57 percent relates to the environmental monitoring supplies.

The prescriptive nature of the budget template, however, limited opportunity to justify the need for each supply item. As a result, we found an alternative, creative way to include those details: the RFP guidelines require a letter of commitment from the consultants. This letter is an ideal venue for the experts to recommend specific supplies, cite a history of working with the supplies, and confirm a willingness to provide training on the supplies. Collectively, these documents provide reviewers with the information necessary to know *what* is needed, *why* it is needed, and *how much* it will cost.

Also of note, the required consultant résumés contained a real bonus—a documented history of service on NEH grant projects. This experience confers individual credibility and reassures the sponsor an awareness exists that budget costs must be allowable, allocable, reasonable, and consistently treated.

Budget					
Applicant Organization:		St. Norbert College			
Consultant Fees.					
Name of Consultant:		Andrea Rolich			**Total:**
No. of days on project: 4		**Daily rate of compensation:** $225			$900
Name of Consultant:		Wayne Gathright			
No. of days on project: 4		**Daily rate of compensation:** $225			$900
Travel.					
From/To:	**No. of persons**	**Total Travel days**	**Subsistence costs**	**Transportation costs**	**Total:**
Madison, WI to De Pere, WI (125 mi)	2	4	$65/day = $520	$250	$770
Supplies, materials, equipment, and workshop registration fees.					
Item: 1 climate control monitor (PEM2) from the Image Permanence Institute web site at $350 each					$350
Item: 1 software (Climate Notebook) from the Image Permanence Institute web site at $500 each					$500
Item: 1 data transport device (SRAM card) from the Image Permanence Institute web site at $100 each					$100
Item: 1 flash drive (PEM2) from the Image Permanence Institute web site at $25 each					$ 25
Item: 1 Foot-candle-LUX meter (Fisher Traceable Dual-Display Light Meter) from Fisher Scientific web site at $200 each					$200
Item: 1 UV Light Meter (UV Elsec Light Monitor from Crawford) from University Products web site at $1,996 each					$1,996
Item: 1 water leak sensor alarm (Flood Detective Pro) from Flood Detective web site at $35 each					$35
Item: 4 water leak sensors (Flood Detective Pro) from Flood Detective web site at $6 each					$24
Item: 4 environmental management books from online bookstore at $50 each					$200
Total of Request: Total requested from NEH (up to $6,000)					**$6,000**

* * *

NEH Application Evaluation: PG50536, St. Norbert College

Panelist 1

The library has a humanities collection that supports the students and faculty of St. Norbert College in their research and curricular needs. In addition the Center for Norbertine Studies was established in 2006 to provide scholars and the wider world access to materials on the Norbertine Order and to promote the study of the Order's history. The materials in the Center's Special Collection can be used by researchers in the fields of Immigrant history, Wisconsin history, European history, Christian monasticism, American Catholicism, American frontier history and Native American/Christian encounters. It houses a relatively large collection of early (pre-1700) imprints.

The Center is a focal point for international research on the Norbertines and there are plans to host scholars from all over the world to do research on the Order. The Center for Norbertine Studies also is exploring the possibility of initiating a series of publications in the area of Norbertine history and spirituality.

As part of the plan for the inauguration of the new Mulva Library, they will highlight items from special collections, including items from the Abbey that were never seen by the public. They will also participate in the Modern Wisconsin Records Collecting Needs project survey, and they have plans, pending funding, to participate in the Wisconsin Association of Independent Colleges and Universities digital Library Collection.

A new library is being built and the applicant wants to have environmental monitors in place as they move into the new space. In 2006 the library had a general preservation assessment survey, awarded as part of the Subsidized Survey Program of the Midwest Art Conservation Center. Purchase of the monitoring equipment allows the applicant to continue to address problems identified in the survey. Equipment includes a climate control monitor with software and peripherals to measure the temperature and relative humidity, light meters, water alarm and sensors.

OK. Consultants will work with staff to assist them in learning to use the computerized monitoring equipment.

Consultants Andrea Rolich and Wayne Gathright served as project leaders for the IPI WebERA (Web Environmental Risk Analysis) project at UW-Madison, they both have experience with the PEM2 climate control monitor. They have been monitoring with PEMs since 2001 and are also experienced in monitoring both UV and visible light levels.

This request from St. Norbert College for environmental monitoring equipment for the new library builds on their multiphase preservation plan. They have demonstrated a solid understanding of preservation issues and have clear priorities in addressing those issues.

Rating: E: Excellent; recommended at highest priority of support

STAGE ONE: FULL APPLICATION

Analyzing Reviewer Comments.

The sponsor had three grant reviewers critique the proposal independently using a five-point scale: excellent, very good, good, some merit, and not competitive. Reviewers' comments are consistent with the three broad criteria identified in section VI "Application Review" of the RFP: (a) the collections and their use in humanities programming, education, or research; (b) the proposed activities and the justification of their importance to the institution, and; (c) the adequacy of the plan of work.

Panelist 1 provided the most extensive feedback, 410 words across seven paragraphs. Approximately two thirds of summary comments reflect sentences and phrases taken verbatim from the project narrative. Every paragraph of commentary touches on one or more sponsor hot buttons:

- Paragraph 1—preservation of humanities collection; accessibility and use of collection.
- Paragraph 2—accessibility and use of collection.
- Paragraph 3—accessibility and use of collection.
- Paragraph 4—preservation of humanities collection; consultations with professionals.
- Paragraph 5—consultations with professionals.
- Paragraph 6—consultations with professionals.
- Paragraph 7—preservation of humanities collection.

Comments also hint at a distinctive feature, future preservation plans. In particular, Panelist 1 saw the project as the next logical step in a multiphase plan, progressing from a past general preservation assessment to the current acquisition of environmental monitoring equipment to a future transition of collections into a new library.

Panelist 2 provided brief feedback, a succinct 187 words across three paragraphs. In the opening paragraph, the first two sentences address directly the sponsor hot buttons of preservation of humanities collection and consultations with professionals. The third sentence is a more subtle hint at the sponsor hot button of accessibility and use of collection. That is to say, the third sentence confirms that the special collections have value "well beyond the campus," thus implying that they will be accessed and used by students locally and scholars worldwide.

Panelist 2 also acknowledges both distinctive features. The final two sentences of the opening paragraph speak to custody of collection and the second paragraph praises "an excellent, comprehensive plan" that builds on prior general assessments and includes transitioning to a new space, a nod to future preservation plans. Of the three grant reviews, Panelist 2 is the only one who commented on custody of collection, which suggests that this distinctive feature may carry more weight with the program officer than with this specific panel of reviewers. Nevertheless, it does seem to be a psychological concern for the sponsor.

Panelist 2

St. Norbert College in DePere, WI, plans to monitor and stabilize the environmental conditions in which its special collections are stored. To accomplish this, the staff requests funding to purchase environmental monitoring equipment and to bring in a pair of consultants to train them in its proper use. St. Norbert's special collections are important to its mission and, as the only Norbertine college in the world, they have value well beyond the campus. In recent years, St. Norbert College has collaborated with St. Norbert Abbey to form the Center for Norbertine Studies. This new entity will care for the special collections of the College and the Abbey as a unified whole.

The environmental monitoring is just one step in an excellent, comprehensive plan following on two consultants' reports. The plans are tied, in part, to the upcoming opening of the College's new library in the Fall of 2009. It is essential that staff and materials are well prepared for the move to the new library.

The plan is well thought out and appropriate. It is especially strong in the context of the other phases of the plan.

Rating: E: Excellent; recommended at highest priority of support

Panelist 3 used 369 words across nine paragraphs to provide feedback. All three sponsor hot buttons are addressed. When the full application was being developed, there was worry that since much of the collection was not currently being used by the public, it would be difficult to show its value. Fortunately, Panelist 3 saw that while the collection is currently "underused," significant potential exists for future use.

Comments by Panelist 3 also highlight applicant credibility: in paragraph three, the reference to "active fund raising from the outside," including a previous NEH grant, bolsters organizational credibility; in paragraph six, the comment

Panelist 3

Primarily the collection supports Norbertine studies, and as the only Norbertine abbey in the world, the institution has the primary responsibility to "gather and share rare documents concerning the life of St. Norbert and the Norbertine Order". The proposal makes an excellent case for preserving an underused though valuable collection. There are titles in the collection available nowhere else in this country.

The Center not only supports the use of the collections for research and for college classes, it has a vigorous program of outreach. They calculate their annual number of visitors at over 225,000.

There is a history in the institution of active fund raising from outside, e.g. an NEH Challenge Grant.

The need for monitoring the environment of these collections is essential at this point to support earlier recommendations of preservation surveys, as well as the imminent opening of a new facility. This data will be fundamental to ensuring the safety of these important materials.

The college and library has a sound short-range preservation plan, which includes the digitization of materials once the collection storage environment is safe and maintained. The intent is to follow those proposed steps with producing a long-range plan.

The plan and budget for two consultants and the associated environmental monitoring equipment are clear and reasonable. The specifics provided in the budget for the proposed equipment show the staff has done its homework. The advice on equipment came from Dr. Andrea Rolich, Preservation Librarian from the University of Wisconsin-Madison, who is overseeing the proposed consultants.

The goal to monitor and ultimately maintain appropriate and stable temperatures, relative humidity, light, and air quality is clearly explained.

The project director, Ms. Maciejewski, as well as the two consultants and the coordinating Preservation Librarian at UofW-M, are extremely well qualified to oversee and carryout the monitoring project.

I applaud this project. This proposal is thoroughly supported in background with the value and use of the collections, the caliber of the associated college, and the need for the environmental monitoring equipment and supporting consultants as part of a soon to be established long-range preservation plan. There is indeed a strong case for the preservation of the collections and it seems well timed for the soon-to-be-opened new facility.

Rating: E: Excellent; recommended at highest priority of support

* * *

"the specifics . . . show that the staff has done its homework" demonstrates project credibility, and; in paragraph eight, the confirmation that the project director and consultants are "extremely well qualified" underscores individual credibility.

In the final paragraph, Panelist 3 offers high praise for the project, recapping the value of the collection, its importance to the scholarly community, and the quality of the preservation plan. More broadly, all three panelists considered the proposal to be "excellent" and recommended the "highest priority of support."

National Endowment for the Humanities Washington, DC 20506

December 2, 2008

Ms. Libby Evelyn Charles
Director of Sponsored Programs
Saint Norbert College
100 Grant Street
De Pere, WI 54115

Ref: PG-50536-090

Dear Ms. Charles:
I am delighted to inform you that the National Endowment for the Humanities has awarded a grant of $6,000.00 in support of your project. Your application was considered carefully during the NEH review process, which includes peer review and specialist review along with deliberation by the National Council on the Humanities and the Office of the Chairman.

I enclose the official notice of action from the NEH Office of Grant Management, which provides information on the grant period and the terms and conditions that apply to your project. Please review this material carefully. Address your questions either to the grants administrator or to the program officer whose names appear on the second page of the award notification.

Congratulations on your award. I wish you every success.

Sincerely,
Bruce Cole
Chairman

Information on the "Preservation Assistance Grants for Smaller Institutions" program can be found online at the National Endowment for the Humanities Web site at http://www.neh.gov/grants/preservation/preservation-assistance-grants-smaller-institutions.

STAGE ONE: FULL APPLICATION

Celebrating the Grant Award Notification.
The RFP guidelines call attention to the fact that the recommendations of grant reviewers are advisory to the sponsor; the program officer synthesizes panel results and assembles a funding slate for consideration by the National Council on Humanities. The NEH chair makes final funding decisions. In this instance, the grant award notification arrived in December, about a month earlier than the RFP indicated, and was a long-awaited delight.

More broadly, the time between reading the RFP for the Preservation Assistance Grants for Smaller Institutions and receiving the grant award notification was approximately nine months. There was intense activity during the first two months to plan and write the full application and there was nervous anticipation for seven months as the application made its way through the sponsor's submission, review, and recommendation processes. The grant award notification is a tangible indicator that we were able to balance successfully the relationship between sponsor values and our organizational capabilities and between proposal logics and psychologics. In short, our proposal was persuasive because it reflected the values of the sponsor.

CHAPTER 8

The Institute of International Education, Fulbright U.S. Scholar Program

FULBRIGHT U.S. SCHOLAR PROGRAM HOME PAGE (COURTESY OF THE COUNCIL FOR INTERNATIONAL EXCHANGE OF SCHOLARS, WWW.CIES.ORG/. USED BY PERMISSION.)

The Fulbright program was established in 1946 and is named in honor of J. William Fulbright, a prominent U.S. senator who was the longest serving chairman of the Senate Foreign Relations Committee. With a goal to "increase mutual understanding and support friendly and peaceful relations between the people of the United States and people of other countries," opportunities for international educational exchanges exist for university faculty, university students, K–12 teachers, and other professionals. Eight hundred faculty participate in core Fulbright U.S. Scholar Program teaching, research, and teaching/research awards annually in more than 125 countries around the world (2014 figure). Comprehensive information about program eligibility, application processes and review criteria, timelines, discipline and regional highlights, and frequently asked questions are available online at http://www.cies.org.

In this chapter we examine a successful proposal to the Institute of International Education, Fulbright U.S. Scholar Program for teaching/research in the health sciences in Finland. The program's emphasis to internationalize campuses and communities is consonant with the project director's commitment to realizing an organizational strategic plan goal to accelerate global learning. Quite simply, this individual fellowship experience has a potential multiplier effect of bringing the world to students and students to the world. The Fulbright U.S. Scholar Program uses a single-stage application process, which requires submission of a three- to five-page, single-spaced project statement. The elements of this chapter include the following.

Stage One: Full Application

- The Request for Proposal
- The Project Statement
- The Letter of Invitation
- The Grant Award Notification

This application is a model of proposal planning and writing; it presents the right balance of logic, emotion, and relationships to connect with the values of the sponsor. Figure 7 overviews the key elements that we brought together to reach the Persuasion Intersection.

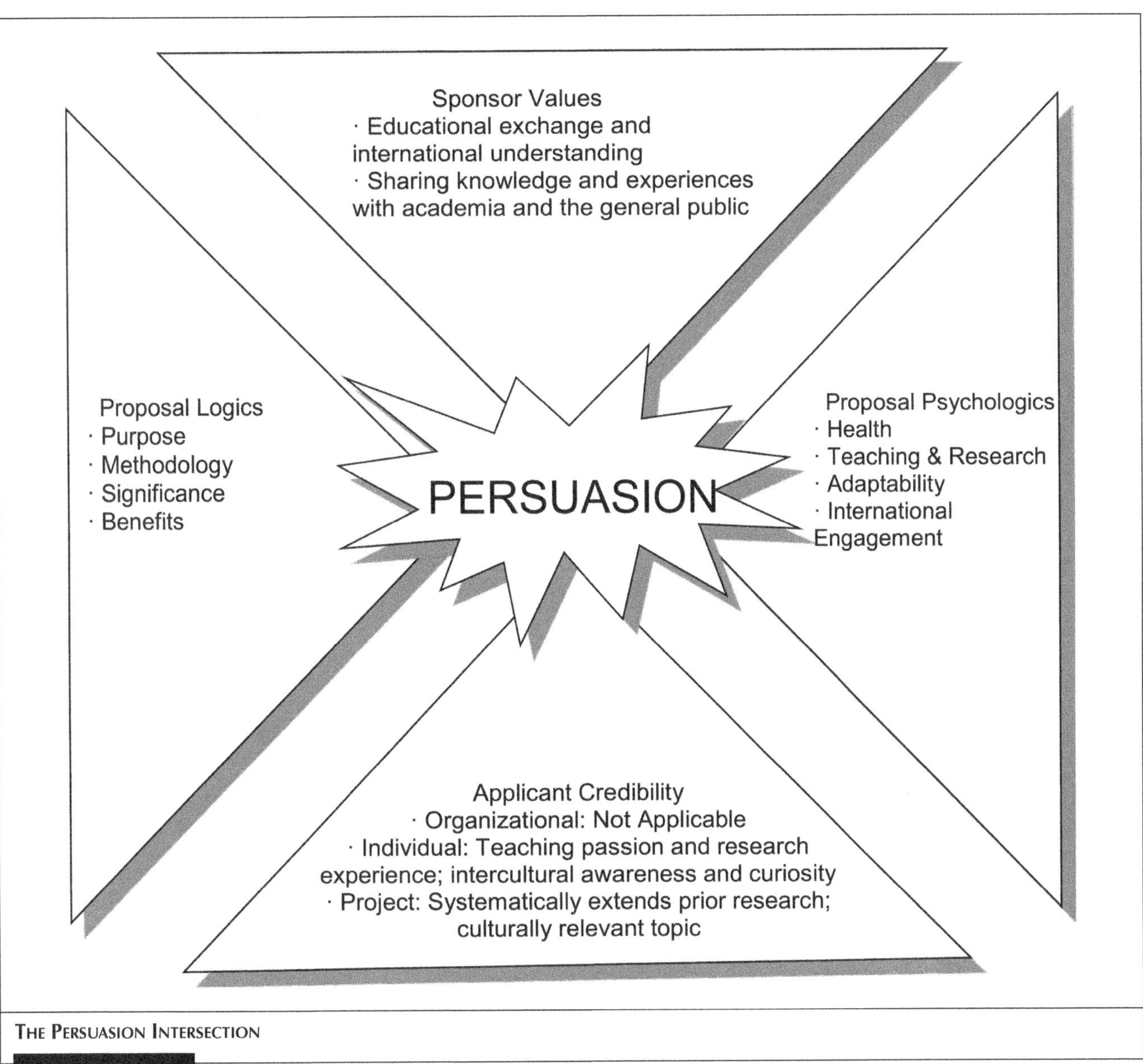

THE PERSUASION INTERSECTION

FIGURE 7

STAGE ONE: FULL APPLICATION

Analyzing the RFP.
The RFP (Request for Proposal) Analysis Process is a systematic way to consider questions about a grant program's *relevance*—Do we want to do this?, *feasibility*—Can we do this?, and *probability*—Will we be competitive in relation to our project ideas? Reading the RFP in recursive fashion helps us methodically identify and answer questions that will make our proposal stand out from the competition.

The following call-out thought bubbles provide insight into the process of planning and writing a successful proposal. Because the RFP Analysis Process is iterative by nature, the three steps may not always appear sequentially.

Step One: Relevance.
According to the RFP guidelines, the Fulbright U.S. Scholar Program, Fulbright-Saastamoinen Foundation Award in Health Sciences offers a living allowance of €2700 a month for five months to engage in research and teaching at the Faculty of Health Sciences at the University of Eastern Finland, starting in either the Fall or Spring semester of the next academic term. A three- to five-page, single-spaced project statement is due by August 2.

Step Two: Feasibility.
Evaluation criteria in RFPs often include consideration of the budget request. However, the Fulbright U.S. Scholar Program is more of an individual fellowship than a project grant, so there is no budget request. The award amount is fixed and includes a monthly stipend and one-time travel allowance that is paid directly to the project director.

Council for International Exchange of Scholars

Institute of International Education

Department of Scholar and Professional Programs

U.S. Fulbright Scholar Catalog of Awards 2011–12

Country Overview

Program Overview:	Fulbright-Saastamoinen Foundation Award in Health Sciences
	The award offers a unique opportunity to engage in international collaboration with Finnish researchers in health sciences. The award includes research and teaching at the Faculty of Health Sciences at the University of Eastern Finland. It is offered for a period of maximum five months, starting in either September 2011 or January 2012. Download brochure at www.fulbright.fi/files/2786_Fulbright-Saastamoinen_brochure.pdf
IIE Staff:	Program Officer Name: Jean McPeek Program Officer Phone: 202-686-6246 Program Officer Email: JMcPeek@iie.org Program Associate Name: Katherine Fox-Boyd Program Associate Phone: 202-686-6240 Program Associate Email: KFox-Boyd@iie.org

Country Benefits

Base Stipend:	n.a.
Maintenance:	The allowance is 2700€ a month, paid out in euros in monthly installments. There are no separate allowances for accompanying dependents.
Travel Relocation:	A one-time travel allowance of $1,800 is provided.
Tuition Assistance:	The Finnish school system is considered one of the best in the world. Finnish schools are free, although some special schools, such as international schools, may charge tuition. Universities do not currently charge tuition for degree students. Instruction in English is available in Helsinki at kindergartens, elementary and secondary schools, as well as at university level.

Other Benefits:	Housing is arranged and paid for by the host institution. Applicants should communicate their housing needs to the host institution so that appropriate housing can be arranged for them. At some institutions Fulbright Scholars have access to the university health care services provided for faculty and staff.
Special Award Benefits:	n.a.

Award Information

Award Code:	1205
World Area:	Europe
Country:	Finland
Award Title:	Fulbright-Saastamoinen Foundation Award in Health Sciences
Category:	Core
Activity:	Teaching/Research
Discipline:	Medical Sciences, Public/Global Health
Ph.D. Required:	Yes
Specializations:	Health sciences, molecular medicine, cardiovascular diseases, neurodegenerative diseases, metabolism-related diseases (type 2 diabetes), chronic, non-communicable diseases, cancer, food and health, safety of food, drug development, drug-like properties of drug substances, new drug formulations and process analysis techniques, evaluation of efficacy of drug treatment, health and well-being of children, youth and families, nursing management, and health services.
Grant Activity:	The award includes research and teaching at the Faculty of Health Sciences at the University of Eastern Finland. It is offered for a period of maximum five months, starting in either September 2011 or January 2012. The academic year runs from September through mid-May (Fall semester: September to mid-December;

Step Two: Feasibility.
Health is a hot button that appears more than two dozen times in the RFP, including prominent placement in the award title.

Step Two: Feasibility.
Teaching and research is an expected activity of the program; *teaching* appears two dozen and *research* appears three dozen times throughout the RFP, making it a clear sponsor hot button.

Step Three: Probability.
Preproposal contact questions might investigate "What is the standard faculty teaching load and which types of classes would best complement current course offerings?" and "What types of physical space, equipment and instrumentation, administrative support, and professional development resources are available to researchers?"

Step Three: Probability.
Strategic thinking questions might include "Do these Web sites reveal additional insights about potential common interests?" and "Does an analysis of faculty publications provide a more in-depth understanding of their current areas of expertise and generate ideas for how to best complement those skill sets?"

	Spring semester: January to mid-May). No teaching is generally offered during June to August. The scholar is expected to teach and participate in research work. Exact teaching to research ratio should be agreed upon by the applicant and the host. The research profile of AIVI is on molecular medicine of major diseases of high importance for health care, including cardiovascular diseases, neurodegenerative diseases, and metabolism-related diseases. http://www.uku.fi/aivi/. Research pursued by the School of Medicine focuses on chronic, non-communicable diseases in a comprehensive manner, from molecular mechanisms to disease prevention and treatment. The medical perspective is complemented by strong research related to food and health, as well as food safety. http://www.uku.fi/laake/english/introduction.shtml. The School of Pharmacy has the following strategic research areas: drug development, drug-like properties of drug substances, new drug formulations and process analysis techniques, and evaluation of efficacy of drug treatment. http://www.uku.fi/farmasia/english/. The main research areas of the Department of Nursing Science are the health and well-being of children, youth and families, learning environments, learning and teaching methods, theoretical and methodological development and evaluation, and research into nursing leadership, management, and health services. http://www.uku.fi/hoitot/english/. Proposals for medical research involving clinical training, patient care, or patient contact are not eligible. Applicants are encouraged to contact the university for more information.
Additional Qualifications:	Rank of full or associate professor
Language:	The language of instruction for the scholar is English. English is widely spoken in academic circles and in the country as a whole.
Locations:	Faculty of Health Sciences, University of Eastern Finland, Kuopio.

	The University of Eastern Finland (UEF) is a multidisciplinary university, which is internationally recognized for its high standard of research and education. The University has a strong profile in its areas of expertise, such as health sciences, molecular medicine, and welfare research. The University of Eastern Finland provides opportunities for a variety of health care and social welfare professionals and scholars. Furthermore, molecular medicine and clinical research are used to develop disease diagnostics and new treatment methods. The university's research on prevention of chronic diseases (e.g. cancer, cardiovascular diseases, type 2 diabetes) is based on its strong expertise in health sciences. The strengths in research are: lifestyle choices, nutrition and health, trials and development of medicinal products, molecular medicine, and neuroscience. The University of Eastern Finland operates on three campuses: Kuopio, Joensuu and Savonlinna. The Faculty of Health Sciences is located on the Kuopio campus in the city of Kuopio, about 400 km North East from Helsinki. Kuopio Science Park is located on the university campus; it offers excellent opportunities for extensive collaboration with the local National Institute of Public Health, the local National Institute of Occupational Health, and other national research institutions, as well. The Faculty of Health Sciences consists of the following units: A.I.Virtanen Institute for Molecular Sciences (AIVI), School of Medicine, School of Pharmacy, and Department of Nursing Science. The city of Kuopio (founded 1775) is a modern, developing center of economic life, scientific knowledge, and technological expertise in Eastern Finland. A unique, natural setting and a high quality of life make it an appealing place to live. It is the eighth largest city in Finland with about 90,000 inhabitants.

Step Three: Probability.
Strategic thinking questions might include "What is the relationship between the University of Eastern Finland and other universities in Finland?" and "Does the University of Eastern Finland share resources, such as access to library acquisitions and laboratory instrumentation, with the University of Helsinki, the largest and oldest institution of higher education in Finland?"

Step Two: Feasibility
The evaluation criteria expect the academic benefits of the scholarship to be described, but the RFP also raises the distinctive feature of international engagement. Consistent with the purpose of the Fulbright U.S. Scholar Program to bridge geographic and cultural boundaries, this distinctive feature encourages connecting with members of the local community to increase mutual understanding.

Step Three: Probability.
Preproposal contact questions might include "Will the three-day orientation be held in Helsinki or in Kuopio?" and "Is there a sample agenda available for the three-day orientation?"

Length of Grant:	5 months
Starting Date:	August or September 2011 or January 2012
Deadline:	August 2, 2010
Special Features:	The Fulbright-Saastamoinen Foundation Award in Health Sciences includes free housing, arranged and paid for by the University of Eastern Finland. The Fulbright Center in Helsinki arranges a 3-day orientation for grantees at the end of August, which grantees arriving for the fall semester are expected to attend. An orientation meeting may also be arranged for grantees arriving in January.
Additional Comments:	The Fulbright Center in Finland encourages potential applicants to visit its website for further information and contact the Center directly with any questions: Sami Krogerus, Program Manager e-mail: sami.krogerus@fulbright.fi tel: +358-9-5494 7402 The Faculty of Health Sciences encourages applicants to contact the UEF/Kuopio Campus beforehand. An invitation letter is recommended as part of the application, but not required. Jukka Mönkkönen, Dean of the Faculty of Health Sciences, UEF e-mail: jukka.monkkonen@uef.fi tel: +358 40 7288057 Anitta Etula, Deputy Director, Centre for International Relations, UEF e-mail: anitta.etula@uef.fi tel: +358 50 590 5012
Helpful Links:	Fulbright Center, Finland - Grant Programs www.fulbright.fi CIES - General information on Finland www.cies.org/country/finland.htm. University of Eastern Finland www.uef.fi/english/ Kuopio Science Park

Step Three: Probability.
Strategic thinking questions might include "What weight does the invitation letter really carry with reviewers if the host institution is free to share letters with multiple candidates?" and "How much lead time is necessary to secure the recommended invitation letter and still meet the application deadline?"

	www.kuopioinnovation.fi City of Kuopio www.kuopio.fi This is Finland – Finnish culture, politics, history, society etc. www.virtual.finland.fi In addition to links provided here, see Description of Activity for additional Web link(s).

U.S. FULBRIGHT SCHOLAR APPLICATION INSTRUCTIONS

APPLICATION FORM

Applicants may only apply for one award per application cycle.

Award Information
Item 1. Country of Interest or Regional Program
Item 2. Award Number
Item 3. Type of Activity

Professional Profile
Item 4. Title
Item 5. Name
Item 6. Preferred Name
Item 7. Current Primary Academic/Professional Title and Starting Date in that Position
Item 8. Professional Address

Citizenship Information
Item 9. Date of Birth
Item 10. City/State/Country of Birth
Item 11. Country of Citizenship
Item 12. Date of Naturalization
Item 13. Gender
Item 14. U.S. Veteran

Academic Credentials
Item 15. Awarded Degree(s)
Item 16. Academic Discipline and Primary Specialization
Item 17. Most Significant Professional Accomplishments—*Maximum 700 characters*
Item 18. Language
Item 19. Residence or Professional Trips Abroad
Item 20. Previous Fulbright Grant(s)

Step Three: Probability.
Strategic thinking questions might include "What additional information can be gleaned from these Web sites and applied to the Personal Statement?" and "Are there dimensions of Finnish culture described on these Web sites that can help address the distinctive feature of international engagement?"

Step Two: Feasibility.
The RFP indicates that a complete submission may include an Application Form, References, Project Statement, Curriculum Vitae or Résumé, Select Bibliography, and Letter of Invitation.

The Application Form contains 38 questions relating to award information, professional profile, citizenship information, academic credentials, project details, and personal information.

Step Two: Feasibility.
The Application Form helps to establish individual credibility in a condensed format. Of all the professional and personal information requested about the project director, Item 17 may be the most significant: a maximum of five professional accomplishments must be summarized in 700 characters, which is approximately 100 words. Since the Project Statement does not request a description of "project director qualifications," outside of the Application Form, reviewers must look to the six-page Curriculum Vitae or Résumé to learn more about key teaching, research, scholarship, public service, and other professional activities.

Step Two: Feasibility.
The Application Form imposes on the abstract (Item 22), the same 700 character limit, roughly 100 words, as it did on the list of most significant professional accomplishments (Item 17). Given the hot button expectation for teaching and research, in practical terms, the abstract will have two sentences on teaching activity and two sentences on research project work, with the hot button of health woven in throughout the description.

Step Three: Probability.
Strategic thinking questions might include "Though technically not required, does the fact that the Application Form has two yes/no questions asking whether a Letter of Invitation has been received (Item 25) or is expected (Item 26) suggest that getting one is a nonoptional option?" and "To expedite the receipt process, would it be considered presumptuous to draft a Letter of Invitation and share it with host institution?"

Step Three: Probability.
Strategic thinking questions might include "Does waiving the right to access submitted reference letters convey to reviewers an increased sense of honesty and legitimacy to what is being written?" and "Does retaining the right to access submitted reference letters also allow the opportunity to correct them for factual accuracy?"

Project Details

Item 21. Project Title
Item 22. Abstract or Summary of Project Statement—*Maximum 700 Characters*
Item 23. Proposed Start Date and Length of Grant
Item 24. Preferred Host Institution
Item 25. Letter of Invitation—received
Item 26. Letter of Invitation—expected
Item 27. Alternate Country and Awards
Item 28. Research Subjects—humans
Item 29. Research Subjects—vertebrate animals

Personal Information

Item 30. Home Mailing Information
Item 31. State of Legal Residence
Item 32. Social Security Number
Item 33. Marital Status
Item 34. Dependent Information
Item 35. Felony
Item 36. Misdemeanor
Item 37. Fulbright Race/Ethnicity Survey
Item 38. Signature

REFERENCES

Please note, this is step one of two required for successful submission of references. You will not be able to submit your application unless both steps are complete.

After completion of the entire application form, you must register references before submitting your application. In this step, once a referee is registered an email will be automatically generated by the system. This email will guide the referees through the process of uploading reference letters. The applicant is responsible for notifying referees of their request for letters and for ensuring those letters are submitted to CIES via the online system by the deadline. Once referees are registered, even if they have not uploaded their letters, you will be able to submit your application.

Reference Letter Instructions

- Indicate whether you waive your right to access your submitted letters of reference. If you do not waive your right, contact CIES on how to view your letters.
- All references must be in English.

- Do not exceed the indicated number of references as stated in the award description. Most awards, this will require three letters of reference. The fourth entry can ***only*** be used for an external language proficiency report.

Reference Letter Guidelines

- Provide your referees with a copy of your project statement.
- Referees should keep an electronic copy of submitted letters.
- References should be from persons able to evaluate your professional work, including teaching effectiveness; the abilities you bring to your project; your ability to adapt; and the merits of the project.
- At least one letter should be from a colleague in your field who is outside your home institution. Such letters help demonstrate the breadth of your scholarly reputation.
- If you are applying for a teaching or teaching/research award, one of your referees should include the departmental chair, dean, or other responsible individual for evaluating your teaching at your home institution.
- If you have recently moved to a new home institution, one of the reference letters should be from your previous institution.
- If your doctorate or master's degree is recent or you are early in your career, one reference should be from the supervisor of your graduate program.

PROJECT STATEMENT

All applications require a project statement. This is your opportunity to explain your specific strengths as a candidate to reviewers and potential hosts. It must be clear and compelling to audiences both inside and outside your field.

Format Requirements:

- 3 to 5 pages, single spaced, 12-point or larger font size
- Submission as a PDF or Word document
- Headers and/or bullets to organize and convey key elements may be helpful

Step Two: Feasibility.
Given the hot button of teaching and research, it is understandable that referees should be able to evaluate the project director's teaching effectiveness, the significance of the research project, or both. However, referees are also invited to assess a more personal quality of the project director—adaptability, which makes it stand out as a distinctive feature.

Referees have the flexibility to interpret the phrase in the third bulleted item "your ability to adapt" to mean broadly "your ability to adapt personally to a new environment, culture, and context" or specifically "your ability to adapt your course materials to the needs of host country students and your research agenda to the needs of the host country and colleagues."

Step Three: Probability.
Strategic thinking questions might include "For an external reference letter, is it better to secure one from a 'big name' in the field with whom only a casual relationship exists or from a junior-level colleague with whom there has been extensive professional engagement?" and "Is it better to select three references who can each attest to health-related teaching and research and international engagement and adaptability, or to select references who complement each other, speaking respectively to teaching, research, and international engagement and adaptability?"

Step Two: Feasibility.
Although the Fulbright U.S. Scholar Program uses a single-stage application process, it uses a three-stage peer review process. Applications are first reviewed by a panel of discipline specialists and categorized

into highly recommended, recommended, and not recommended. Applications and reviewer comments are considered second by a panel of geographic generalists; typically, twice as many applications as award slots available move forward to the next stage. Third, applications are reviewed in the host country and candidate selections are made; the J. W. Fulbright Foreign Scholarship Board makes final approvals. The most persuasive proposals appeal to generalist and specialist reviewers, domestically and internationally.

Step Two: Feasibility.
Evaluation criteria in the RFP indicate that the three- to five-page Project Statement should describe the purpose, methodology, significance, and benefits—individually and institutionally, domestically and internationally, programmatically and disciplinarily.

Step Two: Feasibility.
The bulleted items in this list contain two distinctive features: international engagement and adaptability. The questions in the first bulleted item ask about give-and-take: "What can you contribute to the host institution?" and "What will it mean for you professionally?" The questions in the second, fifth, and sixth bulleted items ask about goodness-of-fit: "What experiences have prepared you to teach in this country?", "How will you adapt your materials to the culture and language of the host country?", and "How will you adapt to a pedagogically different teaching environment in which the first language of the students may not be English?" In essence, the sponsor is looking for individuals who will serve as ambassadors, not ones who will simply teach classes.

Content Guidelines:

- What you propose to do.
- How you propose to do it.
- Why it is important.
- What benefits it will produce for the host, the discipline, the applicant and the home institution.

Project Statements for **Teaching Awards** specifically describe:

- Why this country? What can you contribute to the host institution? What will it mean for you professionally?
- What experiences have prepared you to teach in this country? Highlight experiences that indicate your collegiality, adaptability, cultural sensitivity, ability to serve as a cultural ambassador.
- What have you taught and how do you teach? What is your involvement in curriculum planning, thesis advising, or administrative responsibilities?
- What courses do you propose to teach? Do you plan other teaching activities? (seminars, curriculum and program development, public lectures)
- How you will adapt your materials to the culture and language of the host country?
- How will you adapt to a pedagogically different teaching environment in which the first language of the students may not be English?
- What impact do you expect on your teaching and/or professional work?
- How do you expect to use the experience upon your return? (institutional collaboration, student and faculty exchange)

Project Statements for **Research Awards** specifically describe:

- What do you propose to do? State clearly your objectives, methodology and the nature of your research (quantitative or qualitative).
- What is the academic and professional context of the project? Include a bibliography (not exceeding 3 pages) referring to the leading works by others and the current state of research in the field.
- What professional experience has prepared you to successfully accomplish this project?
- Why does it need to be done? What significance does it hold for your discipline, your development, the host country's benefit?
- How will you carry out the proposed research? (methodology, logistics, time frame)
- How feasible is your project in terms of resources and amount of time allocated?
- Why does it need to be done in this country? What research facilities and resources are found in the host country?
- How could local political or cultural issues impact your work?
- How will your results be disseminated? (publications, conference presentations, joint collaboration)

Step Two: Feasibility.
Just as both distinctive features appeared in the instructions for writing Project Statements for teaching awards, they, too, appear in the instructions for research awards. The distinctive feature of international engagement manifests itself in the fourth and seventh bulleted items, "What significance does it hold for your discipline, your development, the host country's benefit?" and "Why does it need to be done in this country?" The distinctive feature of adaptability shows up in the third and eighth bulleted items, "What professional experience has prepared you to successfully accomplish this project?" and "How could local political or cultural issues impact your work?" The sponsor values gains in mutual understanding, not just advancing individual research productivity.

Project Statements for **Teaching/Research Awards** specifically describe:

- Both the teaching and the research components, using the above suggestions.
- Match your teaching and research time allocations to any specifics given in the award description (e.g., if the award denotes 80% teaching and 20% research, then the project statement should reflect this requirement).
- Lacking a specific percentage requirement, you should address both the teaching and research components adequately. If you have any questions about the percentages, consult with your potential host or contact the appropriate CIES program officer.

Step Three: Probability.
Preproposal contact questions might include "In instances where a specific percentage requirement is not stated in the RFP, is there a typical preferred balance between time spent teaching and time researching?" and "To what extent does flexibility exist to adjust teaching and research time allocations after awards have been made?"

CURRICULUM VITAE OR RÉSUMÉ

All applicants must include a tailored curriculum vitae or résumé with a detailed publications list.

Guidelines

- Curriculum vitae or resume cannot exceed 6 pages for Fulbright Scholar awards, including publications list.
- Publications should be cited fully and listed chronologically starting with the most recent.
- Referred publications should be separated from un-refereed publications.

Step Three: Probability.
Preproposal contact questions might include "Are there any expected categories of information to be listed on the Curriculum Vitae or Résumé beyond the standard: education, positions held, courses taught, publications, professional activities, membership and activities in professional associations, professional honors and awards, and community service?" and "Is there a minimum number of peer-reviewed publications that applicants are expected to have—or more specifically, how will it be received by reviewers if the applicant

has a reasonable number of publications overall, but because of a mid-career change in trajectory, has only a modest number of publications in the current line of research?"

Step Three: Probability.
Preproposal contact questions might include "To what extent will reviewers who are U.S. disciplinary specialists be familiar with pertinent literature in international publications?" and "To what extent will host country experts be familiar with pertinent literature in U.S. publications?"

Step Three: Probability.
Strategic thinking questions might include "Will reviewers react more favorably to syllabi that have been used previously or one that has been developed specifically in response to this RFP?" and "Is there an opportunity cost of developing a syllabus specifically for the host country and then the course is not offered as planned?"

Step Three: Probability.
Strategic thinking questions might include "Will a Letter of Invitation with generic statements of benefits to the host hurt the application more than not including a letter at all?" and "Is it reasonable to communicate via e-mail with the host or should it be via telephone to request a Letter of Invitation, ensuring that they understand the proposed project well enough to detail its expected benefits?"

SELECT BIBLIOGRAPHY

Research or Teaching/Research applicants must submit a bibliography relevant to the proposed topic.

- It should reflect the current state of research on the proposed topic.
- It cannot exceed 3 pages.

For Teaching and Teaching/Research awards, submit two to three course syllabi or course outlines relevant to planned grant activity. The syllabi should be designed by you and expressive of your philosophy of teaching. Indicate whether they have been used previously or have been developed for this application.

- Please merge syllabi or outlines into one PDF or Word document and upload.
- The combined document should not exceed 10 pages.

LETTER OF INVITATION

Not all awards require a letter of invitation. Consult the letter of invitation section of the award description for requirements and any special instructions. If unclear, contact the appropriate CIES program staff.

While there are no specific content requirements for invitation letters, the letter might include:

- The host's interest in the project and how it will benefit the host institution.
- Expected activities (e.g. research at the institution, special lecturing needs, etc.).
- The invitation period.

A single institution is free to send letters of invitation to multiple candidates, so be aware that a letter is not a legally binding pledge, nor does it guarantee an applicant a grant.

Submission Guidelines:

- Upload the letter of invitation in PDF format. If several invitation letters are received, please scan and combine into one PDF file before uploading.
- If the letter of invitation is not in English, include an English translation with the original.
- If a letter of invitation arrives after the application deadline, contact the CIES program officer listed in the award description.

REVIEW CRITERIA

Programs: Core Fulbright U.S. Scholar Program

The Fulbright Core Scholar Program supports activities and projects that recognize and promote the critical relationship between educational exchange and international understanding, in addition to the intellectual merit of the proposals. Applications with broad multiplier effects are particularly welcome, as are projects that are conducive to candidates' sharing of their experiences and knowledge with colleagues, students and, ideally, with the general public in their host country and, upon return, in the United States.

Review Criteria

As reviewers take into account the basic objectives of the Fulbright Scholar Program, they apply the following criteria:

Professional Qualifications

- **Credentials,** training and professional standing.
- **Professional excellence,** as evidenced through the quality of publications, grants, fellowships, honors, awards, conference papers, exhibitions, compositions, and performances.
- **Record of service** to the field and the home institution.

Teaching Awards

- **Match** of academic, professional or artistic expertise to the award.
- **Teaching ability and requisite experience** at the postsecondary level, as evidenced by the applicant's C.V., teaching awards, the quality of submitted syllabi, innovative and effective pedagogical approaches, and/or curriculum projects, and attested to by one of the three letters of reference.
- **Quality and feasibility** of the proposed teaching project: appropriateness of proposed courses to host institution, including demonstrated flexibility in course design to adapt it to the needs of the host student audience; currency in proposed teaching topics; evidence of host institution interest and affiliation, if indicated in the award description.
- **Outcomes, potential impact and benefits:** ability to address the needs and interests of the host institution and host country, and to contribute to curriculum and program development at the host institution, if desired in the award description; benefits to students at home and host institutions; potential for outreach to the public in host and home country, and to establish lasting connections and ties with students, colleagues, and/or institutions in the host country.

Step Three: Probability.
Preproposal contact questions might include "What are some of the biggest dissatisfactions with the current approaches to bridging gaps in international understanding?" and "What kinds of challenges are most glaring—demonstrating intellectual merit, communicating across cultures, engaging general publics, disseminating program experiences widely upon return, sustaining connections with the host country and institution?"

Step Two: Feasibility.
Reviewers consider evaluation criteria holistically and from multiple perspectives, examining individual credibility and project credibility in relation to the overarching aims of the grant program. At the first stage of the peer review process, full applications are examined by a U.S. panel of disciplinary specialists who are knowledgeable in the targeted academic field. At the second stage, applications are appraised by a U.S. panel of geographic generalists who are familiar with the targeted country and region. At the third stage, applications are assessed by experts in the host country who judge the full application and its potential impacts viewed through appropriate local contextual lenses—political, social, economic, legal, environmental, historical, and cultural.

Step Two: Feasibility.
Evaluation criteria under the hot button heading of "Teaching Awards" contain the distinctive features of adaptability and international engagement. The third and fourth bulleted items speak to adaptability: "appropriateness of proposed courses to the host institution, including demonstrated flexibility in course design to adapt it to the needs of the host student audience" and "ability to

address the needs and interests of the host institution and host country." The fourth bulleted item also addresses international engagement: "potential for outreach to the public in the host and home country, and to establish lasting connections and ties with students, colleagues, and/or institutions in the host country."

Step Two: Feasibility.
Just as both distinctive features appear under the hot button heading of "Teaching Awards," they too appear under the hot button heading of "Research Awards." The distinctive feature of adaptability manifests itself subtly in the second bulleted item, "relevant and appropriate research experience and expertise to complete the proposed research activity successfully." The distinctive feature of international engagement shows up in the fourth and sixth bulleted items, respectively, "need for residence in host country to accomplish the project" and "potential for outreach to the public in host and home country, and to establish lasting connections and ties with collaborators, the wider research community, and/or institutions abroad."

Step Three: Probability.
Strategic thinking questions might include "What ways, beyond language, might demonstrate cultural competence, an ability to interact effectively with administrators, faculty, students, and the general public in the host country?" and "Are there other details about Finnish culture and society that can be integrated into the full application to make it stand out from the competition?"

Research Awards

- **Intellectual merits** of the proposal: rigor of research design and methodology; originality and conceptual sophistication; project's significance.
- **Suitability:** relevant and appropriate research experience and expertise to complete the proposed research activity successfully.
- **Feasibility** in terms of resources available and time allocated to the project.
- **Need for residence** in host country to accomplish the project.
- **Evidence of host institution interest and affiliation,** if indicated in the award description.
- **Outcomes, potential impact and benefits:** quality of research output and plans to disseminate research results in the U.S. and abroad; potential to advance knowledge; significance of research to applicant's field and professional development, as well as to the interests and needs of the host country; potential for outreach to the public in host and home country, and to establish lasting connections and ties with collaborators, the wider research community, and/or institutions abroad.

Foreign Language Proficiency

- Foreign language proficiency **as specified** in the award description, or **commensurate with** the requirements of the proposed project. (**Note: in many world areas, English is sufficient for lecturing.**)

Previous Fulbright Awards

- **Compelling justification** for a repeat Fulbright grant: **evidence of outcomes** and **sustained** professional, institutional, and/or personal **ties** resulting from previous Fulbright grant; **explanation** of how **subsequent** Fulbright grant will **build on the previous** one.
- Where there is competition for grants, preference will be given to candidates who have not had previous Fulbright grants, especially within the past ten years. View the J. William Fulbright Foreign Scholarship Board's policies on previous Fulbright Scholar grants.

Previous Experience Abroad

- Preference is generally given to candidates who have not had substantial recent experience abroad in the country to which they are applying (see eligibility). A candidate who has resided abroad for five or more consecutive years in the six-year period preceding the date of application is ineligible for a grant. For the purpose of this section, a candidate who has lived outside the United States for nine months or more during a calendar year is deemed to have resided abroad for that year.
- In-country residence at the time of application or a recent extended stay may reduce chances for an award to that country. Duty abroad in the U.S. Armed Forces, however, is not considered disqualifying within the meaning of this section.

Personal Qualities

- Ability to serve as a cultural ambassador for the United States, including, but not limited to personal attributes of **collegiality, cultural adaptability and sensitivity**.

Geographic Distribution

- Other factors being equal, and to the extent possible, applicants are chosen to represent a broad geographic distribution, by both home state and type of institution.

Veterans of Military Service

- Preference is given to veterans when other factors are equivalent.

Please note, only complete applications, including three letters of reference, will be accepted for consideration.

* * *

Step Three: Probability.
Strategic thinking questions might consider "Would it be valuable to describe how this Fulbright award will build on previous work?" and "Would it be valuable to include examples of outcomes that have been sustained from other grant-funded projects?"

Step Three: Probability.
Preproposal contact questions might include "What levels of commitment to sustainability are reviewers expecting to see in proposals?" and "Is there specific evaluation data you would like to see collected to facilitate a meta-analysis of your grant funding portfolio?"

Step Three: Probability.
Strategic thinking questions might include "Would it be valuable to describe experience living in a comparable geographic and temperate environment as the host country?" and "Which personal international experiences will contribute to success in the host country?"

Step Two: Feasibility.
This "Personal Qualities" section is a direct appeal to the distinctive features of adaptability and cultural engagement. In particular, the terms *cultural adaptability* and *sensitivity* relate to adaptability, and *cultural ambassador* and *collegiality* speak to cultural engagement. The sponsor values bridging geographic and cultural boundaries as a means to fostering mutual understanding, which requires that applicants go beyond demonstrating academic excellence in teaching and research to displaying personal characteristics such as engagement and openness to sharing new ideas that will promote friendly relations and a more peaceful world.

STAGE ONE: FULL APPLICATION

Developing the Project Statement.
The title of the project is presented in boldface type at the top of the page. Health is a hot button that appears prominently in the award title listed in the RFP, so it is especially fitting to include the key word *health* in the project title. The expanded title, "Comparison of U.S. and Finnish Urban-Rural Levels of Heavy Metals in Children's Hair," foreshadows *what* research will be conducted and *where* it will be carried out. What's more, it speaks both to reviewers who are disciplinary specialists and who are geographic generalists, piquing their interest and inviting them to read on.

In 213 words (15 percent of the total), the "Opening Statement" introduces the hot buttons that will be repeated throughout the Project Statement: health and teaching and research. The key word *health* appears more than two dozen times, the same as in the RFP. The key words *teaching* and *research* appear in approximately the same proportion as they do in the RFP, favoring research slightly over teaching.

The third paragraph summarizes *who* is responsible for the project, *who* might be interested in the results of the research activities, and *what* the study is all about: measuring heavy metals in the hair of Finnish children.

This paragraph also alludes to both distinctive features. In the first sentence, "a wealth of information and curiosity" hints at the distinctive feature of adaptability; the project director possesses knowledge and creativity to meet the needs of the host student audience. In the second

Environmental Public Health Perspectives: Comparison of U.S. and Finnish Urban-Rural Levels of Heavy Metals in Children's Hair

I. OPENING STATEMENT

A full understanding of public health requires an appreciation of global health. As I encourage young students in our environmental public health program to take internships across the United States, to study for a semester abroad, and to consider serving internationally in organizations such as the Peace Corps, I realize how much their professor can also grow from such experiences.

Finland, and the University of Eastern Finland at Kuopio in particular, provide excellent learning opportunities in the health sciences. With strong undergraduate and graduate programs that incorporate cutting-edge research on topics including global climate change and chronic disease, Kuopio offers outstanding possibilities for international teaching and research in global health.

As a mid-career health scientist and professor, I would bring both a wealth of information and curiosity to the Fulbright-Saastamoinen Foundation Award in Health Sciences. My proposed research to measure heavy metals in the hair of Finnish children would fit as a natural collaboration with Kuopio researchers. Dietary exposure information collected to determine sources of metal exposure (e.g., mercury in fish) could supplement the comprehensive SYSDIET and HELGA studies. Institutions such as the Laboratory of Applied Environmental Chemistry in Mikkeli would be welcome partners as data on urban vs. rural, and US vs. Finland metal concentrations were analyzed to better protect children's health.

II. PROJECT OVERVIEW

While measurements of toxicants in air, water, soil and food are useful for understanding how we are exposed to dangerous substances, biomarkers of exposure provide an accurate measurement of actual dose, and therefore, risk. Because children are an especially vulnerable subpopulation due to developing organ systems and greater exposure per body weight than adults, they must be carefully monitored and protected. As recognized by the US National Institutes of Health, children are an under-studied group that needs special protection from toxicant exposure.

The heavy metals lead—due to its greater absorption and effects on the CNS—and carcinogenic forms of chromium and arsenic—due to the many years of potential latency in younger people—are of particular concern with regards to children's health.

Previous studies have found differences in children's hair lead levels associated with the use of leaded gasoline, and measured levels near hazardous waste facilities. Others have found that other environmental factors play a role: "Family occupation, direct contact with wastewater, customs and food habits were the most significant factors influencing the metal content of children's hair" (for cadmium and lead). Children's methylmercury hair levels have been associated with gold mining. Others have found an inverse relationship between children's intelligence test scores and arsenic hair levels.

Hair analysis has been shown over the last decade to be a reliable measurement of chronic heavy metal exposure. This project would use non-invasive sampling of hair and questionnaire responses from parents to provide better information about Finnish childrens' exposure to heavy metals.

III. SAMPLES ADDRESSING WHY THE HOST COUNTRY WAS CHOSEN

I would appreciate the opportunity to teach Finnish students elements of environmental public health, sharing hands-on exercises applied to specific concerns in Finland, such as forest sustainability, climate change, industrial pollution and the eutrophication of local lakes. Finnish culture includes respect for environmental resources and a broad commitment to health of all citizens; the application of specific tests and discussion of case studies would thus be well-understood. I have developed and taught a dozen public health courses, supervised research for 52 undergraduate and graduate students, and taught over 10,000 students of all ages and abilities in various dance styles in addition to my academic work. My focus is on hands-on activities and active student involvement in course materials, and I would greatly value the opportunity to work with and learn from Finnish students through teaching environmental health.

sentence, "hair of Finnish children would fit as a natural collaboration with Kuopio researchers," addresses the distinctive feature of international engagement; the project director will connect with the local community as well as the research community.

The "Project Overview" uses 253 words (17 percent of the total) to set the context for and outline the parameters of the research project. The first paragraph explains *why* the study is necessary—to help protect children from toxicant exposure. The fourth paragraph addresses *how* the research will be conducted—noninvasive sampling of hair and questionnaire responses—and *who* is participating in the investigation—Finnish children and their parents.

The third paragraph in this section demonstrates the project director's knowledge of the literature in the field. Preproposal contact revealed that extensive citations were not necessary; a Select Bibliography follows the Project Statement.

The longest section of the Project Statement, "Samples Addressing Why the Host Country Was Chosen," identifies *where* the project will take place and justifies its selection.

The first sentence in this section addresses the hot button of teaching and research and the distinctive feature of adaptability, providing specific examples of how teaching exercises will be made directly relevant to host country students.

The second and third sentences in this section address the hot button of health and tie it to the distinctive feature of adaptability; the project director will select case studies that relate immediately to the values of the host country.

The fourth sentence establishes the credibility of the project director to tailor courses and activities to students' needs: "I have developed and taught a dozen public health courses, supervised research for 52 undergraduate and graduate students . . . ."

The fifth sentence appeals to the distinctive feature of international engagement. The phrase "work with and learn from Finnish students" confirms the mutual exchange of knowledge and ideas.

The second paragraph in this section demonstrates a keen awareness of Finland's climate. It takes a certain disposition and fortitude to withstand Finnish winters, when daylight is short, temperatures can be subzero, and snow accumulation can be heavy. The project director has strategies to thrive in this environment.

The third paragraph in this section raises the possibility of long-term international engagement that could emerge with the host country, namely, "scholarship, student exchange, and international collaboration." A history of successful student internships with Scandinavian universities reinforces the likelihood of sustained stewardship, which relates to the distinctive feature of international engagement.

While my wife and I grew up in the temperate climate of the US west coast, we have lived in the colder climate of Wisconsin for seven years and now enjoy ice skating and cross-country skiing. I also believe an opportunity for our young daughter to learn about Finnish culture would be a benefit.

The opportunity to teach and conduct research at the University of Eastern Finland at Kuopio would also revive a decade-long affiliation between the University of Wisconsin-Eau Claire and Scandinavian universities. My predecessor, Professor Emeritus Robert Nelson regularly visited and gave tours in Sweden, hosted Scandinavian scholars in Wisconsin, gave an environmental health presentation at Kuopio, and set up a decade of student internships. I would like to revive this rich tradition of scholarship, student exchange, and international collaboration.

IV. SAMPLE TEACHING STYLE DESCRIPTIONS

The field of environmental public health is best taught, I believe, through relevant examples and applications. Hands-on equipment use, field trips, and interactive problem-solving discussions are powerful tools for learning the principles and "nuts and bolts" of protecting human health and environmental resources. My teaching also includes extensive use of web-based resources: video clips, simulations and online quizzes and discussions.

Students remember most vividly field trips to local wastewater treatment plants, food processing centers, hospitals, industrial plants, and waste treatment centers. I require students to bring equipment to test temperatures, noise, lower explosivity limits, dust levels, and electromagnetic fields, as they complete an "inspection" report for the field trip. Many of these field trips result in internship opportunities, and some result in job offers for my graduating students.

In classes, students make choices about energy uses to understand health consequences (e.g., coal has the lowest price but causes the greatest health damages). Students learn about the "cap-and-trade" principle by actually trading carbon emission offsets in class as they assume roles of polluters and forest managers. (I am currently evaluating the "Risk Game" at www.environment.fi for possible use in my classes.)

The availability of course materials electronically gives students the opportunity to review and learn at their own pace, and would be of special benefit to give Finnish students time to understand the English text.

The Letter of Invitation that accompanies the Project Statement invites the project director to teach "one or two courses, for example, in Public Health, Environmental Health, Solid and Hazardous Waste Management, Industrial Hygiene, Environmental Toxicology and Risk Assessment, or in Pharmaceutical Toxicology," which is a very broad range from which to choose. In the 224-word "Sample Teaching Style Descriptions" section, rather than selecting beforehand specific courses to teach and preparing syllabi, the project director conveys an overarching teaching philosophy applicable to any course: hands-on learning by doing. Students become proficient by practicing with actual tools of the trade in real-life environments.

The third paragraph contains a noteworthy parenthetical comment, "(I am currently evaluating the 'Risk Game' at www.environment.fi for possible use in my classes.)." The phrase "use in my classes" has a double meaning—courses to be taught in the United States and courses to be taught in Finland. Further, since this Finnish online resource was identified as a direct result of pursuing this award opportunity, the project director is displaying an openness to new ideas and an appreciation for knowledge exchange.

"Sample Descriptions of How Teaching Style Will Be Adapted" represents 10 percent of the total length of the Project Statement. The first paragraph addresses both distinctive features. "Speaking more slowly, learning key Finnish terms, and providing multiple ways in which students can learn material" are examples of adaptability to meet the needs of host country students. "I would expect to learn a great deal about Finnish culture, values, and *sisu* as they relate to public health" illustrate international engagement.

The use of *sisu* was intentional and strategic. This Finnish word doesn't have a direct translation into English, but it shares elements with determination, persistence, inner strength, resoluteness, and stoic toughness, and is a vital concept in Finnish culture. In this instance, more than understanding the Finnish spirit, the project director employs *sisu* to declare his commitment to bridging lab research and life teaching for the benefit of "the health of humans and the environment"—a powerful personal promise that also addresses sponsor hot buttons.

The "Sample of Research Methodology Descriptions" uses a mere 96 words (7 percent of the total) to spell out *how* the research will be accomplished.

The first paragraph in this section justifies the methodological approach, namely, examining hair samples is a noninvasive way to estimate heavy metal exposure.

The second paragraph describes the target population, sample size, and data collection strategies, and the third paragraph explains the analysis process for a recently completed study; the same approach would be used in the host county.

Reviewers who are disciplinary specialists will recognize that this scope of work is feasible and manageable during the five-month project period. They will also take note of the project director's access to an inductively coupled plasma mass spectrometer, a highly advanced instrument that is not widely available in academic environments.

V. SAMPLE DESCRIPTIONS OF HOW TEACHING STYLE WILL BE ADAPTED

Patience is perhaps the most important qualification of a teacher and I have been acknowledged by many students in this regard. Speaking more slowly, learning key Finnish terms, and providing multiple ways in which students can learn material would all be employed to support learning in my classroom. I firmly believe that my students' knowledge, discovery and involvement in courses contribute as much to learning as the material I provide them. As such, I would expect to learn a great deal about Finnish culture, values, and *sisu* as they relate to public health. These principles would be compared to values of cultures around the world as they affect the health of humans and the environment.

The use of visual and mathematical approaches, and hands-on exercises would be emphasized to communicate course material; electronic resources for review would always be available.

VI. SAMPLE OF RESEARCH METHODOLOGY DESCRIPTIONS

Measurement of heavy metal concentrations in human hair is an emerging way to estimate exposure. While blood concentrations of these metals best represent circulating levels, hair concentrations provide a non-invasive measure of long-term exposure.

Urban and rural regions of Wisconsin, US, were identified for sampling. Seventy samples of hair, 1″ by 30 strands, from children 1–17 years old were taken by parents, who also completed a questionnaire on potential sources of heavy metals.

Samples were minced, dissolved in nitric acid and analyzed through inductively-coupled plasma mass spectrometry (ICP-MS) for concentrations of lead, mercury, arsenic and chromium.

VII. SAMPLE DESCRIPTIONS OF HOW RESEARCH WILL BE DISSEMINATED

The results of this research would be submitted for publication in a relevant peer-reviewed journal (e.g., International Archives of Occupational and Environmental Health, Toxicology Letters, Journal of Environmental Health). This study would also be shared at a meeting of the Wisconsin Environmental Health Association.

Student contributions would be acknowledged in a spring 2013 UW-Eau Claire Student Research Day poster, and data would be shared in my US industrial hygiene and toxicology courses as an example of biological monitoring.

The "Sample Descriptions of How Research Will Be Disseminated" is the shortest section of the Project Statement, 5 percent of the total length. It succinctly highlights multiple ways results will be shared for the benefit of the wider research community and future environmental public health students. Note that specific peer-reviewed journals are targeted, offering the potential to advance understanding in the field and professional development for the project director; information, processes, and results will also be integrated into course offerings, contributing to curriculum and program development.

VIII. SAMPLE OUTCOMES AND CONTRIBUTIONS

Analysis of 70 samples in urban and rural communities in Wisconsin found that the levels of Pb, Ar, Hg and Cr in children's hair were similar to those in previous studies conducted around the world. Concentration levels appeared to be lognormally distributed.

We also found that the following factors were predictive of hair metal levels: gender, elevated blood Pb, home age, remodeling, chewing on paint and toys, protective clothing, dental fillings, fishing license, chemicals in well water, knowledge of fish advisories, parental hobbies/jobs, Pb use in the home, fish consumption, and tobacco product use.

Analysis of Finnish children's hair and questionnaires would help to identify how differences in diet, activities within the home, parents' occupations, etc. are related to heavy metal exposure.

Gaining perspective on Scandinavian environmental health practices and policies would enhance my teaching in the US. The Fulbright-Saastamoinen Foundation Award would also provide an opportunity to explore internship opportunities for US students in Finland, and for visiting Finnish scholars to participate in hair analysis and guest lecturing at the University of Wisconsin-Eau Claire.

* * *

The "Sample Outcomes and Contributions" uses 175 words (12 percent of the total length) to identify *who will benefit* from the project: the project director and home country institution will benefit from enhancements to teaching practices, the host country institution will benefit from rich scholarly exchanges, and the discipline will benefit from identification of predictive factors for elevated levels of heavy metals and confirmation of lognormal distribution of concentration levels. The research will broaden participation of underrepresented groups, advance discovery, integrate teaching and research, broaden dissemination, and contribute to public welfare.

The Project Statement ends on a positive, humanistic note. The first sentence addresses both sponsor hot buttons, health and teaching and research. The second sentence touches on the distinctive feature of international engagement, foreshadowing long-term ambassadorial stewardship potential that might emerge from participation in this award.

University of Eastern Finland
Faculty of Health Sciences

29 July 2010

Professor Crispin Pierce
1229 Paakatu
Springfield, WI 20207-0806
USA

Ref: Your application for the Fulbright-Saastamoinen Foundation Award in Health Sciences

Dear Professor Pierce,

On behalf of the Faculty of Health Sciences of the University of Eastern Finland, I would like to invite you to visit our Faculty as a Fulbright scholar for five months during the Academic Year 2011–2012. Your host/contact person at our Faculty will be Professor Jussi Kauhanen, Head of the Department of Public Health (e-mail address: jussi.kauhanen@uef.fi, tel. +358 405525104). The University of Eastern Finland will be responsible for arranging and paying for housing and for providing adequate research facilities for you. The University also has a Research Liaison Office and a Centre for International Relations to which Fulbright scholars can turn for advice and assistance.

The University of Eastern Finland warmly supports your application for the Fulbright-Saastamoinen Foundation Award. Your career and experience, both as a scholar and an instructor, in the field of Health and Environmental Sciences is impressive. During your stay at our institution, we would like to invite you to teach one or two courses, for example, in Public Health, Environmental Health, Solid and Hazardous Waste Management, Industrial Hygiene, Environmental Toxicology and Risk Assessment, or in Pharmaceutical Toxicology. I would like to recommend that you contact Professor Jussi Kauhanen to initially discuss your teaching preferences.

As regards your research plans, we most strongly support your project for a comparative study of sources of heavy metal in the hair of children in Finland and in Wisconsin.

STAGE ONE: FULL APPLICATION

Securing the Letter of Invitation.

While the RFP indicates, "An invitation letter is recommended as part of the application, but not required," preproposal contact emphasized the importance of securing a Letter of Invitation. The peer review process is competitive, and a Letter of Invitation is one more piece of telling evidence that suggests the project will get done.

To solicit the Letter of Invitation, a request was made via e-mail to the host institution contact person identified in the RFP. Attached to the e-mail were an updated curriculum vitae and two excerpts from the Application Form: Item 17 "Most Significant Professional Accomplishments" and Item 22 "Abstract or Summary of Project Statement," each of which was limited to 700 characters in length.

The host institution returned the Letter of Invitation via e-mail in less than one week. What's more, this initial e-mail exchange paved the way for subsequent messages that explored logistical considerations related to conducting research and teaching classes, such as access to research and teaching assistants, availability of lab equipment, and feasibility of coordinating site visits to local environmental facilities.

We are very pleased by your interest in applying for the Fulbright-Saastamoinen Foundation Award and we look forward to mutually beneficial cooperation between you and our Faculty of Health Sciences.

Yours sincerely,

Jukka Mönkkönen, Professor
Dean
Faculty of Health Sciences

* * *

The RFP clarifies that there are "no specific content requirements for invitation letters" and then goes on to recommend possible inclusions, such as the invitation period, expected activities, and the host's interest in the project. The Letter of Invitation follows these suggestions.

The opening paragraph identifies the invitation period—either semester during the academic year—and e-mail and phone contact information for an individual in the host department. Of note, the invitation period is the same as was listed in the RFP; the departmental contact is new information that was used to further build relationships with the host institution.

The second paragraph acknowledges the academic credentials and accomplishments of the project director and provides examples of the types of courses that would meet the needs of host country students. While the RFP establishes the expectation of teaching and research activity, it's the Letter of Invitation that provides valuable information, quantifying the number of courses to be taught.

The third paragraph, in a succinct 30 words, offers a strong endorsement of the proposed research activity and the potential benefits to both countries.

The final paragraph is a warm closing, one that reaffirms the larger purpose of the award in producing "mutually beneficial cooperation" individually, institutionally, and globally.

STAGE ONE: FULL APPLICATION

Celebrating the Grant Award Notification.
Nearly eight months after the full application was submitted, the project director received an award notification from the sponsor. More specifically, the application was submitted in August, a panel of discipline specialists completed their peer review in September, and a panel of geographic generalists completed their review in mid-November and recommended that the application be considered by the host country. Final funding decisions were predicted to occur between March and May and, indeed, the award notification arrived early in this window. It provided an energizing lift right before spring break.

While it is often valuable to examine feedback from peer reviewers, tuning in both to areas in need of improvement and areas identified as strengths, unfortunately the sponsor has a policy which prohibits sharing reviewer comments with applicants and awardees: "It is the policy of the Board not to give to individual applicants, to others inquiring on their behalf, or to the public generally, the specific reasons for selection or nonselection of applicants for awards under the program." (From the "Policy Statements of the J. William Fulbright Foreign Scholarship Board," Section 145.) A phone conversation with the program officer may provide an unofficial snapshot of reviewer reactions.

The J. William Fulbright Foreign Scholarship Board

Office of the Chair
Fulbright

March 7, 2011

Dr. Crispin Pierce
1229 Paakatu
Springfield, WI 20207-0806

Dear Dr. Pierce:

On behalf of the J. William Fulbright Foreign Scholarship Board (FSB), I am pleased to congratulate you on your selection for a Fulbright award to Finland. The FSB is the Presidentially appointed 12-member Board that is responsible for establishing worldwide policies for the Fulbright Program and for selection of Fulbright recipients. Your grant is made possible through funds that are appropriated annually by the U.S. Congress and, in many cases, by contributions from partner countries and/or the private sector.

Your selection for a Fulbright award is, in itself, an achievement for which you can be justly proud. However, please bear in mind that there are several more steps to be accomplished before you become a Fulbright grantee. These include but are not limited to the following. This award is contingent upon your obtaining official research clearance from the host country, where applicable. It is also contingent upon your obtaining a satisfactory medical clearance and the necessary visas. The terms and conditions of your award and other pertinent information will be forwarded to you by the Fulbright Commission in Finland following completion of all formalities. After the necessary grant documents containing the terms of your grant have been provided to you for signature, you must sign them and see that they are returned as instructed.

As a Fulbright grantee, you will join the ranks of distinguished participants in the Program. Fulbright alumni have become heads of state, judges, ambassadors, cabinet ministers, CEOs, university presidents, journalists, artists, professors and teachers. They have been awarded 43 Nobel Prizes. Since its inception more than 60 years ago, approximately 300,000 Fulbrighters have participated in the Program.

Developing international understanding requires a commitment on the part of Fulbright grantees to establish open communication and long-term cooperative relationships. In that way, Fulbrighters enrich the educational, political, economic, social and cultural lives of countries around the world. We expect that you, too, will become involved in the community while on your Fulbright exchange. In so doing, you will demonstrate the qualities of service, excellence and leadership that have been the hallmarks of this Program for more than 60 years. As a representative of your country in Finland, you will help fulfill the principal purpose of the Fulbright Program, which is to increase mutual understanding between the people of the United States and the people of the more than 150 countries that currently participate in the Fulbright Program.

The Bureau of Educational and Cultural Affairs of the United States Department of State, which oversees the operations of this Program throughout the world, joins the Board in congratulating you. If you have any questions about your grant, please contact your program officer at the Council for International Exchange of Scholars.

We hope that your Fulbright experience will be highly rewarding professionally and personally, and that you will share the knowledge you gain as a Fulbrighter with many others throughout your life.

Sincerely,

Anita B. McBride
Chair

Information on the Fulbright-Saastamoinen Foundation Award in Health Sciences is available online at http://catalog.cies.org/viewAward.aspx?n=6196&dc=FI. More information on the Fulbright Program is available on the U.S. State Department Web site at http://eca.state.gov/fulbright. Used by permission of the Institute for International Education.

Fulbright U.S. Scholar awards are markedly competitive and highly prestigious. Unlike grants, which are made to institutions, Fulbright awards are made directly to individuals. Funding odds are highly variable, differing widely by host country; overall success rates average 1:3. Fulbright alumni have gone on to have distinguished careers locally, nationally, and internationally, including winning Nobel Prizes, Pulitzer Prizes, and the Presidential Medal of Freedom.

CHAPTER 9
Final Thoughts

Sponsors vary in their approaches to sharing grant award notifications, as demonstrated in Chapters 4–8. With public sponsors, sometimes a program officer will give you an informal heads up that an official grant award notification is about to be sent out. Occasionally you might receive a telephone call from the office of your congressional representative sharing the good news that you've been selected for a federal grant award and that formal documentation will be arriving shortly. Other times you may receive a simple e-mail message from the sponsor with the grant award notification attached.

With private sponsors, in some cases a program officer may reach out to give you unofficial advanced notice of an impending award. In others, the grant award notification may arrive electronically or in hard copy with no forewarning; among several foundations it is standard practice to enclose a check for the full amount when they mail the grant award notification. In at least one instance, the first indication that an award was imminent was when the sponsor e-mailed to request organizational bank and routing information, a precursor to depositing funds electronically and sending out a grant award notification.

Regardless of whether it arrives as a letter, e-mail message, or attachment, receiving a grant award notification is exciting. It opens up new possibilities, ones you've considered and ones you haven't yet imagined. The funding will allow you to start tackling the problems you convinced the sponsor deserve to be solved right now. In the sponsor's eyes, you are an agent of change. Your project is a means for achieving purposeful good. Though your relationship with the sponsor is just beginning, it's not too early to be thinking about the long term. Undoubtedly, in the future there will be new needs to be addressed, populations to be served, innovative approaches to be tested, economies to be taken to scale, and technologies to be developed. Handled properly, the sponsor will be right beside you through it all. That is to say, excellent ideas helped get you the first grant. Responsible stewardship can help you win the next ones.

STEWARDSHIP

Your grant application presented the right balance of logic, emotion, and relationships to establish a connection with the sponsor. It persuaded the sponsor to invest in you, your project, and your organization. The sponsor expects that you will be a good steward of their funds and there are actions that you can begin taking right away within your organization and with the program officer to reinforce that their confidence is well placed.

Internal Actions

Internal actions at your organization aim to ensure that people, processes, and tools are in place to operationalize your project plan.

Celebrate Success. Celebrating a successful grant award is a crucial first step, and one that is often overlooked. Spread the word: let your board members, supervisors, colleagues, and partners know about the award. Taking a moment to gather your key stakeholders together, whether in person or virtually, to congratulate everyone's hard work shows that grantseeking is valued. You might bring in gourmet coffee and chocolates. You might take partners out for a recognition lunch. You might publish kudos in a staff newsletter. You might recognize staff contributions publicly in department meetings. Conveying thanks and appreciation helps set a positive tone as you begin to move forward with implementing your project.

Consider sharing a final copy of the full proposal with key staff and collaborators to refresh their memories about what was promised (likely) several months earlier. This is an opportunity to reconfirm that staff and partners still have the capacity and inclination to proceed as originally planned. In addition to an awareness that you will be spending time on grant activities from this point forward, supervisors may need to realign human and financial resource allocations toward other organizational priorities. For instance, if you will now be dedicating 20 percent effort to the grant project, a supervisor might need to determine whether some of your traditional duties will go unfulfilled or will be picked up by someone else. Collaborative partners may need to make similar arrangements at their respective organizations.

Review Terms and Conditions. The grant award notification may include specific terms and conditions that must be met as a stipulation of accepting the sponsor's funding. For example, the sponsor may specify cost allowability and payment reimbursement procedures, processes for securing prior approval on scope of work changes and budget modifications, restrictions on acquisition of equipment and ownership of intellectual property, and due dates for financial and technical progress reports. Review the terms and conditions to ensure that your organization can agree to and comply with the provisions; if a provision is incompatible with organizational policy, it's best to negotiate an appropriate remedy with the sponsor prior to accepting and spending funds. Exhibit 5 contains sample "problematic" terms and conditions and potential solutions. Consider setting up tickler files to provide timely reminders of report due dates. At one federal agency, an overdue report can result in delays in reviewing new proposals.

While many sponsors have similar categories of award terms, such as budget revisions, they may vary in their approach. As an illustration, the Robert Wood Johnson Foundation identifies conditions under which a budget revision request must be submitted, including that the program officer requires it, your organization requires it, and the change in a budget category for the given budget year results in an increase of the greater of 10 percent of the category or $10,000. The National Endowment for the Humanities, on the other hand, allows grantees flexibility to make budget revisions at their discretion as long as the project remains consistent with the approved proposal; budget revisions resulting from changes in the scope or objectives of the project require prior written approval from the sponsor.

Establish Accounts and Contracts. The grant award notification is often the only official documentation necessary for your organization's financial office to set up a project account so that authorized individuals can begin spending the funds. Maintaining a separate project account, rather than commingling grant funds with other resources, facilitates financial monitoring, ensuring that expenses are legitimate and balances are accurate. With a project account in place, you may also begin to work with the human resources office to advertise new positions and hire staff, coordinate with the purchasing office to acquire equipment and supplies, make arrangements with the information technology office to order hardware and software, and engage the accounts payable office to organize food and travel arrangements.

To secure the services of individuals outside of your organization, it may be necessary to establish contracts and subawards that define the scope of work and deliverables, period of performance, and budget. The Federal Demonstration Partnership, an association of federal agencies and research institutions that aim to improve productivity of research without compromising its stewardship, provides templates online (www.thefdp.org) that might serve as a springboard for preparing your grant subaward agreements. Templates, of course, should be modified to ensure consistency with your organizational policies and sponsor expectations.

Sponsors include specific terms and conditions to help clarify and enforce their expectations with respect to a grant award. Terms and conditions often fall into three types: programmatic, financial, and administrative. Following are four examples of common "problematic" terms and conditions as well as suggestions for alternative arrangements. Because each grant award is unique, review the clauses carefully and enlist the support of your general counsel as appropriate to identify a workable arrangement.

Publicity Clause: "Neither Party will, without prior approval of the other Party, make any public announcement of or otherwise *disclose the existence* or the terms of this Agreement."

Potential Problem: Public universities may not be able to "hide" the existence of a grant agreement. They may, in accordance with state open records laws, actually be required to make known the existence of the agreement, its purpose, name of sponsor, name of project director, amount of funding received, and project period dates.

Potential Solution: Delete the phrase "or otherwise disclose the existence or the terms."

Liability Clause: "Institution shall *indemnify and hold harmless* the Sponsor and its officers, directors, agents, and employees from claims arising from any infringement by the Institution, its agents or employees pertaining to activities to be carried out pursuant to the obligations of this Agreement."

Potential Problem: By state law, public universities may not be able to indemnify from liability the other party to the grant agreement. Public universities might be able to agree to hold harmless the other party but only to the extent that the liability, loss, or damages arises out of the negligent act or omission of an employee, officer, or agent while acting in the scope of their employment.

Potential Solution: Rewrite the clause to include mutual indemnification and condition the extent of the hold harmless provision.

Publication Clause: "You agree to provide copies to Sponsor of any proposed abstract, publication, or presentation ('Publication') at least 120 days in advance of the submission of said Publication. Sponsor shall have 60 days after receipt of said copies to object to such Publication. *If Sponsor objects because the proposed Publication contains proprietary or patentable information you shall refrain from making such Publication.*"

Potential Problem: Publication restrictions run contrary to the core mission of most academic institutions, which include a commitment to conducting fundamental research and broadly disseminating the results. What's more, the 120-day advance notification may not be practical.

Potential Solution: Rewrite the clause to retain the right to publish and allow the Sponsor 30 days to prereview—but not preapprove—the publication and require deletion of the Sponsor's confidential information. Allow the sponsor an additional 90 days to file a patent application before publication.

Choice of Laws Clause: "This transaction shall be governed by, and this order shall be construed and enforced in accordance with, the internal laws of the State of [State Name]."

Potential Problem: Public institutions may not be able to agree to the governing law of another jurisdiction just to accommodate an out-of-state sponsor.

Potential Solution: Specify the governing law of the applicant's home state or strike the entire clause so the grant agreement remains silent on the issue.

EXHIBIT 5

External Actions

External actions aim to promote trust and open communication with the program officer, laying a solid foundation for long-term project success and continued funding.

Generate Publicity. Help sponsors generate publicity for the good works that you will be doing together: check with your program officer about developing and disseminating a press release that announces the grant award. Prepare a first draft of the press release you would like to issue and then share it with the sponsor to ensure it is in their zone of comfort. Even better, invite the program officer to contribute a quotable quote. Exhibit 6 contains a sample press release that profiles the sponsor, the grantee organization, and the funded project presented in Chapter 6. Of note, be mindful of whether the sponsor prefers to be the first to share the good news and whether you must wait a certain period of time before going public. Even when sponsors intend to issue their own press releases, they often also allow grantees to subsequently disseminate complementary press releases that contain a more local flair.

For some projects it might be appropriate to host a media event. Inviting the program officer to play a prominent role in an announcement may actually help to attract even more attention for otherwise nonbreaking news. A short 30-minute media event on a timely, captivating topic is a powerful way to generate television exposure for your organization, your project, and the sponsor. Furthermore, event photos and video footage could also become a component of a social media campaign. Your communications office may have experience planning major media events, relationships with the media upon which you can draw, and strategies for ensuring consistency with your organization's brand and messaging.

Get Feedback. Ask the program officer for a verbatim copy of reviewer comments. This written feedback may provide insights about exactly what reviewers liked about the proposal as well as which areas they identified as in need of improvement. In instances when reviewer comments are not available, ask the program officer for a verbal debriefing. Clear policies exist, for example, at the Robert Wood Johnson Foundation and for the Fulbright U.S. Scholar Program *not* to provide written reviewer feedback to applicants. That said, program officers may be willing to say things that they might otherwise be reluctant to put in writing. They might speak frankly about your perceived strengths and weaknesses or they might be more reserved, simply encouraging you to compare notes with another grant winner (whom they hold up as the gold standard).

This debriefing is also your opportunity to learn more about the grant review process—who reviewed proposals, how proposals were reviewed, and against what yardstick proposals were measured—so that you will be even better positioned to apply to the sponsor again in a subsequent grant cycle. At one federal grantmaking agency, 100 percent of reviewers turn over annually; at another, reviewers serve three-year terms; at a third, an independent agency is responsible for culling through a pool of potential reviewers each funding cycle and inviting knowledgeable individuals from various backgrounds to serve on panels, irrespective of service in prior years. At one private foundation the review is conducted entirely by board members; at another, a cadre of highly regarded disciplinary experts gather year after year to review proposals; at a third, approximately one third of panelists annually are first-time reviewers. In other words, a future grant application to the same sponsor may use different writing strategies depending on the extent to which the same reviewers will also be reading that proposal.

Build Rapport. No sponsor wants to feel that "you only love me when I give you money." You want to build a lasting relationship with the sponsor. One question you can ask to help establish rapport with the program officer is, "What can I do to make your job easier?" The answer often involves submitting timely reports and providing updates about any possible program changes. Program officers understand that your project will evolve over time. Waiting until the end of the project period to report major changes in scope, personnel, budget, and outcomes puts the program officer in an awkward position when trying to justify continuation funding for you. Asking this question upfront demonstrates that you are committed to mutual success.

A second question you might ask the program officer is, "Beyond the required progress reports, what level and frequency of interaction do you prefer to have with grantees?" It might be appropriate to invite the program officer to visit your organization at key points during the project period, such as to participate in a kick-off event, to see work in progress, and to listen to a final formal presentation. The program officer might value being added to your organizational public relations list for news releases about your agency and project. Notes of appreciation from project participants might be forwarded to the program officer as testimonials of the great work going on. More broadly, getting permission to employ these types of systematic touch points can provide ongoing reassurances that your project is on the right track.

Stewardship is more than making perfunctory contacts at predetermined times. The internal and external stewardship actions cultivate an ongoing relationship with sponsors and program officers. To remain strong, relationships require consistent tending. Pay attention. Invest time. Be involved. Regular communication, critical reflection, and discernible results help to establish trust in a relationship with sponsors and program officers.

Whether you just received your first grant or the next in a series of repeat grants from the same sponsor, stewardship matters. Failing to notify a sponsor about the departure of key personnel, neglecting to secure prior authorization to make a change in project scope, forgetting to invite the program officer to an event funded by the sponsor, attempting to use board member connections to circumvent the grant application process, and submitting progress reports late and poorly written can damage relationships and trust. In more than one instance, a proposal highly rated by grant reviewers was

Nursing professor receives grant to continue community collaborative food insecurity research

EAU CLAIRE—Dr. Mary Canales, a professor of nursing at the University of Wisconsin-Eau Claire, and her colleagues at Feed My People Food Bank and UW–Extension recently received a two-year $50,000 development grant from the UW–Madison School of Medicine and Public Health's Wisconsin Partnership Program to continue a community-academic collaborative research project on food insecurity and hunger in Eau Claire County.

Canales's project was one of five chosen to receive funding out of more than 40 applicants.

Canales, who is interested in food and local justice issues and public health and public policy research, is partnering with Feed My People Food Bank and the Eau Claire County UW–Extension Wisconsin Nutrition Education Program to form a coalition in Eau Claire County to address food insecurity and hunger issues in the area. Members of the coalition will create a five-year strategic plan that will align city, county, and health system plans to streamline efforts dedicated to improving access to healthy and affordable food for low-income residents.

"This is a community-academic partnership project," Canales said. "Invitations to join the coalition will be sent to the Hmong Mutual Assistance Association, Mayo Clinic Health System in Eau Claire, the Eau Claire City-County Health Department, the City of Eau Claire, and other stakeholders and advocacy groups. People who experience food insecurity will provide feedback on the strategic plan and guide the coalition in their work. We will also identify ways to increase community awareness to help reduce the stigma associated with food insecurity in the community."

Work on the project will begin in April and has the potential to make a difference for real people in the Eau Claire County community, Canales said.

"I am most looking forward to bringing people together who are committed and passionate about this issue," Canales said. "We can always accomplish much more working as a committed group than we can working alone. I am excited to make a difference in my own community and want to recognize the UW–Eau Claire Office of Research and Sponsored Programs for sponsoring a grant-writing workshop specifically for the Wisconsin Partnership Program grant and for bringing this program to my attention."

For more information on the community-academic project on food insecurity and hunger, contact Dr. Mary Canales at canalemk@uwec.edu or 123-456-7890.

EXHIBIT 6

removed from funding consideration by a program officer because of poor stewardship on a prior award.

As an extension of stewardship, some sponsors may invite you to become a grant reviewer. The offer could come while you are an active grantee, after you have completed your grant project, or both. Case in point: the Fulbright U.S. Scholar Program actively solicits alumni and other individuals with appropriate disciplinary and regional backgrounds to join peer review committees; reviewers typically serve a three-year term and evaluate up to 30 applications per cycle. Even when sponsors do not publicize widely the opportunity to serve as a grant reviewer, you can still contact the program officer and volunteer. Recall, for example, that the Wisconsin Partnership Program, Community-Academic Partnership Fund went to great lengths in the RFP to encourage preproposal contact; the program officer may welcome your spirit of volunteerism. You often need to submit an updated résumé along with your expression of interest. The review experience is invaluable. Beyond the professional service to the program, you get to network with peers, stay abreast of the latest trends in the field, and see the review process in action, all of which can advance your career development and facilitate your planning for future applications.

PERSISTENCE PAYS

Seasoned grant writers know that it is impossible to have every proposal funded in this competitive environment. They also recognize that sometimes even "excellent" proposals get bumped out of contention due to specific provisions such as the sponsor's preference for a geographic distribution of awards. While being rejected is never fun, it is important to remember that proposals can always be revised and submitted to the same or other sponsors. A "no" does not necessarily mean "never"; it may mean "not right now."

Steps you can take to increase your odds of success with a resubmission include the following:

First, ask for reviewer comments to get a better sense of both what the sponsor liked about the project as well as in which areas they saw room for improvement. Public sponsors usually include reviewers' comments along with the rejection letter. Private sponsors, on the other hand, vary in the extent of their communications. A few private foundations will write detailed rejection letters, spelling out the reason for turndown, but more commonly they send a form letter rebuff: "Due to numerous requests for grants and limited funds, we regret that we are not in a position to be of assistance to you." If reviewer comments are not available, then request a telephone debriefing with the program officer to go over your proposal and explore whether there would be merit in revising and resubmitting in a future grant cycle.

For example, during one telephone debriefing after an application was declined, a sponsor advised that the *worst* strategy is to submit three entirely different proposals in three consecutive years. There was almost an implication that proposals are routinely declined the first time just to see whether applicants are truly committed to their projects. Some applicants who resubmit will be rewarded for their persistence. In another instance, during a presentation at a national conference, a foundation director confessed, "If the proposal was not even close [to the funding line], then my response is 'The program was very competitive this year.' If the proposal was close, then I might hint at what to do [to be more competitive in a future grant cycle]." That is, sometimes what the program officer *doesn't* say during an application debriefing can suggest the extent of revisions necessary to move into consideration for funding on a proposal resubmission.

Second, debrief with the project team to help them process feedback from reviewers and the program officer. Of the weaknesses cited, consider which ones were the most significant and whether they are fixable. Detailed critiques by reviewers might actually provide a roadmap to funding success. For instance, reviewer concerns about organizational credibility might suggest that a new partnership is needed or that a different partner serve as lead applicant; individual credibility might indicate that a blue ribbon advisory council should be established or that an independent consultant be hired; project credibility might signify that more extensive documentation is required or that ideas be reframed as "the next logical steps" rather than as so "highly innovative" that they are deemed "risky." Reviews that contain mixed or contradictory feedback may require large-scale changes to the project design and description.

Because a number of months often pass between when you submit an application and the sponsor makes a funding decision, take a new, open-minded look at the project and the proposal and reflect on ways they could be strengthened. With the benefit of time and some distance, you may recognize that sections weren't as clear as they could have been, details were omitted, or alternative options were not considered. Particularly with collaborative endeavors, it may be necessary to revisit partner commitments to the project, confirming that interest still exists in moving forward together. Further, partners may begin to formalize their relationships in standardized memorandums of understanding rather than relying on verbal promises.

Third, consider the implications of time. Some RFPs are issued only annually, which may mean that you will have to wait nearly a full year to resubmit a revised proposal to a sponsor. It's possible that this delay would necessitate a reconceptualization of your project activities because a few of them might proceed without the benefit of grant funding. For example, grant funding might have allowed an intervention to occur at eight sites but in the absence of sponsor support, your organization will use internal funds to service two sites. A revised proposal, then, may need to identify new activities that could be implemented at the two sites where an intervention already occurred to go along with the initial interventions planned at the other six sites.

As an alternative to waiting, you may determine that it would be more strategic to submit a version of your current proposal to a different sponsor who has a more immediate RFP deadline. Efforts to customize a proposal to a second sponsor, with the benefit of feedback from a first sponsor, may be proportionately less than envisioning new activities to accommodate a timeline delayed by a year or more. Targeting a second sponsor may also produce the benefit of maintaining the momentum of the project and energies of collaborative partners. What's more, the second sponsor may announce their grant awards prior to the deadline for the first sponsor's next funding competition, and if your project is selected for funding, then you would have a powerful detail to include in a revised resubmission.

At one institution of higher education, a young researcher submitted a request to a federal science agency, and it was declined. The researcher secured reviewer comments, made modest revisions and resubmitted in the next cycle. The application was declined a second time. Not to be deterred, the researcher secured reviewer comments again but this time also requested a debriefing with the program officer, a means to get a better understanding of reviewer concerns and to build rapport with the program officer. The reviewers wrote, "The number of users and overall total use may be too low," which the program officer explained meant that the reviewers wanted to see the project having a broader impact. With this understanding, the researcher made significant revisions to the proposal and budget request and resubmitted. The third time proved to be the charm, and the project was selected for funding.

When the grant award notification arrived, however, one of the sponsor's terms was that the budget request be reduced by 20 percent. The researcher followed up with the program officer, puzzled by the seemingly contradictory message of "We want you to have a broader impact but we don't want to pay for it." Through the course of several telephone calls and e-mail messages, together they found a way to maintain the desired impact with only a 9 percent budget reduction. The program officer, in effect, became an in-house hero: rather than impose an arbitrary decrease, the program officer advocated to the sponsor that a more strategic cut would allow the agency and the researcher both to realize their goals. Said differently, the relationship-building efforts with the program officer made a difference that paid off personally, professionally, and financially.

In short, it can pay to be persistent; funding chances usually improve with resubmissions.

YOUR TURN

Over the course of the previous eight chapters you have examined detailed models of proposal planning and writing. You have seen how we applied a three-step process for analyzing RFP guidelines. You have studied approaches we used to develop complete grant applications. You have reviewed the resulting grant award notifications. Now it's your turn.

While there are no guarantees of winning a grant award, the framework and practical strategies presented will move you toward the Persuasion Intersection, thus increasing your likelihood for funding success. Good grant writers follow all the directions in the RFP; great grant writers *analyze* the RFP in iterative passes to forge a persuasive link between their project and the sponsor's values. Successful grant writers also build on previous successes, revise areas of weakness, are not deterred by the occasional rejection, and see sponsors as collaborative partners. By using the available means of logical and psychological persuasion, you can convince sponsors that investments in you, your project, and your organization represent a viable means for realizing a common vision for an improved future.

You have the tools. You made the commitment. Now, go write your best grant ever!

APPENDIX
Summary of Preproposal Contact Questions

The Roads to the Persuasion Intersection highlights the critical nature of gathering information from multiple sources to help you understand the values of sponsors and to persuade them that you can satisfy their logical and psychological needs. Preproposal contact with past grant winners, past grant reviewers, and program officers will help you to obtain key facts, appreciate assorted perspectives, validate impressions, and maximize your likelihood of getting funded.

The list of preproposal contact questions that you could pose is theoretically endless. Chapters 4–8 present 124 examples of questions, which consider past action as well as explore future intentions. For your convenience, the questions are repeated below and organized by type:

Position: what are the baseline situations, present circumstances, and basic facts?
Rationale: what are the problems, needs, and injustices that exist today?
Expectation: what are the implications for addressing these problems?
Priority: what approaches are most likely to lead to an improved situation now?

Use the example questions to springboard development of your own preproposal contact questions. Do you have to ask all questions? Absolutely not! There is no magic number of questions to ask. Rather, experience suggests that asking a few Position questions helps to get the conversation started and that the real value of preproposal contact comes in asking more Rationale, Expectation, and Priority questions. Proportionately, you might target one third to be Position questions and two thirds to be Rationale, Expectation, and Priority questions. Choose the ones that you think will be insightful as you decide whether to submit a proposal to any given sponsor, recognizing that other questions will arise in the natural course of the conversation.

CHAPTER 4: THE ROBERT WOOD JOHNSON FOUNDATION

Position Questions: The Baseline Situation.

- Are "supplies" considered to be office supplies or do they include medical supplies such as spacers and allergy screenings?
- Are these items allowable direct project costs: incentives for community participants, meeting refreshments, postage, telephone, and travel?
- Who are the National Advisory Committee members that will assist in evaluation of proposals?

- Is there an anticipated number of site visits that will occur?
- Who owns evaluation data once it is collected?
- What can you tell us about the review process, such as how many reviewers will be assigned to each proposal, how much time will reviewers have to read proposals, and will they be using a specific reviewer's evaluation form?
- For budget development purposes, would it be appropriate to estimate an October 1 start date?
- Do you anticipate any modifications to the timetable of when proposals will be due, reviewed, and announced?
- To what degree does flexibility exist to rebudget funds as necessary during the project period?
- What are the most common budget challenges faced by grantees?
- Is it expected that an implementation plan must be submitted prior to the release of subsequent funding for implementation activities?
- Will each proposal be reviewed by a panel of 10 National Advisory Committee members?
- As part of the review process, how much time will reviewers have to read proposals and will they be using a specific reviewer's evaluation form?
- Will applicants be expected to respond to additional questions and provide further clarification in advance of or during a site visit?
- What can you tell us about the site visit process, such as how many National Program Office representatives will participate and is there a preset agenda of items for exploration?

Rationale Questions: Problems Existing Today

- Although it is not requested in the RFP, should we describe the magnitude and severity of the asthma problem in our community compared to the national asthma data provided?
- What do you see as essential to improving systems of care for children with asthma that isn't happening now?

Expectation Questions: Basic Implications for Addressing Problems

- Are applicants expected to fulfill all eight of the stated program objectives or would it be appropriate to prioritize the objectives and concentrate on realizing just a few of them?
- Which measures of children's quality of life do you prefer to evaluate?
- Should evaluations be conducted internally, externally, or both?
- Will awards be made on the basis of any special criteria, such as geography, size of target population, or size of the coalition?
- Is there a preferred format and length for resumes of key project staff?
- Are there any expected categories of information to be included on resumes beyond the standard: education, positions held, publications and presentations, professional activities, association memberships, and honors and awards?
- What level of documentation is expected for the "Description of the Application Process"—a brief summary or complete meeting minutes, reports, and correspondence?
- Is there a preferred page length for the "Description of the Application Process"?
- How many letters of support and commitment from collaborating agencies would be appropriate to include as attachments to our application?
- What's the desired local impact you'd like to see, while maintaining a balance across project breadth, depth, and financial resources available?

- Is there a preferred theoretical model for managing a large coalition?
- How many committees are realistic?
- What timeframes are appropriate for "intermediate" and "longer-term" outcomes?
- What level of documentation is expected as evidence of cash and in-kind support?

Priority Questions: Approaches for an Improved Situation

- Are there specific outcomes that are expected of grantees?
- How much change has to occur to be considered having potential to "substantially" change systems for asthma control?
- What types of evaluations are most appropriate for this project—structure, process, outcome, cost-effectiveness, return-on-investment analyses—balancing breadth, depth, and financial resources available?
- Why does the RFP ask applicants to "include and differentiate as relevant goals and objectives for the (1) organization and planning phase, and the (2) implementation phase" when the purpose of the planning phase is to prepare for an effective implementation phase?
- Which survey tools do you recommend that coalitions use to evaluate which specific measures of children's quality of life?
- One selection criterion used in evaluating proposals is the "potential for substantially changing systems for asthma control." What is considered "substantial" change?
- The RFP indicates that model programs must be sustainable. Does that mean activities must be institutionalized, or are there other strategies for supporting project continuation that applicants typically include in their proposals?

CHAPTER 5: THE RETIREMENT RESEARCH FOUNDATION

Position Questions: The Baseline Situation

- Why are the study hypotheses requested in both the "Project Objectives" section and the "Proposed Methods" section?
- Is it reasonable to use the National Institutes of Health's biosketch format for the project director and other key personnel?
- Are there expected categories of information to be included beyond education and training, personal statement, positions and honors, significant contributions to science, and ongoing and completed research support?

Rationale Questions: Problems Existing Today

- Which dimensions of research on financial decision making in older adults are most pressing?
- What difficulties linger that still are not being addressed?

Expectation Questions: Basic Implications for Addressing Problems

- When the Letter of Inquiry asks about "potential regional or national impact of the research finding" is it really asking the same as when the RFP for the full proposal asks about "anticipated contribution to the field"?
- To what extent do reviewers expect to see matching funds already committed to the project?
- Even though the Retirement Research Foundation does not fund theory development, is it expected that applicants elaborate on the theoretical basis for the proposed applied research?

- Is it reasonable to have only two or three objectives given that the project period is only one year in duration?
- What level of detail do reviewers expect to see about plans for funding future phases of research when the results of the proposed project have not yet been realized?

Priority Questions: Approaches for an Improved Situation

- Are there models of development underpinning applied research that are more favorably received?
- Given the Retirement Research Foundation's interest in supporting research "for which federal funding is not available," are there strategies for future funding that will be more favorably received?

CHAPTER 6: THE WISCONSIN PARTNERSHIP PROGRAM, COMMUNITY-ACADEMIC PARTNERSHIP FUND

Position Questions: The Baseline Situation

- Does Institutional Review Board (IRB) approval need to be secured prior to submission or prior to an award?
- What percentage of development grantees have subsequently secured funding for implementation grants?
- To what extent are the same reviewers used in subsequent review cycles?
- What percentage of applications represent first-time submissions compared to resubmissions?
- Historically, what percentage of applicants are invited to submit full proposals?
- Is there an a priori number or percent of Letters of Interest that will move forward to development of Full Applications?
- Will a point system be used for scoring Letters of Interest akin to the one used for scoring Full Applications?
- Does the Oversight and Advisory Committee (OAC) tend to accept the recommendations of the expert review panel without revision?
- How does the project orientation that successful applicants are required to complete fit into the work plan timeframes?

Rationale Questions: Problems Existing Today

- What are some of the biggest dissatisfactions with the current approaches to promoting healthy weight and good nutrition?
- Which dimensions of the problem need to be addressed next?

Expectation Questions: Basic Implications for Addressing Problems

- What is the relationship between the academic partner IRB and the UW-Madison IRB?
- Are there any specific characteristics that development projects shared which positioned them for success as implementation projects?
- What are the most common mistakes that you see in applications that are not invited to submit full proposals?
- Are there preferred levels of cash and in-kind matches?
- What level of cost sharing is expected of grantees?
- Will awards be made on the basis of any special criteria, such as geography, size of target population, or ethnic diversity of the partners?

- Could a higher scoring proposal get bumped out in favor of a lower scoring proposal that meets other special criteria?
- Are there preferred roles for the academic partner to ensure appropriate levels of active engagement?
- Should evaluations be conducted by the academic partner, externally by a consultant, or both?
- Should proposals be written for reviewers with nontechnical backgrounds?
- Do reviewers fill certain roles on the panel as specialists or generalists?
- Who exactly is expected to participate in the project orientation and what is the anticipated time commitment?

Priority Questions: Approaches for an Improved Situation

- Of the six guiding principles, are there any that are considered to be foremost among equals?
- To what extent are partnerships expected to adopt these guiding principles verbatim versus establish collaborative principles of their own that reflect the spirit of prevention, partnership, enhancement, responsiveness, effectiveness, and sustainability?
- What types of concerns have been raised by the OAC in the past prior to making award determinations?
- What would be the key features of an ideal solution?
- Would this approach be useful for cost reasons or something else?

CHAPTER 7: THE NATIONAL ENDOWMENT FOR THE HUMANITIES

Position Questions: The Baseline Situation

- Are there a targeted number of grant awards in each category?
- If individual environmental monitoring units cost less than $5,000, should they be presented on the budget as "equipment" or "supplies"?
- If a suite of environmental monitoring units cost in excess of $5,000, can they be presented as "equipment"?
- How small does an institution need to be to receive preferential consideration?
- What consideration is given to institutions that have not *recently* received an NEH grant?
- Are there page limits associated with supporting documentation—vendor quotes for multiple items could more than triple the length of the application?
- What percentage of awards represent first-time submissions compared to resubmissions?
- Would you review a draft proposal if it was shared four to six weeks in advance of the submission deadline?
- Do you plan to offer a workshop, teleconference, or webinar that offers guidance on how to prepare an application?

Rationale Questions: Problems Existing Today

- What value do reviewers assign to the condition of a collection—is an existing collection that is at-risk perceived as having greater need than a newly acquired collection for which a preventive maintenance approach is being pursued?
- What are the biggest hurdles grantees face in reaching their project goals and objectives?

Expectation Questions: Basic Implications for Addressing Problems

- To what extent is there flexibility to purchase different preservation supplies than originally proposed in the narrative and budget?
- To what extent is there flexibility to change consultants from who was originally proposed in the narrative to who is available at the time of project implementation?
- How much experience is sufficient to justify that expertise exists in-house to rehouse collections?
- Is it reasonable for the preservation assessment to be completed by staff rather than an external consultant?
- Rather than hiring an external consultant, is it permissible to pay an overload to a current staff member for the additional duty of conducting a preservation assessment?
- Are there particular education and training topics that are more in favor with reviewers right now?
- What is the strategic advantage to offering cost sharing when it is not required?
- Though not required, is there a level of cost sharing that reviewers believe applicants should contribute?
- Do reviewers favor applications that focus on a single or a suite of activities?
- Are there specific thresholds for budget and staffing that must be met to be considered small or mid-sized?
- Do reviewers demonstrate a preference for institutions whose missions are more research than public service oriented?
- What degree of "future preservation plans" will reviewers expect to see—one year, five years, 10 years?
- What level of detail will reviewers be expecting in the plan of work if preservation supplies and equipment have already been identified?
- What level of detail is expected in the timetable since purchasing and installation are one-time, short-term events?
- To what extent is it expected that a formal evaluation of the project will be conducted?
- Do reviewers give preferential consideration to applications that include cost sharing?
- If cost sharing is included, is there a preference for organizational funding being used to support consultant fees or preservation supplies?
- What are the most common mistakes in proposals that lead to their rejection?

Priority Questions: Approaches for an Improved Situation

- Do reviewers have a preference for a specific category of grants—general preservation assessments, consultations with professionals, preservation supplies, monitoring equipment, or education and training?
- What outcomes are expected of grantees?
- To what degree are reviewers concerned with exactly which vendors and products are used—that is to say, do they recommend different vendors and products as a means, for example, to reduce budget costs or increase item quality?

CHAPTER 8: THE INSTITUTE OF INTERNATIONAL EDUCATION, FULBRIGHT U.S. SCHOLAR PROGRAM

Position Questions: The Baseline Situation

- What types of physical space, equipment and instrumentation, administrative support, and professional development resources are available to researchers?

- Will the three-day orientation be held in Helsinki or in Kuopio?
- Is there a sample agenda available for the three-day orientation?

Rationale Questions: Problems Existing Today

- What are some of the biggest dissatisfactions with the current approaches to bridging gaps in international understanding?
- What kinds of challenges are most glaring—demonstrating intellectual merit, communicating across cultures, engaging general publics, disseminating program experiences widely upon return, sustaining connections with the host country and institution?

Expectation Questions: Basic Implications for Addressing Problems

- What is the standard faculty teaching load and which types of classes would best complement current course offerings?
- In instances where a specific percentage requirement is not stated in the RFP, is there a typical preferred balance between time spent teaching and time researching?
- To what extent does flexibility exist to adjust teaching and research time allocations after awards have been made?
- Are there any expected categories of information to be listed on the curriculum vitae or résumé beyond the standard: education, positions held, courses taught, publications, professional activities, membership and activities in professional associations, professional honors and awards, and community service?
- Is there a minimum number of peer-reviewed publications that applicants are expected to have—or more specifically, how will it be received by reviewers if the applicant has a reasonable number of publications overall, but because of a mid-career change in trajectory, has only a modest number of publications in the current line of research?
- To what extent will reviewers who are U.S. disciplinary specialists be familiar with pertinent literature in international publications?
- To what extent will host country experts be familiar with pertinent literature in U.S. publications?

Priority Questions: Approaches for an Improved Situation

- What levels of commitment to sustainability are reviewers expecting to see in proposals?
- Is there specific evaluation data you would like to see collected to facilitate a meta-analysis of your grant funding portfolio?

In short, engaging in preproposal contacts is an effective way to begin establishing your credibility with the sponsor. Asking good questions, including ones the program officer has perhaps not considered before, can demonstrate your attention to detail and depth of thinking about project design. Triangulating feedback from past grant winners, past grant reviewers, and program officers can help fine-tune your proposal, so that it closely matches the sponsor's priorities and convinces them to invest in you, your project, and your organization. A proposal does not need to be perfect to garner a grant award; persuasion is the key to funding success.

Index

About the Authors

JEREMY T. MINER, MA, is president of Miner and Associates, Inc., a consulting firm that provides grantseeking and fundraising services to nonprofit organizations. He is also director of grants and contracts in the Office of Research and Sponsored Programs at the University of Wisconsin–Eau Claire. In addition to developing and administering proposals to public and private grantmakers, he has served as a reviewer for federal and state grant programs, helped private foundations streamline their grant application guidelines, and presented grantseeking workshops nationally and internationally to thousands of grant-getters. Miner is an active member of the National Council of University Research Administrators (NCURA) at national and regional levels, serving on committees, presenting workshops and concurrent sessions, and publishing journal and magazine articles; he was awarded an NCURA-SARIMA International Fellowship. Miner authored the ABC-CLIO titles *Proposal Planning & Writing* and *Collaborative Grantseeking: A Guide to Designing Projects, Leading Partners and Persuading Sponsors*.

KELLY C. BALL-STAHL, PhD, is the senior grants specialist at Northeast Wisconsin Technical College, Green Bay, Wisconsin. She has helped organizations successfully secure tens of millions of dollars in grant funding from both government agencies and private foundations. Public sponsors include the National Institutes of Health, the Department of Education, the National Science Foundation, the Department of Labor, the Department of Homeland Security, and the National Endowment for the Humanities. Private sponsors include Lilly Endowment, the Hearst Foundations, and the Bill and Melinda Gates Foundation. She regularly presents workshops on grant seeking and writing persuasive proposals for the National Council of University Research Administrators (NCURA), at local events facilitated by Congressional leaders, and for Northeast Wisconsin Technical College.